HTML5 AND CSS

Seventh Edition

INTRODUCTORY

Gary B. Shelly

Denise M. Woods

COURSE TECHNOLOGY
CENGAGE Learning

Australia • Brazil • Japan • Korea • Mexico • Singapore • Spain • United Kingdom • United States

COURSE TECHNOLOGY
CENGAGE Learning·

HTML5 and CSS
Introductory, Seventh Edition
Gary B. Shelly, Denise M. Woods

Vice President, Publisher: Nicole Pinard

Executive Editor: Kathleen McMahon

Product Manager: Nada Jovanovic

Associate Product Manager: Caitlin Womersley

Editorial Assistant: Angela Giannopoulos

Director of Marketing: Elisa Roberts

Associate Marketing Manager: Adrienne Fung

Print Buyer: Julio Esperas

Director of Production: Patty Stephan

Content Project Manager: Jennifer Feltri-
    George

Development Editor: Karen Stevens

Proofreader: Andrea Schein

Indexer: Michael Brackney

QA Manuscript Reviewers: Jeff Schwartz and
    Danielle Shaw

Art Director: Marissa Falco

Cover Designer: Lisa Kuhn, Curio Press, LLC

Cover Photo: Tom Kates Photography

Compositor: PreMediaGlobal

Library of Congress Control Number: 2011944169

ISBN-13: 978-1-1335-2613-1

ISBN-10: 1-1335-2613-6

Course Technology
20 Channel Center Street
Boston, MA 02210
USA

Cengage Learning is a leading provider of customized learning solutions with office locations around the globe, including Singapore, the United Kingdom, Australia, Mexico, Brazil, and Japan. Locate your local office at:
international.cengage.com/region

Cengage Learning products are represented in Canada by Nelson Education, Ltd.

For your course and learning solutions, visit **www.cengage.com**

To learn more about Course Technology, visit **www.cengage.com/
coursetechnology**

Purchase any of our products at your local collage bookstore or at our preferred online store at **www.CengageBrain.com**

All screen shots are courtesy of Notepad++ and Microsoft Corporation unless otherwise noted.

All rendered figures, including composed art and tables, are © Cengage Learning unless otherwise noted.

Printed in the United States of America
1 2 3 4 5 6 16 15 14 13 11 12

HTML5 Seventh Edition
AND CSS
INTRODUCTORY

Contents

v

Preface

The Shelly Cashman Series® offers the finest textbooks in computer education. We are proud that our previous HTML books have been so well received. With each new edition of our HTML books, we have made significant improvements based on the comments made by instructors and students. The *HTML5 and CSS, Seventh Edition* books continue with the innovation, quality, and reliability you have come to expect from the Shelly Cashman Series.

For this text, the Shelly Cashman Series development team carefully reviewed its pedagogy and analyzed its effectiveness in teaching today's student. Students today read less, but need to retain more. They need not only to be able to perform skills, but to retain those skills and know how to apply them to different settings. Today's students need to be continually engaged and challenged to retain what they're learning.

With this HTML book, we continue our commitment to focusing on the user and how they learn best.

Objectives of This Textbook

HTML5 and CSS: Introductory, Seventh Edition is intended for use in combination with other books in an introductory course on creating Web pages. This book is also suitable for use as a stand-alone text in a one-credit hour course or a continuing education course. No experience with Web page development or computer programming is required. Specific objectives of this book are as follows:

- To teach the fundamentals of developing Web pages using a comprehensive Web development life cycle
- To acquaint students with the HTML5 and CSS (through level 3) languages and creating Web pages suitable for course work, professional purposes, and personal use
- To expose students to common Web page formats and functions
- To promote curiosity and independent exploration of World Wide Web resources
- To develop an exercise-oriented approach that allows students to learn by example
- To encourage independent study and help those who are learning how to create Web pages in a distance education environment

HTML5
AND CSS

Seventh Edition

INTRODUCTORY

The Shelly Cashman Approach

A Proven Pedagogy with an Emphasis on Project Planning

Each chapter presents a practical problem to be solved, within a project planning framework. The project orientation is strengthened by the use of Plan Ahead boxes that encourage critical thinking about how to proceed at various points in the project. Step-by-step instructions with supporting screens guide students through the steps. Instructional steps are supported by the Q&A, Experimental Step, and BTW features.

A Visually Engaging Book that Maintains Student Interest

The step-by-step tasks, with supporting figures, provide a rich visual experience for the student. Call-outs on the screens that present both explanatory and navigational information provide students with information they need when they need to know it.

Supporting Reference Materials (Appendices)

The appendices provide additional information about HTML5 and CSS topics, with appendices such as the HTML Quick Reference, Browser-Safe Color Palette, Accessibility Standards and the Web, CSS Properties and Values, and Publishing Web Pages to a Web Server.

Integration of the World Wide Web

The World Wide Web is integrated into the HTML5 and CSS learning experience by (1) BTW annotations; and (2) the Learn It Online section for each chapter.

End-of-Chapter Student Activities

Extensive end-of-chapter activities provide a variety of reinforcement opportunities for students where they can apply and expand their skills through individual and group work.

Online Companion

The Online Companion includes Learn It Online exercises for each chapter, as well as @Source links, Your Turn links, and Q&As. To access these course materials, please visit **www.cengagebrain.com**. At the CengageBrain.com home page, search for *HTML5 and CSS 7th Edition* using the search box at the top of the page. This will take you to the product page for this book. On the product page, click the Access Now button below the Study Tools heading.

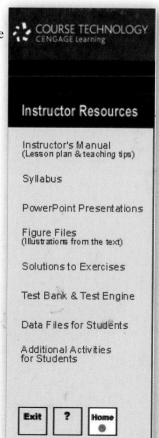

Instructor Resources

The Instructor Resources include both teaching and testing aids and can be accessed via CD-ROM or at login.cengage.com.

Instructor's Manual Includes lecture notes summarizing the chapter sections, figures and boxed elements found in every chapter, teacher tips, classroom activities, lab activities, and quick quizzes in Microsoft Word files.

Syllabus Easily customizable sample syllabi that cover policies, assignments, exams, and other course information.

Figure Files Illustrations for every figure in the textbook in electronic form.

PowerPoint Presentations A multimedia lecture presentation system that provides slides for each chapter. Presentations are based on chapter objectives.

Solutions to Exercises Includes solutions for all end-of-chapter and chapter reinforcement exercises.

Test Bank & Test Engine Test Banks include 112 questions for every chapter, featuring objective-based and critical thinking question types, and including page number references. Also included is the test engine, ExamView, the ultimate tool for your objective-based testing needs.

Data Files for Students Includes all the files that are required by students to complete the exercises.

Additional Activities for Students Consists of Chapter Reinforcement Exercises, which are true/false, multiple-choice, and short answer questions that help students gain confidence in the material learned.

SAM: Skills Assessment Manager

SAM 2010 is designed to help bring students from the classroom to the real world. It allows students to train on and test important computer skills in an active, hands-on environment. SAM's easy-to-use system includes powerful interactive exams, training, and projects on the most commonly used Microsoft Office applications. SAM simulates the Microsoft Office 2010 application environment, allowing students to demonstrate their knowledge and think through the skills by performing real-world tasks such as bolding word text or setting up slide transitions. Add in live-in-the-application projects, and students are on their way to truly learning and applying skills to business-centric documents. Designed to be used with the Shelly Cashman Series, SAM includes handy page references so that students can print helpful study guides that match the Shelly Cashman textbooks used in class. For instructors, SAM also includes robust scheduling and reporting features.

Content for Online Learning

Course Technology has partnered with the leading distance learning solution providers and class-management platforms today. To access this material, Instructors will visit our password-protected instructor resources available at login.cengage.com. Instructor resources include the following: additional case projects, sample syllabi, PowerPoint presentations per chapter, and more. For additional information or for an instructor username and password, please contact your sales representative. For students to access this material, they must have purchased a WebTutor PIN-code specific to this title and your campus platform. The resources for students may include (based on instructor preferences), but are not limited to: topic review, review questions and practice tests.

CourseNotes

Course Technology's CourseNotes are six-panel quick reference cards that reinforce the most important concepts and features of a software application in a visual and user-friendly format. CourseNotes serve as a great reference tool for students, both during and after the course. CourseNotes are available for Adobe Dreamweaver CS5, Web 2.0: Recharged, Buyer's Guide: Tips for Purchasing a New Computer, Best Practices in Social Networking, Hot Topics in Technology and many more. Visit **www.cengagebrain.com** to learn more!

Guided Tours

Add excitement and interactivity to your classroom with "*A Guided Tour*" product line. Play one of the brief mini-movies to spice up your lecture and spark classroom discussion. Or, assign a movie for homework and ask students to complete the correlated assignment that accompanies each topic. "*A Guided Tour*" product line takes the prep-work out of providing your students with information on new technologies and software applications and helps keep students engaged with content relevant to their lives; all in under an hour!

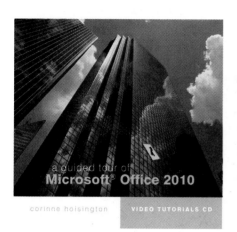

About Our Covers

The Shelly Cashman Series is continually updating our approach and content to reflect the way today's students learn and experience new technology. This focus on student success is reflected on our covers, which feature real students from Bryant University using the Shelly Cashman Series in their courses, and reflect the varied ages and backgrounds of the students learning with our books. When you use the Shelly Cashman Series, you can be assured that you are learning computer skills using the most effective courseware available.

Textbook Walk-Through

The Shelly Cashman Series Pedagogy: Project-Based — Step-by-Step — Variety of Assessments

Plan Ahead boxes prepare students to create successful projects by encouraging them to think strategically about what they are trying to accomplish before they begin working.

Step-by-step instructions now provide a context beyond the point-and-click. Each step provides information on why students are performing each task, or what will occur as a result.

Plan Ahead →

General Project Guidelines

When creating a Web page, the actions you perform and decisions you make will affect the appearance and characteristics of the finished page. As you create a Web page, such as the project shown in Figure 2–1 on the previous page, you should follow these general guidelines:

1. **Complete Web page planning.** Before developing a Web page, you must know the purpose of the Web site, identify the users of the site and their computing environments, and decide who owns the information on the Web page.

2. **Analyze the need for the Web page.** In the analysis phase of the Web development life cycle, you should analyze what content to include on the Web page. In this phase, you determine the tasks and the information that the users need. Refer to Table 1–4 on page HTML 15 in Chapter 1 for information on the phases of the Web development life cycle.

3. **Choose the content for the Web page.** Once you have completed the analysis, you need to determine what content to include on the Web page. Follow the *less is more* principle. The less text, the more likely the Web page will be read. Use as few words as possible to make a point.

4. **Determine the file naming convention that you will use for this Web page.** Before you start creating and saving files, you should decide on a standard way of naming your files. Should you use the .htm or .html extension? As explained later in the chapter, you use the .htm extension when the host Web server only allows short file names. You use .html when the host Web server allows long file names. What name should you give your file to indicate the file's content or purpose? For instance, naming a Web page page1.html does not describe what that Web page is; a more descriptive name is helpful in development of the Web site.

5. **Determine where to save the Web page.** You can store a Web page permanently, or **save** it, on a variety of storage media, including a hard disk, USB flash drive, CD, or DVD. Your instructor or the company for whom you are developing the Web page may have specific storage media requirements.

6. **Determine what folder structure to use on your storage device.** Once you have determined the storage media to use, you should also determine folder location, structure, and names on which to save the Web page. This should be done before you start to save any of your files.

7. ...format various elements of the Web page. The overall appearance of a ...cantly affects its ability to communicate clearly. Examples of how you ...ppearance, or **format**, of the Web page include adding an image, color ...horizontal rules.

8. ...**graphical images.** Eye-catching graphical images help convey the Web ...essage and add visual interest. Graphics can be used to show a product, ...benefit, or visually convey a message that is not expressed easily

9. ...**to position and how to format the graphical images.** The position and ...aphical images should grab the attention of viewers and draw them ...Web page.

10. ...**ge for W3C compliance.** An important part of Web development ...re that your Web page follows standards. The World Wide Web ...) has an online validator that allows you to test your Web page and ...ny errors.

...more specific details concerning the above guidelines are presented ...s in the chapter. The chapter will also identify the actions performed ...egarding these guidelines during the creation of the Web page shown

---

To Save an HTML File

You have entered a lot of text while creating this project and do not want to risk losing the work you have done so far. Also, to view HTML in a browser, you must save the file. The following steps show how to save an HTML file.

1

- With a USB flash drive connected to one of the computer's USB ports, click File on the Notepad++ menu bar (Figure 2–17).

File menu

File menu options

Save As command

recently opened files display in this section

Figure 2–17

2

- Click Save As on the File menu to display the Save As dialog box (Figure 2–18).

Q&A

Do I have to save to a USB flash drive?

No. You can save to any device or folder. A folder is a specific location on a storage medium. Use the same process, but select your device or folder.

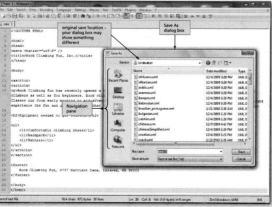

original save location – your dialog box may show something different

Save As dialog box

Navigation pane

Figure 2–18

Textbook Walk-Through

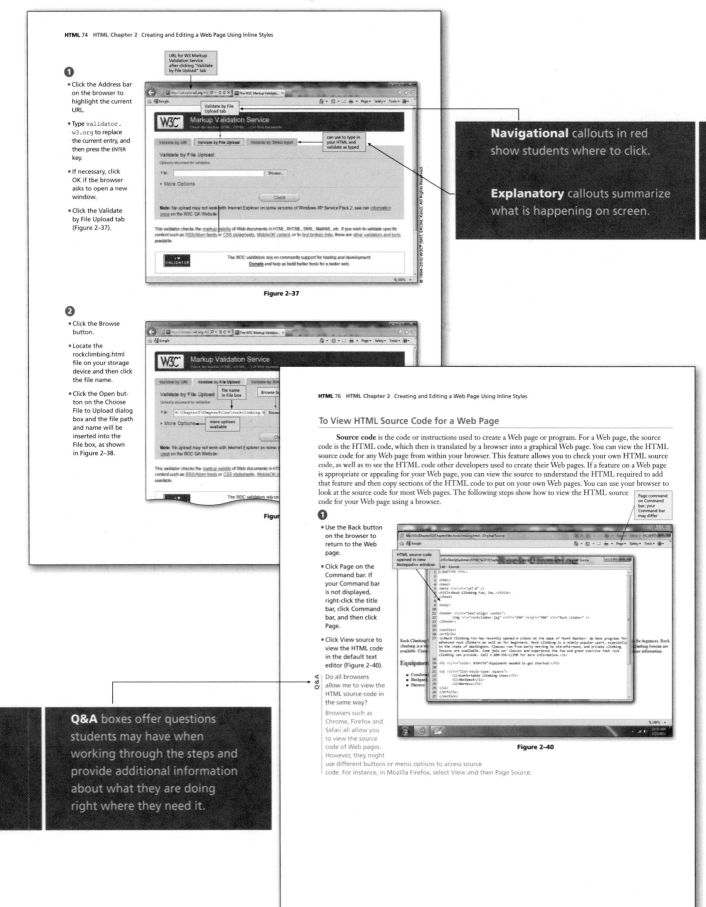

❶

- Click the Address bar on the browser to highlight the current URL.

- Type validator. w3.org to replace the current entry, and then press the ENTER key.

- If necessary, click OK if the browser asks to open a new window.

- Click the Validate by File Upload tab (Figure 2–37).

URL for W3 Markup Validation Service after clicking "Validate by File Upload" tab

Validate by File Upload tab

can use to type in your HTML and validate as typed

Figure 2–37

❷

- Click the Browse button.

- Locate the rockclimbing.html file on your storage device and then click the file name.

- Click the Open button on the Choose File to Upload dialog box and the file path and name will be inserted into the File box, as shown in Figure 2–38.

file name in File box

Browse b...

more options available

Figur...

Navigational callouts in red show students where to click.

Explanatory callouts summarize what is happening on screen.

To View HTML Source Code for a Web Page

Source code is the code or instructions used to create a Web page or program. For a Web page, the source code is the HTML code, which then is translated by a browser into a graphical Web page. You can view the HTML source code for any Web page from within your browser. This feature allows you to check your own HTML source code, as well as to see the HTML code other developers used to create their Web pages. If a feature on a Web page is appropriate or appealing for your Web page, you can view the source to understand the HTML required to add that feature and then copy sections of the HTML code to put on your own Web pages. You can use your browser to look at the source code for most Web pages. The following steps show how to view the HTML source code for your Web page using a browser.

❶

- Use the Back button on the browser to return to the Web page.

- Click Page on the Command bar. If your Command bar is not displayed, right-click the title bar, click Command bar, and then click Page.

- Click View source to view the HTML code in the default text editor (Figure 2–40).

Page command on Command bar; your Command bar may differ

HTML source code opened in new Notepad++ window

Q&A

Do all browsers allow me to view the HTML source code in the same way?

Browsers such as Chrome, Firefox and Safari all allow you to view the source code of Web pages. However, they might use different buttons or menu options to access source code. For instance, in Mozilla Firefox, select View and then Page Source.

Figure 2–40

Q&A boxes offer questions students may have when working through the steps and provide additional information about what they are doing right where they need it.

To Refresh the View in a Browser

As you continue developing the HTML file in Notepad++, it is a good idea to view the file in your browser as you make modifications. Clicking the Refresh button when viewing the modified Web page in the browser, ensures that the latest version of the Web page is displayed. The following step shows how to refresh the view of a Web page in a browser in order to view the modified Web page.

1

- Click the Internet Explorer button on the taskbar to display the rockclimbing.html Web page.

- Click the Refresh button on the Address bar to display the modified Web page (Figure 2–35).

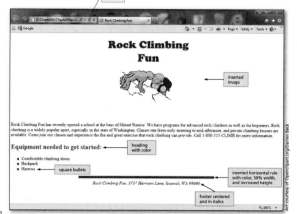

Art courtesy of OpenClipart.org/Darren Beck

Figure 2–35

Other Ways

1. In Internet Explorer, press F5 to refresh

> **Other Ways** boxes that follow many of the step sequences explain the other ways to complete the task presented.

Validating and Viewing HT

BTW

HTML and HTML5 Tags
The Web has excellent sources that list HTML5 tags. For more information about HTML and HTML5, search for "HTML tags" or "HTML5 tags" in a search engine.

In Chapter 1, you read about validating your H available on the Web that can be used to assure This should always be a part of your Web page this book is the W3C Markup Validation Servic the markup validity of Web documents in HTM markup languages. The validator looks at the D of HTML or XHTML you are using, and then version. In this chapter, the project uses the HT

If validation detects an error in your HTM found while checking this document as HTML5 2–36a on the next page). The Result line shows t scroll down the page or click the Jump To: Valida each error.

It is important to note that one error can </h2> tag on line 19 in the rockclimbing.html f Figure 2–36b shows that in this case, one initial be used within the <h2> tag on line 19) resulted

> **Extend Your Knowledge** projects at the end of each chapter allow students to extend and expand on the skills learned within the chapter. Students use critical thinking to experiment with new skills to complete each project.

6. Save the revised HTML file in the Chapter02\Apply folder using the file name apply2-1solution.html.

7. Validate your HTML code at validator.w3.org.

8. Enter g:\Chapter02\Apply\apply2-1solution.html (or the path where your data file is stored) as the URL to view the revised Web page in your browser.

9. Print the Web page.

10. Submit the revised HTML file and Web page in the format specified by your instructor.

Extend Your Knowledge

Extend the skills you learned in this chapter and experiment with new skills.

Creating a Definition List

Instructions: Start Notepad++. Open the file, extend2-1.html from the Chapter02\Extend folder of the Data Files for Students. See the inside back cover of this book for instructions on downloading the Data Files for Students, or contact your instructor for information about accessing the required files. This sample Web page contains all of the text for the Web page. You will add the necessary tags to make this a definition list with terms that are bold, as shown in Figure 2–45.

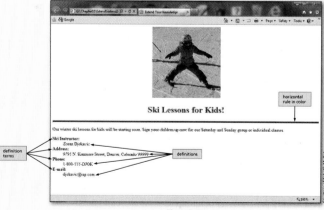

Courtesy of Sabeth Mullet

Figure 2–45

Perform the following tasks:

1. Using the text given in the file extend2-1.html, make changes to the HTML code to change the Web page from a single line of text to a definition list by following the definition list code shown in Table 2–6 on page HTML 52.

Continued >

Textbook Walk-Through

STUDENT ASSIGNMENTS

Extend Your Knowledge continued

2. Add the additional HTML code necessary to make the terms bold. (*Hint:* Review the font-weight property with a value of bold.)

3. Add the image skier.jpg. Find the dimensions of the image by reviewing the image properties.

4. Add a horizontal rule that is 5 pixels high and color #414565. The <h1> heading is also color #414565.

5. Save the revised document in the Chapter02\Extend folder with the file name extend2-1solution. html, validate the Web page, and then submit it in the format specified by your instructor.

Make It Right

Analyze a document and correct all errors and/or improve the design.

Correcting the Star of India Web Page
Instructions: Start Notepad++. Open the file makeitright2-1.html from the Chapter02\MakeItRight folder of the Data Files for Students. See the inside back cover of this book for instructions on downloading the Data Files for Students, or contact your instructor for information about accessing the required files.

The data file is a modified version of what you see in Figure 2–46. Make the necessary corrections to the Web page to make it look like Figure 2–46. Add a background color to the Web page using color #515c7a. (*Hint:* Use an inline style in the <body> tag.) Format the heading to use the Heading 1 style with the color black. Add a paragraph of text in white and four circle bullets also in white. (*Hint:* Use the color property in the heading, paragraph, and bullet tags.) Save the file in the Chapter02\MakeItRight folder as makeitright2-1solution.html, validate the Web page, and then submit it in the format specified by your instructor. Be prepared to discuss the four questions posed in the bullet list.

Make It Right projects call on students to analyze a file, discover errors in it, and fix them using the skills they learned in the chapter.

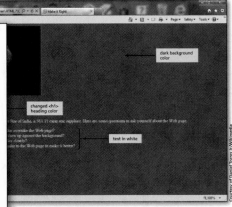

Figure 2–46

STUDENT ASSIGNMENTS

In the Lab continued

3. Insert the image file piggybank.png, stored in the Chapter02\IntheLab folder. You can find the dimensions of an image by clicking on the image using Windows Explorer. You can also right-click the image, click Properties, and then click the Details tab to find out the image's dimensions, or open it in a graphics program. Note that the bullets used for the list are square in shape.

4. Save the HTML file in the Chapter02\IntheLab folder using the file name lab2-3solution.html.

5. Enter g:\Chapter02\IntheLab\lab2-3solution.html (or the path where your data file is stored) as the URL to view the Web page in your browser.

6. Print the Web page from your browser.

7. Submit the revised HTML file and Web page in the format specified by your instructor.

Cases and Places

Apply your creative thinking and problem-solving skills to design and implement a solution.

1: Research HTML5 Structural Tags
Academic
There are many Web sites dedicated to HTML5. Search the Web to find sites that have training modules for HTML5. Discover training specifically targeting the new structural elements discussed in the chapter. How do these new tags differ from the <div> tag? Are there situations in which the <div> tag is a better option? Write a brief report. Identify the URLs for the training Web sites and share them with your fellow students in class.

2: Create a Personal Web Page
Personal ◄
Your class instructor wants to post all of the students' Web pages on the school server to show what his or her students are interested in. Create a Web page of personal information, listing items such as your school major, jobs that you have had in the past, and your hobbies and interests. To make your personal Web page more visually interesting, search the Web for images that reflect your interests. (Remember that if the image is copyrighted, you cannot use it on a personal Web page unless you follow the guidelines provided with the image.) Insert an image or two onto the Web page to help explain who you are.

3: Investigate Methods for Working with Images
Professional
You are creating a new Web site for a local photographer. The photographer has asked that you determine methods to help his Web site load quickly despite having so many large images. To this end, find information on using thumbnail images. Review other photography Web sites and create a list of suggestions for loading large images. Additionally, search the Web for information on adding useful, descriptive alt attributes for images. Write a brief synopsis explaining the information that you found in your research.

Found within the Cases & Places exercises, the **Personal** exercises call on students to create an open-ended project that relates to their personal lives.

1 Introduction to HTML, XHTML, and CSS

Objectives

You will have mastered the material in this chapter when you can:

- Describe the Internet and its associated key terms

- Describe the World Wide Web and its associated key terms

- Describe the types and purposes of Web sites

- Discuss Web browsers and identify their purpose

- Define the Hypertext Markup Language (HTML) and HTML5 standards used for Web development

- Discuss the use of Cascading Style Sheets (CSS) in Web development

- Define the Document Object Model (DOM) and describe its relationship to HTML

- Define Extensible Hypertext Markup Language (XHTML) and describe its relationship to HTML

- Identify tools used to create HTML documents

- Describe the five phases of the Web development life cycle

- Describe the different methods of Web site design and the purpose of each Web site structure

- Discuss the importance of testing throughout the Web development life cycle

- Explain the importance of being an observant Web user

1 | Introduction to HTML, XHTML, and CSS

Introduction

Before diving into the details of creating Web pages with HTML5 and CSS, it is useful to look at how these technologies relate to the development of the Internet and the World Wide Web. The Internet began with the connection of computers and computer networks. This connectivity has had a huge impact on our daily lives. Today, millions of people worldwide have access to the Internet, the world's largest network. Billions of Web pages, providing information on any subject you can imagine, are currently available on the World Wide Web. People use the Internet to search for information, to communicate with others around the world, and to seek entertainment. Students register for classes, pay tuition, and find out final grades via this computer network. Stores and individuals sell their products using computer connectivity, and most industries rely on the Internet and the World Wide Web for business transactions.

Hypertext Markup Language (HTML) and more recently HTML5 and Cascading Style Sheets (CSS) allow the World Wide Web to exist. In order to utilize these technologies effectively, you need to understand the main concepts behind the Internet and HTML. In this chapter, you learn some basics about the Internet, the World Wide Web, intranets, and extranets. You are introduced to Web browsers, definitions of HTML and associated key terms, the five phases of the Web development life cycle, and the tasks that are involved in each phase.

What Is the Internet?

Most people today have had exposure to the Internet at school, in their homes, at their jobs, or at their local library. The **Internet** is a worldwide collection of computers and computer networks that links billions of computers used by businesses, government, educational institutions, organizations, and individuals using modems, phone lines, television cables, satellite links, fiber-optic connections, and other communications devices and media (Figure 1–1).

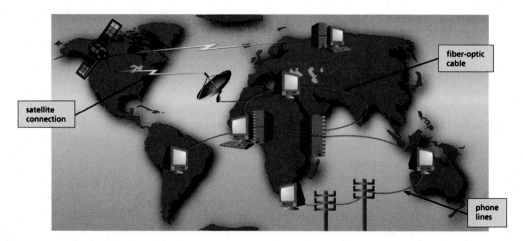

Figure 1–1 The Internet is a worldwide collection of computer networks.

The Internet was developed in the 1960s by the Department of Defense Advanced Research Projects Agency (ARPA). ARPANET (as the Internet was originally called) had only four nodes on it and sent its first message in 1969. Today's Internet has millions of nodes on thousands of networks. A **network** is a collection of two or more computers that are connected to share resources and information. Today, high-, medium-, and low-speed data lines connect networks. These data lines allow data (including text, graphical images, and audio and video data) to move from one computer to another. The **Internet backbone** is a collection of high-speed data lines that connect major computer systems located around the world. An **Internet service provider** (**ISP**) is a company that has a permanent connection to the Internet backbone. ISPs utilize high- or medium-speed data lines to allow individuals and companies to connect to the backbone for access to the Internet. An Internet connection at home generally is a DSL or cable data line that connects to an ISP.

Millions of people in most countries around the world connect to the Internet using computers in their homes, offices, schools, and public locations such as libraries. In fact, the Internet was designed to be a place in which people could share information or collaborate. Users with computers connected to the Internet can access a variety of services, including e-mail, social networking, and the World Wide Web where they can find a variety of information at many different types of Web sites (Figure 1–2).

Figure 1–2 The Internet makes available a variety of services such as the World Wide Web.

What Is the World Wide Web?

Many people use the terms "Internet" and "World Wide Web" interchangeably, but that is not accurate. The Internet is the infrastructure, the physical networks of computers. The **World Wide Web**, also called the **Web**, is the part of the Internet that supports

BTW

Internet and WWW History
The World Wide Web Consortium (W3C or w3.org), the de facto organization that governs HTML, provides a particularly rich history of the Internet and the World Wide Web. Search on "Internet history" or "WWW history" in your browser for many additional sources.

multimedia and consists of a collection of linked documents. To support multimedia, the Web relies on the **Hypertext Transfer Protocol (HTTP)**, which is a set of rules for exchanging text, graphic, sound, video, and other multimedia files. The linked documents, or pages of information, on the Web are known as **Web pages**. Because the Web supports text, graphics, sound, and video, a Web page can include any of these multimedia elements. The Web is ever-changing and consists of billions of Web pages. Because of the ease of creating Web pages, more are being added all the time.

A **Web site** is a related collection of Web pages that is created and maintained by an individual, company, educational institution, or other organization. For example, as shown in Figure 1–3, many organizations, such as the U.S. Department of Labor, publish and maintain Web sites. Each Web site contains a **home page**, which is the first document users see when they access the Web site. The home page often serves as an index or table of contents to other documents and files displayed on the site.

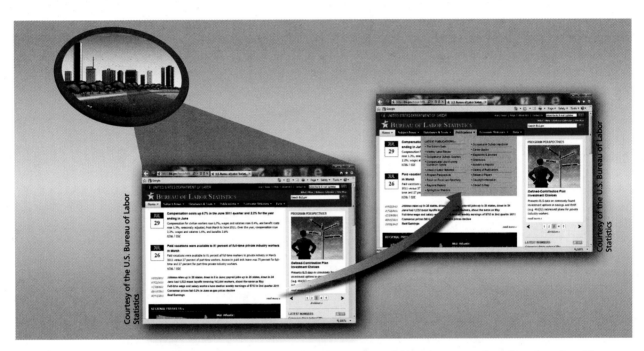

Courtesy of the U.S. Bureau of Labor Statistics

Figure 1–3 A Web site is a related collection of Web pages that is created and maintained by an individual, company, educational institution, or other organization.

Web Servers

Web pages are stored on a **Web server**, or **host**, which is a computer that stores and sends (serves) requested Web pages and other files. Any computer that has Web server software installed and is connected to the Internet can act as a Web server. Every Web site is stored on, and runs from, one or more Web servers. A large Web site may be spread over several servers in different geographic locations.

In order to make the Web pages that you have developed available to your audience, you have to publish those pages. **Publishing** is copying the Web pages and associated files such as graphics and audio to a Web server. Once a Web page is published, anyone who has access to the Internet can view it, regardless of where the Web server is located. For example, although the U.S. Department of Labor Web site is stored on a Web server somewhere in the United States, it is available for viewing by anyone in the world. Once a Web page is published, it can be read by almost any computer: whether you use the Mac, Windows, or Linux operating system, with a variety of computer hardware, you have access to billions of published Web pages.

Web Site Types and Purposes

The three general types of Web sites are Internet, intranet, and extranet. Table 1–1 lists characteristics of each of these three types of Web sites.

An **Internet site**, also known as a **Web site**, is a site generally available to the public. Individuals, groups, companies, and educational institutions use Web sites for a variety of purposes. Intranets and extranets also use Internet technology, but access is limited to specified groups. An **intranet** is a private network that uses Internet technologies to share company information among employees. An intranet is contained within a company or organization's network, which makes it private and only available to those who need access. Policy and procedure manuals usually are found on an intranet. Other documents such as employee directories, company newsletters, product catalogs, and training manuals often are distributed through an intranet.

An **extranet** is a private network that uses Internet technologies to share business information with select corporate partners or key customers. Companies and organizations can use an extranet to share product manuals, training modules, inventory status, and order information. An extranet also might allow retailers to purchase inventory directly from their suppliers or to pay bills online.

Companies use Web sites to advertise or sell their products and services worldwide, as well as to provide technical and product support for their customers. Many company Web sites also support **electronic commerce (e-commerce)**, which is the buying and selling of goods and services on the Internet. Using e-commerce technologies, these Web sites allow customers to browse product catalogs, comparison shop, and order products online. Figure 1–4 shows Cengage.com, which is a company that sells and distributes

BTW

Intranets and Extranets
There are many Web sites that discuss ideas for intranets and extranets. Many companies are already using these technologies and share their "best practice" techniques. Many Web sites provide valuable information on building and maintaining an intranet or extranet, along with additional resources.

BTW

E-Commerce
Today, e-commerce is a standard part of doing business. E-commerce technologies, however, continue to change, offering new applications and potential uses.

Table 1–1 Types of Web Sites			
Type	**Users**	**Access**	**Applications**
Internet	Anyone	Public	Used to share information such as personal information, product catalogs, course information with the public
intranet	Employees or members	Private	Used to share information such as forms, manuals, organization schedules with employees or members
extranet	Select business partners	Private	Used to share information such as inventory updates, product specifications, financial information with business partners and customers

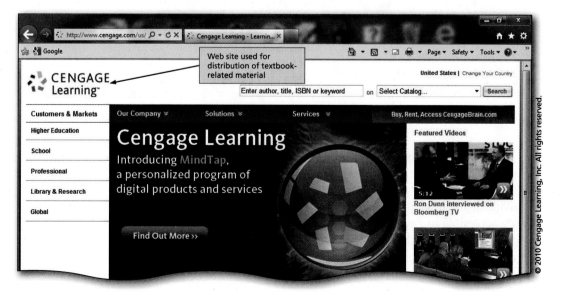

Figure 1–4   Cengage.com is a Web site that provides online educational material.

textbook-related materials online. Many company Web sites also provide job postings and announcements, a frequently asked questions (FAQs) section, customer feedback links to solicit comments from their customers, and searchable technical support databases.

Colleges, universities, and other schools use Web sites to distribute information about areas of study, provide course information, or register students for classes online. Instructors use their Web sites to issue announcements, post questions on reading material, list contact information, and provide easy access to lecture notes and slides. Many instructors today use the course management software adopted by their respective schools to upload course content. Using a standard course management product across a university makes it easier for students to find information related to their various courses. Many course management tools allow instructors to write their own Web content for courses. With many systems, instructors can use Web pages to provide further information for their students within the structure of the course management tool provided by the school. In addition to keeping in contact with current students via the Web, universities also provide a variety of Web site functionality to a variety of visitors as shown in Figure 1–5.

Figure 1–5 University Web sites are varied.

In addition to the use of the Internet by companies and educational institutions, individuals might create personal Web sites that include their résumés to make them easily accessible to any interested employers. Families can share photographs, video and audio clips, stories, schedules, or other information through Web sites (Figure 1–6). Many individual Web sites allow password protection, which makes a safer environment for sharing information.

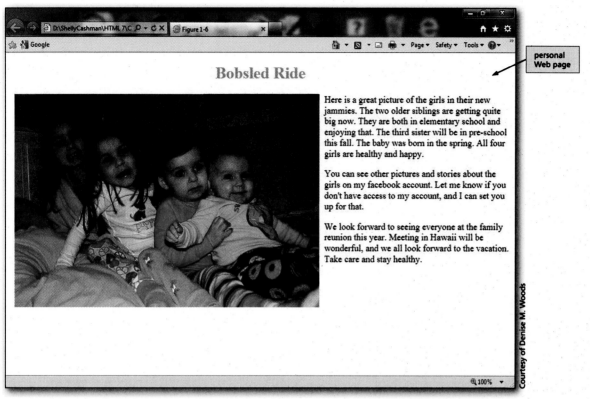

Figure 1–6 Personal Web page used to communicate with family and friends.

Web Browsers

To display a Web page on any type of Web site, a computer needs to have a Web browser installed. A **Web browser**, also called a **browser**, is a program that interprets and displays Web pages and enables you to view and interact with a Web page. Microsoft Internet Explorer, Mozilla Firefox, Google Chrome, and Apple Safari are popular browsers today. Browsers provide a variety of features, including the capability to locate Web pages, to link forward and backward among Web pages, to add a favorite or bookmark a Web page, and to choose security settings.

To locate a Web page using a browser, you type the Web page's Uniform Resource Locator (URL) in the browser's Address or Location bar. A **Uniform Resource Locator (URL)** is the address of a document or other file accessible on the Internet. An example of a URL on the Web is:

http://www.cengagebrain.com/shop/index.html

The URL indicates to the browser to use the HTTP communications protocol to locate the index.html Web page in the shop folder on the cengagebrain.com Web server. Web page URLs can be found in a wide range of places, including school catalogs, business cards, product packaging, and advertisements.

Hyperlinks are an essential part of the World Wide Web. A **hyperlink**, also called a **link**, is an element used to connect one Web page to another Web page on the same server or to Web pages on different Web servers located anywhere in the world. Clicking a hyperlink allows you to move quickly from one Web page to another, and the user does not have to be concerned about where the Web pages reside. You can also click hyperlinks to move to a different section of the same Web page.

With hyperlinks, a Web site user does not necessarily have to view information in a linear way. Instead, he or she can click the available hyperlinks to view the information in a variety of ways, as described later in this chapter. Many different Web page elements, including text, graphics, and animations, can serve as hyperlinks. Figure 1–7 shows examples of several different Web page elements used as hyperlinks.

Figure 1–7 A Web page can use several different Web page elements as hyperlinks.

What Is Hypertext Markup Language?

Web pages are created using **Hypertext Markup Language (HTML)**, which is an authoring language used to create documents for the World Wide Web. HTML uses a set of special instructions called **tags** or **markup** to define the structure and layout of a Web document and specify how the page is displayed in a browser.

A Web page is a file that contains both text and HTML tags. HTML tags mark the text to define how it should appear when viewed in a browser. HTML includes hundreds of tags used to format Web pages and create hyperlinks to other documents or Web pages. For instance, the HTML tags <p> and </p> are used to indicate a new paragraph with a blank line above it, <table> and </table> are used to indicate the start and end of a table, and <hr /> is used to display a horizontal rule across the page. Figure 1–8a shows the HTML tags needed to create the Web page shown in Figure 1–8b. You can also enhance HTML tags by using attributes, as shown in Figure 1–8a. **Attributes** define additional characteristics such as font weight or style for the HTML tag.

HTML is **platform independent**, meaning you can create, or code, an HTML file on one type of computer and then use a browser on another type of computer to view that file as a Web page. The page looks the same regardless of what platform you are using. One of the greatest benefits of Web technology is that the same Web page can be viewed on many different types of digital hardware, including mobile devices like smartphones.

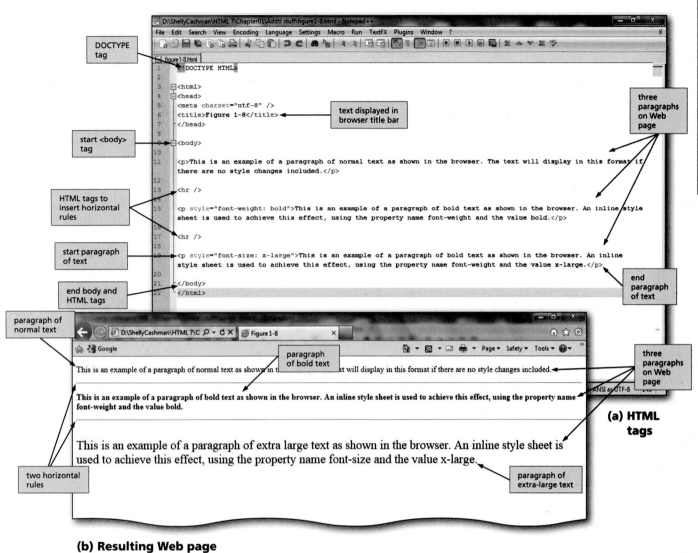

(b) Resulting Web page

Figure 1–8   A Web page is a file that contains both text and HTML tags.

HTML Elements

HTML combines tags and descriptive attributes that define how a document should appear in a Web browser. HTML elements include headings, paragraphs, hyperlinks, lists, images, and more. HTML element syntax is as follows:

- HTML elements begin with a **start tag / opening tag**
- HTML elements finish with an **end tag / closing tag**
- The **element content** is everything inserted between the start and end tags
- Some HTML elements have **empty content** (e.g., <br /> or <hr />)
- Empty elements are **closed in the start tag** (use space-/ to close as in <br />)
- Most HTML elements can have **attributes**

For example, to specify a paragraph of text on a Web page, you would enter the following HTML code:

```
<p>This is a paragraph of text.</p>
```

where <p> is the start or opening tag, </p> is the end or closing tag, and the content is situated between those tags. Table 1–2 shows examples of some HTML elements.

Table 1–2 HTML Elements

Element	Purpose	Code and Content
Title	Indicates title to appear on the title bar in the browser	<title>This is the title text.</title>
Anchor	Creates a link to a Web page named default.html	<a href="default.html">This is text for a link.</a>
Line break	Inserts a line break before the next element (without a blank line); there is no content or closing tag; use space-/ as closing tag	

BTW

HTML Elements
Numerous sources of information about HTML elements are available. The World Wide Web Consortium (w3.org) provides the most comprehensive list of tags and attributes together with examples of their use. One of the main goals of the W3C is to help those building Web sites understand and utilize standards that make the Web accessible to all.

Useful HTML Practices

When creating an HTML file, it is good coding practice to separate sections of the HTML code with spaces and by using the Tab key. Adding space between sections, either with blank lines or by tabbing, gives you an immediate view of the sections of code that relate to one another and helps you view the HTML elements in your document more clearly. HTML browsers ignore spaces that exist between the tags in your HTML document, so the spaces and indentations inserted within the code will not appear on the Web page. Figure 1–9 shows an example of an HTML file with code sections separated by blank lines and code section indentations. Another developer looking at this code can see immediately where the specific sections are located in the code.

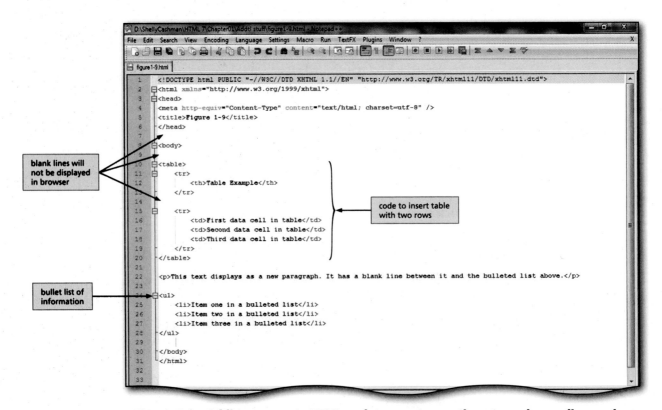

Figure 1–9   Adding spaces to HTML code separates sections to make reading easier.

HTML Versions

HTML has gone through several versions, each of which expands the capabilities of the authoring language. To ensure that browsers can interpret each new version of HTML, the World Wide Web Consortium (W3C) maintains HTML standards, or specifications, which are publicly available on its Web site. HTML5 is the newest version of HTML. HTML5 provides a more flexible approach to Web development. For instance, with HTML5, you can combine lowercase, uppercase, or mixed-case lettering in your tags and attributes. Despite the HTML5 flexibility, this book will adhere to good coding practices that would make it easy to convert to XHTML standards if they should one day override HTML5. The coding practices to which the book adheres are: using all lowercase tags and attributes, enclosing all attribute values in quotation marks, closing all tags, and nesting tags properly (see Table 1–3 on page HTML 13). Although HTML5 has become very popular with Web developers, it is still being developed by the World Wide Web Consortium. The challenge for Web developers, therefore, is to know which new tags and attributes are supported by which browser. This book utilizes HTML5 tags and attributes that are currently supported by Internet Explorer. Additionally, we combine HTML 4.01 tags and attributes with HTML5 to create all of the Web pages in the book. Despite the popularity of HTML5 and HTML 4.01, most browsers continue to support HTML versions 3.2 and 2.0. As described later in this chapter, it is important to verify that Web pages are displayed as intended in a variety of browsers during the testing phase of development.

Cascading Style Sheets

This book has taken a new direction by eliminating deprecated tags and attributes. **Deprecated** tags and attributes are tags and attributes that are being phased out and therefore no longer recommended in the latest W3C standard. Deprecated tags are still used in many Web pages, however, so it is good to know their purpose from a maintenance standpoint. In Appendix A, deprecated tags and attributes are highlighted with an asterisk. In an effort to eliminate deprecated HTML tags, the projects utilize Cascading Style Sheets (CSS) to alter the style (or look) of a Web page. Although HTML allows Web developers to make changes to the structure, design, and content of a Web page, it is limited in its ability to define the appearance, or style, across one or more Web pages. **Cascading Style Sheets** (**CSS**) allow you to specify styles for various Web page elements. A **style** is a rule that defines the appearance of a Web page element. A **style sheet** is a series of rules that defines the style for a Web page or an entire Web site. With a style sheet, you can alter the appearance of a Web page or pages by changing characteristics such as font family, font size, margins, and link specifications, as well as visual elements such as colors and borders. CSS is not used to add any content to your Web site; it just makes your content look more stylish.

With CSS you can specify the style for an element within a single Web page or throughout an entire Web site. For example, if you want all text paragraphs on a Web page to be indented by five spaces, you can use a style sheet to handle the indenting, rather than coding each paragraph with an indentation. And, if you decided you wanted to change the indent to three spaces, you would change just one style sheet line rather than changing the coding for each paragraph. So you can see that using CSS saves a lot of time and makes it much easier to make style changes.

CSS is not HTML; it is a separate language used to enhance the display capabilities of HTML. The World Wide Web Consortium, the same organization that defines HTML standards, defines the specifications for CSS. This book will provide information about CSS3, the newest version of CSS that is currently being developed. We address the new features that CSS3 brings to the world of Web development. Be forewarned that this is a moving target and

BTW

CSS, DOM, and XHTML
The w3.org Web site has an extensive amount of information and tutorials about Cascading Style Sheets (CSS), Document Object Model (DOM), and Extensible HTML (XHTML). The standards suggested in the W3C Web site are the ones that most Web developers follow.

not all browsers support the latest selector syntax provided by CSS3. Appendix A at the back of this book and available online provides a list of HTML tags and corresponding attributes that will allow you to alter the Web page elements as needed, and Appendix D has complete information on the properties and values associated with different CSS elements.

Document Object Model (DOM)

HTML can be used with other Web technologies to provide additional Web page functionality. For example, the term **Document Object Model (DOM)** describes a combination of HTML tags, CSS, and a scripting language such as JavaScript. DOM allows JavaScript and other languages to manipulate the structure of the underlying document to create interactive, animated Web pages. This is a model in which the Web page (or document) contains objects (elements, links, etc.) that can be manipulated. DOM allows a Web developer to add, delete, or change an element or attribute. Web pages enhanced with DOM can be more responsive to visitor interaction than basic HTML Web pages. Not all interactive Web pages require DOM, but if you have a need for extensive interactivity, then this might be a model to consider. CSS, JavaScript, and DOM are covered in later chapters in the Comprehensive (12-chapter) version of this book.

Extensible Hypertext Markup Language (XHTML)

As you have learned, HTML uses tags to describe how a document should appear in a Web browser, or the Web page format. HTML is used to display data, whereas **Extensible Markup Language (XML)** is designed to transport and store data. XML provides a set of rules that are used to encode documents in machine-readable form. XML is not a replacement for HTML, but it is a software- and hardware-independent tool that is used to carry information. Chapter 12 discusses XML in depth and is used to teach XML specifics to students. **Extensible Hypertext Markup Language (XHTML)** is a reformulation of HTML formatting so it conforms to XML structure and content rules. By combining HTML and XML, XHTML combines the display features of HTML and the stricter coding standards required by XML.

As mentioned previously, the projects in this book utilize some of the new tags and attributes introduced with HTML5. The XHTML standards do not apply to HTML5, but we will adhere to the XHTML coding practices as per Table 1–3 because these practices create a uniformity of coding styles. Applying the XHTML coding practices together with any new HTML5 tags or attributes will not cause a problem when you validate your code as long as you use the HTML5 <!DOCTYPE> statement:

```
<!DOCTYPE HTML>
<html>
```

at the start of your Web page.

An important step in Web development is to check that your Web pages are compliant with HTML5 standards as defined by W3C. You will validate your Web pages starting in Chapter 2, using the new HTML5 <!DOCTYPE> statement noted above, and continue that process throughout the book. Most Web pages already developed do not validate. However, it is best that you begin your Web development training using the standards recommended by W3C.

Table 1–3 lists some of the coding rules that Web developers should follow to ensure that their HTML code conforms to XHTML standards when using a combination of HTML 4.01 and HTML5 tags and attributes. All of the projects in this book follow XHTML standards (except for the <!DOCTYPE>) and adhere to the rules outlined in Table 1–3. The specifics of each rule are explained in detail when used in a project.

Table 1–3 XHTML Coding Practices

Practice	Invalid Example	Valid Example
All tags and attributes must be written in lowercase	<TABLE WIDTH="100%">	<table width="100%">
All attribute values must be enclosed by single or double quotation marks	<table width=100%>	<table width="100%">
All tags must be closed, including tags such as img, hr, and br, which do not have end tags, but which must be closed as a matter of practice	 <hr><p>This is another paragraph	 <hr /><p>This is another paragraph</p>
All elements must be nested properly	<p><strong>This is a bold paragraph</p></strong>	<p><strong>This is a bold paragraph</strong></p>

Tools for Creating HTML Documents

You can create Web pages using HTML with a simple text editor, such as Notepad++, Notepad, TextPad, or TextEdit. A **text editor** is a program that allows a user to enter, change, save, and print text, such as HTML. Text editors do not have many advanced features, but they do allow you to develop HTML documents easily. For instance, if you want to insert the DOCTYPE tags into the Web page file, type the necessary text into any of the text editors, as shown in Figure 1–10a and Figure 1–10b on the next page. Although Notepad (Figure 1–10b) is an adequate text editor for Web development, note its differences from Notepad++. Notepad++ is a more robust text editor that uses color schemes for HTML code as it is entered.

You can also create Web pages using an HTML text editor, such as EditPlus or BBEdit (Mac OS). An **HTML text editor** is a program that provides basic text-editing functions, as well as more advanced features such as color-coding for various HTML tags, menus to insert HTML tags, and spell checkers. An **HTML object editor**, such as EiffelStudio object editor, provides the additional functionality of an outline editor that allows you to expand and collapse HTML objects and properties, edit parameters, and view graphics attached to the expanded objects.

Many popular software applications also provide features that enable you to develop Web pages easily. Microsoft Word, Excel, and PowerPoint, for example, have a Save as Web Page option that converts a document into an HTML file by automatically adding HTML tags to the document. Using Microsoft Access, you can create a Web page that allows you to view data in a database. Adobe Acrobat also has an export feature that creates HTML files. Each of these applications also allows you to add hyperlinks, drop-down boxes, option buttons, or scrolling text to the Web page.

These advanced Web features make it simple to save any document, spreadsheet, database, or presentation to display as a Web page. Corporate policy and procedures manuals and PowerPoint presentations, for example, can be easily saved as Web pages and published to the company's intranet. Extranet users can be given access to Web pages that allow them to view or update information stored in a database.

You can also create Web pages using a WYSIWYG editor such as Adobe Dreamweaver, Amaya, or CoffeeCup HTML Editor. A **WYSIWYG editor** is a program that provides a graphical user interface that allows a developer to preview the Web page during its development. WYSIWYG (pronounced wizzy-wig) is an acronym for What You See Is What You Get. A WYSIWYG editor creates the HTML code for you as you

BTW

Free HTML WYSIWYG Editors
There are a number of popular WYSIWYG editors that are being used by many novice Web developers to create well-designed, interactive Web sites. You can find these by searching for "WYSIWYG HTML editor" in most search engines.

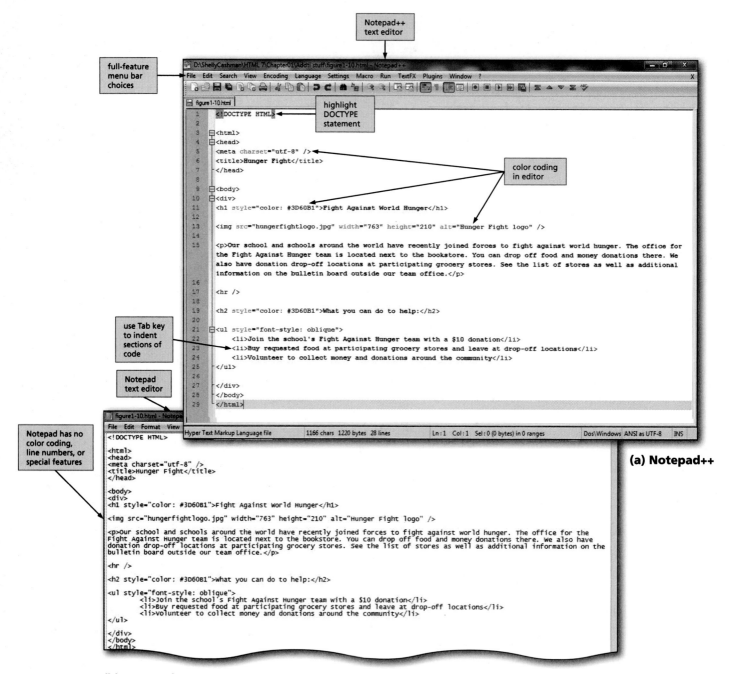

Figure 1–10 With text editors such as Notepad++ or Notepad, you can type HTML tags directly in the files.

add elements to the Web page, which means that you do not have to enter HTML tags directly. The main problem with WYSIWYG editors is that they often create "puffed-up" HTML code (HTML tags with many lines of unnecessary additional code surrounding them).

Regardless of which type of program you use to create Web pages, it is important to understand the specifics of HTML so you can make changes outside of the editor. For instance, you may be able to create a Web page with Dreamweaver, but if you want to make some minor changes, it is very helpful to know the HTML tags themselves. It is also important to understand the Web development life cycle so the Web pages in your Web site are consistent and complete.

Web Development Life Cycle

For years, university and college information technology courses have stressed the importance of following the Systems Development Life Cycle when designing and implementing new software to ensure consistency and completeness. The Web development process should follow a similar cycle. Comprehensive planning and analysis ensure that developers will provide what the users want. If you start to code your Web pages without thorough planning and analysis, you run the risk of missing pertinent information. It is much less expensive to make corrections to a Web site in the early phases of project development than it is to alter Web pages that are completed.

The Web development life cycle outlined in this section is one that can be utilized for any type or size of Web development project. The **Web development life cycle** is a process that can be used for developing Web pages at any level of complexity. The Web development life cycle includes the following phases: planning, analysis, design and development, testing, and implementation and maintenance. Table 1–4 lists several questions that should be asked during each phase in the Web development life cycle. Throughout this book, you will follow this systematic cycle as you develop your Web pages.

Table 1–4 Web Development Phases and Questions

Web Development Phase	Questions to Ask
Planning	• What is the purpose of this Web site? • Who will use this Web site? • What are the users' computing environments? • Who owns and authors the information on the Web site? • Who decides if/where the information goes on the Web site?
Analysis	• What tasks do the users need to perform? • What information is useful to the users? • What process considerations must be made?
Design and Development	• How many Web pages will be included in the Web site? • How will the Web pages be organized? • What type of Web site structure is appropriate for the content? • How can I best present the content for ease of use? • What file naming convention will be employed for this Web site? • What folder structure will be used for the Web page files? • How do I apply standards throughout the development process? • What forms of multimedia contribute positively to the Web site? • How can accessibility issues be addressed without limiting usability? • Will there be an international audience?
Testing	• Do the Web pages pass the World Wide Web Consortium (W3C) validation process as HTML5 compliant? • Is the Web site content correct? • Does the Web site function correctly? • Are users able to find the information they need to complete desired tasks? • Is navigation clear and easy to use?
Implementation and Maintenance	• How is the Web site published? • How can users be attracted to visit and revisit the Web site? • How is the Web site updated? • Who is responsible for content updates? • Who is responsible for structure updates? • How will users be notified about updates to the Web site? • Will the Web site be monitored?

Web Site Planning

Web site planning, which is the first phase of the Web development life cycle, involves identifying the goals or purpose of the Web site. The first step in the Web site planning phase is to answer the question "What is the purpose of this Web site?" As you have learned, individuals and groups design and publish Web sites for a variety of purposes. Individuals develop Web sites to share their hobbies, to post résumés, or just to share ideas on personal interests. Organizations create Web sites to keep members informed of upcoming events or to recruit new members. Businesses create Web sites to advertise and sell products or to give their customers 24-hour online support. Instructors publish Web sites, or add information to their courses using the school's online course management software, to inform students of course policies, assignments, and due dates, as well as course requirements. Until you can adequately identify the intended purpose of the Web site, you should not proceed with the Web development project.

In addition to understanding the Web site's purpose, you should also understand who will use the Web site and the computing environments of most of the users. Knowing the makeup of your target audience — including age, gender, general demographic background, and level of computer literacy — will help you design a Web site appropriate for the target users. Understanding users' computing environments will determine what types of Web technologies to use. For example, if most users have low-speed Internet connections, you would not want to create pages with large graphics or multimedia elements.

A final aspect to the Web site planning phase is to identify the content owners and authors. To determine this, you need to ask the questions:

• Who owns and authors the information on the Web site?

• Who decides if/where the information goes on the Web site?

Once you have identified who will provide and authorize the Web site content, you can include those individuals in all aspects of the Web development project.

Web Site Analysis

During the analysis phase, you make decisions about the Web site content and functionality. To help define the appropriate Web site content and functionality, you should first identify the tasks that users need to perform. Answering that question allows you to define necessary content to facilitate those tasks and determine useful information for the users. Extraneous content that does not serve any purpose should be eliminated from the Web site.

In the analysis phase, it is also important to consider the processes required to support Web site features. For example, if you determine that users should be able to order products through the Web site, then you also need to define the processes or actions to be taken each time an order is submitted. For instance, after an order is submitted, how will that order be processed throughout the back-office business applications such as inventory control and accounts payable? Will users receive e-mail confirmations with details about their orders? The analysis phase is one of the more important phases in the Web development life cycle. Clearly understanding and defining the desired content and functionality of the Web site will direct the type of Web site that you design and reduce changes during Web site development.

Web Site Design and Development

After determining the purpose of the Web site and defining the content and functionality, you need to consider the Web site's design. Some key considerations in Web site design are defining how to organize Web page content, selecting the appropriate Web site structure, determining how to use multimedia, addressing accessibility issues, and designing pages for an international audience. One of the most important aspects of Web site design is determining the best way to provide navigation on the Web site. If users cannot easily find the information that they are seeking, they will not return to your Web site.

Many ways to organize a Web page exist, just as many ways to organize a report or paper exist. Table 1–5 lists some organizational standards for creating a Web page that is easy to read and navigate.

BTW

Accessibility Standards
Creating a Web site that is accessible to all users allows your Web site to reach the widest audience. Further, under Section 508 law, any Web site or technology used by a U.S. federal agency must be usable by people with disabilities. See Appendix C for Section 508 guidelines.

Table 1–5 Web Page Organizational Standards

Element	Organizational Standard	Reason
Titles	Use simple titles that clearly explain the purpose of the page	Titles help users understand the purpose of the page; a good title explains the page in the search engine results lists
Headings	Use headings to separate main topics	Headings make a Web page easier to read; simple headlines clearly explain the purpose of the page
Horizontal Rules	Insert horizontal rules to separate main topics	Horizontal rules provide graphical elements to break up Web page content
Paragraphs	Use paragraphs to help divide large amounts of text	Paragraphs provide shorter, more readable sections of text
Lists	Utilize bulleted or numbered lists when appropriate	Lists provide organized, easy-to-read text that readers can scan
Page Length	Maintain suitable Web page lengths	Web users do not always scroll to view information on longer pages; appropriate page lengths increase the likelihood that users will view key information
Information	Emphasize the most important information by placing it at the top of a Web page	Web users are quick to peruse a page; placing critical information at the top of the page increases the likelihood that users will view key information
Other	Incorporate a contact e-mail address; include the date of the last modification	E-mail addresses and dates give users a way to contact a Web site developer with questions; the date last modified helps users determine the timeliness of the site information

Web sites can use several different types of structures, including linear, hierarchical, and webbed. Each structure links, or connects, the Web pages in a different way to define how users navigate the site and view the Web pages. You should select a structure for the Web site based on how users will navigate the site and view the Web site content.

A **linear** Web site structure connects Web pages in a straight line, as shown in Figure 1–11 on the next page. A linear Web site structure is appropriate if the information on the Web pages should be read in a specific order. For example, if the information on the first Web page, Module 1, is necessary for understanding information on the second Web page, Module 2, you should use a linear structure. Each page would have links from one Web page to the next, as well as a link back to the previous Web page. There are many cases in which Web pages need to be read one after the other, such as in the case of training material in which Module 1 needs to be completed before Module 2 can be attempted.

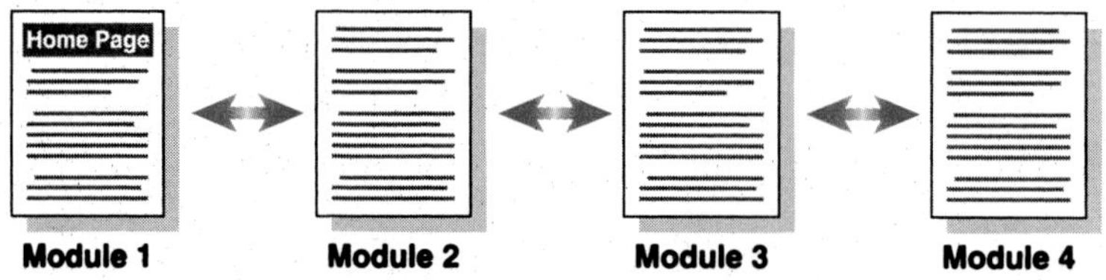

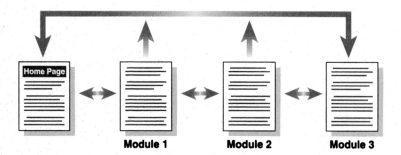

Figure 1–11 Linear Web site structure.

A variation of a linear Web site structure includes the addition of a link to the home page of the Web site, as shown in Figure 1–12. For some Web sites, moving from one module to the next module is still important, but you also want to provide users with easy access to the home page at any time. In this case, you would still provide links from the module Web pages to the previous and next module, but each Web page would also have a link back to the home page. In this way, the user does not have to click the previous link multiple times in order to get back to the home page.

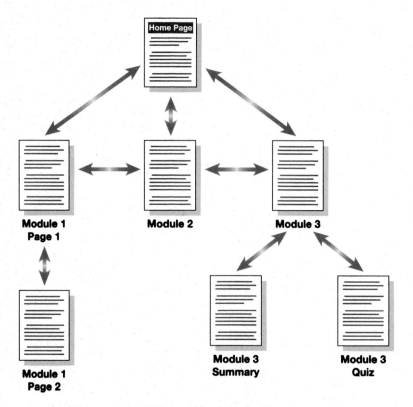

Figure 1–12 Linear Web site structure with links to home page.

> **BTW**
> **User Interface Design**
> The user interface design is an important aspect of a Web site. If a site is designed poorly, users may not be able to find the desired information or complete a task, which makes the Web site ineffective.

A **hierarchical** Web site structure connects Web pages in a treelike structure, as shown in Figure 1–13. A hierarchical Web site structure works well on a site with a main

Figure 1–13 Hierarchical Web site structure.

index or table of contents page that links to all other Web pages. With this structure, the main index page would display general information, and secondary pages would include more detailed information. Notice how logically the information in Figure 1–13 is organized. A Web page visitor can easily go from the home page to any of the three modules. In addition, the visitor can easily get to the Module 3 Quiz by way of the Module 3 link. One of the inherent problems with this structure, though, is the inability to move easily from one section of pages to another. As an example, to move from Module 1 Page 2 to the Module 3 Summary, the visitor would have to use the Back button to get to the Home Page and then click the Module 3 link. This is moderately annoying for a site with two Web pages, but think what it would be like if Module 1 had 100 Web pages!

To circumvent the problems with the hierarchical model, you can use a webbed model. A **webbed** Web site structure has no set organization, as shown in Figure 1–14. A webbed Web site structure works best on sites with information that does not need to be read in a specific order and with many navigation options. The World Wide Web uses a webbed structure, so users can navigate among Web pages in any order they choose. Notice how the Web site visitor can more easily move between modules or module summaries with this structure. With this model, you most often provide a link to the Home Page from each page, resulting in an additional arrow going from each individual Web page back to the home page (which is difficult to depict in these small figures). Many Web sites today utilize a graphical image (usually the company or institutional logo) in the top-left corner of each Web page as a link to the home page. You will use that technique later in the book.

Most Web sites are a combination of the linear, hierarchical, and webbed structures. Some information on the Web site might be organized hierarchically from an index page, other information might be accessible from all areas of the site, and still other information might be organized linearly to be read in a specific order. Using a combination of the three structures is appropriate if it helps users navigate the site easily. The key is to get the right information to the users in the most efficient way possible.

Regardless of the structure or structures that you use, you should balance the narrowness and depth of the Web site. A **broad Web site** is one in which the home page

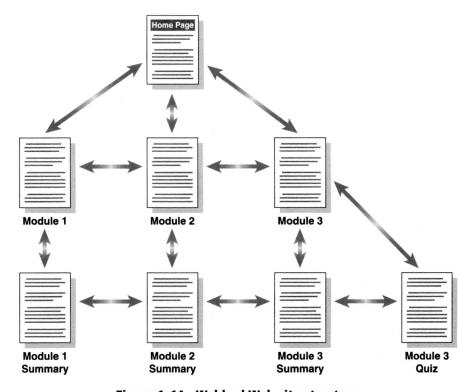

Figure 1–14 Webbed Web site structure.

is the main index page, and all other Web pages are linked individually to the home page (Figure 1–15). By making the other Web pages accessible only through the home page, a broad Web site forces the user to return to the home page to move from one Web page to another. The structure makes navigation time-consuming and limiting for users. A better structure would present a user with navigation alternatives that allow for direct movement between Web pages.

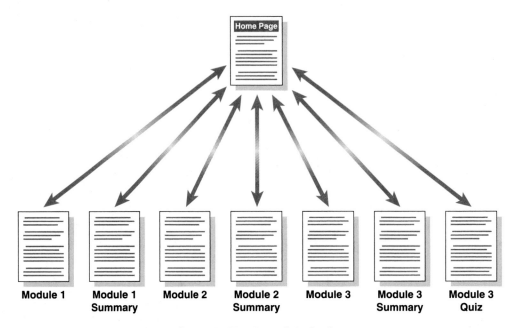

Figure 1–15 Broad Web site.

A **deep Web site** is one that has many levels of pages, requiring the user to click many times to reach a particular Web page (Figure 1–16). By requiring a visitor to move through several Web pages before reaching the desired page, a deep Web site forces a user to spend time viewing interim pages that may not have useful content. As an example, note the difference between finding the Module 3 Summary in Figure 1–13 on page HTML 18 as compared to finding the same Web page (Module 3 Summary) in Figure 1–16. Assume that the user went through the Figure 1–13 Web site once to study the Module 3 material. When the user returns to the Web site using the Figure 1–16 structure, however, to review the Module 3 Summary Web page and then take the Module 3 Quiz, the user would have to go completely through the Module 3 material, Web page by Web page, in order to get to the Module 3 Summary page. You probably want to give users easier access to that Web page.

As a Web developer, you must select an appropriate structure for the Web site and work to balance breadth and depth. Users go to a Web site looking for information to complete a task. Good design provides ease of navigation, allowing users to find content quickly and easily. In addition to planning the design of the Web site itself, a Web developer should always plan the specifics of the file naming and storage conventions early on in the design phase. Once you determine the structure of the Web site and the approximate number of pages necessary to fulfill the site purpose, then you need to identify what standards to use with file naming and the folder structure. For instance, saving your Web pages with names such as page1.html and page2.html does not tell you the purpose of those Web pages. A better option would be to name the Oceanside Hotel Web site's home page oceansidehome.html or oceanside.html, and the Web page with the reservation form could be named reservation.html. Those file names tell the developer, as well as future developers maintaining the Web site, the purpose of those Web pages.

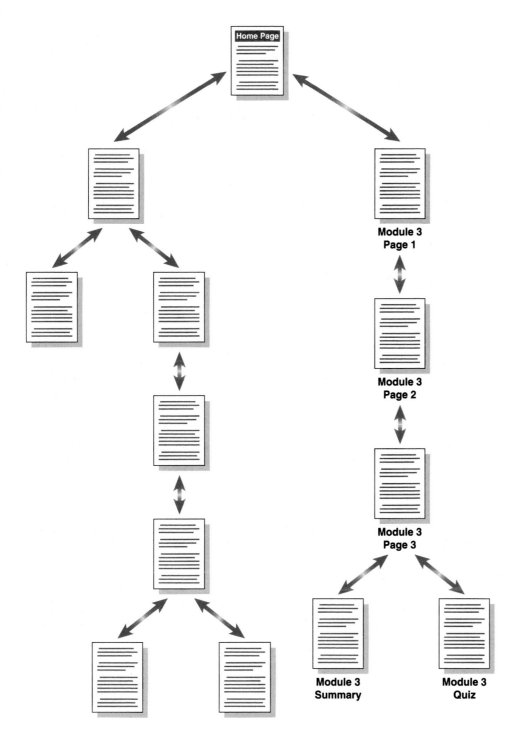

Figure 1–16 Deep Web site.

The same principle applies to the folder structure that you use in your Web development. The projects in this book have so few Web page files and graphic files that all content (Web pages and graphics) is stored together in one folder. With a large Web site, however, you may want to put the Web page files in a separate folder from the graphics files. Larger, more complex Web sites might also require a folder just to store video or audio clips. Where you store the files will affect how you access those files in your HTML code. Determining a good folder structure in the planning phase of the Web development life cycle is important. You'll learn more about effective folder structures in Chapter 3.

During the design and development phase, you should also consider what, if any, types of multimedia could contribute positively to the Web site experience. For instance,

BTW

Web Page Structure
There are many resources available on the Web that further discuss Web site structures. In addition to general design information, there are a number of tools available for sale or free download that can help you design your Web sites. Enter the phrase "Web site structure" into a search engine to find many valuable design sources.

adding a video message from the company CEO might be useful, but if the computing environment of your users cannot accommodate video playback, then the video serves no purpose. In general, do not use advanced multimedia technologies in a Web site unless they make a positive contribution to the Web site experience. Today, more Web sites are using audio and video content. The addition of multimedia can enhance the overall purpose of the Web site, but it sometimes detracts from the message.

Finally, consider accessibility issues and internationalization. A Web developer should always design for viewing by a diverse audience, including physically impaired and global users. A key consideration is that the software used by physically impaired individuals does not work with some Web features. For instance, if you use graphics on the Web site, always include alternative text for each graphic. To support an international audience, use generic icons that can be understood globally, avoid slang expressions in the content, and build simple pages that load quickly over lower-speed connections.

The design issues just discussed are only a few of the basic Web page design issues that you need to consider. Throughout this book, design issues will be addressed as they relate to each project. Many excellent Web page design resources are also available on the Internet.

Once the design of the Web site is determined, Web development can begin. The rest of the chapters in this book discuss good Web page standards, in addition to the actual development of Web pages. You will learn many development techniques, including links, tables, graphics, image maps, and Web forms. The umbrella that covers all of the development techniques taught in this book is the use of Cascading Style Sheets (CSS).

BTW

Web Site Testing
Testing should be done on all pages in a Web site. You should also test the links within the Web page, to other Web pages in the Web site, and to external Web sites. Testing is an important part of Web development and assures that your Web pages work as intended.

Web Site Testing

A Web site should be tested at various stages of the Web design and development processes. The testing process should be comprehensive and include a review of Web page content, functionality, and usability. Web sites with broken links, missing graphics, and incorrect content create a poor impression. You want to attract users to your Web site and maintain their interest. If visitors find that your Web site is poorly tested and maintained, they will be less likely to return. You cannot get your message out if users don't frequently visit the Web site. Some basic steps to test content and functionality include:

- Validating each Web page by running it through the W3C markup validation service
- Proofreading page content and titles to review for accurate spelling and grammar
- Checking links to ensure they are not broken and are linked correctly
- Checking graphics to confirm they appear properly and are linked correctly
- Ensuring that accessibility and internationalization issues are addressed
- Testing forms and other interactive page elements
- Testing pages to make sure they load quickly, even over lower-speed connections
- Printing each page to check how printed pages look

Usability is the measure of how well a product, such as a Web site, allows a user to accomplish his or her goals. **Usability testing** is a method by which users of a Web site or other product are asked to perform certain tasks in an effort to measure the product's ease-of-use and the user's perception of the experience. Usability testing for a Web site should focus on three key aspects: content, navigation, and presentation.

Usability testing can be conducted in several ways; one effective way is to directly observe users interfacing with (or using) the Web site. As you observe users, you can track the links they click and record their actions and comments. You can even ask the users to explain what tasks they were trying to accomplish while navigating the site. The information gained by observing users can be invaluable in helping identify potential problem areas in the Web site. For example, if you observe that users have difficulty finding the

Web page that lists store locations and hours of operation, you may want to clarify the link descriptions or make the links more prominent on the home page.

Another way to conduct usability testing is to give users a specific task to complete (such as finding a product price list) and then observe how they navigate the site to complete the task. If possible, ask them to explain why they selected certain links. Both of these observation methods are extremely valuable, but require access to users.

Usability testing can also be completed using a questionnaire or survey. When writing a questionnaire or survey, be sure to write open-ended questions that can give you valuable information. For instance, asking the yes/no question "Is the Web site visually appealing?" will not gather useful information. If you change that question to use a scaled response, such as, "Rate the visual appeal of this Web site, using a scale of 1 for low and 5 for high," you can get more valuable input from the users. Make sure, however, that the scale itself is clear and understandable to the users. If you intend that a selection of 1 equates to a "low" rating, but the users think a 1 means "high," then your survey results are questionable. A usability testing questionnaire should always include space for users to write additional explanatory comments.

Figure 1–17 shows some examples of types of questions and organization that you might include in a Web site usability testing questionnaire.

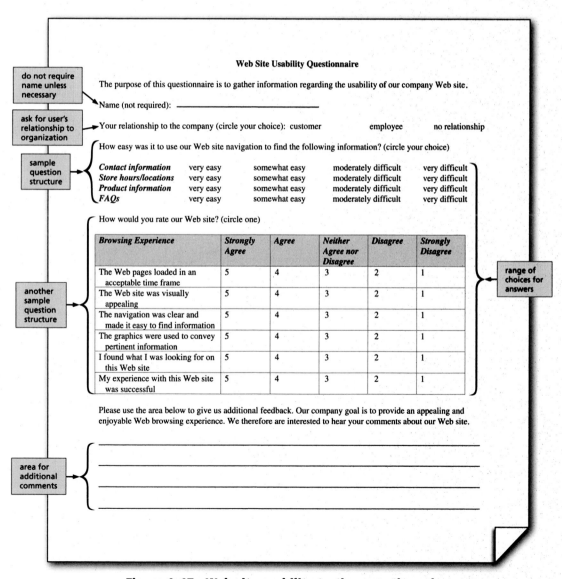

Figure 1–17 Web site usability testing questionnaire.

In addition to content, functionality, and usability testing, there are other types of testing. For a newly implemented or maintained Web site, two other types of tests should be conducted: compatibility testing and stress testing. **Compatibility testing** is done to verify that the Web site works with a variety of browsers and browser versions. Initially, test using the browsers that your audience is most likely to use. Different browsers display some aspects of Web pages differently, so it is important to test Web pages in several different browsers to verify they appear correctly in each browser. If you have used technologies that are not supported by older browsers or that require plug-ins, consider changing the content or providing alternative Web pages for viewing in older browsers. If your audience uses both PC and Macintosh computers, you need to test the Web pages using browsers on both platforms. You may also want to test the Web pages in several versions of the same browser (usually the two most recent versions), in the event users have not yet upgraded.

Stress testing determines what happens on your Web site when greater numbers of users access the site. A Web site with 100 users accessing it simultaneously may be fine. When thousands of users use the Web site at once, it may operate at an unacceptably slow speed. Stress testing verifies that a Web site runs at an acceptable speed with many users. There are many cases in which companies did not effectively stress test their Web sites. The results of this lack of testing have been disastrous, with Web sites locking up when too many users tried to access the same Web site function. Especially in the case of Web sites used for e-commerce, it is imperative for the Web site to stay online. A crashed or locked-up Web site will not sell products or services, and the company stands to lose a lot of money.

Web Site Implementation and Maintenance

Once Web site testing is complete and any required changes have been made, the Web site can be implemented. Implementation of a Web site involves the actual publishing of the Web pages to a Web server. Many HTML editors and WYSIWYG editors provide publishing capabilities. You can also use FTP software, such as WS_FTP or CuteFTP, to publish your Web pages to a Web server. After you publish a Web site, you should test the Web pages again to confirm no obvious errors exist such as broken links or missing graphics.

After a site is tested and implemented, you need to develop a process to maintain the Web site; users will undoubtedly request changes and timely content will require updates. You need to ensure, however, that updates to the Web site do not compromise the site's integrity and consistency. For example, if you have several different people updating various Web pages on a large Web site, you might find it difficult to maintain a consistent look on pages across the Web site. You should plan to update your Web site on a regular basis to keep content up-to-date. This could mean hourly, daily, weekly, or less often, depending on the site's purpose. Do not allow your content to become stale, outdated, or include broken links to Web pages that no longer exist. As a user looking for information related to a specific topic, how likely are you to believe the information found on a Web site that says "Last update on December 10, 1998" comes from a reliable source?

To help manage the task of Web site maintenance, first determine who is responsible for updates to content, structure, functionality, and so on. Then, limit update responsibilities to specific users. Be sure the implementation is controlled by one or more Web developers who can verify that the Web pages are tested thoroughly before they are published.

As updates and changes are made to a Web site, consider notifying users with a graphic banner or a "What's New" announcement, explaining any new features and how the features will benefit them. This technique not only keeps users informed, but also encourages them to come back to the Web site to see what is new.

Finally, Web site monitoring is another key aspect of maintaining a Web site. Usually, the Web servers that host Web sites keep logs of information about Web site usage. A **log** is the file that lists all of the Web pages that have been requested from the Web site. Web site logs are an invaluable source of information for a Web developer. Obtaining and analyzing the logs allow you to determine such things as the number of visitors, browser types and versions, connection speeds, pages most commonly requested, and usage patterns. With this information, you can design a Web site that is effective for your targeted audience, providing visitors with a rich and rewarding experience.

Be an Observant Web User

As you embark on this course, and perhaps start your Web development career, one useful practice is to be an observant Web user. Most of us use the Web several times a day (or more often) to complete our daily tasks. As a Web developer, you should review the Web pages that you access with an eye on functionality and design. As described in the first In the Lab exercise at the end of the chapter, you can bookmark Web sites you think are effective and ineffective, good and bad, and use them as references for your own Web development efforts. Watch for trends on the Web as you search for information or make online purchases. For example, blinking text and patterned backgrounds used to be very popular on the Web, but now other design techniques have taken over. Being an observant Web user can help you become a more effective Web developer.

> **BTW**
>
> **Quick Reference**
> For a list of HTML tags and their associated attributes, see the HTML Quick Reference (Appendix A) at the back of this book, or visit the HTML Quick Reference on the Book Companion Site Web page for this book at www.cengagebrain.com.

Chapter Summary

In this chapter, you have learned about the Internet, the World Wide Web, and associated technologies, including Web servers and Web browsers. You learned the essential role of HTML in creating Web pages and reviewed tools used to create HTML documents. You also learned that most Web development projects follow a five-phase life cycle. The items listed below include all the new concepts you have learned in this chapter.

1. Describe the Internet (HTML 2)
2. Describe the World Wide Web (HTML 3)
3. Define Web servers (HTML 4)
4. Describe the Internet, intranets, and extranets (HTML 5)
5. Discuss Web browsers (HTML 7)
6. Define Hypertext Markup Language (HTML 8)
7. Describe HTML elements (HTML 9)
8. List useful HTML practices (HTML 10)
9. Explain HTML versions (HTML 11)
10. Describe Cascading Style Sheets (HTML 11)
11. Define the Document Object Model (HTML 12)
12. Define Extensible Hypertext Markup Language (XHTML) (HTML 12)
13. Describe tools for creating HTML documents (HTML 13)
14. Discuss the Web development life cycle (HTML 15)
15. Describe steps in the Web development planning phase (HTML 16)
16. Explain the Web development analysis phase (HTML 16)
17. Discuss Web design and development (HTML 17)
18. Describe various Web site structures (HTML 17)
19. Discuss the importance of Web site testing, including usability testing, compatibility testing, and stress testing (HTML 22)
20. Discuss Web site implementation and maintenance (HTML 24)
21. Explain the importance of being an observant Web user (HTML 25)

Learn It Online

Test your knowledge of chapter content and key terms.

Instructions: To complete the following exercises, please visit www.cengagebrain.com. At the CengageBrain.com home page, search for *HTML5 and CSS 7th Edition* using the search box at the top of the page. This will take you to the product page for this book. On the product page, click the Access Now button below the Study Tools heading. On the Book Companion Site Web page, select chapter 1, and then click the link for the desired exercise.

Chapter Reinforcement TF, MC, and SA
A series of true/false, multiple choice, and short answer questions that test your knowledge of the chapter content.

Flash Cards
An interactive learning environment where you identify chapter key terms associated with displayed definitions.

Practice Test
A series of multiple choice questions that test your knowledge of chapter content and key terms.

Who Wants to Be a Computer Genius?
An interactive game that challenges your knowledge of chapter content in the style of a television quiz show.

Wheel of Terms
An interactive game that challenges your knowledge of chapter key terms in the style of the television show *Wheel of Fortune*.

Crossword Puzzle Challenge
A crossword puzzle that challenges your knowledge of key terms presented in the chapter.

Apply Your Knowledge

Reinforce the skills and apply the concepts you learned in this chapter.

Understanding Web Page Structures
Instructions: Figure 1–18 shows the Web site of OnGuardOnline.gov. As you learned in this chapter, three common Web site structures include linear, hierarchical, and webbed. Based on that information, determine the structure used in the OnGuardOnline.gov Web site. Review other similar Web sites and determine which Web site design features are beneficial to a user. Incorporate those ideas into a new Web site design for OnGuardOnline.gov. Use paper to sketch the new Web site design for the OnGuardOnline.gov Web site.

Perform the following tasks:
1. Start your browser. Open the OnGuardOnline.gov Web site in your browser. Print the home page by clicking Print on the File menu or by clicking the Print icon.
2. Explore the OnGuardOnline.gov Web site, determine the structure that the Web site utilizes (linear, hierarchical, or webbed), and then write that on the printout.
3. Find two other government Web sites. Print the home pages for each of those sites. Navigate these Web sites to identify any design features that are beneficial to a user.
4. Using ideas from the government Web sites that you found in Step 3, sketch a new Web site structure and design for the OnGuardOnline.gov site on paper.
5. Submit your answers in the format specified by your instructor.

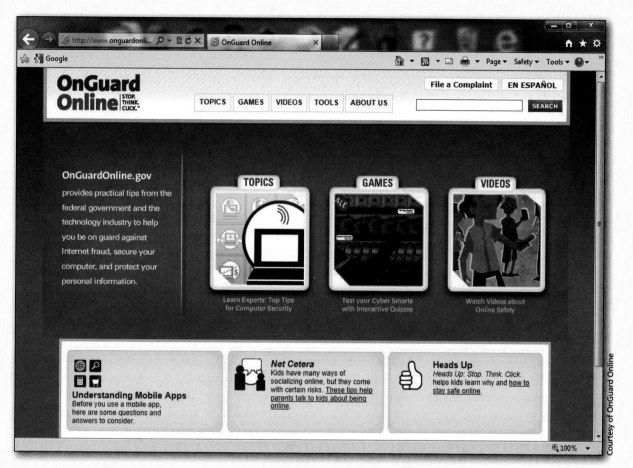

Courtesy of OnGuard Online

Figure 1–18

Extend Your Knowledge

Extend the skills you learned in this chapter and experiment with new skills.

Evaluating a User Survey

Instructions: Start your word-processing program. Open the document extend1-1.docx from the Chapter01\Extend folder of the Data Files for Students. See the inside back cover of this book for instructions on downloading the Data Files for Students, or contact your instructor for information about accessing the required files. This sample Web site survey shows various questions that could be asked in gathering feedback on Web site usability. It is important to assess the usability of your Web site, as mentioned in the chapter.

You will evaluate the user survey and modify the questions or add new questions that apply to the Web site that you have chosen. Then you will ask five people to take your survey.

Perform the following tasks:

1. Determine if the survey questions would provide you with valuable information about a Web site. Why or why not?

2. Identify what you can do to improve the Web site survey. Using a word processor, type your analysis into a new file, and save the file as extend1-1solution.docx.

3. Once you have analyzed the questions in the original survey, make changes to the user survey by following some of the guidelines provided in Figure 1–17 on page HTML 23. Type your new

Continued >

Extend Your Knowledge *continued*

survey questions into the new extend1-1solution.docx file after the analysis completed in step 2. Add questions to the survey that will help you determine a user's opinion of the selected Web site. Remember that the purpose of using surveys is to improve a Web site. Your questions therefore have to provide you with information that can help you achieve that goal.

4. After you have completed these steps, submit the extend1-1solution.docx file in the format specified by your instructor.

Make It Right

Analyze a document and correct all errors and/or improve the design.

Correcting the Web Site Type Table

Instructions: Start your word-processing program. Open the file makeitright1-1.docx from the Chapter01\MakeItRight folder of the Data Files for Students. See the inside back cover of this book for instructions on downloading the Data Files for Students, or contact your instructor for information about accessing the required files. The document, shown in Table 1–6, is a modified version of Table 1–5 (on page HTML 17). The table, which intentionally contains errors, lists the Web page organizational standards discussed in this chapter. Without referring to Table 1–5, make the necessary corrections to Table 1–6 by identifying the correct organizational standard and reason for each of the seven elements listed. Save the revised document as makeitright1-1solution.docx and then submit it in the form specified by your instructor.

Table 1–6 Web Page Organizational Standards		
Element	**Organizational Standard**	**Reason**
Titles	Use these to separate main topics	These provide graphical elements to break up Web page content
Headings	Use simple ones that clearly explain the purpose of the page	These provide shorter, more-readable sections of text
Horizontal Rules	Utilize these in bulleted or numbered format when appropriate	Web users do not always scroll to view information on longer pages; appropriate page lengths increase the likelihood that users will view key information
Paragraphs	Maintain suitable Web page lengths	Web users are quick to peruse a page; placing critical information at the top of the page increases the likelihood that users will view key information
Lists	Insert these graphical elements to separate main topics	These provide organized, easy-to-read text that readers can scan
Page Length	Use these to help divide large amounts of text	Titles help users understand the purpose of the page; a good title explains the page in the search engine results lists
Information	Emphasize the most important information by placing it at the top of a Web page	These make a Web page easier to read; simple headlines clearly explain the purpose of the page

In the Lab

Design and/or create a document using the guidelines, concepts, and skills presented in this chapter. Labs are listed in order of increasing difficulty.

Lab 1: Evaluating Web Sites

Problem: In this chapter, you learned the importance of being an observant Web user, which can help you become a more effective Web developer. To further develop that concept, find and then discuss "good" and "bad" ("effective" and "ineffective") Web sites. Start your browser and your word-processing program. Open the file lab1-1.docx from the Chapter01\IntheLab folder of the Data Files for Students. See the inside back cover of this book for instructions for downloading the Data Files for Students, or contact your instructor for information on accessing the required files for this book.

Instructions: Perform the following steps using your browser and the file listed.

1. Browse the Internet and find one "good" (i.e., effective) and one "bad" (i.e., ineffective) Web site. Determine, based on your own opinion, what is "good" and what is "bad" in these Web sites. You will identify the specific reason for your opinion in Step 2 below.

2. Using the lab1-1.docx file, rate the usability of the good and bad Web sites that you selected. Be sure to add additional comments in the survey to specifically identify your positive or negative feelings about the Web site. Save the documents using the file names lab1-1goodsolution.docx and lab1-1badsolution.docx.

3. Team up with one other student and discuss your survey results while reviewing the Web sites that you selected. Also review your student partner's Web sites and surveys.

4. Open the word-processing document named lab1-1comparison.docx and note any differences of opinion in your survey results and the opinion of your student partner. Make sure to include the URLs of the four Web sites that you and your partner reviewed in this new document. Save the document using the file name lab1-1comparison.docx.

5. Submit your own solutions (lab1-1goodsolution.docx and lab1-1badsolution.docx) and the team document (lab1-1comparison.docx) in the format specified by your instructor.

In the Lab

Lab 2: Designing a Web Site for a Flower Shop

Problem: Your neighborhood flower shop wants you to design a Web site that will give visitors access to a full range of information. To do this, you must complete the planning and analysis phases by answering such questions as:

- What tasks do flower shop visitors want to complete on the Web site?
- What tasks will the flower shop owner want to complete on the Web site?
- What types of information should be included?
- Who will provide information on the Web site content?

Interview several friends or relatives who have visited flower shops in the past and determine the answers to these questions. Based on that information, you will draw a sketch of a design for the home page of the flower shop's Web site, such as the design shown in Figure 1–19 on the next page.

Continued >

In the Lab *continued*

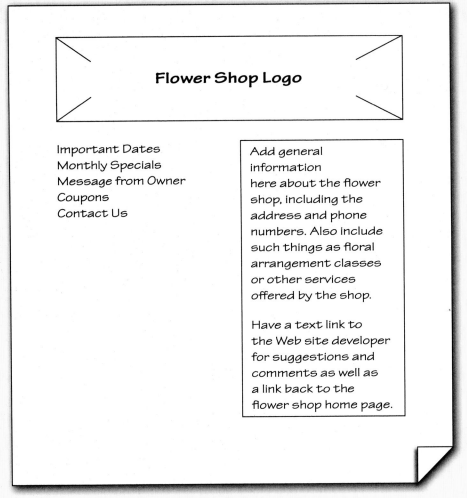

Flower Shop Logo

Important Dates
Monthly Specials
Message from Owner
Coupons
Contact Us

Add general
information
here about the flower
shop, including the
address and phone
numbers. Also include
such things as floral
arrangement classes
or other services
offered by the shop.

Have a text link to
the Web site developer
for suggestions and
comments as well as
a link back to the
flower shop home page.

Figure 1–19

Instructions: Perform the following tasks using your word-processing program and paper.

1. Review the questions in the planning and analysis phases of the Web development life cycle, as shown in Table 1–4 on page HTML 15.

2. Assess the value of those questions listed in the table. Add other questions that you think are relevant to the planning and analysis of a flower shop Web site.

3. Start your word-processing program. If necessary, open a new document. Enter the questions you will use for planning and analysis. Save the document using the file name lab1-2solution.docx. Print the document.

4. Using the questions that you developed, interview friends and family who have visited flower shops to determine what information should be included in the Web site, who will provide the information, and so on.

5. After gathering the required information, sketch a design for the home page of the Web site on paper.

6. Share your design sketch with the people who you interviewed to get their opinions on your design.

7. Redraw the design on paper, making any changes based on the input from the friends and relatives with whom you have worked.

8. Write Original Design on the first design sketch.

9. Write Second Design on the second design sketch.

10. Submit your solution (lab1-2solution.docx) in the format specified by your instructor.

In the Lab

Lab 3: Asking Planning Phase Questions: Internet, Intranet, and Extranet Designs

Problem: Three different types of Web sites were discussed in this chapter — Internet, intranet, and extranet. Each type of Web site is designed for a different target audience. Think of a retail business that you frequently visit and how that business might use an Internet, intranet, and extranet site. The Planning phase questions found in Table 1–4 on page HTML 15 have been reproduced in Table 1–7. Determine the answers to these questions and enter your ideas in the table. If there are questions that are difficult/impossible to answer directly (for example, What are users' computing environments?), list ways that you can find the answers to those questions.

Instructions: Start your word-processing program. Open the file lab1-3.docx from the Chapter01\ IntheLab folder of the Data Files for Students. See the inside back cover of this book for instructions for downloading the Data Files for Students, or contact your instructor for information on accessing the required files. Perform the following tasks using your word-processing program.

1. Enter the type of business in the first row of the table. Determine the answers to the first question for all three types of Web sites and then enter the answers in the appropriate table cells. If the business you chose has no reason to maintain one of the three types of Web sites (Internet, intranet, or extranet), thoroughly identify in your answer why they would not need it.

2. Continue answering the other four questions.

3. Save the file using the file name lab1-3solution.docx and then submit it in the format specified by your instructor.

Table 1–7 Planning Phase Questions

Type Of Business			
Planning Question	**Internet**	**Intranet**	**Extranet**
What is the purpose of this Web site?			
Who will use this Web site?			
What are users' computing environments?			
Who owns and authors the information on the Web site?			
Who decides if/where the information goes on the Web site?			

Cases and Places

Apply your creative thinking and problem-solving skills to design and implement a solution.

Note: To complete these assignments, you may be required to use the Data Files for Students. See the inside back cover of this book for instructions on downloading the Data Files for Students, or contact your instructor for information about accessing the required files.

1: Create a Usability Survey

Academic

Your school recently updated its Web site. The school administration has selected a team to develop a usability survey or questionnaire that you can give to a group of users (including students, parents, and teachers) to evaluate the new Web site. What types of information do you hope to gain by distributing this survey or questionnaire? How can you convey information on the survey or questionnaire so it clearly identifies what you are asking? Create a usability survey using your word-processing program. Give the survey or questionnaire to at least five people, including at least one from each group identified above. Allow participants to complete the survey or questionnaire and then look at the results. If possible, ask the users what they thought the various questions conveyed. Is that what you wanted to convey? If not, think of clearer, more relevant questions and redistribute the survey to another group of participants.

2: Learn More About HTML5

Personal

This chapter introduced the use of HTML5 in Web development. You will utilize HTML5 throughout this book, so it is important that you become familiar with it. Visit the W3Schools Web site (w3schools.com) to learn more about HTML5. Find three other sources of information about HTML5 on other Web sites. Using a word-processing program, create a document that briefly describes the Web sites that you found and an explanation about how you could utilize these three Web sites for Web development.

3: Learn More About Web Access Issues

Professional

Your company wants to offer online courses to employees. Several employees have physical challenges, and it is imperative that the online courses be accessible to everyone. Your manager has asked you to learn more about accessibility guidelines to determine what changes are needed to make the company's online courses accessible to those with physical challenges. Research accessibility issues on the Web and determine what needs should be considered to satisfy accessibility requirements. Make sure to visit the w3.org Web site. Consider the following questions when doing your research: What types of physical challenges do you have to consider when developing Web pages? What recommendations do the Web sites make for accessibility? Why is this important to you as a Web developer?

2 | Creating and Editing a Web Page Using Inline Styles

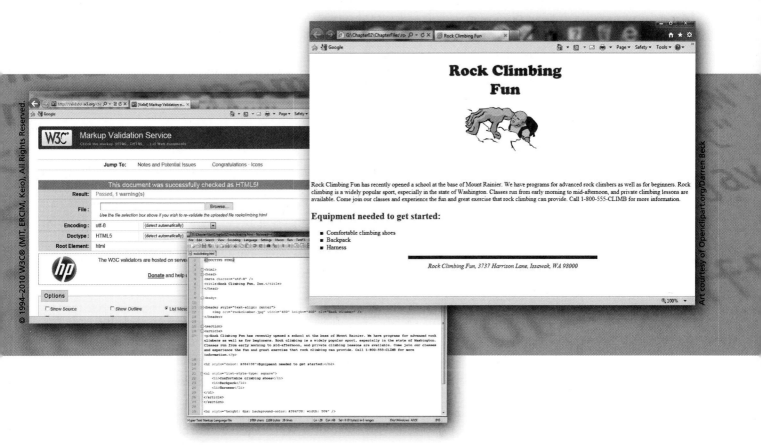

Objectives

You will have mastered the material in this chapter when you can:

- Identify elements of a Web page

- Start Notepad++ and describe the Notepad++ window

- Enable word wrap in Notepad++

- Enter HTML tags

- Enter a centered heading and a paragraph of text

- Create an unordered, ordered, or definition list

- Save an HTML file

- Use a browser to view a Web page

- Activate Notepad++

- Identify Web page image types and attributes

- Add an image, change the color of headings on a Web page, change a bulleted list style, and add a horizontal rule using inline styles

- View the HTML source code in a browser

- Print a Web page and an HTML file

- Quit Notepad++ and a browser

2 | Creating and Editing a Web Page Using Inline Styles

Introduction

With an understanding of the Web development life cycle, you should have a good idea about the importance of proper Web site planning, analysis, and design. After completing these phases, the next phase is the actual development of a Web page using HTML. As discussed in Chapter 1, Web pages are created by using HTML tags and attributes to define the structure, layout, and appearance of a Web page. In this chapter, you create and edit a Web page using basic HTML tags.

Project — Rock Climbing Fun Web Page

Chapter 2 illustrates how to use HTML to create a Web page for a rock climbing company, as shown in Figure 2–1a. As an employee of the company, one of your tasks is to develop a Web page to advertise the company's rock climbing classes. The Rock Climbing Fun Web page will include general information about the company along with information on the equipment needed to start rock climbing.

To enter text and HTML tags used to create the Web page, you will use a program called Notepad++, as shown in Figure 2–1b. **Notepad++** is a basic text editor that you can use for simple documents or for creating Web pages using HTML. Previous editions of this book used Notepad, a text editor that is a part of the Windows operating system. Notepad worked well to enter the HTML elements and Web page content, but Notepad++ is a more sophisticated text editor with more features. Notepad++ has line numbering, which is very helpful when reading code. It also highlights code and text with different colors, as you will see later in the chapter. Because of this added versatility, Notepad++ is the chosen text editor for this edition. You will use the Microsoft Internet Explorer browser to view your Web page as you create it. By default, Internet Explorer is installed with Windows, and Notepad++ can be downloaded for free on the Web. If you do not have Notepad++ on your computer, you can download it from the notepad-plus-plus.org Web site. If you do not have Internet Explorer available on your computer, another browser program will work.

Overview

As you read this chapter, you will learn how to create the Web page shown in Figure 2–1 by performing these general tasks:

- Enter HTML code into the Notepad++ window.
- Save the file as an HTML file.
- Enter basic HTML tags and add text to the file.
- Organize the text by adding headings and creating a bulleted list.
- Enhance the Web page's appearance with an image and inline styles.
- View the Web page and HTML code in your browser.
- Validate the Web page.
- Print the Web page.

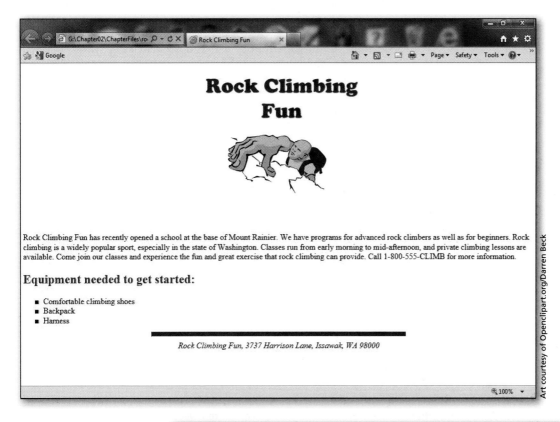

(a) Rock Climbing Fun Web page.

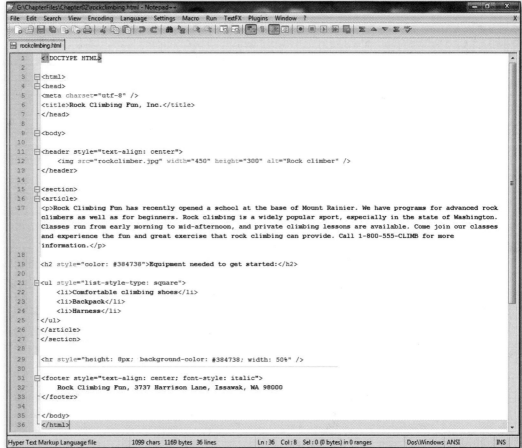

(b) HTML code used to create the Web page.

Figure 2–1

**Plan
Ahead**

General Project Guidelines

When creating a Web page, the actions you perform and decisions you make will affect the appearance and characteristics of the finished page. As you create a Web page, such as the project shown in Figure 2–1 on the previous page, you should follow these general guidelines:

1. **Complete Web page planning.** Before developing a Web page, you must know the purpose of the Web site, identify the users of the site and their computing environments, and decide who owns the information on the Web page.

2. **Analyze the need for the Web page.** In the analysis phase of the Web development life cycle, you should analyze what content to include on the Web page. In this phase, you determine the tasks and the information that the users need. Refer to Table 1–4 on page HTML 15 in Chapter 1 for information on the phases of the Web development life cycle.

3. **Choose the content for the Web page.** Once you have completed the analysis, you need to determine what content to include on the Web page. Follow the *less is more* principle. The less text, the more likely the Web page will be read. Use as few words as possible to make a point.

4. **Determine the file naming convention that you will use for this Web page.** Before you start creating and saving files, you should decide on a standard way of naming your files. Should you use the .htm or .html extension? As explained later in the chapter, you use the .htm extension when the host Web server only allows short file names. You use .html when the host Web server allows long file names. What name should you give your file to indicate the file's content or purpose? For instance, naming a Web page page1.html does not describe what that Web page is; a more descriptive name is helpful in development of the Web site.

5. **Determine where to save the Web page.** You can store a Web page permanently, or **save** it, on a variety of storage media, including a hard disk, USB flash drive, CD, or DVD. Your instructor or the company for whom you are developing the Web page may have specific storage media requirements.

6. **Determine what folder structure to use on your storage device.** Once you have determined the storage media to use, you should also determine folder location, structure, and names on which to save the Web page. This should be done before you start to save any of your files.

7. **Identify how to format various elements of the Web page.** The overall appearance of a Web page significantly affects its ability to communicate clearly. Examples of how you can modify the appearance, or **format**, of the Web page include adding an image, color to headings, and horizontal rules.

8. **Find appropriate graphical images.** Eye-catching graphical images help convey the Web page's overall message and add visual interest. Graphics can be used to show a product, service, result, or benefit, or visually convey a message that is not expressed easily with words.

9. **Establish where to position and how to format the graphical images.** The position and format of the graphical images should grab the attention of viewers and draw them into reading the Web page.

10. **Test the Web page for W3C compliance.** An important part of Web development is testing to assure that your Web page follows standards. The World Wide Web Consortium (W3C) has an online validator that allows you to test your Web page and clearly explains any errors.

When necessary, more specific details concerning the above guidelines are presented at appropriate points in the chapter. The chapter will also identify the actions performed and decisions made regarding these guidelines during the creation of the Web page shown in Figure 2–1a.

Elements of a Web Page

Today, many people — individuals, students, teachers, business executives, Web developers, and others — are developing Web pages for personal or professional reasons. Each person has his or her own style and the resulting Web pages are as diverse as the people who create them. Most Web pages, however, include several basic features, or elements, as shown in Figure 2–2.

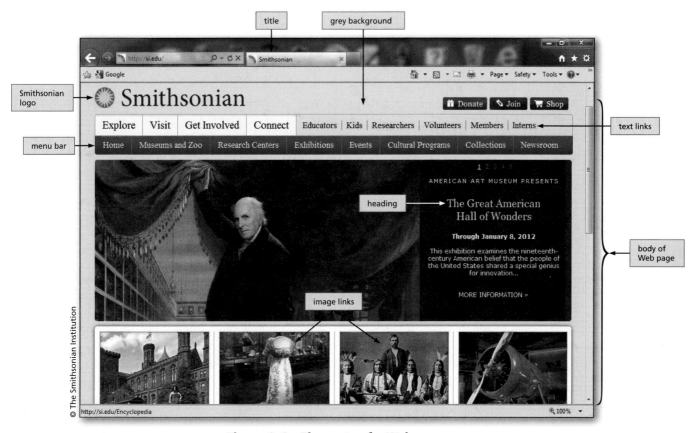

Figure 2–2 Elements of a Web page.

Browser Window Elements

The **title** of a Web page is the text that appears on the title bar and taskbar of the browser window when the Web page appears. The title is also the name assigned to the page if a user adds the page to the browser's list of **favorites**, or **bookmarks**. Because of its importance, you should always include a title on your Web page. The title, which usually is the first element you see, should identify the subject or purpose of the page. The title should be concise, yet descriptive, and briefly explain the page's content or purpose to the visitor.

The **body** of the Web page contains the information that is displayed in the browser window. The body can include text, graphics, and other elements. The Web page displays anything that is contained within the <body> (start body) and </body> (end body) tags. The **background** of a Web page is a solid color, a picture, or a graphic against which the other elements on the Web page appear. When choosing your background, be sure it does not overpower the information on the Web page. As you surf the Web, watch for background colors or images that do not allow the content of the Web page to show through. This is certainly a "what not to do" guideline for Web developers.

BTW

Favorites and Bookmarks
Internet Explorer, Google Chrome, and Mozilla Firefox have a feature that allows you to add Web pages to a list so you can quickly access them in the future. Internet Explorer refers to these as Favorites, while Chrome and Firefox calls them Bookmarks. Web developers need to make sure that they include a descriptive title on their Web pages because that is the title that is shown in the bookmark or favorite.

Text Elements

Normal text is the default text format used for the main content of a Web page. Normal text can be used in a standard paragraph or formatted to appear as: bold, italic, or underlined; in different colors; and so on. You can also use inline styles to alter the format of the text, an approach used throughout this book. Normal text can also be used in a series of text items called a **list**. Typically, lists are bulleted or numbered. Various attributes of lists can be altered. For example, you might want to have square bullets rather than the default round bullets, or to have your list text in italic or bold.

Headings are used to set off paragraphs of text or different sections of a page. Headings are a larger font size than normal text and are often bold or italic or a different color than normal text. Heading sizes run from 1 (the largest) to 6 (the smallest). You generally go from one heading size to the next smallest when setting up a Web page.

Image Elements

Web pages typically use several different types of graphics, or images, such as an icon, bullet, line, photo, illustration, or other picture. An image used in a Web page is also called an **inline image**, which means that the image or graphic file is not part of the HTML file. Instead, the Web browser merges the separate graphic file into the Web page as it is displayed in the browser window. The HTML file contains <img> tags that tell the browser which graphic file to request from the server, where to insert it on the page, and how to display it.

Web pages typically use several different types of inline images. An **image map** is a special type of inline image in which you define one or more areas as hotspots. A **hotspot** is an area of an image that activates a function when selected. For example, each hotspot in an image map can link to a different Web page. Some inline images are **animated**, meaning they include motion and can change in appearance.

Horizontal rules are lines that are displayed across a Web page to separate different sections of the page. Although the appearance of a horizontal rule can vary, many Web pages use an inline image as a horizontal rule. Alternatively, you can use the horizontal rule tag (<hr />) to add a simple horizontal rule, such as the one used in this chapter project.

Hyperlink Elements

One of the more important elements of a Web page is a hyperlink, or link. A **link** is text, an image, or another Web page element that you click to instruct the browser to go to a location in a file or to request a file from a server. On the Web, links are the primary way to navigate between Web pages and among Web sites. Links point not only to Web pages, but also to graphics, sound, video, program files, e-mail addresses, and parts of the same Web page. Text links, also called hypertext links, are the most commonly used hyperlinks. For example, the text "Volunteers" in Figure 2–2 on the previous page links to opportunities for volunteer service. When text identifies a hyperlink, it usually appears as underlined text, in a color different from the rest of the Web page text. Image links are also very common. For example, there are two image links identified in Figure 2–2. Clicking either of those image links sends (or links) the user to another Web page that contains further information about those items. A corporate or organizational logo, such as the Smithsonian logo, often serves as an image link to the home page or corporate information.

Defining Web Page Structure

To create an HTML document, you use a text editor to enter information about the structure of the Web page, the content of the Web page, and instructions for how that content should be displayed. This book uses the Notepad++ text editor to enter the HTML elements and content for all projects and exercises.

Before you begin entering the content for this project, you must start by entering tags that define the overall structure of the Web page. You do this by inserting a <!DOCTYPE> tag and five tags (<html>, <head>, <meta />, <title>, and <body>) together with the closing tags (</html>, </head>, </title>, and </body>). These tags define the structure of a standard Web page and divide the HTML file into its basic sections: header information and the body of the page that contains text and graphics.

The **<!DOCTYPE>** tag is used to tell the browser which HTML or XHTML version and type the document uses. Throughout this book, we will utilize the HTML5 <!DOCTYPE> tag. In addition to that tag, the World Wide Web Consortium (W3C) supports three document types for other versions of HTML or XHTML: strict, transitional, and frameset. The **strict** document type is specified when you want to prohibit the use of deprecated tags. **Deprecated tags** are tags that the W3C has earmarked for eventual removal from their specifications, because those tags have been replaced with newer, more functional tags, attributes, or CSS properties. The **transitional** document type allows the use of deprecated tags. The **frameset** document type, which is used to support frames on a Web page, also allows the use of deprecated tags although the frame tags have been eliminated by HTML5. The <!DOCTYPE> tag includes a URL that references a Document Type Definition found on the w3.org Web site. Although this book does not use deprecated tags, the projects do use HTML5, which does not require a URL reference to a Document Type Definition.

BTW

The <!DOCTYPE> Tag
The w3schools.com Web site provides additional information about the <!DOCTYPE> tag used for the HTML5 or XHTML strict, transitional, and frameset document types. To learn more about the <!DOCTYPE> tag, visit the W3C Web site at w3.org. It provides a wealth of information on this and other HTML tags.

Defining the HTML Document

The first set of tags beyond the <!DOCTYPE> tag, **<html>** and **</html>**, indicates the start and end of an HTML document. This set of tags contains all of the content of the Web page, the tags that format that content, and the tags that define the different parts of the document. Software tools, such as browsers, use these tags to determine where the HTML code in a file begins and ends.

The Head   The next set of tags, **<head>** and **</head>**, contains the Web page title and other document header information. One of the tags inserted into the <head> </head> container is the meta tag. The **<meta />** tag has several functions. In this chapter, it is used to declare the character encoding UTF-8. The **Unicode Transformation Format (UTF)** is a compressed format that allows computers to display and manipulate text. When the browser encounters this meta tag, it will display the Web page properly, based on the particular UTF-8 encoding embedded in the tag. UTF-8 is the preferred encoding standard for Web pages, e-mail, and other applications. The encoding chosen is also important when validating the Web page. The meta tag has other purposes that are described in subsequent chapters of the book. The <title> tag is another tag inserted into the <head> </head> container. The **<title>** and **</title>** tags indicate the title of the Web page, which appears on the browser title bar and taskbar when the Web page is displayed in the browser window. The title is also the name given to the page when a user adds the page to a favorites or bookmarks list.

The Body   The final set of tags, **<body>** and **</body>**, contains the main content of the Web page. All text, images, links, and other content are contained within this final set of tags. Table 2–1 on the next page lists the functions of the tags described so far, as well as other tags that you will use in this chapter.

Table 2–1 Basic HTML Tags and Their Functions	
HTML Tag	**Function**
<!DOCTYPE>	Indicates the version and type of HTML used; may include a URL reference to a DTD
<html> </html>	Indicates the start and end of an HTML document
<head> </head>	Indicates the start and end of a section of the document used for the title and other document header information
<meta />	Indicates hidden information about the Web page
<title> </title>	Indicates the start and end of the title. The title does not appear in the body of the Web page, but appears on the title bar of the browser.
<body> </body>	Indicates the start and end of the body of the Web page
<hn> </hn>	Indicates the start and end of the text section called a heading; sizes range from <h1> through <h6>. See Figure 2–9a on page HTML 47 for heading size samples.
<p> </p>	Indicates the start and end of a new paragraph; inserts a blank line above the new paragraph
<ul> </ul>	Indicates the start and end of an unordered (bulleted) list
<li> </li>	Indicates that the item that follows the tag is an item within a list
<hr />	Inserts a horizontal rule
 	Inserts a line break at the point where the tag appears

Most HTML start tags, such as <html>, <head>, <title>, and <body>, have corresponding end tags, </html>, </head>, </title>, and </body>. Note that, for tags that do not have end tags, such as <meta />, <hr />, and <br />, the tag is closed using a space followed by a forward slash.

To Start Notepad++

With the planning, analysis, and design of the Web page complete, you can begin developing the Web page by entering the HTML code and Web page content using a text editor.

The following steps, which assume Windows 7 is running and Notepad++ is installed, start Notepad++ based on a typical installation. You may need to ask your instructor how to download, install, and start Notepad++ for your computer.

1

- Click the Start button on the Windows taskbar to display the Start menu.

- Click All Programs at the bottom of the left pane on the Start menu to display the All Programs list.

- Click the Notepad++ folder in the All Programs list (Figure 2–3).

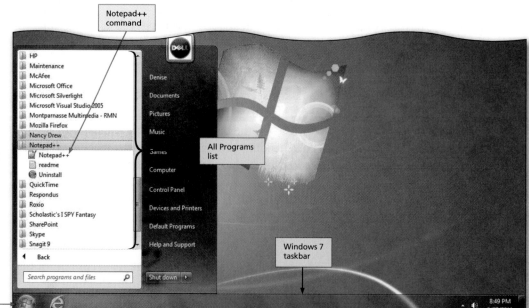

Figure 2–3

2

- Click Notepad++ in the list to display a blank Notepad++ window (Figure 2–4).

- If the Notepad++ window is not maximized, click the Maximize button on the Notepad++ title bar to maximize it. Note that by default, Notepad++ starts with the most recently used file open, so your Notepad++ screen may not look like Figure 2–4. To close all open files, click File and then click Close All.

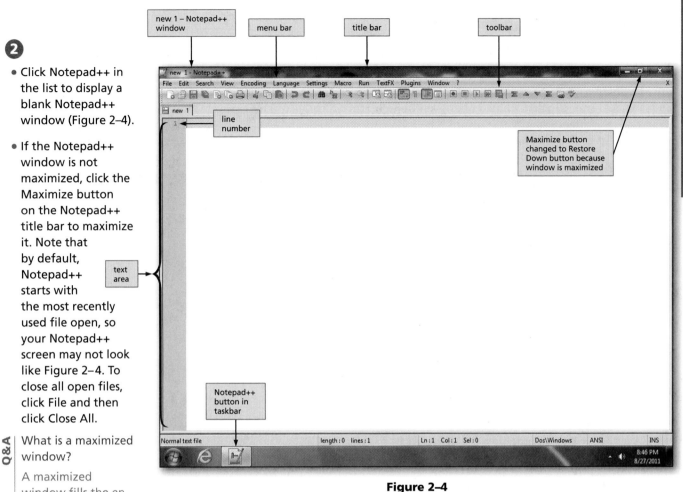

Figure 2–4

Q&A What is a maximized window?

A maximized window fills the entire screen. When you maximize a window, the Maximize button changes to a Restore Down button.

Q&A How can I add Notepad++ to my Start menu or the taskbar?

To add Notepad++ to the Start menu or taskbar, complete Step 1 above, right-click Notepad++, and then click Pin to Start Menu or Pin to Taskbar.

Other Ways	
1. Double-click Notepad++ icon on desktop, if one is present	2. Click Notepad++ on Start menu, if it is present

To Enable Word Wrap in Notepad++

In Notepad++, the text entered in the text area scrolls continuously to the right unless the word wrap feature is enabled, or turned on. **Word wrap** causes text lines to break at the right edge of the window and appear on a new line, so all entered text is visible in the Notepad++ window. When word wrap is enabled, a paragraph of text will be assigned a single logical line number even though it may display on multiple physical lines in Notepad++. Word wrap does not affect the way text prints. The following step shows how to enable word wrap in Notepad++.

1

- Click View on the menu bar (Figure 2–5).

- If word wrap does not have a check mark next to it, click word wrap.

Q&A How do I know if word wrap is enabled?

When word wrap is enabled, a check mark precedes the word wrap command on the View menu, and when you type, your words remain on the screen.

Q&A What happens to the text if word wrap is not enabled?

The text of a paragraph would appear all on one line in Notepad++ and scroll off the screen, though the Web page would still be displayed correctly in the browser. For readability in Notepad++, you should enable word wrap.

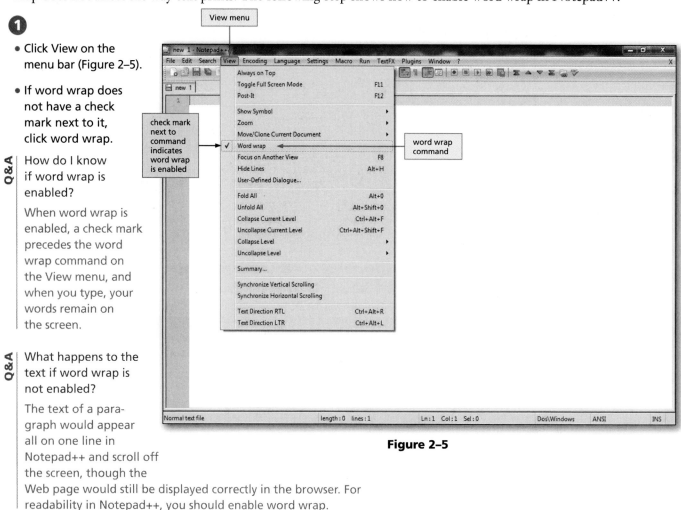

Figure 2–5

To Define the Web Page Structure Using HTML Tags

The first task is to enter the initial tags that define the Web page structure. Table 2–2 contains the HTML tags and text used to create the Web page shown in Figure 2–1a on page HTML 35. In this chapter and throughout this book, where large segments of HTML code or text are to be entered, you will find this code or text in tables with line number references, rather than within the steps. The steps will direct you to enter the text shown in the tables.

Table 2–2 Initial HTML Tags

Line	HTML Tag and Text
1	`<!DOCTYPE HTML>`
2	
3	`<html>`
4	`<head>`
5	`<meta charset="utf-8" />`
6	`<title>Rock Climbing Fun</title>`
7	`</head>`

The following steps illustrate how to enter the initial tags that define the structure of the Web page.

1

- Enter the HTML code shown in Table 2–2 (Figure 2–6). Press ENTER at the end of each line. If you make an error as you are typing, use the BACKSPACE key to delete all the characters back to and including the incorrect characters, and then continue typing.

- Press the ENTER key to start the next line of code, leaving one blank line after the </head> tag.

- Compare what you typed to Figure 2–6. If you notice errors, use your mouse pointer or arrow keys to move the insertion point to the right of each error and use the BACKSPACE key to correct the error.

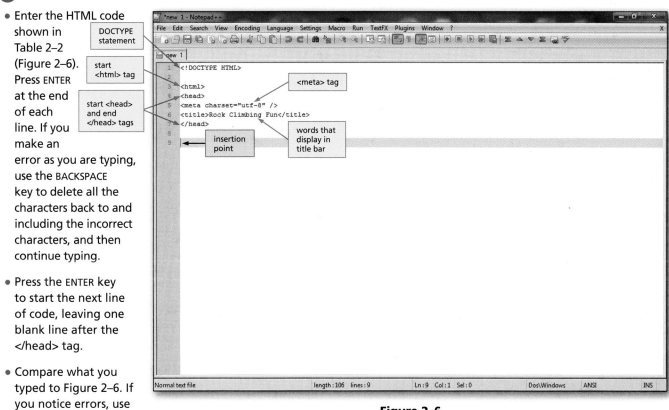

Figure 2–6

2

- On line 9, type `<body>` and then press the ENTER key twice.

- Type `</body>` and then press the ENTER key.

- Type `</html>` as the end tag (Figure 2–7).

- Compare what you typed to Figure 2–7 and correct errors in your typing if necessary.

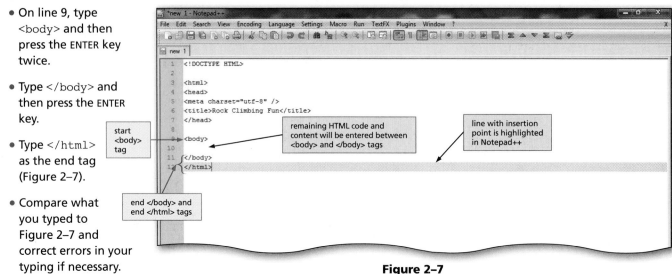

Figure 2–7

Do I have to type the initial HTML tags for every Web page that I develop?

The same initial HTML tags are used in many other chapters. To avoid retyping these tags, you can save the code that you just typed, and give it a new file name, something like structure. html or template.html. If you save this file at the root level of your folders, you will have easy access to it for other chapters.

Can I use either uppercase or lowercase letters for my HTML code?

HTML5 allows tags to be entered in upper-, lower-, or mixed-case. However, in this book, the project directions follow the guidelines presented in Table 1–3 on page HTML 13 in Chapter 1.

Plan Ahead

Identify how to format various elements of the text.
By formatting the characters and paragraphs on a Web page, you can improve its overall appearance. On a Web page, consider the following formatting suggestions.

- **Determine the Web page layout.** HTML5 has introduced new tags to format the layout of the Web page. The tags include the head, section, articles, and footer divisions.

- **Use default text size when appropriate.** The body text consists of all text between the heading and the bottom of the Web page. This text highlights the key points of the message in as few words as possible. It should be easy to read and follow. While emphasizing the positive, the body text must be realistic, truthful, and believable. The default font size and style are appropriate to use for the body of text.

- **Effectively utilize headings.** The main heading is generally the first line of text on the Web page. It conveys the purpose of the Web page, such as identifying the company name. In this project, the company name is part of the image that is used at the top of the page, so a heading size 1 is not needed. Heading size standards should be followed, as shown in Figure 2–9 on page HTML 47. The main heading should be size 1, and subtopics or subheadings should be size 2. For the Web site in this chapter, you start with heading size 2 because the main heading is part of the image. That heading identifies the equipment needed. It is generally not a good idea to jump from one heading size to a heading two sizes smaller. For instance, if your main heading is size 1, then the next heading down should be heading size 2, not heading size 4.

- **Highlight key points with a bulleted list.** A **bullet** is a dot or other symbol positioned at the beginning of a list item. The bulleted list contains specific information that is more clearly identified by a list versus a paragraph of text.

Formatting the Web Page

In HTML 4.01, <div> </div> tags were introduced to separate sections within a Web page. This works well, and we utilize the <div> tag throughout the book. HTML5 has introduced new semantic elements to help Web developers structure the layout of a Web page. These tags are **semantic** in that the name of the tag reflects the purpose of the tag. For instance, the new <footer> tag is used to display content at the bottom (or footer) of the Web page. The <aside> tag is used to add content that is **tangential** or a side issue to the main Web page content. These new HTML5 tags, including <article>, <aside>, <footer>, <header>, <nav>, and <section>, are used for layout in the Web page projects in this book. Although the <div> tags, together with an id attribute (see Figure 2-8a), achieve the same results in layout, the future of Web development includes the new HTML5 layout tags. Figure 2-8b shows the new structural elements provided in HTML5 and how they help structure a Web page. Note that the <nav> (navigation) tag can also be used across the top of the page under the header depending on the Web page design.

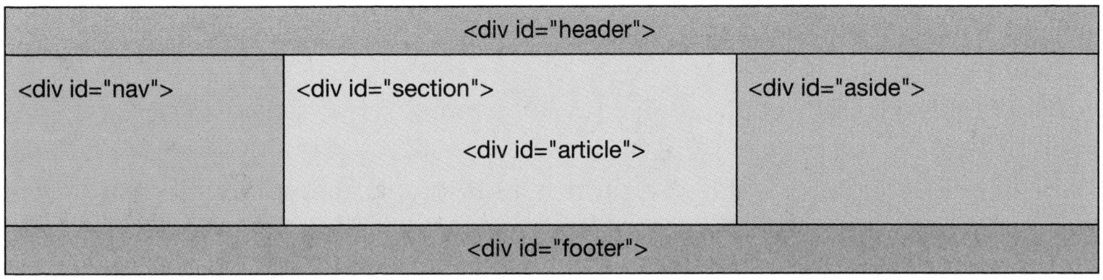

<div id="header">		
<div id="nav">	<div id="section"> <div id="article">	<div id="aside">
<div id="footer">		

(a) Structural elements with HTML 4.01 tags

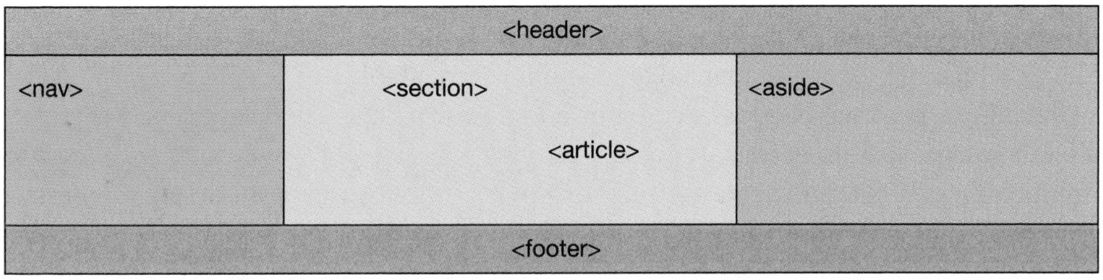

<header>		
<nav>	<section> <article>	<aside>
<footer>		

(b) Structural elements with new HTML5 tags

Figure 2–8

The header section is the top area of a Web page and is generally used for company logos, main heading text, or navigation. The <nav> tag identifies a section of the Web page that can alternately be used for navigation. The <section> tag is used as a generic document or application section. A section can be used to incorporate Web page content together with heading tags (i.e., h1 through h6). Articles are inserted within sections, adding to the content. An <aside> tag is used to represent content that is slightly related to the rest of the page, such as comments, biography, or background information. The footer is generally used for company information. Table 2–3 on the next page describes the purpose for each of these new tags. The project in this chapter contains a header, a footer, and one section that contains one article.

Table 2–3 HTML5 Structural Elements

Element	Purpose
Header	Information placed at the top of the Web page, such as logos or main headings
Navigation	Navigation structure that links to other parts of the Web page, Web site, or external to the Web site
Section	Major content area on the Web page
Article	Content that represents an independent piece of information
Aside	Content that is tangential or slightly related to the main topic of the Web page
Footer	Content placed at the bottom of the Web page, such as copyright or contact information

Entering Web Page Content

Once you have established the Web page structure, it is time to enter the content of the Web page, including headings, an informational paragraph of text, a subtopic heading, and a bulleted list.

Web pages generally contain a significant amount of text. Because you turned word wrap on (Figure 2–5 on page HTML 42) in Notepad++, you will see all of the text that you type in one Notepad++ window. If there is a substantial amount of information, you can break the text into paragraphs that help to separate key ideas and make the text easier to read. Paragraphs are separated with a blank line by using <p> (start paragraph) and </p> (end paragraph) tags. Putting too much text on one Web page is not a good choice. Your audience can get lost in large amounts of text. If you find that you have to press the Page Down key dozens of times to get to the bottom of the Web page, you need to think about restructuring your Web page. You can split up large pieces of information under more headings, which will be more manageable and more readable.

Headings are used to separate text or add new topics on the Web page. Several styles and sizes of headings exist, indicated by the tags <h1> through <h6>, with <h1> being the largest. Generally, you use the Heading 1 style for the main heading unless you use a graphical image for the heading (as we do in later steps). Figure 2–9a on the next page shows a Web page using various sizes of headings. A Web page usually has only one main heading; therefore, the HTML file for that Web page usually has only one set of <h1> </h1> tags. One method of maintaining a consistent look on a Web page is to use the same heading size for headings at the same topic level (Figure 2–9b). The header image that is inserted later in the chapter takes the place of the Main heading at the top of the Web page in Figure 2–9b. The complete Web page will therefore not have any <h1> headings. Notice that the paragraphs of text and the bulleted lists are all separated by size 2 headings in Figure 2–9b. This separation indicates that the text (i.e., two paragraphs plus one bulleted list) is all at the same level of importance on the Web page.

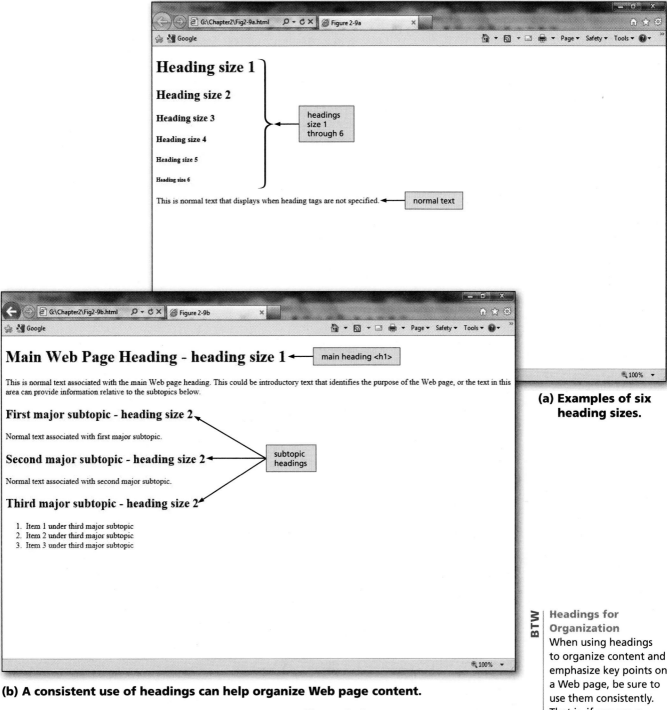

(a) Examples of six heading sizes.

(b) A consistent use of headings can help organize Web page content.

Figure 2–9

Sometimes text on a Web page is easier for users to read and understand when it is formatted as a list, instead of as a paragraph. HTML provides several types of lists, but the most popular are unordered (bulleted) and ordered (numbered) lists. During the design phase of the Web development life cycle, you decide on the most effective way to structure the Web content and format the text on the Web page. Your main goal is to give Web page visitors an effective way to find the information that they need. If users cannot easily find what they need, they will not revisit your Web site.

To Enter a Paragraph of Text

After you enter the initial HTML tags, you next add a paragraph of text using the <p> tag. When the browser finds a <p> tag in an HTML file, it starts a new line and inserts a blank line above the new paragraph. The </p> end tag indicates the end of the paragraph. When you enter this paragraph of text, do not press the ENTER key at the end of each line. Because word wrap is turned on, your text will wrap to the next line even without pressing the ENTER key. Table 2–4 contains the HTML tags and text used in the paragraph.

Table 2–4 Adding a Paragraph of Text	
Line	**HTML Tag and Text**
11	`<section>`
12	`<article>`
13	`<p>Rock Climbing Fun has recently opened a school at the base of Mount Rainier. We have programs for advanced rock climbers as well as for beginners. Rock climbing is a widely popular sport, especially in the state of Washington. Classes run from early morning to mid-afternoon, and private climbing lessons are available. Come join our classes and experience the fun and great exercise that rock climbing can provide. Call 1-800-555-CLIMB for more information.</p>`

The following step illustrates how to enter a paragraph of text in an HTML file.

1

- Click line 10 and then press the ENTER key.

- With the insertion point on line 11, enter the HTML code, as shown in Table 2–4. Do not press ENTER at the end of each line when entering the text in line 13 and use only one space after periods.

- Press the ENTER key twice to position the insertion point on line 15 (Figure 2–10).

Q&A

Why do you not press the ENTER key after each line of code in line 13 in Table 2–4?

Because you turned on word wrap right after you started Notepad++, the text that you enter as the paragraph will automatically wrap to the next line. The text goes to the end of the Notepad++ window and then wraps. If you had not turned on word wrap, your text would continue scrolling to the right as you type, and text to the left would scroll off the screen. With word wrap on, all text remains visible in the Notepad++ window.

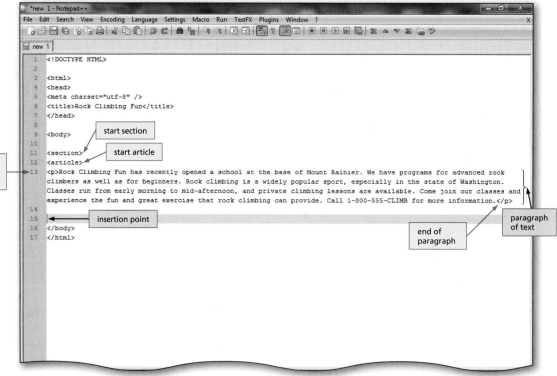

Figure 2–10

To Enter a Heading

The heading, Equipment needed to get started, is the heading that separates the paragraph of text from the bulleted list. You use an <h2> heading because it is not really the main heading of the Web page. You insert an image as the main heading later in the chapter. The following step illustrates how to enter a heading on the Web page.

- With the insertion point on line 15, type `<h2>Equipment needed to get started:</h2>` in the text area, and then press the ENTER key twice (Figure 2–11).

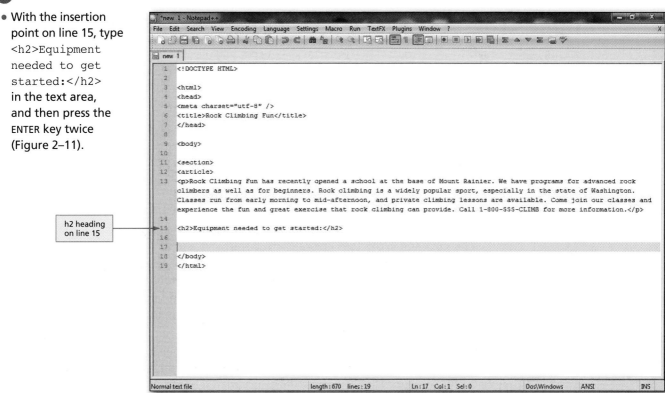

h2 heading on line 15

Figure 2–11

Using Lists to Present Content

Lists structure text into an itemized format. Typically, lists are bulleted (unordered) or numbered (ordered). An **unordered list**, which also is called a **bulleted list**, formats information using small images called bullets. Figure 2–12 shows Web page text formatted as unordered, or bulleted, lists and the HTML code used to create the lists.

An **ordered list**, which also is called a **numbered list**, formats information in a series using numbers or letters. An ordered list works well to organize items where

BTW

List Styles
It is sometimes helpful to structure the text of a Web page in a list. There are several list options that you can use. The Web page purpose determines which would be more effective. See the section on List Styles in Appendix D for style options that can be used with lists.

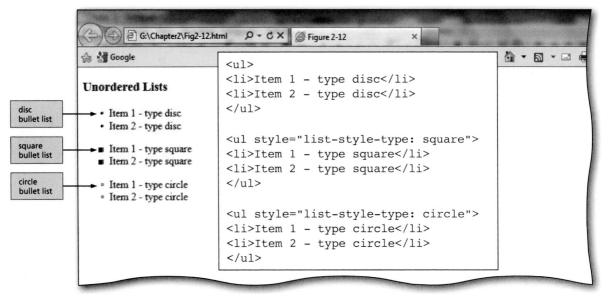

Figure 2–12

order must be emphasized, such as a series of steps. Figure 2–13 shows Web page text formatted as ordered, or numbered, lists and the HTML tags used to create the lists.

The **<ul>** and **</ul>** tags must be at the start and end of an unordered or bulleted list. The **<ol>** and **</ol>** tags are used at the start and end of an ordered or numbered list. Unordered and ordered lists have optional bullet and number types. As shown in Figure 2–12, an unordered list can use one of three different bullet options: disc, square, or circle. If no type is identified, the default, disc, is used. You can also use an image as a bullet as is shown in a later chapter. An ordered list can use numbers, letters, or Roman numerals, as shown in Figure 2–13. The default option is to use Arabic numbers, such as 1, 2, and 3. After the <ul> or <ol> tag is entered to define the type of list, the **<li>** and **</li>** tags are used to define each list item within an ordered or unordered list.

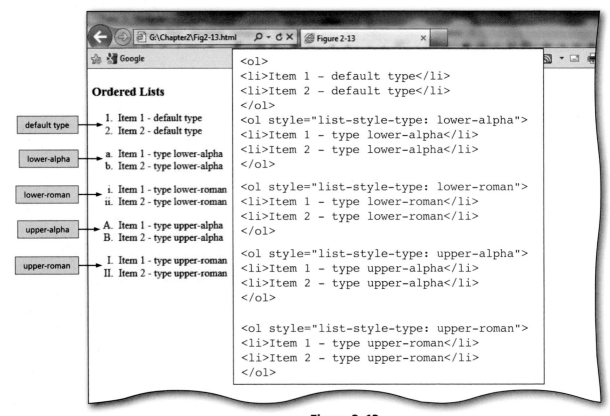

Figure 2–13

To Create an Unordered List

To highlight what Web site visitors will need for equipment when taking a class with Rock Climbing Fun you will create a bulleted (unordered) list using the HTML tags and text shown in Table 2–5. Remember that each list item must start with <li> and end with </li>.

Line	HTML Tag and Text
Table 2–5 Adding an Unordered List	
17	`<ul>`
18	`<li>Comfortable climbing shoes</li>`
19	`<li>Backpack</li>`
20	`<li>Harness</li>`
21	`</ul>`
22	`</article>`
23	`</section>`

The following step illustrates how to create an unordered, or bulleted, list using the default bullet style.

- With the insertion point on line 17, enter the HTML code, as shown in Table 2–5. When you type the text on line 18, make sure to press the TAB key at the start of the line (also on lines 19 and 20 if they are not automatically indented). Press ENTER at the end of each line.

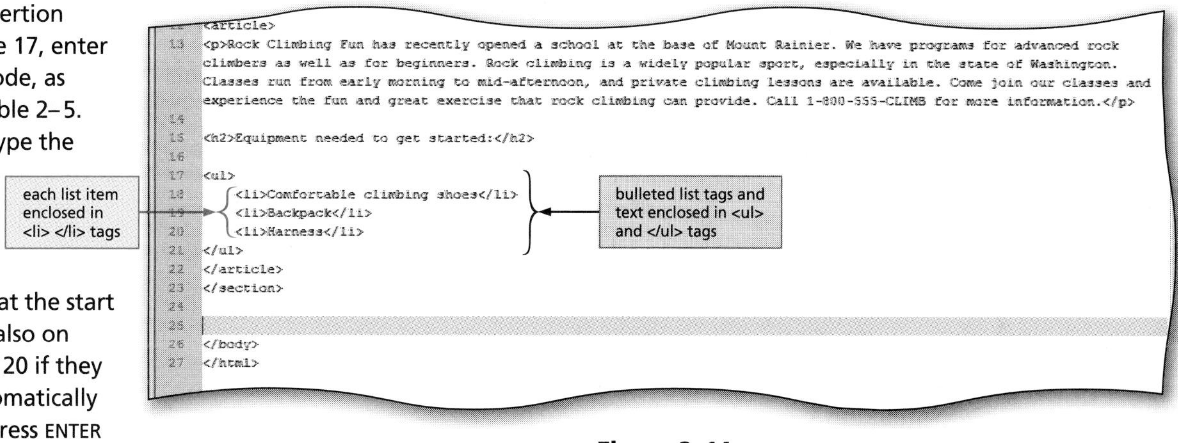

each list item enclosed in <li> </li> tags

bulleted list tags and text enclosed in <ul> and </ul> tags

Figure 2–14

- On line 23, press the ENTER key twice, positioning the cursor on line 25 and leaving a blank line on 24 (Figure 2–14).

Q&A

Why do you press the TAB key at the start of the lines with the <li> (list item) code?

Using the TAB key (to indent) when you enter list items helps format the text so that you can easily see that this text is different from the paragraph of text. Indenting text helps the Web developer see that certain segments of code are related to each other.

More About List Formats

If you use the <ul> or <ol> start tags without attributes, you will get the default bullet (disc) or number style (Arabic numerals). To change the bullet or number type, the **list-style-type** property is entered within the <ol> or <ul> tags. To create a list with square bullets, you would type the line

```
<ul style="list-style-type: square">
```

as the inline style (CSS) code. You can find other list-style properties and values in Appendix D.

In addition to ordered and unordered lists, there is a third kind of list, called a **definition list**, which offsets information in a dictionary-like style. Although they are used less often than unordered or ordered lists, definition lists are useful to create a glossary-like list of terms and definitions, as shown in Figure 2–15a. Figure 2–15b shows the HTML code used to create the definition list.

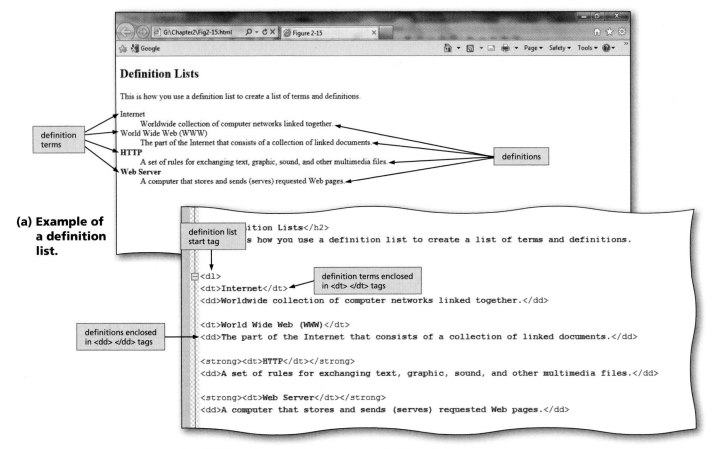

(a) Example of a definition list.

(b) HTML code used to create a definition list.

Figure 2–15

The syntax for definition lists is not as straightforward as the <ul>, <ol>, or <li> structure that is used in the unordered and ordered list styles. With definition lists, you use the **<dl>** and **</dl>** tags to start and end the list. A **<dt>** tag indicates a term, and a **<dd>** tag identifies the definition of that term by offsetting the definition from the term. Table 2–6 lists definition list tags and their purposes.

Table 2–6 Definition List Tags and Purposes	
Definition List Tags	**Purpose**
<dl> </dl>	Start and end a definition list
<dt> </dt>	Identify a term
<dd> </dd>	Identify the definition of the term directly above

As shown in Figure 2–15, by default, the definition term is left-aligned on the line and the definition for each term is indented so it is easily distinguishable as the definition for the term above it. In order to more clearly identify the definition term, you may want to make the term bold, as shown in the last two definitions (HTTP and Web Server) in Figure 2–15. You could do this by wrapping the term inside a <strong></strong>

container. That gives the term a strong emphasis, so text is usually displayed as bold text. The following code would do that for the HTTP definition term.

```
<strong><dt>HTTP</dt></strong>
```

Adding a Footer

As mentioned earlier in the chapter, HTML5 introduced several new structural elements that help to enhance the layout of a Web page. One of these new elements, the footer, is inserted in the next section of the chapter. The footer tag is used to position text toward the bottom of a Web page. Content placed there generally has to do with the company's address, copyright, or contact information.

To Add a Footer

It is important for Web site visitors to be able to contact the company. In the next step, you enter company contact information onto the Web page by inserting a tag in the HTML file using the tags and text shown in Table 2–7.

Line	HTML Tag and Text
Table 2–7 Adding a Footer	
25	`<footer>`
26	`Rock Climbing Fun, 3737 Harrison Lane, Issawak, WA 98000`
27	`</footer>`

- With the insertion point on line 25, enter the HTML code, as shown in Table 2–7. Press ENTER at the end of each line (Figure 2–16).

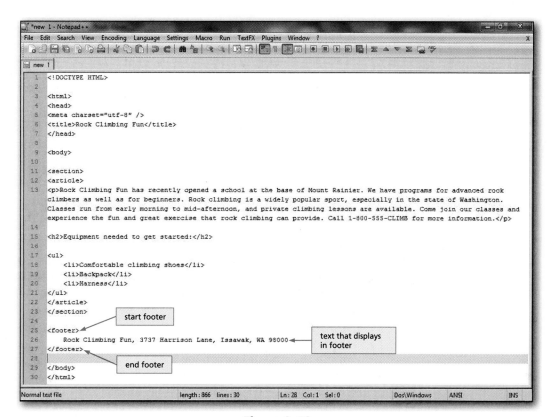

Figure 2–16

BTW

HTML File Names
HTML files have an extension of .html or .htm. The home page of a Web site is often called index.html, index.htm, default.html, or default.htm. Check with your Web hosting service provider to find out which name they use.

BTW

Saving Your Work
It is a good idea to save your HTML file periodically as you are working to avoid the risk of losing your work completed thus far. You should get into the habit of saving your file after any large addition of information (i.e., a paragraph or image). You might also want to save the file after typing in several HTML tags that would be difficult to re-do.

BTW

Storing Your Files
Many schools provide students with space on a Web server to store their Web pages. However, saving your Web pages to another medium (e.g., a USB flash drive) assures that you have a backup copy of the files that you created. Saving Web page files to the hard drive on a computer in a school lab runs the risk of it not being there the next time you are in that lab. Many schools delete all files at the start-up of each computer.

Saving and Organizing HTML Files

Before you can see how your HTML file looks in a Web browser, you must save it. It is also important to save your HTML file for the following reasons:

- The document in memory will be lost if the computer is turned off or you lose electrical power while the text editor is open.
- If you run out of time before completing your project, you may finish your document at a future time without starting over.

To save your file, you use the Notepad++ File, Save command. When you save a file, you give your file a name and follow that with the file extension. As mentioned earlier in the book, file names should always make sense relative to their purpose. For instance, naming a file page1 does not indicate the purpose of that file. Naming the file rockclimbing immediately identifies that this file has something to do with that topic. The Web page files in this book are always named with all lowercase letters and with no spaces. This is a standard that is followed throughout the book.

HTML files must end with an extension of **.htm** or **.html**. Many older Web page servers can only display pages with the .htm extension, or short file names (i.e., file names that are only up to eight characters in length). HTML files with an extension of .html can be viewed on Web servers running an operating system that allows long file names (i.e., file names that can be up to 255 characters in length). Almost all current operating systems allow long file names, including Windows 7, Windows Vista, Windows XP, Windows Server 2003/2008, Windows 2000, Mac OS X, and Linux. For Web servers that run an operating system that does not accept long file names, you need the .htm extension. In this book, all files are saved using the .html extension.

You will use a very simple folder structure with all the projects in this book. It is therefore important to organize your files in folders so that all files for a project or end-of-chapter exercise, including HTML code and graphical images, are saved in the same folder. If you correctly downloaded the files from the Data Files for Students (see the inside back cover of this book), you will have the required file structure. When you initially save the rockclimbing.html file, you will save it in the ChapterFiles subfolder of the Chapter02 folder. The graphical image used in Chapter 2, rockclimbing.jpg, will be stored in that same folder — Chapter02\ChapterFiles. Because the chapter projects in this book are relatively simple and use few images, images and HTML code are stored in the same folder. In real-world applications, though, hundreds or thousands of files might exist in a Web site, and it is more appropriate to separate the HTML code and graphical images into different subfolders. You will learn more about organizing HTML files and folders in Chapter 3.

Plan Ahead

> **Determine where to save the Web page.**
> When saving a Web page, you must decide which storage medium to use.
>
> - If you always work on the same computer and have no need to transport your projects to a different location, then your computer's hard drive will suffice as a storage location. It is a good idea, however, to save a backup copy of your projects on a separate medium in case the file becomes corrupted or the computer's hard disk fails.
>
> - If you plan to work on your projects in various locations or on multiple computers, then you should save your projects on a portable medium, such as a USB flash drive or CD. The projects in this book use a USB flash drive, which saves files quickly and reliably and can be reused. CDs are easily portable and serve as good backups for the final versions of projects because they generally can save files only one time.
>
> The above are general guidelines about saving your files. Your instructor may give you specific instructions for saving your work that differ from the steps that follow.

To Save an HTML File

You have entered a lot of text while creating this project and do not want to risk losing the work you have done so far. Also, to view HTML in a browser, you must save the file. The following steps show how to save an HTML file.

1

- With a USB flash drive connected to one of the computer's USB ports, click File on the Notepad++ menu bar (Figure 2–17).

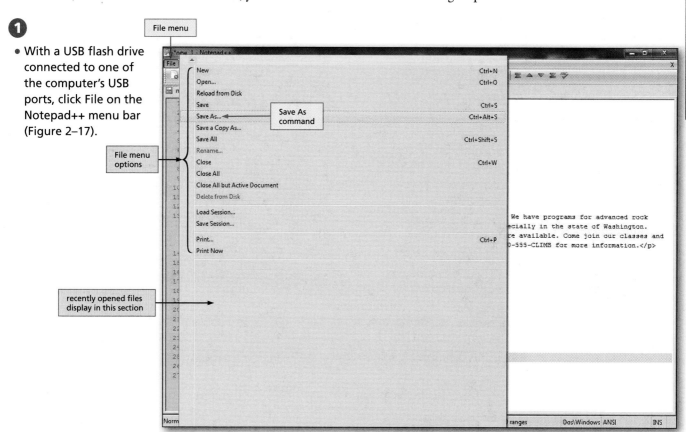

Figure 2–17

2

- Click Save As on the File menu to display the Save As dialog box (Figure 2–18).

Q&A

Do I have to save to a USB flash drive?

No. You can save to any device or folder. A folder is a specific location on a storage medium. Use the same process, but select your device or folder.

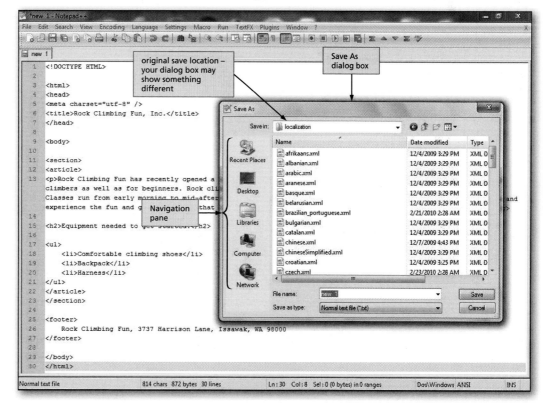

Figure 2–18

• Type
`rockclimbing.html`
in the File name text
box to change the
file name. Do not
press ENTER after
typing the file name.

• Click Computer in the
left side of the dialog
box to display a list
of available drives
(Figure 2–19).

• If necessary, scroll
until your USB flash
drive, such as UDISK
2.0 (G:), appears in
the list of available
drives.

Q&A Why is my list of
files, folders, and
drives arranged and
named differently
from those shown in
the figure?

Your computer's
configuration determines
how the list of files and folders is displayed and how drives are named.

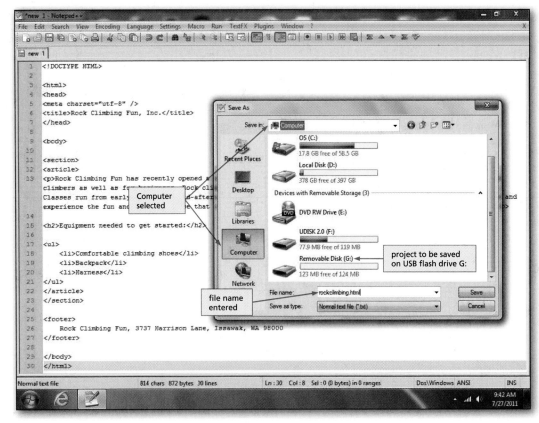

Figure 2–19

Q&A How do I know the drive and folder in which my file will be saved?

Notepad++ displays a list of available drives and folders. You then select
the drive and/or folder into which you want to save the file.

4

- Double-click UDISK 2.0 (G:) (or your storage device) in the Computer list to select the USB flash drive, drive G in this case, as the new save location.

Q&A What if my USB flash drive has a different name or letter?

It is likely that your USB flash drive will have a different name and drive letter and be connected to a different port. Verify that the device in your Computer list is correct.

- If necessary, open the Chapter02\ ChapterFiles folder (Figure 2–20).

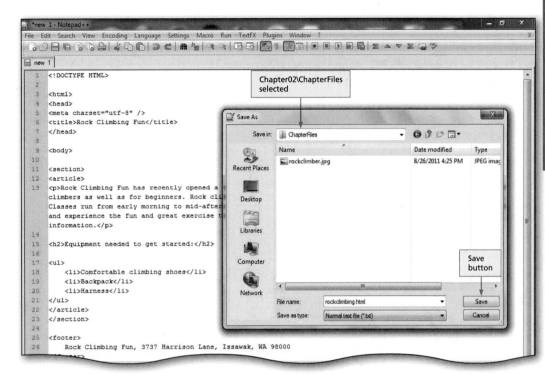

Figure 2–20

Q&A What if my USB flash drive does not have a folder named Chapter02\ChapterFiles?

If you followed the steps to download the chapter files from the Data Files for Students, you should have a folder named Chapter02\ChapterFiles. If you do not, check with your instructor.

5

- Click the Save button in the Save As dialog box to save the file on the USB flash drive with the name rockclimbing.html (Figure 2–21).

Q&A Is my file only on the USB drive now?

No, although the HTML file is saved on a USB drive, it also remains in memory and is displayed on the screen (Figure 2–21). Notepad++ displays the new file name on the title bar and on the document tab.

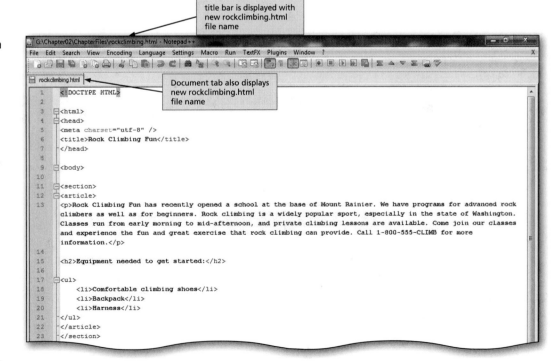

Figure 2–21

Other Ways
1. Press CTRL+ALT+S, type file name, click Computer, select drive or folder, click Save button

BTW

Developing Web Pages for Multiple Browsers
When developing Web pages, you must consider the types of browsers visitors will use. Popular browsers include Internet Explorer, Google Chrome, Mozilla Firefox, and Apple Safari. Part of thorough testing includes reviewing your Web pages in multiple versions of different browsers.

Using a Browser to View a Web Page

After saving the HTML file, you should view the Web page in a browser to see what the Web page looks like up to this point. The HTML file is displayed in the browser as if the file were available on the Web. In general, viewing the Web page periodically during development is good coding practice, because it allows you to see the effect of various HTML tags on the text and to check for errors in your HTML file. If your computer is connected to the Internet when the browser window opens, it displays a **home page**, or **start page**, which is a Web page that appears each time Internet Explorer starts.

To Start a Browser

With the HTML file saved on the USB drive, the next step is to view the Web page using a browser. Because Windows is **multitasking**, you can have more than one program running at a time, such as Notepad++ and your browser. The following steps illustrate how to start a browser to view a Web page.

1
• Click the Internet Explorer icon on the taskbar (Figure 2–22).

2
• If necessary, click the Maximize button to maximize the browser window (Figure 2–23).

Q&A

Why does my browser display a different window?

Because it is possible to change the Web page that appears as the home page using browser settings, the home page that is displayed by your browser may be different. Schools and organizations often customize the home page for browsers installed on lab or office computers.

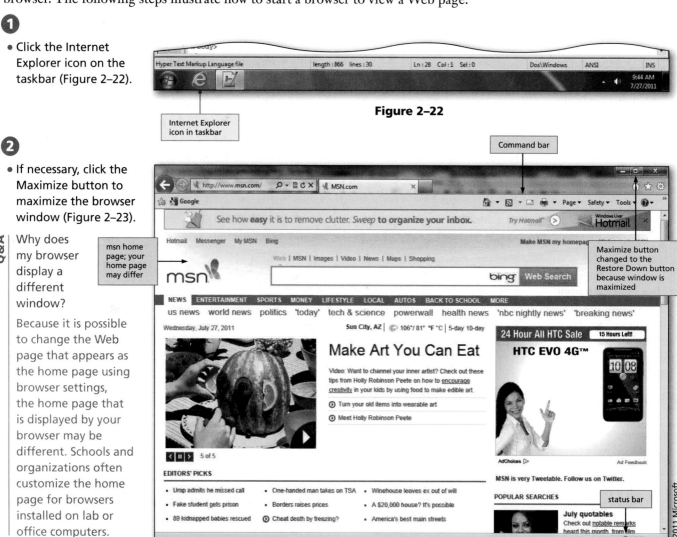

Figure 2–22

Figure 2–23

Other Ways

1. Click Start, click All Programs, click Internet Explorer

2. Double-click Internet Explorer icon on desktop, if one is present

To View a Web Page in a Browser

A browser allows you to open a Web file located on your computer and have full browsing capabilities, as if the Web page were stored on a Web server and made available on the Web. The following steps use this technique to view the HTML file, rockclimbing.html, in a browser.

1

- Click the Address bar to select the URL.

- Type `g:\Chapter02\ ChapterFiles\ rockclimbing.html` to enter the path of the HTML file in the Address bar (Figure 2–24).

URL of Web page entered on Address bar

Figure 2–24

Q&A
What if my file is in a different location?

You can type in the path to your file in the Address bar or browse to your file, as shown in Other Ways.

2

- Press the ENTER key to display the rockclimbing.html page as if it were available on the Web (Figure 2–25).

Q&A
What if my page is not displayed correctly?

Check your rockclimbing.html file carefully against Figure 2–26 on the next page to make sure you have not made any typing errors or left anything out. Correct the errors, resave the file, and try again by refreshing the Web page in the browser.

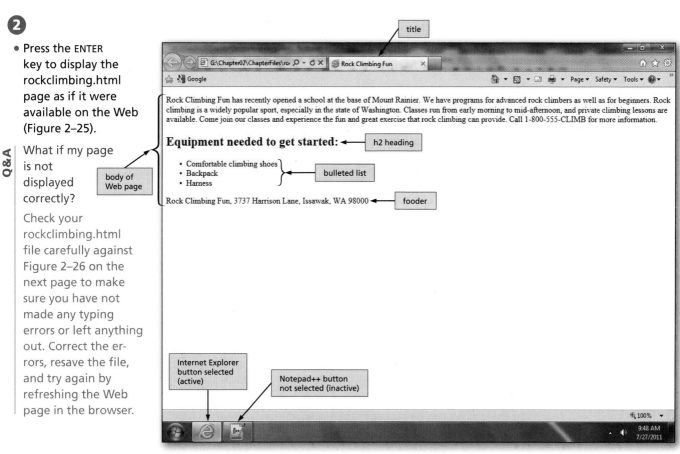

title

h2 heading

bulleted list

footer

body of Web page

Internet Explorer button selected (active)

Notepad++ button not selected (inactive)

Figure 2–25

Other Ways	
1. In Windows Explorer, double-click HTML file name to open in default browser	2. In Windows Explorer, right-click HTML file name, point to Open with, click browser name

To Activate Notepad++

After viewing the Web page, you can modify it by adding additional tags or text to the HTML file. To continue editing, you first must return to the Notepad++ window. The following step illustrates how to activate Notepad++.

- Click the Notepad++ button on the task-bar to maximize Notepad++ and make it the active window (Figure 2–26).

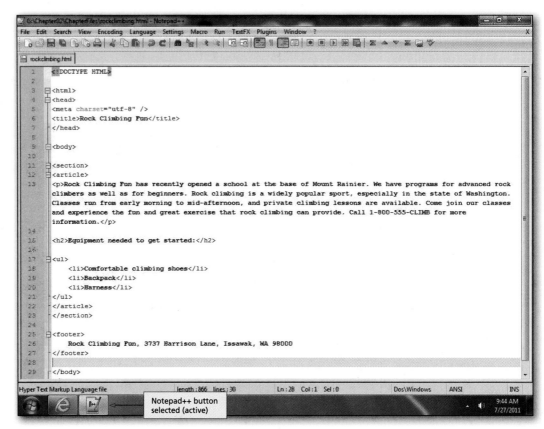

Figure 2–26

Improving the Appearance of Your Web Page

One goal in Web page development is to create a Web page that is visually appealing and maintains the interest of the visitors. The Web page developed thus far in the chapter is functional, but lacks visual appeal. In this section, you will learn how to improve the appearance of the Web page from the one shown in Figure 2–27a to the one shown in Figure 2–27b by adding an image, adding color to a heading, changing the style of the footer, adding a horizontal rule, and changing the list style type of the bulleted list. Many of these tasks can be accomplished by using style sheets.

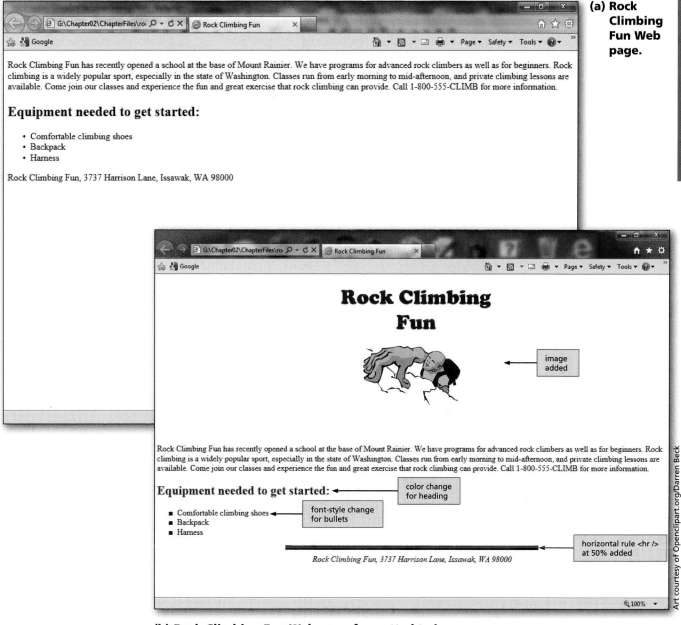

(a) Rock Climbing Fun Web page.

(b) Rock Climbing Fun Web page formatted to improve appearance.

Figure 2–27

Using Style Sheets

Although HTML allows Web developers to make changes to the structure, design, and content of a Web page, HTML is limited in its ability to define the appearance, or style, across one or more Web pages. As a result, style sheets were created.

As a review, a **style** is a rule that defines the appearance of an element on a Web page. A **Cascading Style Sheet (CSS)** is a series of rules that defines the style for a Web page or an entire Web site. With a style sheet, you can alter the appearance of a Web page or pages by changing characteristics such as font family, font size, margins, and link specifications.

The latest version of CSS is CSS3. As with HTML5, CSS3 is still in a working draft status at the World Wide Web Consortium (W3C). CSS3 adds many new style features, including column-based layouts, rounded borders, and enhanced text effects. For full CSS3 styles, visit w3.org. We will utilize some of the new styles in later chapters.

BTW

Inline Styles
Using an inline style is helpful when you want to alter the appearance (or style) of a single HTML element. Appendix D contains the Cascading Style Sheet Properties and Values supported by most browsers. The inline styles used in this chapter can be found in the appendix. For more information on CSS, look at w3.org.

CSS supports three types of style sheets: inline, embedded (or internal), and external (or linked). With an **inline style**, you add a style to an individual HTML tag, such as a heading or paragraph. The style changes that specific tag, but does not affect other tags in the document. With an **embedded style sheet**, or **internal style sheet**, you add the style sheet within the <head> tags of the HTML document to define the style for an entire Web page. With an **external style sheet**, or **linked style sheet**, you create a text file that contains all of the styles you want to apply, and save the text file with the file extension .css. You then add a link to this external style sheet on any Web page in the Web site. External style sheets give you the most flexibility and are ideal to apply the same formats to all of the Web pages in a Web site. External style sheets also make it easy to change formats quickly across Web pages. You will use inline styles in this chapter's project to enhance the styles of the heading (change the color) and the bulleted list (change the font style).

Style Sheet Precedence As shown in Table 2–8, the three style sheets supported by CSS control the appearance of a Web page at different levels. Each type of style sheet also has a different level of precedence or priority in relationship to the others. An external style sheet, for example, is used to define styles for multiple pages in a Web site. An embedded style sheet is used to change the style of one Web page, and overrides or takes precedence over any styles defined in an external style sheet. An inline style is used to control the style within an individual HTML tag and takes precedence over the styles defined in both embedded and external style sheets.

Table 2–8 Style Sheet Precedence

Type	Level and Precedence
Inline	• To change the style within an individual HTML tag • Overrides embedded and external style sheets
Embedded	• To change the style of one Web page • Overrides external style sheets
External	• To change the style of multiple pages in a Web site

Because style sheets have different levels of precedence, all three types of style sheets can be used on a single Web page. For example, you may want some elements of a Web page to match the other Web pages in the Web site, but you also may want to vary the look of certain sections of that Web page. You can do this by using the three types of style sheets.

Style Statement Format No matter what type of style sheet you use, you must use a **style statement** to define the style. The following code shows an example of a style statement used in an inline style:

```
<h1 style="font-family: Garamond; font-color: navy">
```

A style statement is made up of a selector and a declaration. The part of the style statement that identifies the page elements is called the **selector**. In this example, the selector is h1 (header size 1). The part of the style statement that identifies how the element(s) should appear is called the **declaration**. In this example, the declaration is everything between the quotation marks: the font-family and font-color properties and their values (Garamond and navy, respectively). A declaration includes at least one type of style, or **property**, to apply to the selected element. Examples of properties include color, text-indent, border-width, and font-style. For each property, the declaration includes a related **value**, which specifies the display parameters for that specific property.

Each property accepts specific values, based on the styles that property can define. The property, font-color, for example, can accept the value, navy, but cannot accept the value, 10%, because that is not a valid color value. In the next section of this chapter, you will change the heading color to the color #384738 for the h2 heading. Using an inline style in this case is appropriate because there is only one heading to change on the Web page. If you had many headings to change, an embedded or external style sheet would be more appropriate. This will be discussed in later chapters.

Inline Styles   An inline style is used to define the style of an individual HTML tag. For example, to change the style of a horizontal rule, you could add an inline style with the <hr /> (horizontal rule) tag as the selector and a declaration that defines new height, width, and background-color styles, as shown here:

```
<hr style="height: 8px; background-color: #384738; width: 50%" />
```

Because inline styles take precedence over the other types of style sheets and affect the style for individual HTML tags, they are helpful when one section or one element of a Web page needs to have a style different from the rest of the Web page. In this chapter's project, an inline style is used to change the color of the <h2> heading, the bullet list type, the footer, and the horizontal rule styles on the Web page.

Now that you understand how style sheets and inline styles function, it is time to think about adding an image to enhance the appearance of your Web page.

Using Web Page Divisions

It can be helpful to break up your Web page into divisions (or sections), which allows you to apply styles to different Web page elements. Throughout this book, you sometimes use the start <div> and end </div> division tags as a container in which to insert images. You also use the new HTML5 layout elements to help structure your Web page into sections. As mentioned earlier, these new semantic elements are useful because the name of the tag actually reflects the purpose of the tag. For example, the <header> tag is used to display text at the top (or the header) of the Web page. Utilizing structural and division tags allows you to add styles such as centering your image or adding background color to your images.

Find appropriate graphical images.

To use graphical images, also called graphics, on a Web page, the image must be stored digitally in a file. Files containing graphical images are available from a variety of sources:

- Some Web sites offer images that are free and are not subject to copyright; these images are considered to be in the **public domain**. Other Web sites offer images that require permission from the copyright owner or a fee for use.

- You can take a picture with a digital camera and **download** it, which is the process of copying the digital picture from the camera to your computer.

- With a scanner, you can convert a printed picture, drawing, or diagram to a digital file.

   If you receive a picture from a source other than yourself, do not use the file until you are certain it does not contain a virus. A **virus** is a computer program that can damage files and programs on your computer. Use an antivirus program to verify that any files you use are virus free.

(continued)

Plan Ahead

Plan Ahead

(*continued*)

Establish where to position and how to format the graphical image. The content, size, shape, position, and format of a graphic should capture the interest of viewers, enticing them to stop and read the Web page. Often, the graphic is the center of attraction and visually the largest element on a page. If you use colors in the graphical image, be sure they are part of the Web page's color scheme.

Identify the width and height of the image. The width and height (measured in pixels) of an image should always be identified in the <img> tag. These dimensions are used by the browser to determine the size to display the image.

Provide alternate text for the image. Text describing the image, known as alternate text, should always be used for each image. This text is especially useful to users with visual impairments who use a screen reader, which translates information on a computer screen into audio output. The length of the alternate text should be reasonable.

Types of Web Page Images

Images are used in many ways to enhance the look of a Web page and make it more interesting and colorful. Images can be used to add background color, to help organize a Web page, to help clarify a point being made in the text, or to serve as links to other Web pages. Images are often also used to break up Web page sections (such as with a horizontal rule) or as directional elements that allow a visitor to navigate a Web site.

Web pages use three types of files as images: GIF, JPEG, and PNG (Table 2–9). **Graphics Interchange Format (GIF)** files have an extension of .gif. A graphic image saved as a GIF (pronounced *jiff* or *giff*) uses compression techniques, called LZW compression, to make it smaller for download on the Web. Standard (or noninterlaced) GIF images are displayed one line at a time when loading. Interlaced GIF images load all at once, starting with a blurry look and becoming sharper as they load. Using interlaced GIFs for large images is a good technique, because a Web page visitor can see a blurred outline of the image as it loads.

A second type of image file is **Portable Network Graphics (PNG)**, which has a .png extension. The PNG (pronounced *ping*) format is also a lossless compressed file format that supports multiple colors and resolutions. The PNG format is a patent-free alternative to the GIF format. Most newer browsers support PNG images.

Finally, **Joint Photographic Experts Group (JPEG)** files have an extension of .jpg, .jpe, or .jpeg. A JPEG (pronounced *JAY-peg*) is a graphic image saved using a lossy compression technique that discards some data during the compression process and is best suited for images with smooth variations of tone and color. JPEG files are often used for more complex images, such as photographs, because the JPEG file format supports more colors and resolutions than the other file types.

BTW

Images
Images on Web pages are viewed in a variety of environments, including on computers with slow connctions to the Internet. Optimizing your images is important to increase the speed of download for all of your Web page visitors. Search the Web for more information on image optimization.

Table 2–9 Image Types and Uses	
Image Type	**Use**
Graphics Interchange Format (GIF)	• Use for images with few colors (<256) • Allows for transparent backgrounds
Portable Network Graphics (PNG)	• Newest format for images • Use for all types of images • Allows for variation in transparency
Joint Photographic Experts Group (JPEG)	• Use for images with many colors (>256), such as photographs

If an image is not in one of these formats, you can use a paint or graphics-editing program to convert an image to a .gif, .jpg, or .png format. Some paint programs even allow you to save a standard GIF image as interlaced. A number of paint and graphics-editing programs, such Adobe Photoshop and Corel Paint Shop Pro, are available in the marketplace today.

Image Attributes

You can enhance HTML tags by using attributes. **Attributes** define additional characteristics for the HTML tag. For instance, you should use the width and height attributes for all <img> tags. Table 2–10 lists the attributes that can be used with the <img> tag. In this chapter, the src and alt attributes are used in the <img> tag. Image attributes will be explained in detail, because they are used in later chapters.

BTW

Overusing Images
Be cautious about overusing images on a Web page. Using too many images may give your Web page a cluttered look or distract the visitor from the purpose of the Web page. An image should have a purpose, such as to convey content, visually organize a page, provide a hyperlink, or serve another function.

Table 2–10 Image Attributes	
Attribute	**Function**
alt	• Alternative text to display when an image is being loaded • Especially useful for screen readers, which translate information on a computer screen into audio output • Should be a brief representation of the purpose of the image • Generally should stick to 50 characters or fewer
height	• Defines the height of the image, measured in pixels • Improves loading time
src	• Defines the URL of the image to be loaded
width	• Defines the width of the image, measured in pixels • Improves loading time

To Add an Image

In the early days when the Web was used mostly by researchers needing to share information with each other, having purely functional, text-only Web pages was the norm. Today, Web page visitors are used to a more graphically oriented world, and have come to expect Web pages to use images that provide visual interest. The following step illustrates how to add an image to a Web page by entering an <img> tag in the HTML file using the tags and text shown in Table 2–11.

Table 2–11 Adding an Image	
Line	**HTML Tag and Text**
11	`<header style="text-align: center">`
12	`<img src="rockclimber.jpg" width="450" height="300" alt="Rock climber" />`
13	`</header>`

- Click the blank line 10 and then press the ENTER key.

- With the insertion point on line 11, enter the HTML code, as shown in Table 2–11. Press ENTER at the end of each line (Figure 2–28).

Q&A

What is the purpose of the alt attribute?

The alt attribute has three important purposes. First, screen readers used by users with visual impairments read the alternate text out loud. Second, the alternate text is displayed while the image is being loaded. Finally, the alt tag is required for compliance to good programming standards.

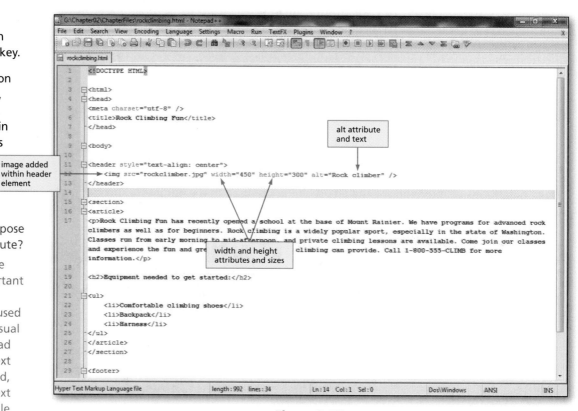

Figure 2–28

Q&A

What is the purpose of the inline style used in the <header> tag?

You use the style="text-align: center" statement to center the header on the Web page.

Plan Ahead

Make other visual enhancements.
In addition to images, there are several ways to add visual interest.

Add color to headings. Web developers often use colors to call attention to elements on a Web page. The color selected should coordinate with the images selected for the page. It should also allow the Web page text to be read easily. Some colors, such as dark colors, may not be appropriate because the default black text cannot be displayed effectively on a dark background. When changing the color of an element such as a heading, it is usually best to apply the same style to all headings on the Web page for consistency.

Change the list style type of a bulleted list. It is sometimes aesthetically pleasing to change the style of the bullet in a bulleted list. When you want to call attention to the information, you might also want to italicize or bold the bullet text.

Insert a horizontal rule. It is useful to use a horizontal rule to break up text on a Web page. A horizontal rule is used as a divider for a page to separate text sections.

Alter the footer style. A footer contains content, such as contact information, that does not have to be strongly highlighted. Changes can be made to that tag to make its style different from the other content on the page.

Other Visual Enhancements

One way to help capture a Web page visitor's attention is to use color. Many colors are available for use as a Web page background, text, border, or link. Figure 2–29 shows colors often used on Web pages, with the corresponding six-digit number codes. The six-digit number codes, known as **hexadecimal** codes, can be used to specify a color for a background, text, or links. The heading on the Rock Climbing Fun Web page is currently black (the default color). You will spruce up the Web page by adding color to the heading and the horizontal rule using inline styles.

BTW

Colors
Figure 2–29 does not list all possible Web colors. Many other colors are available that you can use for Web page backgrounds or text fonts. For more information about colors, see Appendix B or search the Web for browser colors.

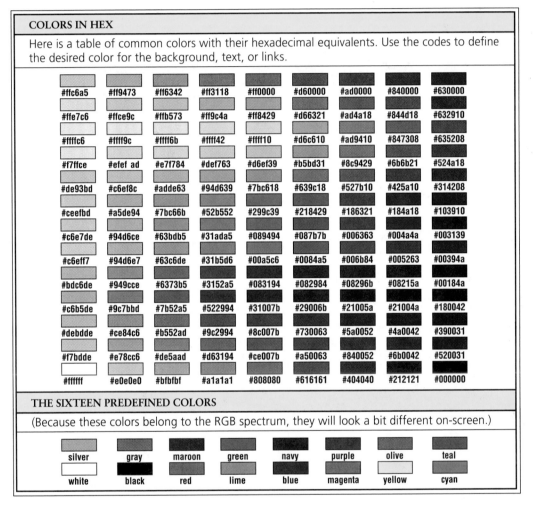

Figure 2–29

The color codes and names shown in Figure 2–29 can be used for background, text, border, and link colors. The color property is used in the <h2> tag to specify the color for the heading. The color #384738 will be used for the heading because it is one of the colors found in the graphical image inserted in the steps above.

Another way to visually enhance the Web page is to change the style of some of the text. This calls attention to that particular text on the Web page. In this section, you will change the text in the footer to an italic style using an inline style. This change helps call attention to that tangential content.

BTW

Browser-safe Colors
Web developers used to have to make sure that they used browser-safe colors (Appendix B). The trend for monitors today is to display "true color", which means that any of 16 million colors can be displayed on the monitor. Few people use 8-bit monitors anymore, so you generally do not have to limit yourself to browser-safe colors.

Finally, you will add a horizontal rule and an inline style to further enhance this Web page. As discussed earlier in the chapter, horizontal rules are lines that act as dividers on a Web page to provide a visual separation of sections on the page. You can use an inline image to add a horizontal rule, or you can use the horizontal rule tag (<hr />) to add a simple horizontal rule, as shown in the following steps. To make the horizontal rule more apparent, you will give it a height of 8 pixels and color the background the same color as the <h2> heading. You will also set the width of the horizontal rule to 50% of the Web page. You do all three of those changes to the horizontal rule using an inline style. Figure 2–30 shows examples of a variety of horizontal rules and the HTML code used to add them. The default horizontal rule is shown in the first rule on the page. Dimension is added to a horizontal rule by increasing the number of pixels that are displayed.

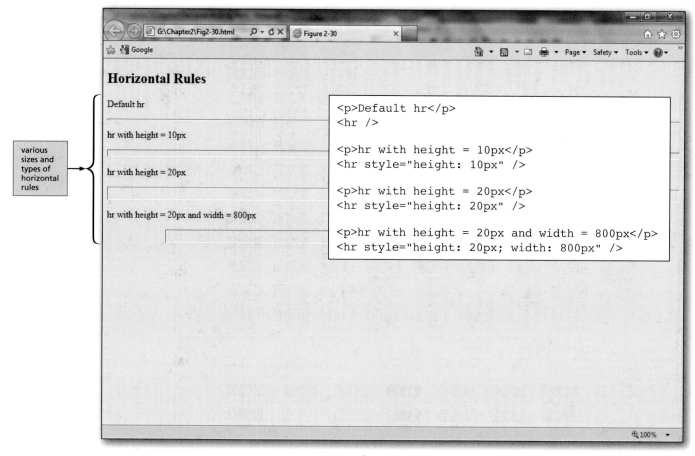

Figure 2–30

To Add Color to a Web Page Heading

To change the color of a heading on a Web page, the color property must be added in the <h2> tag of the HTML file. The **color** property lets you change the color of various elements on the Web page. The following step shows how to add a color using the color property in an inline style.

- Click after the "2" but before the closing bracket in <h2> on line 19 and then press the SPACEBAR.

- Type style="color: #384738" as the color code for the heading (Figure 2–31).

Q&A

Can I use any hexadecimal code or color name to change colors of headings?

Although you may use any of the hexadecimal codes or color names available, you have to make sure that the color is appropriate for the headings of your Web page. You do not want a heading that is too light in color or otherwise diminishes the headings.

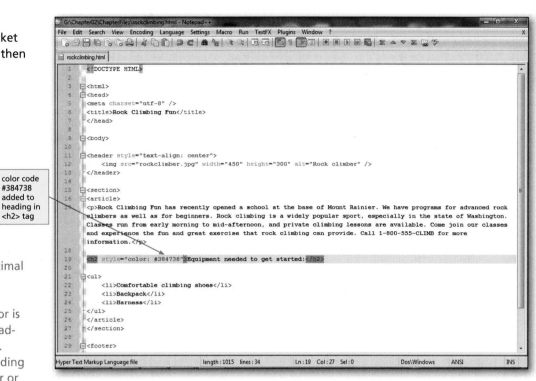

Figure 2–31

To Change the Bulleted List Style

To change the style of the bulleted list, you again use an inline style with the list-style-type property. The list-style-type property lets you change the style of the bullet type from the default disc to other options. There are several values for the list-style-type, as shown in Appendix D. The following step shows how to change the list-style-type property using an inline style.

- Click after the "l" but before the closing bracket in <ul> on line 21 and then press the SPACEBAR.

- Type style="list-style-type: square" as the code (Figure 2–32).

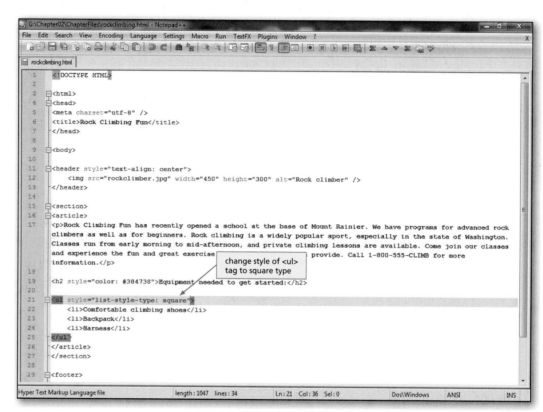

Figure 2–32

To Add a Horizontal Rule

You next insert a horizontal rule to separate the top part of the Web page from the footer area. You also give the horizontal rule more height (8 pixels) than the default, change the background color to match the heading, and make the width 50%. The following step illustrates how to add a horizontal rule to a Web page.

- Click the blank line 28 and then press the ENTER key.

- Type `<hr style="height: 8px; background-color: #384738; width: 50%" />` and then press the ENTER key (Figure 2–33).

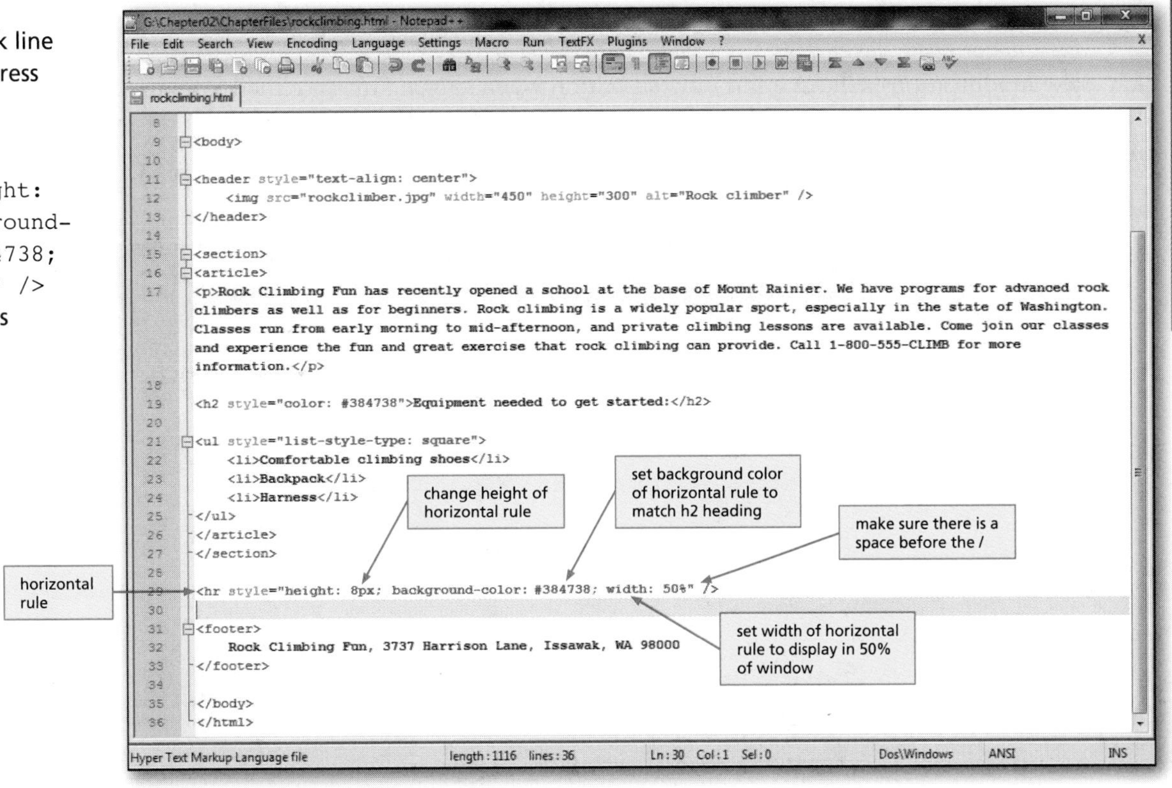

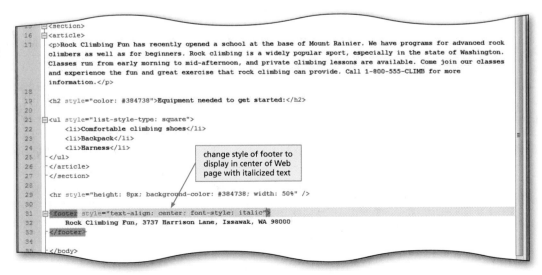

Figure 2–33

To Change the Footer Style

To change the style of the footer element, you again use an inline style with the font-style property. In this step, you center the footer across the Web page and change the font style to italic. Footer information is not generally intended to be the highlight of the Web page, so making the footer content italic is appropriate. The following steps show how to center and change the text using an inline style.

- Click after the "r" but before the closing bracket in `<footer>` on line 31 and then press the SPACEBAR.

- Type `style="text-align: center; font-style: italic"` as the code (Figure 2–34).

- Click File on the menu bar and then click Save.

Figure 2–34

To Refresh the View in a Browser

As you continue developing the HTML file in Notepad++, it is a good idea to view the file in your browser as you make modifications. Clicking the Refresh button when viewing the modified Web page in the browser, ensures that the latest version of the Web page is displayed. The following step shows how to refresh the view of a Web page in a browser in order to view the modified Web page.

- Click the Internet Explorer button on the taskbar to display the rockclimbing.html Web page.

- Click the Refresh button on the Address bar to display the modified Web page (Figure 2–35).

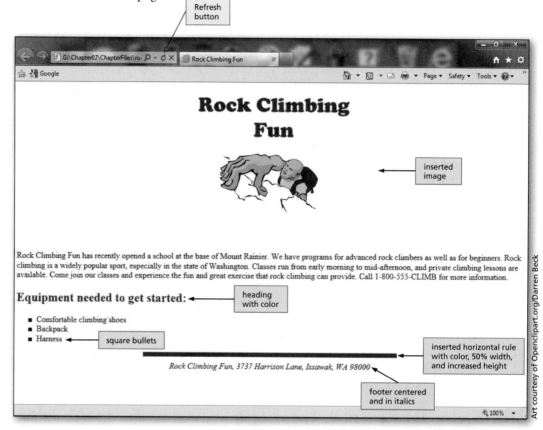

Figure 2–35

Art courtesy of Openclipart.org/Darren Beck

Validating and Viewing HTML Code

HTML and HTML5 Tags
The Web has excellent sources that list HTML5 tags. For more information about HTML and HTML5, search for "HTML tags" or "HTML5 tags" in a search engine.

In Chapter 1, you read about validating your HTML code. Many validation services are available on the Web that can be used to assure that your HTML code follows standards. This should always be a part of your Web page testing. The validation service used in this book is the W3C Markup Validation Service (validator.w3.org). This validator checks the markup validity of Web documents in HTML and XHTML, along with some other markup languages. The validator looks at the DOCTYPE statement to see which version of HTML or XHTML you are using, and then checks to see if the code is valid for that version. In this chapter, the project uses the HTML5 DOCTYPE.

If validation detects an error in your HTML code, you will see the warning "Errors found while checking this document as HTML5!" in the header bar, which is in red (Figure 2–36a on the next page). The Result line shows the number of errors that you have. You can scroll down the page or click the Jump To: Validation Output link to see detailed comments on each error.

It is important to note that one error can result in more errors. As an example, the </h2> tag on line 19 in the rockclimbing.html file was removed to show code with an error. Figure 2–36b shows that in this case, one initial error (that the <ul> tag on line 21 cannot be used within the <h2> tag on line 19) resulted in a total of three errors and one warning.

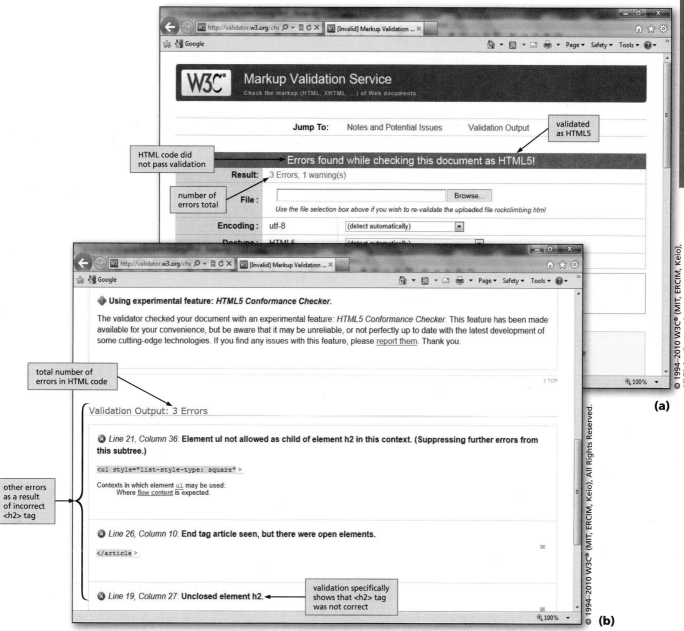

Figure 2–36

To Validate HTML Code

Now that you have added all the basic elements to your Web page and enhanced it with images, color, italics, and rules, you need to validate your code. The current validation process for HTML5 returns not just errors, but informational warnings, as shown in Figure 2–39a on page HTML 75. Although the validator says the code "was successfully checked as HTML5" it also displays a warning for the code. Figure 2–39b explains that warning, which says that the HTML5 Conformance Checker used for validation on HTML5 code is experiemental. As mentioned earlier in the chapter, HTML5 is still experimental as are associated support features, and this warning is just telling you that. The warning is fine though, so your code has passed the validation process. The following steps illustrate how to validate your HTML code using the W3 validator.

1

- Click the Address bar on the browser to highlight the current URL.

- Type `validator.w3.org` to replace the current entry, and then press the ENTER key.

- If necessary, click OK if the browser asks to open a new window.

- Click the Validate by File Upload tab (Figure 2–37).

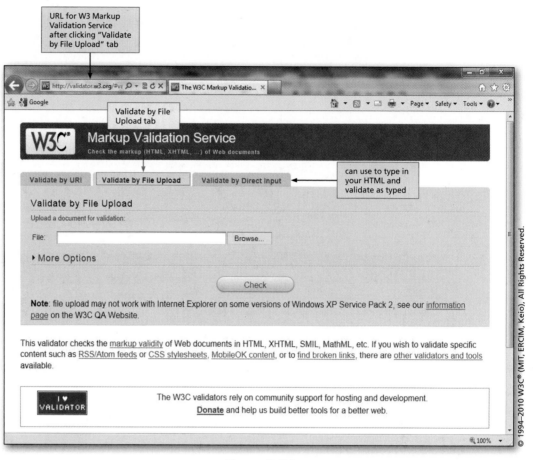

Figure 2–37

2

- Click the Browse button.

- Locate the rockclimbing.html file on your storage device and then click the file name.

- Click the Open button on the Choose File to Upload dialog box and the file path and name will be inserted into the File box, as shown in Figure 2–38.

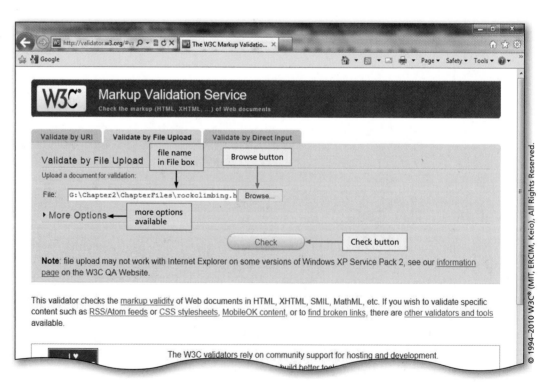

Figure 2–38

3

- Click the Check button. The resulting validation should be displayed, as shown in Figure 2–39a and 2–39b.

- Return to the Rock Climbing Fun Web page, either by clicking the Back button on your browser or by clicking the Internet Explorer button in the taskbar.

Q&A How do I know if my HTML code is valid?

The notification header will be green, and in the Result area, you should see the word "Passed."

Q&A What can I do if my HTML code is not validated?

If your code has errors, edit your HTML file to correct the errors. The Markup Validation Service report lists what is wrong with your code. Once you make the necessary changes and save the file, you can use the Browse button to open the corrected HTML file, then scroll down and click the Revalidate button to validate the changed code.

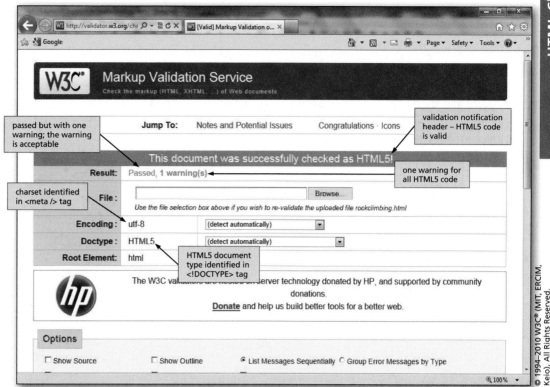

(a)

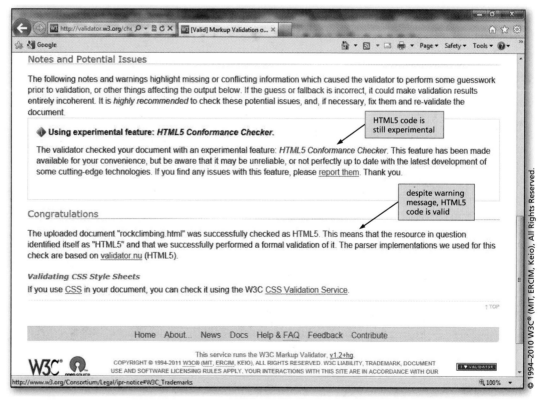

(b)

Figure 2–39

To View HTML Source Code for a Web Page

Source code is the code or instructions used to create a Web page or program. For a Web page, the source code is the HTML code, which then is translated by a browser into a graphical Web page. You can view the HTML source code for any Web page from within your browser. This feature allows you to check your own HTML source code, as well as to see the HTML code other developers used to create their Web pages. If a feature on a Web page is appropriate or appealing for your Web page, you can view the source to understand the HTML required to add that feature and then copy sections of the HTML code to put on your own Web pages. You can use your browser to look at the source code for most Web pages. The following steps show how to view the HTML source code for your Web page using a browser.

1

- Use the Back button on the browser to return to the Web page.

- Click Page on the Command bar. If your Command bar is not displayed, right-click the title bar, click Command bar, and then click Page.

- Click View source to view the HTML code in the default text editor (Figure 2–40).

Q&A

Do all browsers allow me to view the HTML source code in the same way?

Browsers such as Chrome, Firefox and Safari all allow you to view the source code of Web pages. However, they might use different buttons or menu options to access source code. For instance, in Mozilla Firefox, select View and then Page Source.

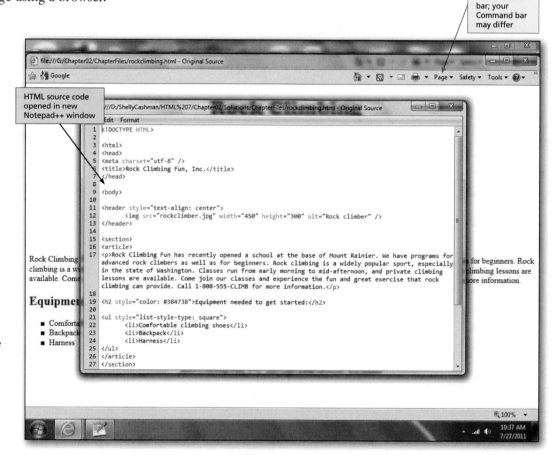

Figure 2–40

2

- Click the Close button on the text editor menu bar to close the active text editor window (Figure 2–41).

Q&A What is the default text editor?

It is likely to be Notepad for Internet Explorer, but could be Notepad++ or another editor depending on your browser setup.

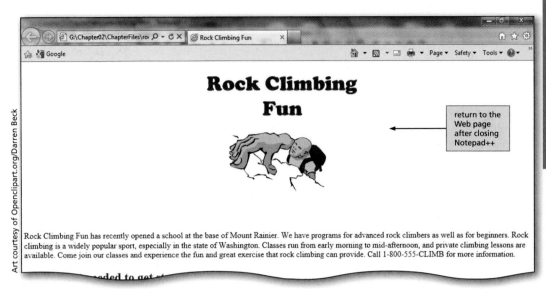

Art courtesy of Openclipart.org/Darren Beck

return to the Web page after closing Notepad++

Figure 2–41

To Print a Web Page and an HTML File

After you have created the HTML file and saved it, you might want to print a copy of the HTML code and the resulting Web page. A printed version of a file, Web page, or other document is called a **hard copy** or **printout**. Printed copies of HTML files and Web pages can be kept for reference or to distribute. The following steps show how to print a Web page and its corresponding HTML file.

1

- Ready the printer according to the printer instructions.

- With the Rock Climbing Fun Web page open in the browser window, click the Print icon on the Command bar.

- When the Print dialog box appears, click the Print button.

- When the printer stops printing the Web page, retrieve the printout (Figure 2–42).

Q&A Are there other ways to print a Web page?

Pressing CTRL+P opens the Print dialog box, where you can select print options. You can also use the Print option in the File menu on the menu bar.

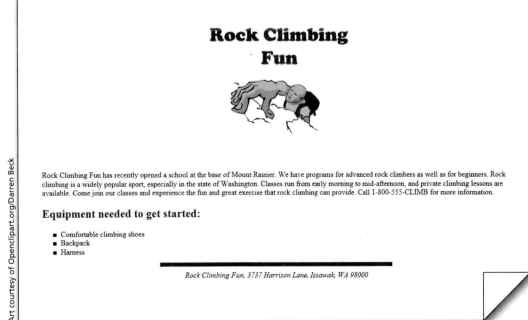

Art courtesy of Openclipart.org/Darren Beck

Figure 2–42

2

- Click the Notepad++ button on the task-bar to activate the Notepad++ window.

- Click File on the menu bar, click the Print command, and then click the Print button to print a hard copy of the HTML code (Figure 2–43).

Q&A

Why do I need a printout of the HTML code?

Having a hard-copy printout is an invaluable tool for be-ginning developers. A printed copy can help you immediately see the relationship be-tween the HTML tags and the Web page that you view in the browser.

```
<!DOCTYPE HTML>

<html>
<head>
<meta charset="utf-8" />
<title>Rock Climbing Fun, Inc.</title>
</head>

<body>

<header style="text-align: center">
    <img src="rockclimber.jpg" width="450" height="300" alt="Rock climber" />
</header>

<section>
<article>
<p>Rock Climbing Fun has recently opened a school at the base of Mount Rainier. We have
programs for advanced rock climbers as well as for beginners. Rock climbing is a widely
popular sport, especially in the state of Washington. Classes run from early morning to
mid-afternoon, and private climbing lessons are available. Come join our classes and
experience the fun and great exercise that rock climbing can provide. Call
1-800-555-CLIMB for more information.</p>

<h2 style="color: #384738">Equipment needed to get started:</h2>

<ul style="list-style-type: square">
    <li>Comfortable climbing shoes</li>
    <li>Backpack</li>
    <li>Harness</li>
</ul>
</article>
</section>

<hr style="height: 8px; background-color: #384738; width: 50%" />

<footer style="text-align: center; font-style: italic">
    Rock Climbing Fun, 3737 Harrison Lane, Issawak, WA 98000
</footer>

</body>
</html>
```

Figure 2–43

BTW

Quick Reference
For a list of HTML tags and their associated attributes, see the HTML Quick Reference (Appendix A) at the back of this book, or visit the HTML Quick Reference on the Book Companion Site Web page for this book at www.cengagebrain.com. For a list of CSS properties and values, see Appendix D.

To Quit Notepad++ and a Browser

The following steps show how to quit Notepad++ and a browser.

1 In Notepad++, click the File menu, then Close All.

2 Click the Close button on the Notepad++ title bar.

3 Click the Close button on the Internet Explorer title bar.

Chapter Summary

In this chapter, you have learned how to identify the elements of a Web page, define the Web page structure, and enter Web page content using a text editor. You enhanced the appearance of your Web page using inline styles, saved and validated your code, and viewed your Web page and source code in a browser. The items listed below include all the new HTML skills you have learned in this chapter.

1. Start Notepad++ (HTML 40)
2. Enable word wrap in Notepad++ (HTML 42)
3. Define the Web Page Structure Using HTML Tags (HTML 42)
4. Enter a Paragraph of Text (HTML 48)
5. Enter a Heading (HTML 49)
6. Create an Unordered List (HTML 51)
7. Add a Footer (HTML 53)
8. Save an HTML File (HTML 55)
9. Start a Browser (HTML 58)
10. View a Web Page in a Browser (HTML 59)
11. Activate Notepad++ (HTML 60)
12. Add an Image (HTML 65)
13. Add Color to a Web Page Heading (HTML 69)
14. Change the Bulleted List Style (HTML 70)
15. Add a Horizontal Rule (HTML 70)
16. Change the Footer Style (HTML 71)
17. Refresh the View in a Browser (HTML 72)
18. Validate HTML Code (HTML 73)
19. View HTML Source Code for a Web Page (HTML 76)
20. Print a Web Page and an HTML File (HTML 77)

Learn It Online

Test your knowledge of chapter content and key terms.

Instructions: To complete the following exercises, please visit www.cengagebrain.com. At the CengageBrain.com home page, search for *HTML5 and CSS 7th Edition* using the search box at the top of the page. This will take you to the product page for this book. On the product page, click the Access Now button below the Study Tools heading. On the Book Companion Site Web page, select Chapter 2, and then click the link for the desired exercise.

Chapter Reinforcement TF, MC, and SA
A series of true/false, multiple choice, and short answer questions that test your knowledge of the chapter content.

Flash Cards
An interactive learning environment where you identify chapter key terms associated with displayed definitions.

Practice Test
A series of multiple choice questions that test your knowledge of chapter content and key terms.

Who Wants To Be a Computer Genius?
An interactive game that challenges your knowledge of chapter content in the style of a television quiz show.

Wheel of Terms
An interactive game that challenges your knowledge of chapter key terms in the style of the television show, *Wheel of Fortune.*

Crossword Puzzle Challenge
A crossword puzzle that challenges your knowledge of key terms presented in the chapter.

Apply Your Knowledge

Reinforce the skills and apply the concepts you learned in this chapter.

Editing the Apply Your Knowledge Web Page

Instructions: Start Notepad++. Open the file apply2-1.html from the Chapter02\Apply folder of the Data Files for Students. See the inside back cover of this book for instructions for downloading the Data Files for Students, or contact your instructor for information about accessing the required files for this book.

The apply2-1.html file is a partially completed HTML file that you will use for this exercise. Figure 2–44 shows the Apply Your Knowledge Web page as it should be displayed in a browser after the additional HTML tags and attributes are added.

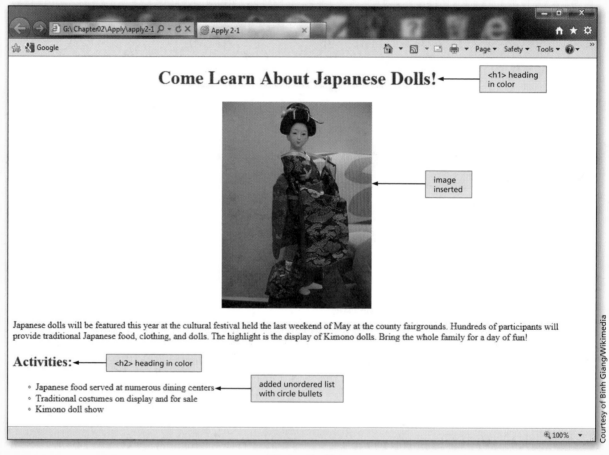

Figure 2–44

Perform the following tasks:

1. Enter g:\Chapter02\Apply\apply2-1.html as the URL to view the Web page in your browser.

2. Examine the HTML file and its appearance in the browser.

3. Using Notepad++, change the HTML code to make the Web page look similar to the one shown in Figure 2–44. Both headings are the color #910603. (*Hint:* Use the style="color: #910603" property and value.)

4. Add the image kimono_doll.jpg (in the Chapter02\Apply folder) to the Web page. It has a width of 260 pixels and a height of 346 pixels. (*Hint:* Include the image in a <header> </header> container and remember to use the alt attribute.)

5. Make the bulleted list using bullet type "circle" as shown in Figure 2–44.

6. Save the revised HTML file in the Chapter02\Apply folder using the file name apply2-1solution.html.

7. Validate your HTML code at validator.w3.org.

8. Enter g:\Chapter02\Apply\apply2-1solution.html (or the path where your data file is stored) as the URL to view the revised Web page in your browser.

9. Print the Web page.

10. Submit the revised HTML file and Web page in the format specified by your instructor.

Extend Your Knowledge

Extend the skills you learned in this chapter and experiment with new skills.

Creating a Definition List

Instructions: Start Notepad++. Open the file, extend2-1.html from the Chapter02\Extend folder of the Data Files for Students. See the inside back cover of this book for instructions on downloading the Data Files for Students, or contact your instructor for information about accessing the required files. This sample Web page contains all of the text for the Web page. You will add the necessary tags to make this a definition list with terms that are bold, as shown in Figure 2–45.

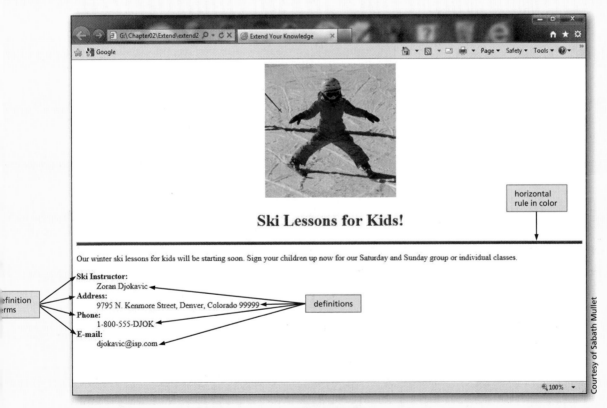

Figure 2–45

Perform the following tasks:

1. Using the text given in the file extend2-1.html, make changes to the HTML code to change the Web page from a single line of text to a definition list by following the definition list code shown in Table 2–6 on page HTML 52.

Continued >

Extend Your Knowledge *continued*

2. Add the additional HTML code necessary to make the terms bold. (*Hint:* Review the font-weight property with a value of bold.)

3. Add the image skier.jpg. Find the dimensions of the image by reviewing the image properties.

4. Add a horizontal rule that is 5 pixels high and color #414565. The <h1> heading is also color #414565.

5. Save the revised document in the Chapter02\Extend folder with the file name extend2-1solution. html, validate the Web page, and then submit it in the format specified by your instructor.

Make It Right

Analyze a document and correct all errors and/or improve the design.

Correcting the Star of India Web Page

Instructions: Start Notepad++. Open the file makeitright2-1.html from the Chapter02\MakeItRight folder of the Data Files for Students. See the inside back cover of this book for instructions on downloading the Data Files for Students, or contact your instructor for information about accessing the required files.

The data file is a modified version of what you see in Figure 2–46. Make the necessary corrections to the Web page to make it look like Figure 2–46. Add a background color to the Web page using color #515c7a. (*Hint:* Use an inline style in the <body> tag.) Format the heading to use the Heading 1 style with the color black. Add a paragraph of text in white and four circle bullets also in white. (*Hint:* Use the color property in the heading, paragraph, and bullet tags.) Save the file in the Chapter02\MakeItRight folder as makeitright2-1solution.html, validate the Web page, and then submit it in the format specified by your instructor. Be prepared to discuss the four questions posed in the bullet list.

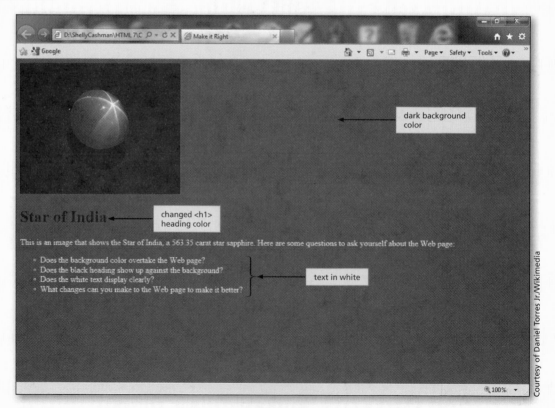

dark background color

changed <h1> heading color

text in white

Figure 2–46

Courtesy of Daniel Torres Jr./Wikimedia

In the Lab

Lab 1: Creating an Informational Web Page

Problem: You enjoy volunteering and decide to prepare a Web page announcement, such as the one shown in Figure 2–47, to promote the latest food drive.

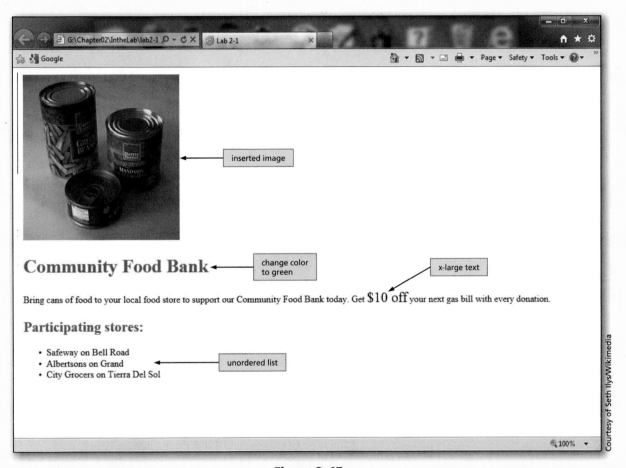

Figure 2–47

Instructions: Perform the following steps:

1. Create a new HTML file in Notepad++ with the title Lab 2-1 within the \<title> \</title> tags.

2. Add the donations.jpg image file, which has a width of 272 and a height of 277. Place the image on the left side of the Web page. Use the color green for both headings.

3. Add the paragraph of text, as shown in Figure 2–47. Make the words "$10 off" x-large style of font. (*Hint:* Review the \<span> HTML tag in Appendix A.)

4. Create one bulleted list with the information shown.

5. Save the file in the Chapter02\IntheLab folder using the file name lab2-1solution.html.

6. Print the lab2-1solution.html file.

7. Enter g:\Chapter02\IntheLab\lab2-1solution.html (or the path where your data file is stored) as the URL to view the Web page in your browser.

8. Print the Web page.

9. Submit the revised HTML file and Web page in the format specified by your instructor.

In the Lab

Lab 2: Creating a Healthy Living Web Page

Problem: You work for the Healthy Living Commission in your city. You would like to create a Web page showing two great ideas for healthy living, as shown in Figure 2–48.

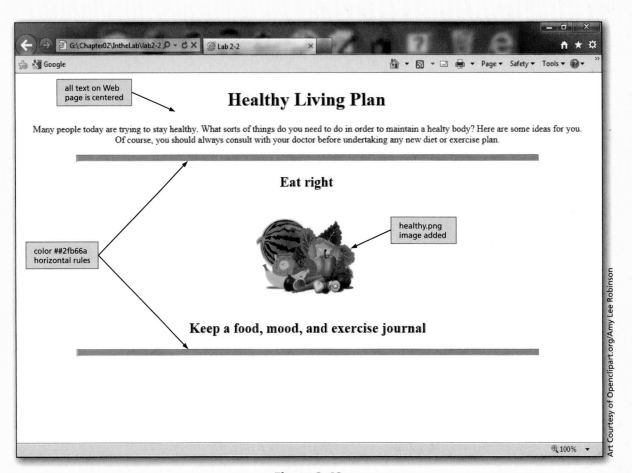

Figure 2–48

Art Courtesy of Openclipart.org/Amy Lee Robinson

Instructions: Perform the following steps:

1. Create a new HTML file in Notepad++ with the title, Lab 2-2, within the <title> </title> tags. For the initial HTML tags, you can use the structure.html file if you created one at the start of this chapter's project, otherwise type the initial tags.

2. Begin the body section by adding an <h1> heading, Healthy Living Plan. Format the heading to use the heading 1 style center-aligned on the Web page. (*Hint:* See the text-align property in Appendix D to center the heading.)

3. Add the centered paragraph of text shown in Figure 2–47. Make sure the fourth sentence displays on the next line with no blank line in between. (*Hint:* Use the <br /> tag.)

4. Add a horizontal rule with a height of 10 pixels, a width of 80%, and a background color of #2fb66a.

5. Add a centered heading, as shown, using the heading 2 style.

6. Add the healthy.png image. Find the height and width properties for that image and include them together with alternate text.

7. Add another <h2> heading and horizontal rule.

8. Save the file in the Chapter02\IntheLab folder as lab2-2 solution.html.

9. Print the lab2-2.html file.

10. Enter g:\Chapter02\IntheLab\lab2-2solution.html (or the path where your data file is stored) as the URL to view the Web page in your browser.

11. Print the Web page.

12. Submit the revised HTML file and Web page in the format specified by your instructor.

In the Lab

Lab 3: Composing a Personal Web Page

Problem: Your friends are concerned that they aren't able to save money. They have asked you for help, since you seem to always have money saved for a rainy day. You decide to compose a Web page with some advice for them. You plan to use a paragraph of text, an image and a bulleted list, as shown in Figure 2–49. The text and bullets in the figure should be replaced with your own money-saving experience and tips.

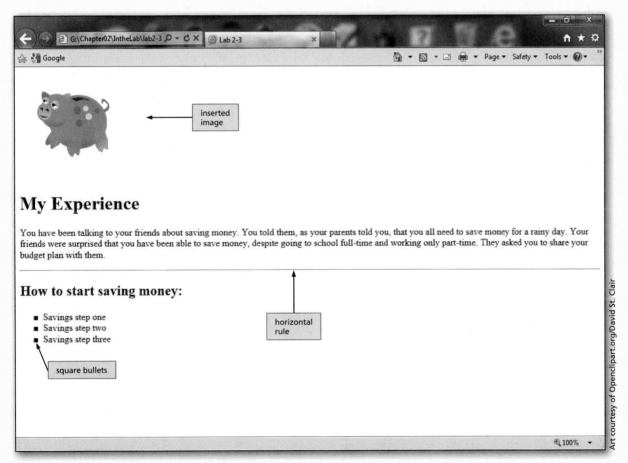

Art courtesy of Openclipart.org/David St. Clair

Figure 2–49

Instructions: Perform the following steps:

1. Create a new HTML file with the title Lab 2-3 within the <title> </title> tags.

2. Include a short paragraph of information and a bulleted list, using a format similar to the one shown in Figure 2–49, to provide information about your money-saving experience.

Continued >

In the Lab *continued*

3. Insert the image file piggybank.png, stored in the Chapter02\IntheLab folder. You can find the dimensions of an image by clicking on the image using Windows Explorer. You can also right-click the image, click Properties, and then click the Details tab to find out the image's dimensions, or open it in a graphics program. Note that the bullets used for the list are square in shape.

4. Save the HTML file in the Chapter02\IntheLab folder using the file name lab2-3solution.html.

5. Enter g:\Chapter02\IntheLab\lab2-3solution.html (or the path where your data file is stored) as the URL to view the Web page in your browser.

6. Print the Web page from your browser.

7. Submit the revised HTML file and Web page in the format specified by your instructor.

Cases and Places

Apply your creative thinking and problem-solving skills to design and implement a solution.

1: Research HTML5 Structural Tags

Academic

There are many Web sites dedicated to HTML5. Search the Web to find sites that have training modules for HTML5. Discover training specifically targeting the new structural elements discussed in the chapter. How do these new tags differ from the <div> tag? Are there situations in which the <div> tag is a better option? Write a brief report. Identify the URLs for the training Web sites and share them with your fellow students in class.

2: Create a Personal Web Page

Personal

Your class instructor wants to post all of the students' Web pages on the school server to show what his or her students are interested in. Create a Web page of personal information, listing items such as your school major, jobs that you have had in the past, and your hobbies and interests. To make your personal Web page more visually interesting, search the Web for images that reflect your interests. (Remember that if the image is copyrighted, you cannot use it on a personal Web page unless you follow the guidelines provided with the image.) Insert an image or two onto the Web page to help explain who you are.

3: Investigate Methods for Working with Images

Professional

You are creating a new Web site for a local photographer. The photographer has asked that you determine methods to help his Web site load quickly despite having so many large images. To this end, find information on using thumbnail images. Review other photography Web sites and create a list of suggestions for loading large images. Additionally, search the Web for information on adding useful, descriptive alt attributes for images. Write a brief synopsis explaining the information that you found in your research.

3 Creating Web Pages with Links, Images, and Embedded Style Sheets

Courtesy of Sabath Mullet

Objectives

You will have mastered the material in this chapter when you can:

- Describe linking terms and definitions
- Create a home page and enhance a Web page using images
- Change body and heading format using embedded (internal) style sheets
- Align and add color to text using embedded and inline styles
- Add a text link to a Web page in the same Web site
- Add an e-mail link
- Add a text link to a Web page on another Web site

- Use absolute and relative paths
- Save, validate, and view an HTML file and test the links
- Use style classes to add an image with wrapped text
- Add links to targets within a Web page
- Use an inline style to change the default bullet list type to square bullets
- Copy and paste HTML code
- Add an image link to a Web page in the same Web site

3 | Creating Web Pages with Links, Images, and Embedded Style Sheets

Introduction

One of the most useful and important aspects of the World Wide Web is the ability to connect (link) one Web page to other Web pages — on the same server or on different Web servers — located anywhere in the world. Using hyperlinks, a Web site visitor can move from one page to another, and view information in any order. Many different Web page elements, including text, graphics, and animations, can serve as hyperlinks. In this chapter, you will create Web pages that are linked together using both text links and image links. In the last chapter, you used inline styles to change the appearance of individual elements or HTML tags. In this chapter, you will also use embedded style sheets (also called internal style sheets) to set the appearance of elements such as headings and body text for the entire Web page. Before starting on this project, you would have already completed the Web site planning, analysis, and design phases of the Web Development Life Cycle.

Project — Underwater Tours by Eloise Web Site

Chapter 3 illustrates how to use HTML to create a home page for the Underwater Tours by Eloise Web site (Figure 3–1a) and to edit the existing samplephotos.html Web page (Figure 3–1b) to improve its appearance and function. Your older sister, Eloise, recently opened an underwater tour company and named it Underwater Tours by Eloise. She would like to advertise her company on the Web and show sample pictures of sea creatures. She knows that you have studied Web development in college and asks you to develop two Web pages that are linked together: a home page and a Web page with the sample pictures. During your analysis, you determined that there are four basic types of links to use. The first type is a link from one Web page to another in the same Web site. The second type is a link to a Web page on a different Web site. The third type is an e-mail link. The fourth type is a link within one Web page. You plan to utilize all four of these types of links for your sister's Web site.

The Underwater Tours by Eloise home page (Figure 3–1a) includes a logo image, headings, an e-mail link, and a text link to a Web page on another Web site. This page also includes a link to the samplephotos.html Web page. The Sample Photographs Web page (Figure 3–1b) contains two images with text wrapped around them and internal links that allow visitors to move easily from section to section within the Web page. The Web page also has an image link back to the Underwater Tours by Eloise's home page.

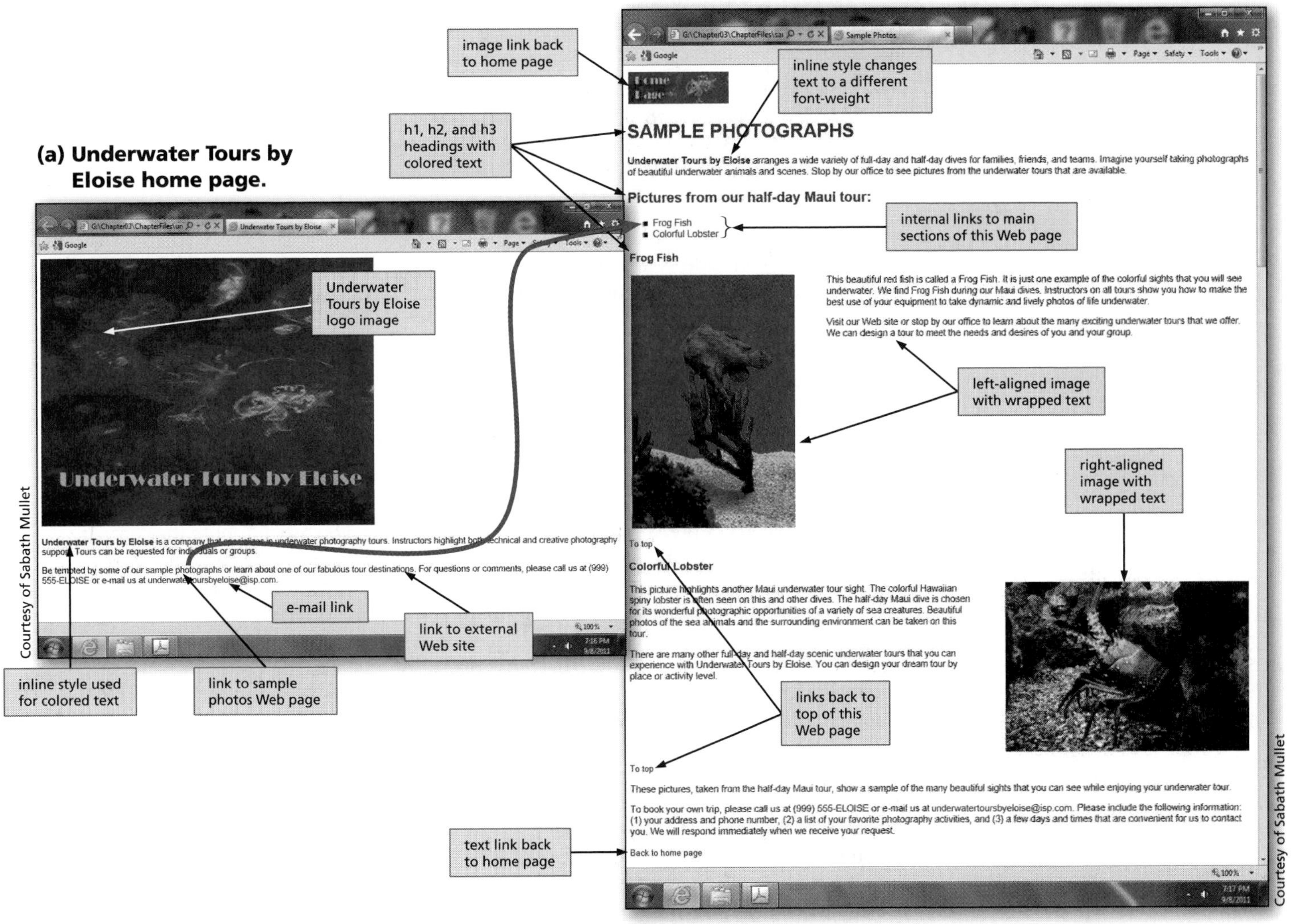

(b) Sample Photographs Web page.

image link back to home page

inline style changes text to a different font-weight

h1, h2, and h3 headings with colored text

(a) Underwater Tours by Eloise home page.

SAMPLE PHOTOGRAPHS

Underwater Tours by Eloise arranges a wide variety of full-day and half-day dives for families, friends, and teams. Imagine yourself taking photographs of beautiful underwater animals and scenes. Stop by our office to see pictures from the underwater tours that are available.

Pictures from our half-day Maui tour:

- Frog Fish
- Colorful Lobster

internal links to main sections of this Web page

Frog Fish

This beautiful red fish is called a Frog Fish. It is just one example of the colorful sights that you will see underwater. We find Frog Fish during our Maui dives. Instructors on all tours show you how to make the best use of your equipment to take dynamic and lively photos of life underwater.

Visit our Web site or stop by our office to learn about the many exciting underwater tours that we offer. We can design a tour to meet the needs and desires of you and your group.

Underwater Tours by Eloise logo image

left-aligned image with wrapped text

right-aligned image with wrapped text

To top

Colorful Lobster

This picture highlights another Maui underwater tour sight. The colorful Hawaiian spiny lobster is often seen on this and other dives. The half-day Maui dive is chosen for its wonderful photographic opportunities of a variety of sea creatures. Beautiful photos of the sea animals and the surrounding environment can be taken on this tour.

There are many other full-day and half-day scenic underwater tours that you can experience with Underwater Tours by Eloise. You can design your dream tour by place or activity level.

Underwater Tours by Eloise is a company that specializes in underwater photography tours. Instructors highlight both technical and creative photography support. Tours can be requested for individuals or groups.

Be tempted by some of our sample photographs or learn about one of our fabulous tour destinations. For questions or comments, please call us at us at (999) 555-ELOISE or e-mail us at underwatertoursbyeloise@isp.com.

e-mail link

link to sample photos Web page

link to external Web site

links back to top of this Web page

To top

These pictures, taken from the half-day Maui tour, show a sample of the many beautiful sights that you can see while enjoying your underwater tour.

To book your own trip, please call us at (999) 555-ELOISE or e-mail us at underwatertoursbyeloise@isp.com. Please include the following information: (1) your address and phone number, (2) a list of your favorite photography activities, and (3) a few days and times that are convenient for us to contact you. We will respond immediately when we receive your request.

Back to home page

inline style used for colored text

text link back to home page

Figure 3–1

Overview

As you read this chapter, you will learn how to create the Web page shown in Figure 3–1 by performing these general tasks:

- Use embedded style sheets, inline styles, and classes to change the format of text, links, images, and headings.
- Use an inline style to create a bulleted list with a square bullet style.
- Add a link to another Web page in the same Web site.
- Add a link to an external Web site.
- Add an e-mail link.
- Add targets and links within the same Web page.

Project Planning Guidelines

As you create Web pages, such as the project shown in Figure 3–1 on the previous page, you should follow these general guidelines:

1. **Plan the Web site**. Before developing a multiple-page Web site, you must plan the purpose of the site. Refer to Table 1–4 on page HTML 15 for information on the planning phase of the Web Development Life Cycle. In this phase, you determine the purpose of the Web site, identify the users of the site and their computing environments, and decide who owns the information on the Web page.

2. **Analyze the need**. In the analysis phase of the Web Development Life Cycle, you analyze what content to include in the Web page. The Web development project in Chapter 3 is different than the one completed in Chapter 2 because it contains two Web pages that will be linked together. Part of the analysis phase then includes determining how the multiple Web pages work together to form a Web site.

3. **Design the Web site.** Once the analysis is complete, you design the Web site. In this phase, you determine the content of the site, both text and graphics. Design steps specific to this chapter also include determining links within the site and to external Web sites.

   a. **Choose the content for the Web pages**. This part of the life cycle also differs from the previous chapter's project because all of the content does not have to appear on one Web page, as it did in Chapter 2. With a multiple-page Web site, you can distribute the content as needed throughout the Web site. Because of the nature of this Web site, pictures are a large part of the content. The Web site owner wants to show a sample of her company's work. Pictures help to highlight what sea creatures might be seen on a tour.

   b. **Determine the types of Cascading Style Sheets (CSS) that you will use**. You already learned how to use inline styles to best support the design and purpose of the Web site. In this chapter, you utilize both inline and embedded (internal) style sheets to alter the appearance (or style) of various Web page elements. You also incorporate classes with your embedded style sheets to further control the style of elements on the Web page. You need to consider which of these options is best suited for the styles of your Web site.

   c. **Determine how the pages will link to one another**. This Web site consists of a **home page** (the first page in a Web site) and a secondary Web page to which you will link. You need to determine how to link (e.g., with text or a graphic) from the home page to the secondary page and how to link back to the home page.

   d. **Establish what other links are necessary**. In addition to links between the home page and secondary Web page, you need an e-mail link. It is standard for Web developers to provide an e-mail link on the home page of a Web site for visitor comments or questions. Additionally, the secondary Web page (samplephotos.html) is a long page that requires visitors to scroll down for navigation. Because of its length, it is important to provide easy and quick ways to navigate the Web page. You do this using links within the Web page.

4. **Develop the Web page(s) and insert all links**. Once the analysis and design is complete, the Web developer creates the Web page(s) using HTML and CSS. Good Web development standard practices should be followed in this step. Examples of good practices include utilizing the proper initial HTML tags, as shown in the previous chapter, and always identifying alt text with images.

5. **Test all Web pages within the Web site**. An important part of Web development is testing to assure that you are following the standards outlined in the previous chapter. For the projects in this book, you will use the World Wide Web Consortium (W3C) validator that allows you to test your Web pages and clearly explains any errors it finds. When testing, you should check all content for accuracy. Also, all links (external, internal, and page to page within the same Web site) should be tested.

When necessary, more specific details concerning the above guidelines are presented at appropriate points in the chapter. The chapter will also identify the actions performed and decisions made regarding these guidelines during the creation of the Web page shown in Figure 3–1.

Using Links on a Web Page

As you have learned, many different Web page elements, including text, images, and animations, can serve as links. Text and images are the elements most widely used as links. Figure 3–2 shows examples of text and image links.

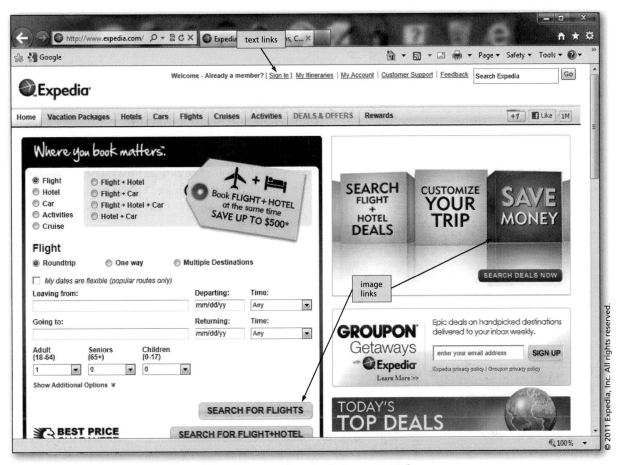

Figure 3–2 Text and image links on a Web page.

When using text links on a Web page, use descriptive text as the clickable word or phrase. For example, the phrase "Click here" does not explain the purpose of the link to the visitor. By contrast, the phrase "SAVE MONEY" (in Figure 3–2) indicates that the link connects to a Web page with discounted airline tickets.

When a link is identified with text, it often appears as underlined text, in a color different from the main Web page text. Unless otherwise changed in the anchor <a> or <body> tags, the browser settings define the colors of text links throughout a Web page. For example, with Internet Explorer, the default color for a normal link that has not been clicked (or visited) is blue, a visited link is purple, and an active link (a link just clicked by a user) varies in color. Figure 3–3 on the next page shows examples of text links in normal and visited states. Generally, moving the mouse pointer over a link causes the mouse pointer to change to a pointing hand. This change notifies the user that a link is available from that text or image.

BTW

Link Help
Many Web sites provide help for new HTML5 developers. For more information about links, search for keywords such as "HTML5 Tutorials" or "HTML5 Help" in any good search engine.

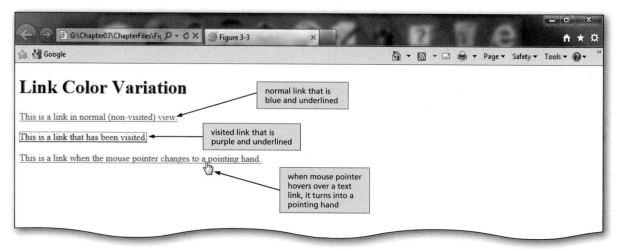

Figure 3–3   Examples of text link color and hover variations.

The same color defaults apply to the border color around an image link. A border makes the image appear as if it has a frame around it. If the image has no border, no frame will appear around the image. The color of the border shows whether the border is a link, and whether the link has been visited (Figure 3–4).

Figure 3–4   Normal and visited link colors.

The <a> tag also is called the **anchor tag** because it is used to create anchors for links to another page in the same Web site, to a Web page in an external Web site, within the same Web page, and for e-mail links. This is the tag that you will use throughout the project for the four types of links inserted in the Web pages.

If you want to change the color of text links or image link borders to override the browser defaults, you can designate those changes in the anchor <a> or <body> elements using an embedded or external style sheet, or by using an inline style. Recall that you use an inline style to change the appearance (or style) of a single element. An embedded (or internal) style sheet is used to change the styles of similar elements in one Web page. Finally, an external style sheet is contained in a separate .css document and is used to change the style in an entire Web site. (You will use an external style sheet in the next chapter.) To use an embedded or external style sheet in the anchor element to change normal, visited, and active link colors from the default, you would use the following format:

```
a        {color: black;}
```

where color is a designated color name, such as black, or a hexadecimal color code. To make the same change with an inline style, the tag format is:

```
<a style="color: black">
```

Links, by default, are underlined to indicate that they are links. You can disable the underlining of a link with the text-decoration property within the anchor tag. The **text-decoration property** allows text to be "decorated" with one of five values: underline, overline, line-through, blink, or none. This property can be used in a variety of tags including the anchor tag.

In the design phase you should carefully consider the benefits and disadvantages of any style change, especially to a default style. Be sure that users are still able to immediately see that specific text is used as a link before turning off link underlines or changing the default link color. If you determine that you can effectively turn the underline off on a link (as you do for the image link that you create later in this chapter), you can change the text-decoration attribute to none. To do this with an embedded or external style, you would enter the following code:

```
a        {text-decoration: none;}
```

To change text-decoration to none with an inline style, enter:

```
<a style="text-decoration: none">
```

Linking to Another Web Page Within the Same Web Site

Web pages often include links to connect one Web page to another page within the same Web site. For example, a visitor can click a link on the home page of a Web site (Figure 3–5a on the next page) to connect and view another Web page on the same Web site (Figure 3–5b). The Web pages created in this project include links to other pages in the same Web site: (1) the Underwater Tours by Eloise home page includes a text link to the Sample Photographs Web page; and (2) the Sample Photographs Web page includes both text and image links back to the Underwater Tours by Eloise home page. To link the words "sample photographs" on the underwatertours.html home page to the samplephotos.html Web page, you need the following HTML code:

```
<a href="samplephotos.html">sample photographs</a>
```

The href in the anchor <a> tag indicates that when the words "sample photographs" are clicked, the visitor links to the samplephotos.html Web page. You end the link with the </a> tag. If you did not add the </a> tag, then all text after the words "sample photographs" would be linked.

BTW

Link Colors
You can change the link colors in popular browsers. In Internet Explorer, click the Tools button on the Command bar, click Internet Options, General tab, and the Colors button under Appearance. In Mozilla Firefox, click the Tools menu, Options, Content tab, and the Colors button under Fonts & Colors. In both browsers, you change colors by selecting a color from a color palette.

BTW

Links on a Web Page
An anchor tag also allows visitors to move within a single Web page. Use the id attribute to allow movement from one area to another on the same page. This linking technique is useful, particularly on long pages. An index of links can also provide easy access to various areas within the Web page.

(a) Web site home page.

(b) Linked Web page in same Web site.

Figure 3–5

Linking to a Web Page in Another Web Site

One of the most powerful features of Web development is the ability to link to Web pages outside of your Web site. Web developers use these links to connect their Web pages to other Web pages with information on the same topic. The links are what give the Web its value as an interconnected resource and provide its "webbiness." In this project, the home page (Figure 3–6a) includes a link to a page on another Web site where the visitor can find additional information about Hawaii's national parks (Figure 3–6b). To link the words "one of our fabulous tour destinations" on the underwatertours.html home page to an external Web site, you need the following HTML code:

```
<a href="http://www.nps.gov/state/hi/index.htm">one of our
fabulous tour destinations</a>
```

Notice that the code is basically the same as that used to link to a Web page within the same Web site. However, you have to add the complete URL (http://www.nps.gov/state/hi/index.htm) when you link to an external Web site.

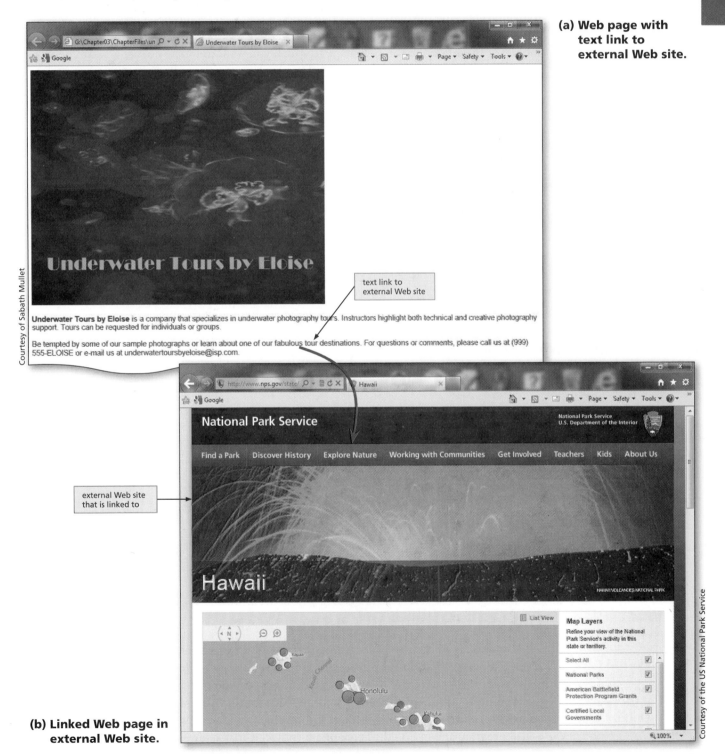

(a) Web page with text link to external Web site.

text link to external Web site

Underwater Tours by Eloise is a company that specializes in underwater photography tours. Instructors highlight both technical and creative photography support. Tours can be requested for individuals or groups.

Be tempted by some of our sample photographs or learn about one of our fabulous tour destinations. For questions or comments, please call us at (999) 555-ELOISE or e-mail us at underwatertoursbyeloise@isp.com.

external Web site that is linked to

(b) Linked Web page in external Web site.

Courtesy of Sabath Mullet

Courtesy of the US National Park Service

Figure 3–6

Linking Within a Web Page

Links within a Web page allow visitors to move quickly from one section of the Web page to another. This is especially important in Web pages that are long and require a visitor to scroll down to see all of the content. Many Web pages contain a list of links like a menu or table of contents at the top of the page, with links to sections within the Web page (Figure 3–7). In this project, the Sample Photographs Web page includes links from the top section of the Web page to other sections within the page, as well as links back to the top of the Web page. There are two steps to link within a Web page. First, you have to set a target using a name that makes sense to the purpose of the link. Then, you create a link to that target using the name given. The following HTML code shows an example of a target named fish and then the use of that target as a link. The first statement is inserted at the top of the section of the Web page to which you want to link. The second statement is inserted into the bulleted list at the top of the Web page where you want the link to appear.

```
<a id="fish"></a>
<a href="#fish">Frog Fish</a>
```

Again, notice that you also use the anchor <a> tag for this type of link. However, with this inner-page link, you insert the # before the target id to indicate that you want to link to a specific section of the Web page, not necessarily the top of the page. Sometimes when you are browsing the Web, you might see a # used in a link address. That generally links you to a specific section of the Web page.

Figure 3–7 Web page with internal links.

BTW

E-mail Links
You can assign more than one e-mail address to a mailto: tag. Use the form "mailto:first@isp.com, second@isp.com" in the <a href=> tag. Some older browsers may not support this tag.

Linking to an E-mail Address

A well-designed Web page always provides a way for visitors to contact the person at the company responsible for maintaining the Web site or addressing customer questions and comments. An easy way to provide contact information is to include an e-mail link on the Web site's home page, as well as on other pages in the Web site. As shown in Figure 3–8, when a visitor clicks the **e-mail link**, it automatically opens a new message in the default e-mail program and inserts the appropriate contact e-mail address in the To field. Visitors then can type and send an e-mail to request additional information, comment on the

Web site, or notify the company of a problem with its Web site. (*Note*: If your browser is not configured to send e-mail, the e-mail link will not work.) The following HTML code shows an example of how to link the words underwatertoursbyeloise@isp.com to an e-mail link.

```
<a href="mailto:underwatertoursbyeloise@isp.com">
underwatertoursbyeloise@isp.com</a>
```

You again use the anchor <a> tag for this type of link. In the href attribute, though, you use the mailto:*e-mail address* as the value. It may seem strange to have the e-mail address underwatertoursbyeloise@isp.com twice in this code. The first occurrence of the e-mail address is for the link itself. The second occurrence of underwatertoursbyeloise@isp.com is used for the words on the Web page that you use as the link.

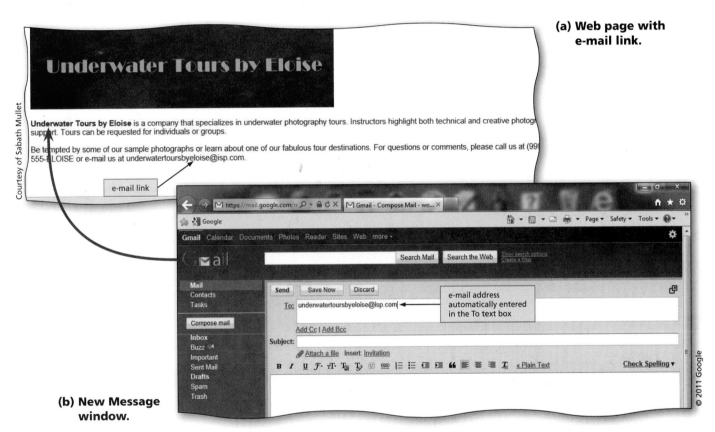

(a) Web page with e-mail link.

(b) New Message window.

Courtesy of Sabath Mullet

© 2011 Google

Figure 3–8

Creating a Home Page

The first Web page developed in this chapter is the home page of the Underwater Tours by Eloise Web site. A home page is the main page of a Web site, which visitors to a Web site will generally view first. A Web site home page should identify the purpose of the Web site by briefly stating what content, services, or features it provides. The home page also should indicate clearly what links the visitor should click to move from one page on the site to another. A Web developer should design the Web site in such a way that the links from one Web page to another are apparent and the navigation is clear. The Web site home page most often includes an e-mail link, so visitors can easily find contact information for the individual or organization. Many Web sites now include an additional e-mail link to the Web development team. Users can utilize this e-mail link to notify the Web developers of any problems with the Web site or to comment on the site.

You begin creating the home page by starting Notepad++ and entering the initial HTML tags. Then you add an image, heading, text, and an unordered list to your home page. Finally, you add text and e-mail links, and then test the links.

To Start Notepad++

The following steps, which assume Windows 7 is running, start Notepad++ based on a typical installation. You may need to ask your instructor how to start Notepad++ for your computer.

1 Click the Start button on the Windows taskbar to display the Start menu.

2 Click All Programs at the bottom of the left pane on the Start menu to display the All Programs list.

3 Click Notepad++ in the All Programs list to open the Notepad++ folder.

4 Click Notepad++ in the list to display the Notepad++ window. If there are files already open in Notepad from previous projects, close them all now by clicking the Close button on each open file.

5 If the Notepad++ window is not maximized, click the Maximize button on the Notepad++ title bar to maximize it (Figure 3–9).

6 Click View on the menu bar. If the Word wrap command does not have a check mark next to it, click Word wrap.

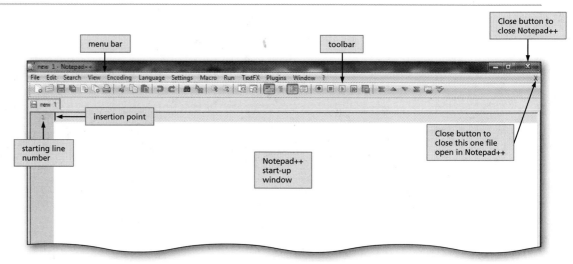

Figure 3–9

To Enter Initial HTML Tags to Define the Web Page Structure

Just as you did in Chapter 2, you start your file with the initial HTML tags that define the structure of the Web page. Table 3–1 contains the tags and text for this task.

BTW

Copy Initial Structure
Remember that you can type in the initial HTML tags and save that code in a file called structure.html, which you can then open and use as the basis for all HTML files. This eliminates the need for you to type this same code at the beginning of every HTML file. Just remember to save structure.html with a new name as soon as you open it.

Table 3–1 Initial HTML Tags	
Line	**HTML Tag and Text**
1	`<!DOCTYPE HTML>`
2	
3	`<html>`
4	`<head>`
5	`<meta charset="utf-8" />`

Table 3–1 Initial HTML Tags (continued)

Line	HTML Tag and Text
6	`<title>Underwater Tours by Eloise</title>`
7	`</head>`
8	
9	`<body>`
10	
11	`</body>`
12	`</html>`

The following steps illustrate how to enter the initial tags that define the structure of the Web page.

1 Enter the HTML code shown in Table 3–1. Press ENTER at the end of each line. If you make an error as you are typing, use the BACKSPACE key to delete all the characters back to and including the incorrect characters, then continue typing.

2 Position the insertion point on the blank line between the <body> and </body> tags (line 10) and press the ENTER key (Figure 3–10).

3 Compare what you typed to Figure 3–10. If you notice errors, use your mouse pointer or arrow keys to move the insertion point to the right of each error and use the BACKSPACE key to correct the error.

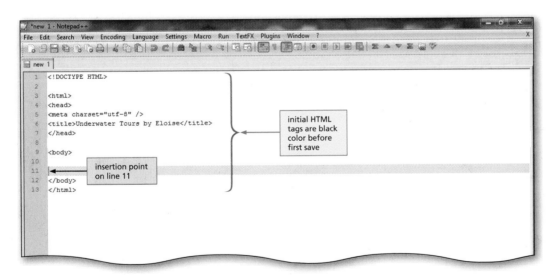

Figure 3–10

To Save an HTML File

With the initial HTML code for the Underwater Tours by Eloise home page entered, you should save the file. Saving the file frequently ensures you won't lose your work. Saving a file in Notepad++ also adds color to code that can help you identify different elements more easily. The following step illustrates how to save an HTML file in Notepad++.

① With a USB flash drive connected to one of the computer's USB ports, click File on the Notepad++ menu bar and then click Save.

② Type `underwatertours.html` in the File name text box (do not press ENTER).

③ Click Computer in the left pane of the Save As dialog box to display a list of available drives.

④ If necessary, scroll until UDISK 2.0 (G:) or the name of your storage device is displayed in the list of available drives.

⑤ Open the Chapter03\ChapterFiles folder.

⑥ Click the Save button in the Save As dialog box to save the file on the USB flash drive in the Chapter03\ChapterFiles folder with the name underwatertours.html.

Plan Ahead

Identify how to format various elements of the text.
Before inserting the graphical and color elements on a Web page, you should plan how you want to format them. By effectively utilizing graphics and color, you can call attention to important topics on the Web page without overpowering it. Consider the following formatting suggestions.

- **Effectively utilize graphics.** An important part of Web development is the use of graphics to call attention to a Web page. Generally, companies utilize the same logo on their Web site as they use on print material associated with the company, such as business cards and letterheads. Using the same graphical image on all marketing materials, including the Web site, is a good way to provide a consistent visual and brand message to customers.

- **Utilize headings that connect to the graphics.** In many cases, companies use a logo image as the main heading on their home page, as opposed to using an <h1> heading. It is sometimes good to coordinate the color of the headings and graphics contained on the Web page to the logo. This can bring attention to the company logo image, and it makes the Web page look cohesive with coordinating colors. Heading size standards should generally be followed from h1 (the largest) to h6 (the smallest). In this project, though, you use the company logo image as your main heading, so you have no h1 heading. Figure 3–1b on page HTML 89 shows the use of h1 and h2 headings in appropriate precedence.

To Add a Banner Image

The Underwater Tours by Eloise home page includes a logo image to provide visual appeal, catch the visitor's interest, and promote the company's brand. The following steps illustrate how to add an image to a Web page using the <header></header> container. Table 3–2 contains the code for adding the logo image.

Table 3–2 HTML Code for Adding a Banner Image	
Line	**HTML Tag and Text**
11	`<header>`
12	`<img src="underwaterlogo.jpg" width="581" height="450" alt="Underwater Tours logo" />`
13	`</header>`

1

• With the insertion point on line 11, enter the HTML code shown in Table 3–2, pressing ENTER at the end of each line. Make sure to indent the second line of code by using the TAB key. This separates the start and end <header> tags from the <img> tag, highlighting the image insertion. Press the ENTER key twice at the end of line 13 to position the insertion point on line 15 (Figure 3–11).

start and end <header> </header> tags to indicate header section

code to add an image

insertion point on line 15

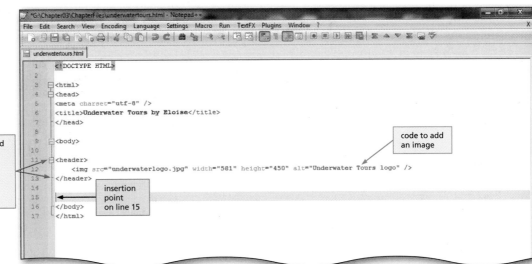

Figure 3–11

Q&A

Why should I include the width, height, and alt attributes?

Adding width and height attributes can improve page loading time because the browser does not have to figure the width and height before loading the image. Avoid using the height and width attributes to resize an image when possible. Use graphic editing software to resize it and save it with a different filename. The height and width attributes as used in the img tag should reflect the actual image size. The alt attribute provides information about the purpose of the image for assistive technology such as screen readers.

Identify how to format text elements of the home page.

Plan Ahead

You should always make a plan before inserting the text elements of a Web page. By formatting the characters and paragraphs on a Web page, you can improve its overall appearance. Effectively formatting the text also makes the message or purpose of the Web page clearer to the users. On a Web page, consider the following formatting suggestions.

• **Use default text size when appropriate**. The body text consists of all text between the heading and the bottom of the Web page. This text is the main content of the Web page and should be used to highlight the key points of your message. You can vary your content by utilizing both paragraphs of text and lists.

• **Determine what text formatting to use**. In a long Web page, it may help to vary your text as a way to break information up between headings. Using bold, color, or italicized text sparingly gives the Web page a more interesting look. Make sure not to overdo the formatting of text because you can make the page look cluttered. It is more difficult to find the content for which you are searching in a cluttered Web page.

• **Determine what style sheets to use**. Consider using style sheets to vary the format of text elements. If the text varies across paragraphs, an inline style is good to use. If you want all of the text in the Web page to be the same, an embedded style sheet is appropriate. If the text is common across more than one Web page, an external style sheet (discussed in the next chapter) should be used.

• **Determine other information suitable for the home page**. Other information that is suitable for a home page includes: the company address (often found in the logo), a phone number, and an e-mail link.

To Add Paragraphs of Text

After the underwater tours image for the Underwater Tours by Eloise home page is inserted, you need to add two paragraphs of text introducing Underwater Tours by Eloise. Table 3–3 shows the tags and text to enter.

Line	HTML Tag and Text
	Table 3–3 HTML Code for Adding Two Paragraphs of Text
15	`<section>`
16	`<article>`
17	`<p>Underwater Tours by Eloise is a company that specializes in underwater photography tours. Instructors highlight both technical and creative photography support. Tours can be requested for individuals or groups.</p>`
18	
19	`<p>Be tempted by some of our sample photographs or learn about one of our fabulous tour destinations. For questions or comments, please call us at (999) 555-ELOISE or e-mail us at underwatertoursbyeloise@isp.com.</p>`
20	`</article>`
21	`</section>`

1 With the insertion point on line 15, enter the HTML code shown in Table 3–3. Press ENTER twice after the </p> tag on line 17 and once after the </section> tag on line 21. After entering the closing </article> and </section> tags, the insertion point is on line 22 (Figure 3–12).

Q&A Do I have to end all paragraphs of text with the </p> tag?

A Web page without </p> tags would display in the browser correctly. This Web page would not pass validation using the W3C Markup Validation Service, however. One missed </p> tag will result in many errors during validation.

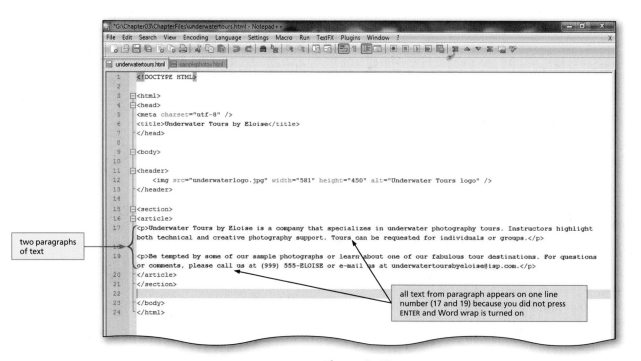

Figure 3–12

Plan
Ahead

> **Plan how and where to use the four types of links.**
>
> - **Identify how to link from the home page to another page in the same Web site.**
>   Linking to another Web page in the same Web site is often done with text links. When
>   determining what words to use, make sure that the text links are clear and easy to
>   understand. Using a phrase such as "click here" is not one that clearly identifies where
>   the link will go. Choosing words such as "sample photographs" tells the Web site
>   visitor to click that link if they want to see sample photographs.
>
> - **Use an e-mail link on the home page.** A good standard practice is to include an e-mail
>   link on the home page. Again, using words such as "click here" are not as effective
>   as using a company's actual e-mail address (underwatertoursbyeloise@isp.com in this
>   case) as the e-mail link text.
>
> - **Determine external links for the home page.** Visitors to a Web site might want additional
>   information on a topic, so a link can also be included on the home page (or any other
>   Web page in the Web site). Linking to an external Web site (i.e., one that is outside of
>   the boundaries of the current Web site) is appropriate to provide additional information.
>   Again, it is important to select words or phrases that make sense for that link.
>
> - **Use internal links on long Web pages.** Another good standard practice is to include
>   links within a Web page when the page is long (i.e., when you have to use the scroll
>   bar or press the PAGE DOWN key several times to get to the end of the Web page).
>   Internal links help visitors navigate more easily within long Web pages. Also consider
>   using links to help the visitor easily return back to the top of a long Web page.

Adding a Text Link to Another Web Page Within the Same Web Site

For the purpose of this Web site, the <a> and </a> tags are used to create links on
a Web page. As mentioned earlier, the <a> (anchor) tag is used to create anchors for the
links. The anchor tag can also be used to specify the base language of the target URL or
to specify the media type of the link. The href attribute stands for a hyperlink reference.
This is a reference (an address) to a resource on the Web. Hyperlinks can point to any
resource on the Web, including an HTML page, an image, a sound file, or a video. The
basic form of the tag used to create a link is:

```
<a href="URL">linktext</a>
```

where *linktext* is the clickable word or phrase that is displayed on the Web page and
the value for href (hypertext reference) is the name or URL of the linked page or file.
Table 3–4 shows some of the <a> tag attributes and their functions.

BTW

Other Links
You also can create links
to other locations on the
Internet (that is, non-http)
such as FTP sites, and
newsgroups. To link to
an FTP site, type ftp://
URL rather than http://
URL as used in this
project. For a newsgroup,
type news:newsgroup
name, and for any
particular article within
the newsgroup, type
news:article name as
the entry.

Table 3–4 <a> Tag Attributes and Functions	
Attribute	**Function**
href	Specifies the URL of the linked page or file.
id	Defines a name (or id) for the current anchor so it may be the target or destination of another link. Each anchor on a Web page must use a unique id.
rel	Specifies the relationship between the current document and the linked document. The value of the rel attribute is a link type, such as prev, next, author, or license. For example, the Web page chapter3.html might include the tag <a rel="next" href="chapter4.html"> to indicate a link to the Web page for the next chapter, chapter4.html.

Table 3–4 <a> Tag Attributes and Functions (continued)	
Attribute	**Function**
type	Specifies the content type (also known as media types or MIME types) of the linked page or file to help a browser determine if it can handle the resource type. Examples of content types include text/html, image/jpeg, video/quicktime, application/java, text/css, and text/javascript.

Before creating a link, be sure you know the URL or name of the file to be linked and the text that will serve as the clickable word or phrase. The words should be descriptive and tell the Web page visitor the purpose of the link. For the Underwater Tours by Eloise home page, the text link is a phrase in a paragraph at the bottom of the Web page.

To Add a Text Link to Another Web Page Within the Same Web Site

The Underwater Tours by Eloise home page includes a text link to the Sample Photographs Web page, which is part of the same Web site. The following step illustrates how to add a text link to another Web page within the same Web site.

- Click immediately to the left of the s in the word sample on line 19.

- Type <a href= "samplephotos .html"> to start the link, setting the Web page samplephotos.html as the linked Web page.

- Click immediately to the right of the s in photographs on line 19. Type </a> to close the link (Figure 3–13).

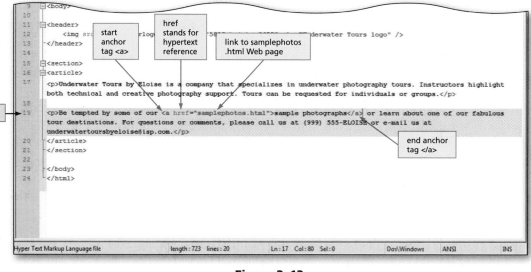

Figure 3–13

Q&A

What is the href attribute for?

The href stands for "hypertext reference" and precedes the URL of the destination Web page.

Q&A

How will I know if my text is a link when it is displayed in the browser?

In the browser, the mouse pointer turns into a pointing finger where there is a link. Also, as the default, text used as a link will be blue and underlined. You can change the color and style of a link, and you do that later in the chapter.

Q&A

What happens if I forget to insert the </a> tag on a link?

A text link without the </a> tag will not display correctly in the browser. If you forget to use the </a> tag to end this text link, all of the text beyond the <a href=""> tag will serve as that link. In this example, all of the text that follows the s in sample will link to the samplephotos.html Web page, which is certainly not what you want.

Adding an E-mail Link

BTW

E-mail Links
E-mail Links may not work in a lab setting because there may not be an e-mail client installed on the school servers. You therefore may not be able to test this link.

Adding an e-mail link is similar to adding a text link, but instead of using a URL as the href attribute value, the href attribute value for an e-mail link uses the form:

```
<a href="mailto:address@email.com">linktext</a>
```

where the href attribute value uses the word mailto to indicate it is an e-mail link, followed by a colon and the e-mail address to which to send the e-mail message. When the browser recognizes a **mailto** URL in a clicked link, it automatically opens a new message in the default e-mail program and inserts the appropriate contact e-mail address in the To field. The clickable text used for an e-mail link typically is the e-mail address used in the e-mail link. The Web page should also provide some information before the link, so visitors know the purpose of the e-mail link.

To Add an E-mail Link

The Underwater Tours by Eloise home page includes an e-mail link so customers can contact Underwater Tours by Eloise for additional information or to comment on the Web page. The <a> and </a> tags used to create a text link to a Web page are also used to create an e-mail link. The following step shows how to add an e-mail link to a Web page.

- Click immediately to the left of the u in the beginning of underwatertours-byeloise@isp.com on line 19. Type `<a href="mailto: underwatertours-byeloise@isp .com">` as the start of the e-mail link. This will link to the e-mail address underwater-toursbyelo-ise@isp.com when the link is clicked.

- Click immediately after the m in isp.com and before the period in the e-mail address text on line 19.

- Type `</a>` to end the e-mail link, as shown in Figure 3–14.

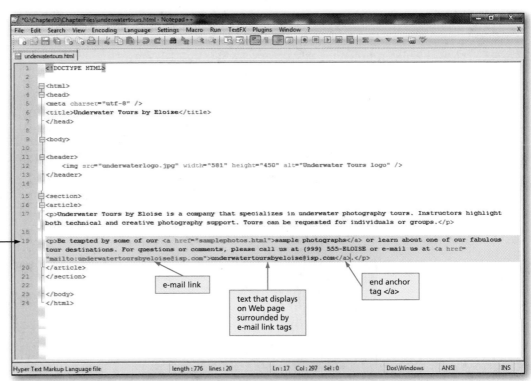

Figure 3–14

Q&A

I see two occurrences of underwatertoursbyeloise@isp.com on line 19. Why do I need two?

The first occurrence of underwatertoursbyeloise@isp.com (the one within the link <a> tag following the mailto:) is the destination of the link. The second occurrence of the e-mail address is the text link itself that will be displayed in the browser.

Adding Other Information to an E-mail Link

Sometimes, you need to add a subject to the e-mail message. This technique can be very helpful when more than one e-mail link is positioned on a Web page, and each link has a different purpose. For instance, one e-mail might be used for general questions, whereas another link might be used for specific information. You can also include a carbon-copy (cc) address. For instance, to include a subject in the above mailto:, you would use the form:

```
<a href="mailto:underwatertoursbyeloise@isp.com?subject=Maui
tours">
```

Sometimes, you need to add a message in the body of the e-mail in addition to the subject. This technique can be very helpful when more than one e-mail link is positioned on a Web page, and each link has a different purpose. For instance, one e-mail might be used for general questions, whereas another link might be used for specific information. Using the subject and body attributes can be helpful for this scenario. Notice that the two attributes (subject and body) are separated by an ampersand in the following form:

```
<a href="mailto:underwatertoursbyeloise@isp.com?subject=Maui
tours&body=Do you have half-day group tours?">
```

Figure 3–15 shows how the subject "Maui tours" and the message text "Do you have half-day group tours?" would appear in an e-mail program.

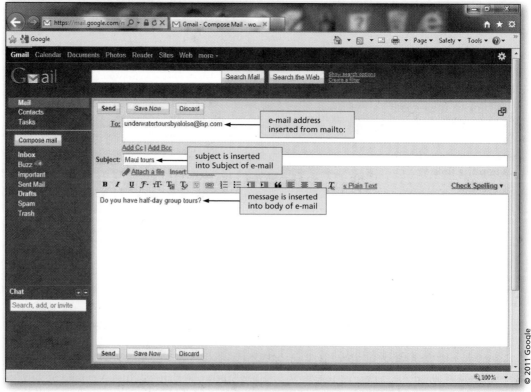

Figure 3–15

To Add a Text Link to a Web Page in Another Web Site

The <a> and </a> tags used to create a text link to a Web page within the same Web site are also used to create a link to a Web page in another Web site. The following step illustrates how to add a text link on the Underwater Tours by Eloise Web page to an external Web page that describes Hawaii's national parks.

1

- Click immediately to the left of the o in the word, one, on line 19 and type <a href="http:// www.nps.gov/ state/hi/index .htm"> to add the URL for the external Web site when clicked.

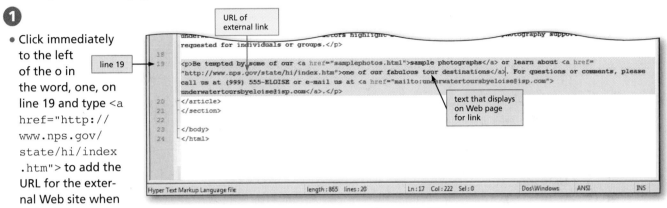

URL of external link

line 19

text that displays on Web page for link

Figure 3–16

- Click immediately to the right of the last letter s in destinations on line 19 and type </a> to end the tag, as shown in Figure 3–16.

Q&A When I type in the URL in the Address box of my browser, I never type in the http:// part of the URL. Why do I have to add the http:// in the link? I did not need the http:// for the sample photographs link.

Although you do not need to type the http:// into the URL on the browser, you always must include this as part of the href when creating external links. The Sample Photographs Web page is stored in the same folder as the home page from which you are linking. You therefore do not need to include any information other than the name of the Web page file. See the discussion on absolute and relative paths below for more information.

Q&A When I link to the external Web page (www.nps.gov), I have to use the Back button on the browser to return to my home page. Is that the only way to get back?

Yes. You have to use the Back button to return to the home page because this is an external Web site. There is no way to provide a link back to your home page from an external Web site. In later chapters, you will learn how to open a new window for external.

Using Absolute and Relative Paths

At this point, it is appropriate to revisit the overall concept of how the files are organized and saved. As noted in the last chapter, the projects in this book use a very simple folder structure. In this book, the graphical images are stored in the same folder as the HTML files, for example, in the Chapter03\ChapterFiles folder. For most real-world applications, however, it would be more appropriate to separate the HTML code and the graphical images into different folders. Figure 3–17 on the next page shows an example of a more complex file structure that could be used for this book.

To understand how to use this sort of folder structure, you need to identify the folder location, or path, to the files. A **path** describes the location (folder or external Web site) where the files can be found, beginning with the UDISK G:\ drive (or another drive on your computer). This beginning location is also known as the **root** location. You can use either an absolute or relative path when identifying the location of the files. An **absolute path** specifies the exact address for the file to which you are linking or displaying a graphic. You can think of an absolute path as the complete address of

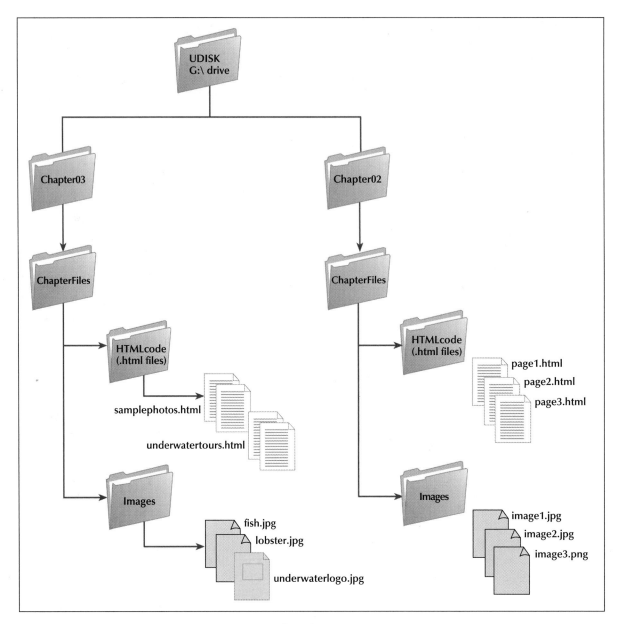

Figure 3–17

a house, including the house number, street name, city, state, and zip. In order to use that absolute address, you would have to give the entire path (or address) to a person who wants to get to that particular house. When you are referencing a Web page from a server outside of the server on which your Web pages reside, you have to use an absolute path. In this chapter, you use the absolute path to the National Park Service Web site for Hawaii. This is because that Web page is located outside of the server (or storage media) on which the Web pages created in the chapter reside. Your link statement for this external Web site is:

```
<a href="http://www.nps.gov/state/hi/index.htm">one of our
fabulous tour destinations</a>
```

Although absolute paths indicate the specific addresses of files, they can be cumbersome. For instance, if you use absolute paths for specific addressing of external Web pages, and those Web pages are moved to a different folder or different Web server, then all of the absolute paths would have to be changed. In the example above, if the home page for href="http://www.nps.gov/state/hi/index.htm" moved to a new Web server, your link would not work and would therefore have to be changed.

Relative paths specify the location of a file, relative to the location of the file that is currently in use. This is analogous to telling someone your house is located four doors down from the only gas station on that street. Your address in this case is relative to the beginning point, the gas station. Because your user has a beginning point (the gas station), you can describe the ending address (the house) relative to the beginning. A relative path allows you to move up the folder structure. So in the example shown in Figure 3–17, to display the image underwaterlogo.jpg (stored in the Images subfolder) from the Web page underwatertours.html (stored in the HTMLcode subfolder) within the Chapter03\ChapterFiles folder, you would use the following relative path structure:

```
\Images\underwaterlogo.jpg
```

Looking at Figure 3–17, you would store the image underwaterlogo.jpg in the Images subfolder and store the Web page itself, the underwatertours.html file, in the HTMLcode subfolder. If you moved the image to the HTMLcode subfolder and viewed the underwatertours.html file, the image underwaterlogo.jpg would not appear because it is not in the original folder.

Another example is storing one file at the root level and one in a subfolder. If you stored the underwatertours.html file in the HTMLcode subfolder, but stored the image underwaterlogo.jpg in the ChapterFiles folder, you would use the following relative path structure, in which the two dots (..) indicate one directory level up:

```
..\underwaterlogo.jpg
```

To display the underwatertours.html file with the underwaterlogo.jpg image, you would use the following relative path when identifying the image:

```
<img src="underwaterlogo.jpg" width="581" height="450"
alt="Underwater Tours logo" />
```

Another example is the relative addressing that you use in this chapter to link to the second Web page from the home page, and vice versa. The HTML code to link from the home page, underwatertours.html, to the second Web page is:

```
<a href="samplephotos.html">sample photographs</a>
```

and to go from the samplephotos.html Web page back to the home page, the HTML code is:

```
<a href="underwatertours.html">home page</a>
```

You currently have one folder ChapterFiles in the Chapter03 folder. Because HTML code and images are all in the same folder, your HTML code to access those images would look like this:

```
<img src="fish.jpg" width="259" height="387" alt="Frog fish" />
<img src="lobster.jpg" width="387" height="259" alt="Lobster" />
```

It is better to use relative paths for flexibility whenever feasible. If the root folder (i.e., the "highest" folder in the hierarchy) must change for some reason, you do not have to change all addressing if you used relative paths.

Adding Interest and Focus with Styles

In Chapter 2, you learned how to vary the size of headings with the <h1> through <h6> tags. Any text on a Web page, including headings, can be formatted with a different color or style to make it stand out by using style properties. Table 3–5 lists some properties that can be used to enhance standard text on a Web page using styles. Remember that CSS and inline styles are the preferred technique to alter the style of the content on a Web page.

BTW

Font Properties
Refer to Appendix D for a more complete list of CSS font properties and values. You can also set font characteristics with the HTML <font> tag (see Appendix A), but this tag has been removed from the HTML5 specification.

Table 3–5 Font Properties and Values

Property	Function
color	• Changes the font color • Values include six-digit (hexadecimal) color codes, color names, or RGB values
font-family	• Changes the font face or type • Values include fonts, such as Verdana or Arial; text appears using the default font if the font face is not specified
font-size	• Changes the font size • Value can be an actual numeric size, a percentage, or values such as large, medium, small, etc.
font-style	• Changes the style of a font • Values include normal, italic, and oblique
font-weight	• Changes the weight of a font • Values include normal, bold, bolder, and lighter

Figure 3–18 shows how several of these attributes affect the appearance of text.

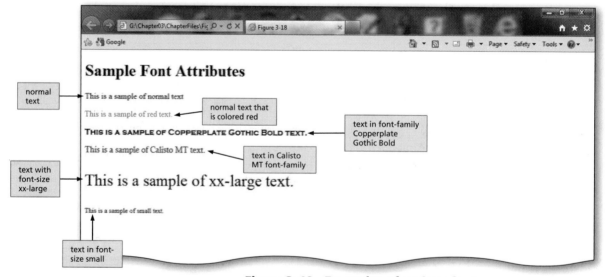

Figure 3–18   Examples of various fonts.

Adding Interest and Focus with HTML Tags

There is another way to format text in addition to the inline styles used in Chapter 2. Web pages that use the HTML5 DOCTYPE statement allow the use of deprecated tags, as explained in Chapter 2. These Web pages validate the HTML elements and attributes, including deprecated elements, successfully. Text can also be formatted using the formatting tags in HTML. In Chapter 2, you changed the font-style of some text on the Web page using an inline style. Instead of using an inline style, you could have used the HTML bold tags (<b> </b>) that make text bold. HTML provides a number of tags that can be used to format text, several of which are listed in Table 3–6.

Table 3–6 Text Formatting Tags

HTML Tag	Function
`<b> </b>`	Physical style tag that displays text as bold
`<blockquote> </blockquote>`	Designates a long quotation; indents margins on sections of text
`<em> </em>`	Logical style tag that displays text with emphasis (usually appears as italicized)
`<i> </i>`	Physical style tag that displays text as italicized
`<pre> </pre>`	Sets enclosed text as preformatted material, meaning it preserves spaces and line breaks; often used for text in column format in another document pasted into HTML code
`<small> </small>`	Decreases the font-size in comparison to the surrounding text
`<strong> </strong>`	Logical style tag that displays text with strong emphasis (usually appears as bold)
`<sub> </sub>`	Displays text as subscript (below normal text)
`<sup> </sup>`	Displays text as superscript (above normal text)

BTW

Deprecated and Non supported Tags
A deprecated element or attribute is one that has been outdated. Deprecated elements may become obsolete in the future, but most browsers continue to support deprecated elements for backward compatibility. You can still use deprecated tags with an HTML5 document type as used in this book. There are many tags and attributes not supported by HTML5, as noted in Appendx A.

Figure 3–19 shows a sample Web page with some HTML text format tags. These tags fall into two categories: logical style tags and physical style tags. **Logical style tags** allow a browser to interpret the tag based on browser settings, relative to other text on a Web page. The `<h2>` heading tag, for example, is a logical style that indicates the heading text should be larger than regular text but smaller than text formatted using an `<h1>` heading tag. The `<strong>` tag is another logical style, which indicates that text should have a strong emphasis, and which most browsers interpret as displaying the text in bold font. **Physical style tags** specify a particular font change that is interpreted strictly by all browsers. For example, to ensure that text appears as bold font, you would enclose it between a start `<b>` and end `</b>` tag. The `<strong>` tag is a better fit because it does not dictate how the browser displays the text. In practice, the `<strong>` and `<b>` tags usually have the same result when the Web page is displayed.

BTW

Logical versus Physical Tags
For more information about the differences between logical and physical tags, search the Web for the keywords "HTML logical tags" or "HTML physical tags."

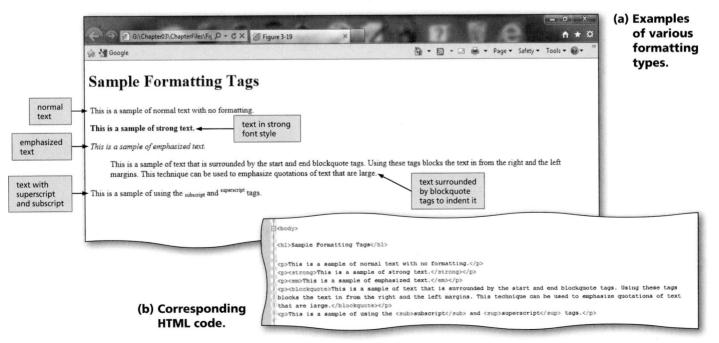

(a) Examples of various formatting types.

(b) Corresponding HTML code.

Figure 3–19

Types of Styles
Remember that an inline style changes the style of an individual element; an embedded style sheet changes the style of an entire Web page; and an external style sheet changes the style in multiple Web pages in the same Web site. If you want to change the style of a single element, use an inline style.

Style Sheet Precedence Review

In Chapter 2, you learned how to insert an inline style. The project in this chapter uses an inline style and also introduces you to embedded style sheets. You will learn about the third and final form of style, external style sheets, in Chapter 4. It will be helpful at this point to review the information from Chapter 2 on the precedence of styles (see Table 2-6 on page HTML 53). An inline style is used to control the style within an individual HTML tag and takes precedence over both embedded and external style sheets. An embedded sheet is used to change the style of an element over one Web page, but overrides or takes precedence over any styles defined in an external style sheet. An external style sheet is a separate document with a .css extension that is used to define styles for multiple pages in a Web site.

Because styles have different levels of precedence, all three types of styles can be used on a single Web page. For example, in this part of the chapter, you define body, anchor, and heading styles with embedded style sheets that are used for both the underwatertours.html file and the samplephotos.html file. You also insert a few inline styles on each Web page. Because of the precedence rules, the inline styles take precedence over the embedded style sheets. For instance, if you use an embedded style sheet to make all paragraphs Garamond font-family in normal text type and size 12, you can override that font-family, style, and size for a specific paragraph with an inline style within that paragraph's <p> tag. Maybe there is a paragraph that you want to highlight, so you make it bold with an inline style. Or maybe there is a paragraph that you want to downplay, and you make it smaller and italic with an inline style. It is important to determine how and when to use the various styles in the design phase of Web development.

Plan Ahead

Identify which level of style or style sheet to use.
Because of precedence rules, it is generally better to look at the broadest level style first. In this chapter project, you use inline and embedded style sheets, with embedded being the broader level. In other words, an embedded style sheet is used for the entire Web page, and an inline style is used in a particular HTML tag. In Chapter 4, you will add an external style sheet (the broadest level) to your chapter project.

- **Identify what styles need to be different than the standards used across the Web site.** Sometimes you need to vary a style in order to call attention to the content or pull attention away from it. Many Web sites have a legal statement on the bottom of the home page. That is not necessarily something that needs to be the same font-size as the rest of the content on that Web page. So you may choose a smaller font-size and maybe make the text italic for that content. Two types of style sheets are used for styles that are different across a Web site: embedded and inline.

- **Use embedded style sheets to affect a single Web page.** This type of style is good to use if you want the style to affect just one (or a few) Web pages, and not all pages across the Web site.

- **Use inline styles for individual styles.** If you want to change the style of one or a few elements of one Web page, then using inline styles is the most appropriate. If a style is intended for most (or all) of the Web page, consider using an embedded or external style sheet.

Using Embedded Style Sheets

An embedded style sheet is used to control the style of a single Web page. To add an embedded style sheet to a Web page, you insert a start <style> tag at the top of the Web page within the <head> </head> tags that define the header section. After adding the desired style statements, you end the embedded style sheet by adding an end </style> tag.

The following code shows an example of an embedded style sheet to set the h1 heading to the Garamond font-family, point size 32. This code would be added between the <head> and </head> tags within <style> </style> tags:

```
<style type="text/css">
<!--
h1 {font-family: Garamond;
    font-size: 32pt;}
-->
</style>
```

In this embedded style, you identify the code as a style sheet by using the "text/css" type. You should also use comment tags in your embedded (internal) style sheet. The comment tags are positioned just after the start style <style> and just before the end style </style> tags. The <!-- is used to start a comment, and the --> code is used to end the comment. These comment lines tell the browser to ignore whatever is between the comment lines if the browser cannot interpret the code between. So if your Web page user has a browser that is not current, it may not be able to interpret embedded style sheets. An older browser would see the start of the comment <!-- and disregard anything between that line and the end of the comment -->. Enclosing your style sheet within comment lines is a good Web development technique. The h1 (header size 1) element is the **selector**, and the remainder of the code is the **declaration**. The declaration sets the values for two different properties. The first property-value statement sets the h1 font-family to Garamond. The second property-value statement sets the font size to 32 point. The style statement is enclosed in curly brackets and each property-value statement ends with a semicolon. This statement tells the browser to display all h1 headers in 32-point Garamond font. You could use this embedded style sheet to easily change all h1 headings, in lieu of making the same change with an inline style in each individual heading tag.

The various types of Cascading Style Sheets allow you to control many different property values for various elements on a Web page. Table 3–7 lists six main properties and related options that are used in CSS. A complete list of properties and property values that can be used in CSS is included in Appendix D.

Table 3–7 CSS Properties and Options

Property Name	Options That Can Be Controlled
background	• color • image • position
border	• color • style • width
font	• family • size • style • variant • weight
list	• image • position • type

BTW

HTML/CSS Terminology
In HTML, a *tag* is a special instruction to the browser to specify how the Web page is displayed. Many tags have attributes that help to further modify what is displayed. In CSS, a style *statement* is made up of a selector and a declaration. The part of the style statement that identifies the page element(s) is called the *selector*. The part of the style statement that identifies how the element(s) should appear is called the *declaration*. A declaration includes at least one type of style, or property, to apply to the selected element.

Property Name	Options That Can Be Controlled
margin	• length • percentage
text	• alignment • color • decoration • indentation • spacing • white space

Table 3–7 CSS Properties and Options (continued)

Specifying Alternative Fonts

If a Web page font is not available on users' computers, you can create a list of fonts and the browser will determine the font to use. For example, if the Web page uses a Geneva font, but Arial or Helvetica would also work well, you create a comma-separated list of acceptable fonts, using <font face="geneva, arial, helvetica"> *your text*</font> as the code. If a Web page uses a font that Web page visitors do not have on their computers, the Web page appears using a default font (usually Times New Roman).

The following code shows an example of an embedded style sheet that you will use in the chapter project:

```
<style type="text/css">
<!--
body            {font-family: Arial, Verdana, Garamond;
                font-size: 11pt;}
h1, h2, h3      {color: #020390;}
a               {text-decoration: none;
                color: #020390;}
a:hover         {background: #020390;
                color: #01d3ff;}
-->
</style>
```

This embedded style sheet defines four elements on the page: body, headings, links, and the link-hover property. The first style statement uses the **body** selector to specify that all text on the Web page should be one of the font families: Arial, Verdana, or Garamond, in 11-point size. Computers do not always have every font-family installed, so Web developers usually specify multiple font-families. If the first font-family is not available, then the next takes effect. If none of the named font-families are installed, the computer's default font is used. Separate the font-families by commas.

The second style statement defines values for the h1, h2, and h3 properties. The value #020390 will give all h1, h2, and h3 headings on this Web page the color dark blue. On the home page, there are no headings, but there are headings on the second Web page, and later in the chapter you will use this same embedded style sheet for that Web page, which has h1, h2, and h3 headings.

The third style statement defines one property of the link element. The selector **a** is used to indicate the link element. The property-value statement text-decoration: none; color: #020390; changes the appearance of links from the default underlined, blue color text. The default style for text links is underlined text. In order to eliminate that underline, you can set text-decoration to none. There are several values for text-decoration, including: none, underline, overline, and line-through. Also as a default, linked text is blue before being visited. With the inline style, you can change that color. Because the style statement uses **a** as the selector, it changes all link states (normal, visited, active) to these property values. You can also define a unique style for normal, visited, and active links by creating three separate style statements with **a:link**, **a:visited**, and **a:active** as the selectors.

The last style statement uses the **a:hover** selector to define the style of a link when the mouse pointer points to, or **hovers** over, a link. In this statement, you use a pseudo-class (hover) to have more control over the anchor (link) element. A **pseudo-class** is attached to a selector with a colon to specify a state or relation to the selector to give the Web developer more control over that selector. The format to use with a pseudo-class is entered in the form:

```
selector:pseudo-class {property: value;}
```

with a colon between the selector and the pseudo-class. There are four pseudo-classes that can be used when applied to the anchor or link selector:

- link, for an unvisited link
- visited, for a link to a page that has already been visited
- active, for a link when it gains focus (for example, when it is clicked)
- hover, for a link when the cursor is held over it.

The hover statement tells the browser to display light blue (color #01d3ff) link text on a dark blue (#020390) background when the mouse hovers over the link as shown in Figure 3–20. Adding a link-hover style significantly changes the look of the links and adds a dimension of interactivity to the Web page.

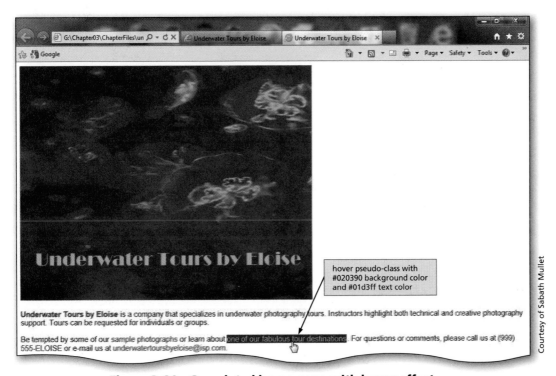

Figure 3–20 Completed home page with hover effect.

As mentioned earlier, the <!-- and --> code used in the embedded style sheet (just after the start style <style> and just before the end style </style> tags) are comment lines. These comment lines tell the browser to ignore whatever is between the comment lines if the browser cannot interpret the code between.

Recall that embedded style sheets have the second-highest level of precedence of the three types of styles. Although an inline style overrides the properties of an embedded style sheet, the embedded style sheet takes precedence over an external style sheet.

To Add Embedded Style Sheet Statements

Table 3–8 on the next page shows the CSS code for an embedded style sheet to specify the font-family and font-size for the body text on the underwatertours.html Web page.

Table 3–8 CSS Code for an Embedded Style Sheet	
Line	CSS Selectors and Declarations
7	`<style type="text/css">`
8	`<!--`
9	
10	`body      {font-family: Arial, Verdana, Garamond;`
11	`           font-size: 11pt;}`
12	
13	`h1, h2, h3      {color: #020390;}`
14	
15	`a        {text-decoration: none;`
16	`         color: #020390;}`
17	
18	`a:hover {background: #020390;`
19	`         color: #01d3ff;}`
20	
21	`-->`
22	`</style>`

The following step shows how to enter the embedded style sheet code to change h1, h2, and h3 headings to blue, change all links to blue with no text-decoration, and change the color of the link hover to a dark blue background with light blue text to provide visual impact.

- Click immediately to the right of the > in </title> on line 6 and press the ENTER key.

- Type the code in Table 3–8 but do not press the ENTER key at the end of line 22 (Figure 3–21).

Q&A

What other styles can I use on my Web pages?

Appendix D lists available CSS properties and values. You can also search the Web for examples of how CSS

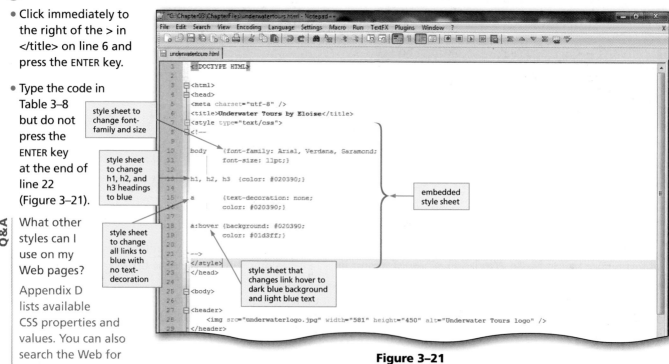

style sheet to change font-family and size

style sheet to change h1, h2, and h3 headings to blue

style sheet to change all links to blue with no text-decoration

embedded style sheet

style sheet that changes link hover to dark blue background and light blue text

Figure 3–21

are used for Web development. Finally, be an active Web page visitor and review the source code on Web pages with styles that you think are particularly effective or ineffective.

To Add an Inline Style for Color

The following step shows how to enter an inline style to add a blue color (#020390) in a bold font-weight to provide visual impact and call attention to the company name, Underwater Tours by Eloise. With this inline style, you use the <span> </span> tags. The **<span> </span>** tags create a container into which a user can add an inline style. The <span> tag provides a finer level of control for styles than the <div> </div> tags, which define block-level structure or division in the HTML document. The <span> tag tells the browser to apply the chosen styles to whatever is within the <span></span> container.

1

- With the insertion point right after the > in <p> on line 33, type <span style="color: #020390; font-weight: bold"> (Figure 3–22).

- With the insertion point right after the last e in Eloise on line 33, type </span> (Figure 3–22).

Q&A What other font-weights could I have used?

The font-weights are normal, bold, bolder, and lighter. Additionally, you can add values of 100–900 in which 400 is the same as normal, and 700 is the same as bold. If you don't specify a font-weight, normal is the default.

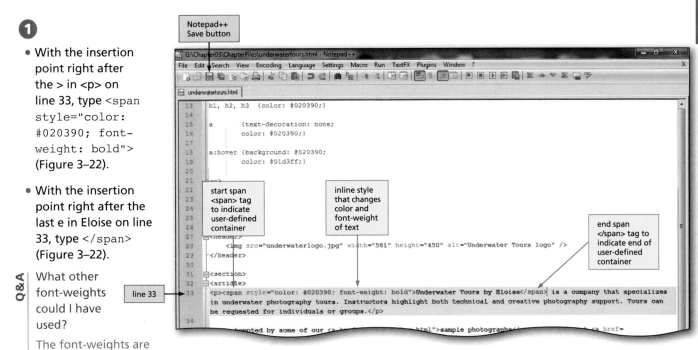

Figure 3–22

Q&A What different colors can I use for text?

There are a variety of colors that you can use for headings, text, and backgrounds. You can name the color by color name or hexadecimal code. See Figure 2–27 on page HTML 64 for examples.

To Save an HTML File

With the HTML code for the Underwater Tours by Eloise home page complete, you should save the changes to the file. The following step shows how to save an HTML file that has been previously saved.

1 Click the Save button on the Notepad++ toolbar to save the most recent version of underwatertours.html on the same storage device and in the same folder as the last time you saved it.

Validating the HTML, Viewing the Web Page, and Testing Links

After you save the HTML file for the Underwater Tours by Eloise home page, it should be validated to ensure that it meets current HTML5 standards and viewed in a browser to confirm the Web page is displayed as desired. It is also important to test the two links in the Underwater Tours by Eloise home page to verify that they function as expected.

To Validate HTML Code

1 Open Internet Explorer.

2 Navigate to the Web site validator.w3.org.

3 Click the Validate by File Upload tab.

4 Click the Browse button.

5 Locate the underwatertours.html file on your storage device and click the file name.

6 Click the Open button.

7 Click the Check button. A successful validation should be displayed, as shown in Figure 3–23. If you have errors in your code, you may see a screen similar to Figure 3–24. In this example, the errors relate to a missing </p> tag.

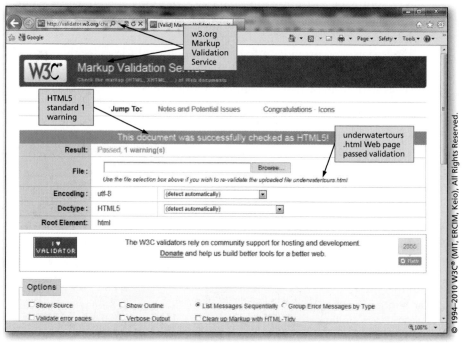

Figure 3–23

Q&A What if my HTML code does not validate?

If your code has errors, you should edit your HTML file to correct the errors. The Markup Validation Service report lists clearly what is wrong with your code. Once you make the necessary changes and save the file, you can again use the Browse button to open the corrected HTML file. You then use the Revalidate button to validate the changed code.

Q&A Why is there a warning noted on the validation screen, but it still says that it passed HTML5 validation?

As you learned in Chapter 2, all HTML5 files result in a warning in validation because HTML5 is still under development.

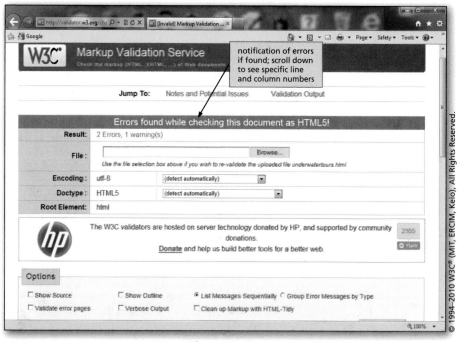

Figure 3–24

BTW **Common Validation Errors**
Common validation errors include not spelling tags, selectors, or attributes correctly; using uppercase letters (except for DOCTYPE); and not nesting tags correctly. A single coding error can cause many lines of errors during validation. For instance, Figure 3-24 shows a Web page that has two errors.

To Print an HTML File

After your HTML code has passed validation, it's a good idea to make a hard copy printout of it to have a record of that file.

1 Click the Notepad++ button on the taskbar to activate the Notepad++ window.

2 Click File on the menu bar, click Print, and then click the Print button to print a hard copy of the HTML code (Figure 3–25).

```
<!DOCTYPE HTML>

<html>
<head>
<meta charset="utf-8" />
<title>Underwater Tours by Eloise</title>
<style type="text/css">
<!--

body     {font-family: Arial, Verdana, Garamond;
          font-size: 11pt;}

h1, h2, h3  {color: #020390;}

a         {text-decoration: none;
          color: #020390;}

a:hover {background: #020390;
          color: #01d3ff;}

-->
</style>
</head>

<body>

<header>
    <img src="underwaterlogo.jpg" width="581" height="450" alt="Underwater Tours logo" />
</header>

<section>
<article>
<p><span style="color: #020390; font-weight: bold">Underwater Tours by Eloise</span> is
a company that specializes in underwater photography tours. Instructors highlight both
technical and creative photography support. Tours can be requested for individuals or
groups.</p>

<p>Be tempted by some of our <a href="samplephotos.html">sample photographs</a> or
learn about <a href="http://www.nps.gov/state/hi/index.htm">one of our fabulous tour
destinations</a>. For questions or comments, please call us at (999) 555-ELOISE or
e-mail us at <a href="mailto:underwatertoursbyeloise@isp.com">
underwatertoursbyeloise@isp.com</a>.</p>
</article>
</section>

</body>
</html>
```

-1-

Figure 3–25

To View a Web Page

The following steps illustrate how to view the HTML file in a browser.

1 Open Internet Explorer.

2 In Internet Explorer, click the Address bar to select the URL in the Address bar.

3 Type `G:\Chapter03\ChapterFiles\underwatertours.html` (or the specific path to your file) to display the new URL in the Address bar and then press the ENTER key (Figure 3–26).

Q&A

What if my page does not display correctly?

Check your underwatertours.html code carefully in Notepad++ to make sure you have not made any typing errors or left anything out. Correct the errors, save the changes, and try again.

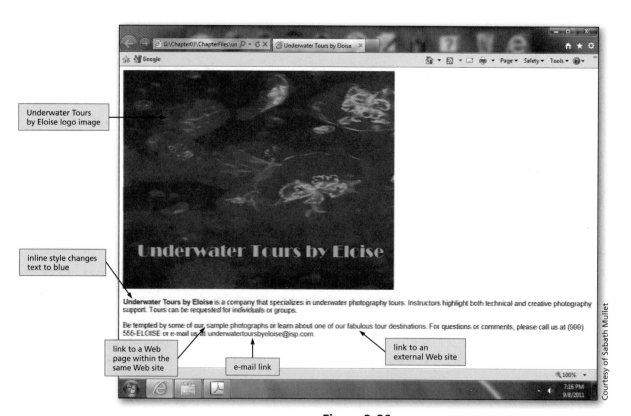

Figure 3–26

**Plan
Ahead**

Test your Web page.

- **Determine what you need to test.** It is important to have a test plan when you test your Web pages. Planning what to test assures that all functionality of the Web page is tested. You should specifically test the display of the Web page itself on multiple browsers and test that all of the links on the Web page work correctly.

- **Test the Web page as displayed in multiple browsers.** Certainly the first part of testing is to verify that your Web page is displayed in each browser as intended. Ask yourself the following questions: (1) Are the images all displayed where they should be? (2) Is the text presented as intended? (3) Are the links displayed as intended?

- **Test the links.** In your testing plan, you need to address all of the links that you have inserted into the Web page. It is especially important to test external links, that is, those over which you have no control. If you need to link outside of the Web pages that you developed, then periodically test the links to make sure they are still valid.

- **Have a test plan.** A test plan can be as simple as a matrix that includes three columns of information. The first column contains information about all of the links on the Web page. The second column contains information about the intended results of those links. The third column is the one that you complete during testing. If a link tests as it should, you can note that by putting a check mark in the third column. If a link test result is not as it should be, you can note in the third column what the result is. Using a technique such as this makes it easier to do thorough testing. When you know what the results of the test should be, it helps you verify valid links. This is an excellent technique to use when there are different people developing and testing the Web pages. The matrix will notify the developers of the test results clearly.

BTW

Web Page Testing
An important part of Web page development is testing Web page links. For more information about link testing, search the Web for keywords such as "HTML testing" or look at the World Wide Web Consortium (w3.org) Web site.

To Test Links on a Web Page

The following steps show how to test the links in the Underwater Tours by Eloise home page to verify that they work correctly. (Note that you might not be able to test the e-mail link if your browser is not configured to work with an e-mail client.)

- With the Underwater Tours by Eloise home page displayed in the browser, point to the e-mail link, underwatertoursbyeloise@isp .com and then click the link to open the default e-mail program with the address underwatertoursbyeloise@isp .com in the To: text box, as shown in Figure 3–27.

- Click the Close button in the Compose Mail window. If a dialog box asks if you want to save changes, click No.

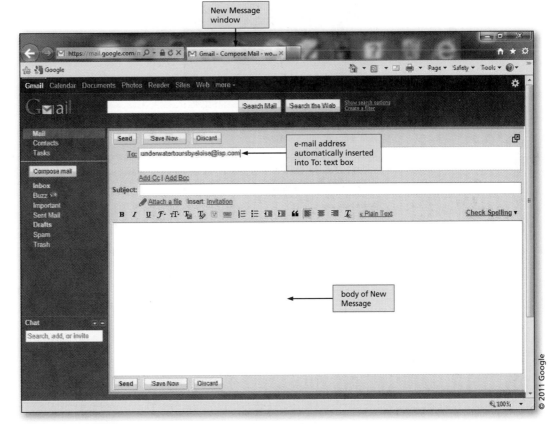

Figure 3–27

© 2011 Google

2

- Click the 'one of our fabulous tour destinations' link to test the external link on the Web page. Use the Back button to return to the Underwater Tours by Eloise home page.

- With the USB flash drive in drive G, point to the sample photographs link and click the link. The secondary Web page, samplephotos .html, is displayed (Figure 3–28), although it is not completed.

Q&A

My e-mail does not work when I click the link. Why does that happen?

You may not have an e-mail client installed on your computer or your school's servers. You therefore may not be able to test this e-mail link.

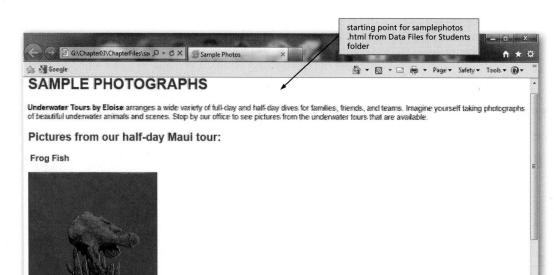

starting point for samplephotos .html from Data Files for Students folder

SAMPLE PHOTOGRAPHS

Underwater Tours by Eloise arranges a wide variety of full-day and half-day dives for families, friends, and teams. Imagine yourself taking photographs of beautiful underwater animals and scenes. Stop by our office to see pictures from the underwater tours that are available.

Pictures from our half-day Maui tour:

Frog Fish

This beautiful red fish is called a Frog Fish. It is just one example of the colorful sights that you will see underwater. We find Frog Fish during our Maui dives. Instructions on all tours show you how to make the best use of your equipment to visit our Web site or stop by our office to learn about the many exciting underwater tours that we offer. We can design a tour to meet the needs and desires of you and your group.

Colorful Lobster

This picture highlights another Maui underwater tour sight. The colorful Hawaiian spiny lobster is often seen on this and other dives. The half-day Maui dive is chosen for its wonderful photographic opportunities of a variety of sea creatures. Beautiful photos of the sea animals and the surrounding environment can be taken on this tour.

There are many other full-day and half-day scenic underwater tours that you can experience with Underwater Tours by Eloise. You can design your dream tour by place or activity level.

These pictures, taken from the half-day Maui tour, show a sample of the many beautiful sights that you can see while enjoying your underwater tour.

To book your own trip, please call us at (999) 555-ELOISE or e-mail us at underwatertoursbyeloise@isp.com. Please include the following information: (1) your address and phone number, (2) a list of your favorite photography activities, and (3) a few days and times that are convenient for us to contact you. We will respond immediately when we receive your request.

Back to home page

Figure 3–28

Courtesy of Sabath Mullet

To Print a Web Page

Print the Web page for future reference.

1 Click the Back button on the Standard toolbar to return to the Underwater Tours by Eloise home page.

2 Click the Print button on the Command bar.

3 Once the Underwater Tours by Eloise home page is printed (Figure 3–29), click the sample photographs link to return to that Web page.

Underwater Tours by Eloise

Courtesy of Sabath Mullet

Figure 3–29

Editing the Second Web Page

With the home page complete, the next step is to enhance the Sample Photographs Web page. For this part of the project, you will download an existing Web page file and edit the HTML code to create the Web page shown in Figure 3–30 on the next page. You will insert a class id in both image tags that set text to wrap around the images. You also will add two additional types of links: links within the same Web page and an image link to a Web page in the same Web site.

As you have learned, the <a> tag used to create a link must specify the page, file, or location to which it links. In the case of a link within a Web page, the <a> tag specifies a **target**, or named location, in the same file. Before adding the links and targets in the Sample Photographs Web page, you need to add an unordered (bulleted) list that uses the square list style type as the bullets. This list contains two items — Frog Fish and Colorful Lobster — and must be added to the page. The list items will serve as the links that are directed to the heading at the top of each major section of the Sample Photographs Web page. When clicked, these links will move the Web page visitor to the targets, which are named fish and lobster, respectively.

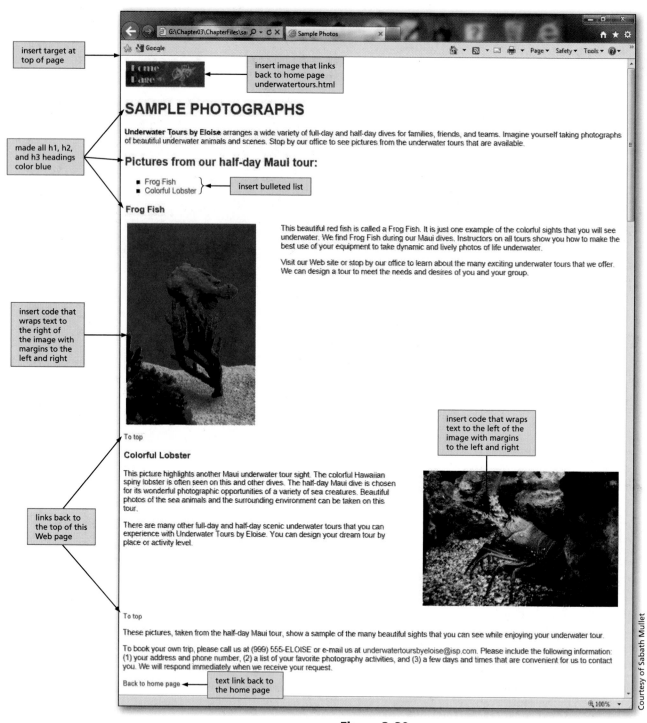

insert target at top of page

insert image that links back to home page underwatertours.html

made all h1, h2, and h3 headings color blue

insert bulleted list

insert code that wraps text to the right of the image with margins to the left and right

insert code that wraps text to the left of the image with margins to the left and right

links back to the top of this Web page

text link back to the home page

SAMPLE PHOTOGRAPHS

Underwater Tours by Eloise arranges a wide variety of full-day and half-day dives for families, friends, and teams. Imagine yourself taking photographs of beautiful underwater animals and scenes. Stop by our office to see pictures from the underwater tours that are available.

Pictures from our half-day Maui tour:

- Frog Fish
- Colorful Lobster

Frog Fish

This beautiful red fish is called a Frog Fish. It is just one example of the colorful sights that you will see underwater. We find Frog Fish during our Maui dives. Instructors on all tours show you how to make the best use of your equipment to take dynamic and lively photos of life underwater.

Visit our Web site or stop by our office to learn about the many exciting underwater tours that we offer. We can design a tour to meet the needs and desires of you and your group.

To top

Colorful Lobster

This picture highlights another Maui underwater tour sight. The colorful Hawaiian spiny lobster is often seen on this and other dives. The half-day Maui dive is chosen for its wonderful photographic opportunities of a variety of sea creatures. Beautiful photos of the sea animals and the surrounding environment can be taken on this tour.

There are many other full-day and half-day scenic underwater tours that you can experience with Underwater Tours by Eloise. You can design your dream tour by place or activity level.

To top

These pictures, taken from the half-day Maui tour, show a sample of the many beautiful sights that you can see while enjoying your underwater tour.

To book your own trip, please call us at (999) 555-ELOISE or e-mail us at underwatertoursbyeloise@isp.com. Please include the following information: (1) your address and phone number, (2) a list of your favorite photography activities, and (3) a few days and times that are convenient for us to contact you. We will respond immediately when we receive your request.

Back to home page

Courtesy of Sabath Mullet

Figure 3–30

BTW

Web Page Improvement Web page development is an ongoing process. In Web page development, you create a Web page, view it in a browser, and then look for ways to improve the appearance of the page.

Because this Web page is so long, it is a good design practice to provide users with a quick way to move back to the top of the Web page without scrolling back. For this purpose, the Web page includes two text links named To top. These links are located just below the Frog Fish and Colorful Lobster sections. When clicked, any To top link takes the Web page visitor back to the top of the page.

To complete the Sample Photographs Web page, you will create an image link, so users can click the back to home page link to return to the Underwater Tours by Eloise home page. There is already a text link inserted at the bottom of the Web page that can be used to return to the home page. It is always important to provide a link back to the home page from subsequent Web pages. Your visitors should not have to use the Back button on the browser to return to the home page.

To Open an HTML File

The following steps illustrate how to open the samplephotos.html file in Notepad++.

1 Click the Notepad++ button on the taskbar.

2 With a USB flash drive connected to one of the computer's USB ports, click File on the menu bar and then click Open.

3 Click Computer in the navigation pane to display a list of available drives.

4 If necessary, scroll until UDISK 2.0 (G:) is displayed in the list of available drives.

5 If necessary, navigate to the USB drive (G:). Click the Chapter03 folder, and then click the ChapterFiles folder in the list of available folders.

6 Click samplephotos.html in the list of files.

7 Click the Open button in the Open dialog box to display the HTML code for the samplephotos.html Web page, as shown in Figure 3–31.

Q&A If I open another file in Notepad++, will I lose the underwatertours.html file?

The last saved version of underwatertours.html will still be on the USB drive, even though another HTML file is open in Notepad++. Additionally, even after you open the new file in Notepad++ the other file (underwatertours.html) remains open in another tab in Notepad++. That is one of the benefits of Notepad++; you can have more than one file open at the same time.

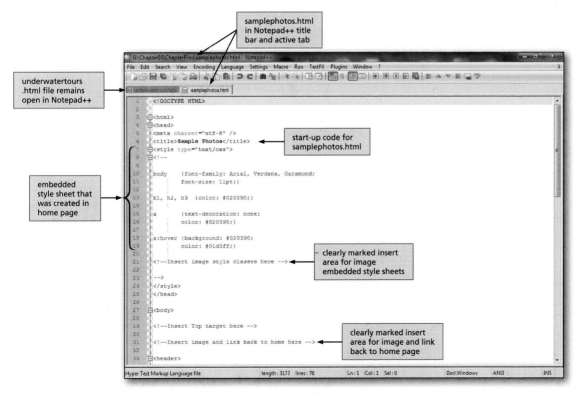

Figure 3–31

Plan Ahead

- **Determine what graphic images will be used and how to format them.** They say that a picture is worth a thousand words. In Web development, it sometimes makes your message clearer and more attractive if you use pictures. In the planning stage, you have to consider which pictures will help (and not hinder) your content. You also have to decide how to align the text relative to the pictures. Sometimes it makes sense to put the text above or below the picture. It might also be appropriate to wrap the text around the picture. You need to determine all of these specifics before you create the Web page.

- **Identify what links are needed on a long Web page.** When you have an especially long Web page (one in which the visitor has to use the PAGE DOWN key), you should provide links within the Web page for easier navigation. You need to decide where it makes sense to put page breaks. Often it is best to put a link to major topics within the Web page. Make sure that the Web page visitor can easily move to those areas by providing links close to the top of the Web page.

- **Use links back to the top of the page.** Another good technique for long Web pages is to allow visitors to link back to the top of the Web page easily from several places on the page. Providing links back to the top of a long Web page makes browsing more enjoyable.

- **Create a link back to the home page.** If possible, you should always provide a link from secondary Web pages back to the home page. Your visitors should not have to use the Back button on the browser to get back to the home page of the Web site. A common Web development practice is to use a company logo (often a smaller version) to navigate back to the home page. Again, the purpose of this image link as well as other links mentioned here is to make your Web site easy to navigate.

Working with Classes in Style Statements

Notice that the samplephotos.html file contains the same embedded style sheet that you created in the underwatertours.html file earlier in this chapter. For the second Web page, you will add one additional element (img) to the embedded style sheet. In order to utilize the image element as needed on the second Web page (samplephotos.html), you need to understand the concept of classes as used with CSS. CSS classes give you more control over the style on a Web page.

Recall that a style statement is made up of a selector and a declaration. The part of the style statement that identifies the page elements is called the selector.

```
a        {text-decoration: none; color: #020390;}
```

The example above shows a section of the embedded style sheet used in the samplephotos.html Web page. The selector in the example is the a (the anchor or link). The part of the style statement that identifies how the element(s) should appear is called the declaration. In this example, the declaration is everything between the curly brackets. This includes the text-decoration property and a value of none together with the property named color and the value of #030290.

There is another level of control that you can have over the styles that display on a Web page. For example, rather than having all paragraphs of text appear in the same style, you might want the style of the first paragraph on a page to be different from the other paragraphs of text. To gain more control for these purposes, you can define specific elements of an HTML file as a category, or **class**. You can then create a specific style for each class. Using classes in CSS thus allows you to apply styles to HTML tags selectively.

Using a class, for example, you could apply one style to a beginning paragraph and a different style to a closing paragraph on the same Web page.

Defining and using classes in CSS is a two-step process. First, any elements that belong to the class are marked by adding the tag:

```
class="classname"
```

where *classname* is the identifier or name of the class.

Any word can be used as a class name, as long as it does not contain spaces. In general, however, you should use descriptive names that illustrate the purpose of a class (for example, beginning, legallanguage, or copyrighttext), rather than names that describe the appearance of the class (for example, bluetext, largeritalic, or boldsmallarial). Using names that describe the purpose makes the code easier to read and more flexible. For this chapter, you will use the class names align-left and align-right in the img element. This immediately tells someone reviewing the code that the styles defined by those classes are used to align images either left or right.

After you have named the classes, you can use the class names in a selector and define a specific style for the class. For example, within the <style> and comment tags in an embedded or internal style sheet, you enter a style statement in the format:

```
p.beginning {color: red;
            font-size: 20pt;}
```

where the p indicates that the class applies to a specific category of the paragraph tag and beginning is the class name. The tag and the class name are separated by a period. Together, the tag and the class name make up the selector for the style statement. The declaration then lists the property-value statements that should be applied to elements in the class.

For instance, if you want to display the beginning paragraph text in a 20-point red font, you would add a style statement like the one shown in the sample code in Figure 3–32 on the next page and then use the tag, <p class="beginning">, to apply the style defined by the declaration associated with the p.beginning selector. If the paragraph <p> tag is used without the class name, the paragraph appears in the default format or other format as defined by a style. To use this class name in an HTML tag, you would type:

```
<p class="beginning">
```

as the code.

In addition to the style for the beginning paragraphs, Figure 3–32a shows an example of HTML code with classes defined for and applied to the middle and end paragraphs. Figure 3–32b shows how the resulting Web page appears in the browser.

You can add as many classes to your Web pages as you need. This is a very useful Web development technique that allows flexibility and variety in a Web page. One drawback is that classes can be defined for use only in embedded or external style sheets. Because the purpose of using classes is to format a group of elements, not individual elements, classes do not work in inline styles.

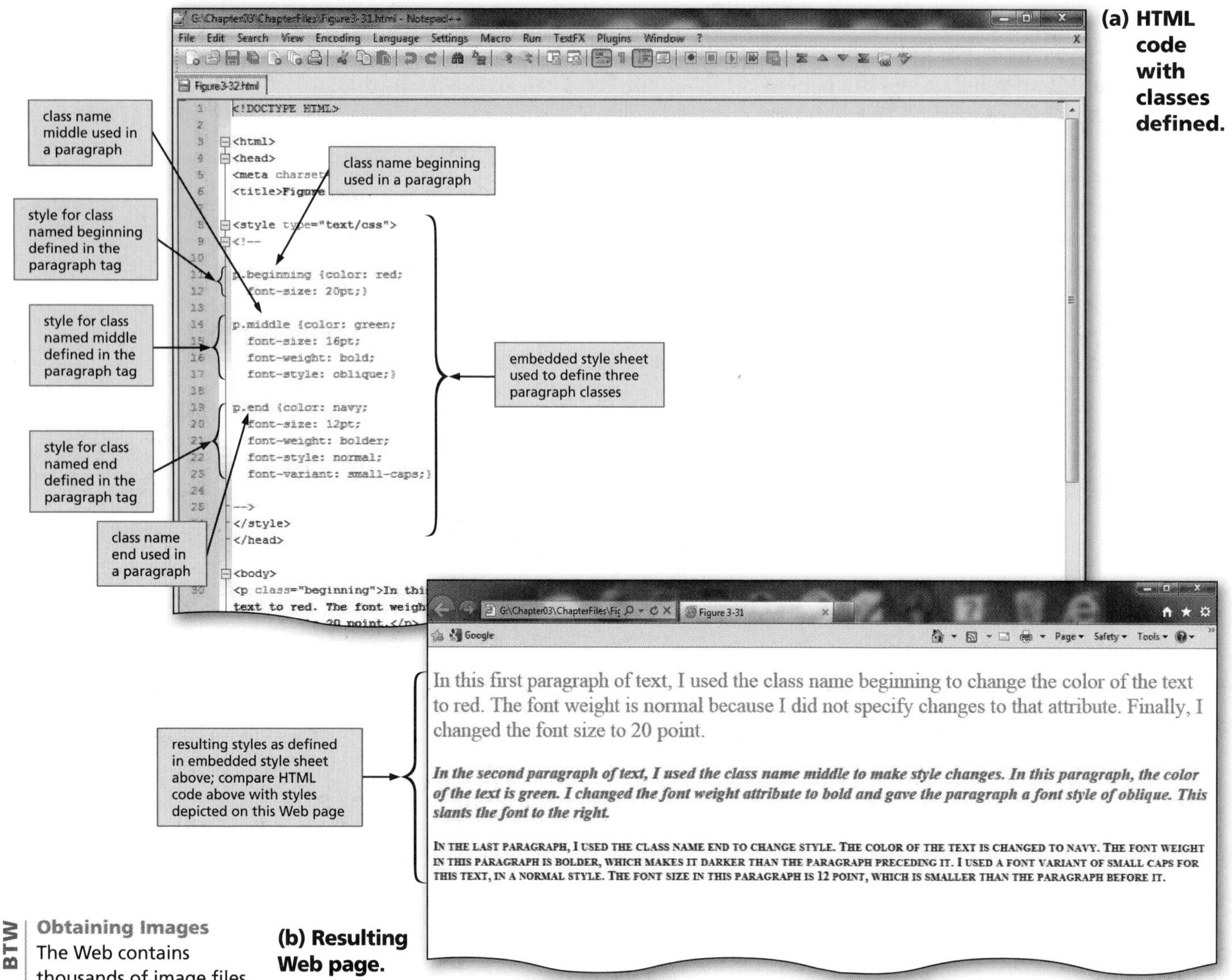

(a) HTML code with classes defined.

class name middle used in a paragraph

class name beginning used in a paragraph

style for class named beginning defined in the paragraph tag

style for class named middle defined in the paragraph tag

embedded style sheet used to define three paragraph classes

style for class named end defined in the paragraph tag

class name end used in a paragraph

resulting styles as defined in embedded style sheet above; compare HTML code above with styles depicted on this Web page

(b) Resulting Web page.

Figure 3–32

Adding an Image with Wrapped Text

As shown in Appendix A, the <img> tag has many attributes, including attributes to specify height, width, and alternative text.

Alignment is also a key consideration when inserting an image. Alignment can give an image and the surrounding text completely different looks. Figure 3–33 shows two images, the first of which is left-aligned and wraps any text to the right of the image. In this chapter, you use an embedded style sheet to align (float) the image to the left or right and wrap the text to the right or left of the positioned image. You will also add some space (margins) around the image so that it is separated from the text. To accomplish these tasks, you use the float and margin properties.

The float property indicates in which direction (in this case left and right) to display (or float) an element being inserted on a Web page. **Floating** an element like an image allows the element to move to the side indicated in the float statement. As a result of that repositioning (floating), the other elements, like text, are moved up and allowed to wrap next to the floated element. When you first open the samplephotos.html file in Internet Explorer (Figure 3–28 on page HTML 122), both images are left-aligned. Notice that the text is aligned beneath each image, leaving a lot of white space to the right of the images. The text does not surround the images in Figure 3–28, as it does in Figure 3–30 on page HTML 124. You achieve this text wrap by applying the float property to the image. In addition to floating the element, you should also provide some space around the image. The margin-left and margin-right properties indicate how many pixels of space to put around each element. In this case, you will have five pixels of space around the right and left of each image. Figure 3–33 shows examples of images with margin spacing.

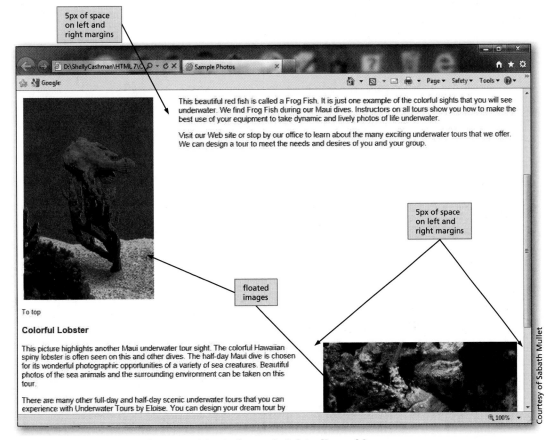

Figure 3–33 Left- and right-aligned images.

There are several ways to align text around images using styles. You can do this with an inline style (HTML code shown below) or with an embedded style sheet. The format of the HTML code to add the left- and right-aligned images with an inline style is:

```
<img style="float: left; margin-left: 5px; margin-right:
5px" src="fish.jpg" width="259" height="387" alt="Frog fish" />
<img style="float: right; margin-left: 5px; margin-right:
5px" src="lobster.jpg" width="387" height="259" alt="Lobster"
align="right" />
```

where the float property tells the browser on which side to float the image element, and the margin properties tell the browser how much space (5 pixels) to add around the image. Using an inline style is a perfectly acceptable way to float an image element, wrap the text, and add margins of space around the image, but there may be a more efficient way to do it.

If you have numerous images to float on the page, it is better to use classes in an embedded style sheet than to use inline styles.

This project uses an embedded style sheet with a two-step approach. First, you will insert the class names align-left and align-right into the image <img> tags that will use the classes. Then, you will add those class names (align-left and align-right) to an image <img> element in the embedded style sheet. To use this two-step approach, first you will add the HTML code for the left-align and right-align class names in the <img> tag itself within the Web page content:

```
<img class="align-left" src="fish.jpg" width="259"
height="387" alt="Frog fish" />
<img class="align-right" src="lobster.jpg" width="387"
height="259" alt="Lobster" />
```

which aligns the first image to the left, and the second image to the right.

Second, you have to insert the img (image) property in the embedded style sheet and add those two class names (align-left and align-right) where you define the style that you will use for images. This involves the following code that is inserted into the embedded style sheet:

```
img.align-left     {float: left;
                    margin-left: 5px;
                    margin-right: 5px;}
img.align-right    {float: right;
                    margin-left: 5px;
                    margin-right: 5px;}
```

where img is the property element and align-right and align-left are the class names. The class names align-right and align-left are arbitrary; you could name them anything. When naming classes, use names that make sense. Notice that the class names are separated from the element img with a period.

Using Thumbnail Images

Many Web developers use thumbnail images to improve page loading time. A **thumbnail image** is a smaller version of the image itself. The thumbnail is used as a link that, when clicked, will load the full-sized image. Figure 3–34a shows an example of a thumbnail image. When the image is clicked, the browser loads the full-sized image (Figure 3–34b). Loading images can take a long time, depending on the size and the complexity of the image. Using a thumbnail image gives a visitor the opportunity to decide whether to view the full-sized image.

To create a thumbnail version of an image, the image can be resized to a smaller size in a paint or image-editing program and then saved with a different file name. The thumbnail image then is added to a Web page as an image link to the larger version of the image. The HTML code to add a thumbnail image that links to a larger image takes the form:

```
<a href="largeimage.gif"><img src="thumbnail.gif" /></a>
```

where largeimage.gif is the name of the full-sized image and thumbnail.gif is the name of the smaller version of the image. In the case of this simple thumbnail example, a visitor clicks the thumbnail image to view the larger image, but there is no "return" button or link on the full-sized image Web page for the user to return to the original Web page.

In this case, the visitor would have to use the Back button on the browser's toolbar to return to the original Web page displaying the thumbnail image. For most Web development projects, however, you always want to provide a link for visitors and not force them to use the Back button.

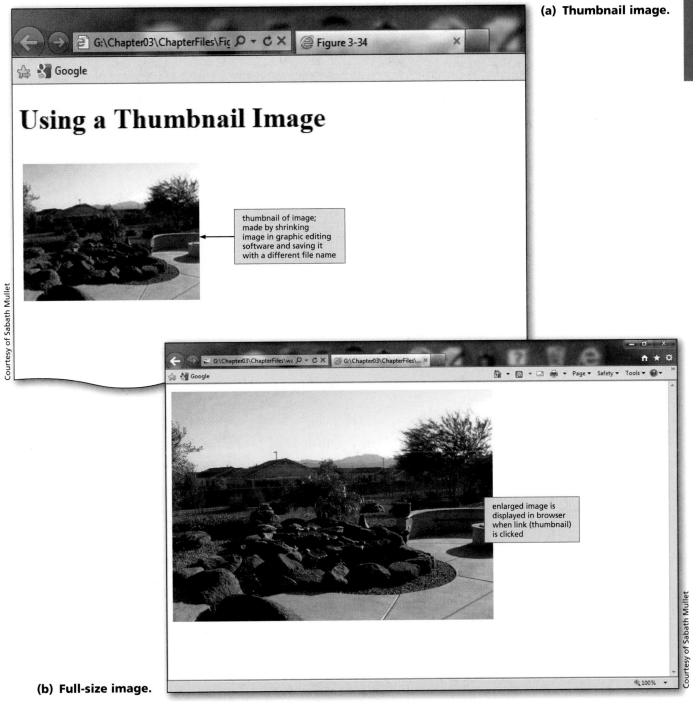

(a) Thumbnail image.

(b) Full-size image.

Figure 3–34

To Wrap Text Around Images Using CSS Classes

Now you will use an embedded style sheet to wrap the text around the two images on the samplephotos.html Web page. Remember that an embedded style sheet affects only the Web page into which it is embedded. The embedded style sheet is placed within the <head> </head> container at the top of the Web page file.

The following steps show you how to insert left- and right-aligned images with wrapped text by adding class names to the img tags and then defining the classes within the embedded style sheets. Table 3–9 shows the code you'll need to define the classes in Step 3.

- With the sample-photos.html file displayed in Notepad++, click immediately to the left of the s in src on line 45 to begin adding the class name to the first <img> tag.

- Type `class="align-left"` and press the SPACEBAR so that there is a space between what you just typed and src.

- Click immediately to the left of the s in src on line 57, to begin adding the class name to the second <img> tag.

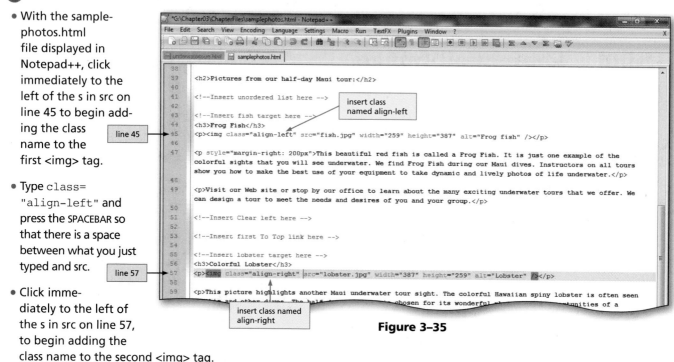

Figure 3–35

- Type `class="align-right"` and press the SPACEBAR so that there is a space between what you just typed and src (Figure 3–35).

- Highlight the line <! Insert image style classes here --> on line 21, as shown in Figure 3–36, to begin adding image classes.

Q&A

Do I have to press the DELETE key to delete the text that I highlighted in Step 2?

No, you do not have to press the DELETE key to delete the text on line 21. As long as the text is high-lighted, the text is automatically deleted as soon as you start typing the HTML code in Step 3.

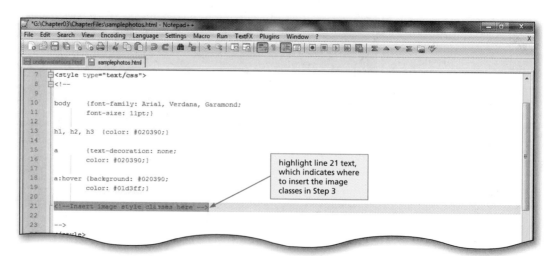

Figure 3–36

Table 3–9 CSS Code to Insert Class Definitions in Embedded Style Sheets

Line	CSS Selectors and Declarations	
21	`img.align-left`	`{float: left;`
22		`margin-left: 5px;`
23		`margin-right: 5px;}`
24		
25	`img.align-right`	`{float: right;`
26		`margin-left: 5px;`
27		`margin-right: 5px;}`

3

- Type the HTML code in Table 3–9 but do not press the ENTER key at the end of line 27. This HTML code inserts the embedded style sheets that will be used by the align-left and align-right class names inserted in the previous step. This will align the images left or right on the Web page, with text wrapped to the right or left and with five pixels of horizontal space around the image (Figure 3–37).

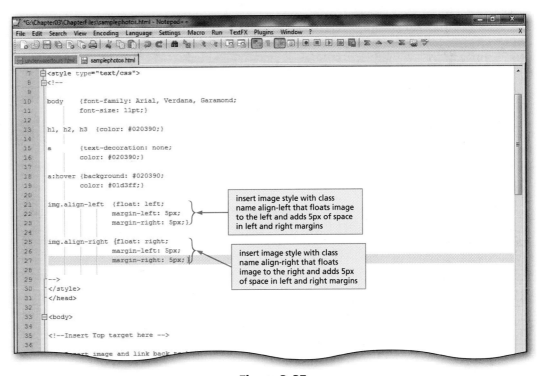

insert image style with class name align-left that floats image to the left and adds 5px of space in left and right margins

insert image style with class name align-right that floats image to the right and adds 5px of space in left and right margins

Figure 3–37

Q&A What does the float property do?

The float property allows you to position elements (in this case photographs) on the Web page.

Q&A Why do we need margin-left and margin-right properties?

These properties add five pixels (in this case) of space around the left and right sides of the image that is being inserted. If those are not entered, then the text aligns itself right next to the image. Allowing a bit of space between these two elements makes the image and text neater.

To Clear Text Wrapping

After specifying an image alignment and defining how text wraps, you must enter a break (<br />) tag to stop the text wrapping. You use the <br style="clear: left" />" and the <br style="clear: right" /> tags to reset the margins after you used code to wrap text around an image. If you did not insert this code to clear the wrapping, then all text would continue to wrap. For instance, without the <br style="clear: left" /> code inserted below, the following text (Colorful Lobster and the paragraphs beyond it) would continue just after the paragraphs about the Frog Fish. The following steps show how to enter code to clear the text wrapping.

- Highlight the line <Insert Clear left here --> on line 57, and then type <br style="clear: left" /> as the tag (Figure 3–38).

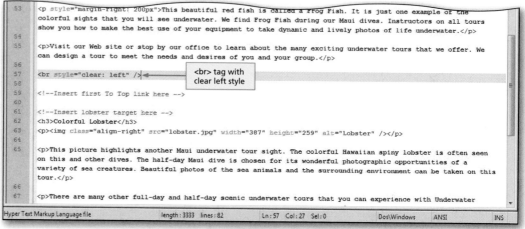

Figure 3–38

- Highlight the line <!--Insert Clear right here --> on line 69, and then type <br style="clear: right" /> as the tag to clear the text wrapping for both left- and right-aligned images, as displayed in Figure 3–39.

What happens if you do not use the <br style="clear: direction" /> tag?

Your text following the wrapped image will not be displayed as you intended. The following text will continue to wrap beyond the end of the text and image combination.

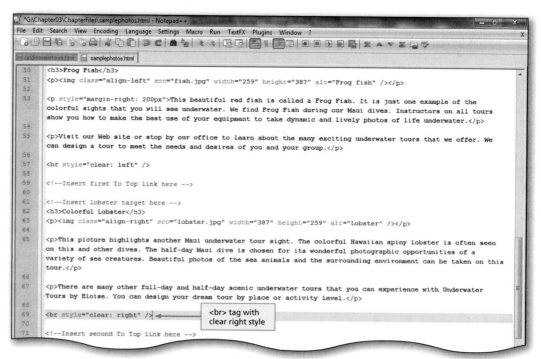

Figure 3–39

Is there one tag to clear all alignments?

Yes. The <br style="clear: both" /> tag clears all text alignments.

Adding Links Within a Web Page

The final links to be added in this project are links within the Sample Photographs Web page and a link back to the Underwater Tours by Eloise home page. Because the Sample Photographs Web page is quite long, it would be easier for visitors to have a menu or list at the top of the Web page that facilitates immediate movement to another section. Figure 3–40 shows how clicking the text link Frog Fish in the bulleted list near the top of the page links to the Frog Fish section in another part of the Web page. When the mouse pointer is moved over the words Frog Fish and is clicked, the browser repositions, or links, the page to the target named fish. Notice when the mouse hovers over the link, the link changes to a dark blue background with light blue text. That is because of the a:hover styles that are embedded on this Web page.

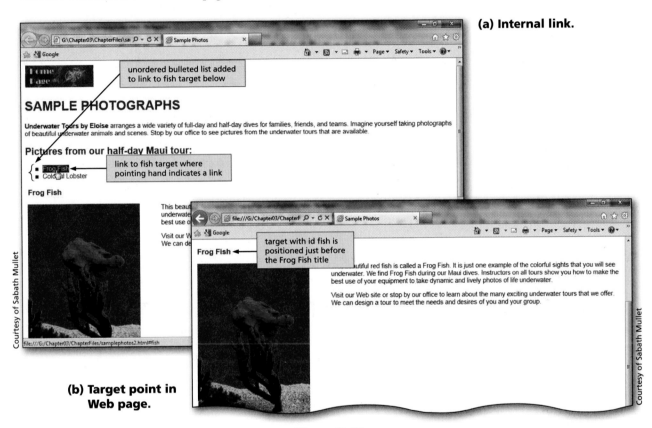

(a) Internal link.

(b) Target point in Web page.

Courtesy of Sabath Mullet

Courtesy of Sabath Mullet

Figure 3–40

To create links within the same Web page, the targets for the links must first be created. Link targets are created using the <a> tag with the id attribute, using the form:

```
<a id="targetname"></a>
```

where targetname is a unique name for a link target within that Web page. Notice that the tag uses the id attribute, rather than the href attribute, and that no text is included between the start <a> and end </a> tag, because the target is not intended to appear on the Web page as a clickable link. Instead, the link target is intended to mark a specific area of the Web page, to which a link can be directed.

Links to targets are created using the <a> tag with the href attribute, using the form:

```
<a href="#targetname">
```

where targetname is the name of a link target in that Web page. Notice that the tag uses the href attribute, followed by the pound sign (#) and the target name enclosed in quotation marks.

To Set Link Targets

The next step is to set link targets to the Frog Fish and Colorful Lobster sections of the Web page. The following steps show how to set the two link targets in the Sample Photographs Web page.

- Highlight the line `<!-- Insert fish target here -->` on line 49.

- Type `<a id="fish"></a>` to create a link target named fish (Figure 3–41).

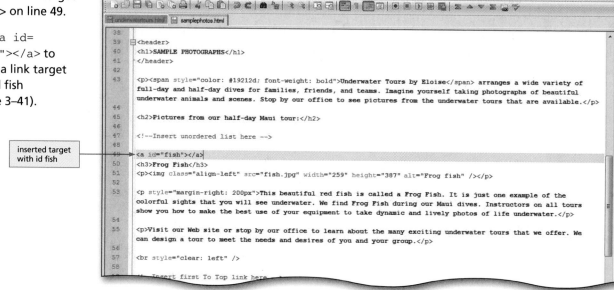

inserted target with id fish

Figure 3–41

- Highlight the line `<!--Insert lobster target here -->` on line 61.

- Type `<a id="lobster"></a>` to create a link target named lobster (Figure 3–42).

Q&A

There is nothing between the start anchor and end anchor tags for these targets. Will they work?

These targets are just placeholders, so they do not need any words or phrases; they only need a target name, as shown in the anchor tag.

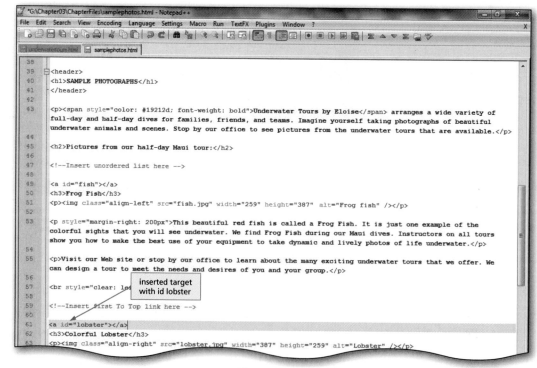

inserted target with id lobster

Figure 3–42

To Add Links to Link Targets Within a Web Page

The next step is to add link targets using the code shown in Table 3–10.

Line	HTML Tag and Text
	Table 3–10 HTML Code to Insert Bulleted List with Links to Link Targets
47	`<ul style="list-style-type: square">`
48	`<li><a href="#fish">Frog Fish</a></li>`
49	`<li><a href="#lobster">Colorful Lobster</a></li>`
50	`</ul>`

The following step shows how to add the code to create an unordered (bulleted) list and then to use the list items as links to link targets within the Web page.

- Highlight the line `<!--Insert unordered list here -->` on line 47.

- Type the HTML code in Table 3–10 but do not press the ENTER key at the end of line 50. This HTML code inserts the bulleted list that provides links to the two targets (fish and lobster) inserted above.

Q&A

Do I have to use a bulleted list for the links?

No, you can use any text for the links to the targets created in the step above. The bulleted list makes the links easy to see and keeps the links in one area of the Web page.

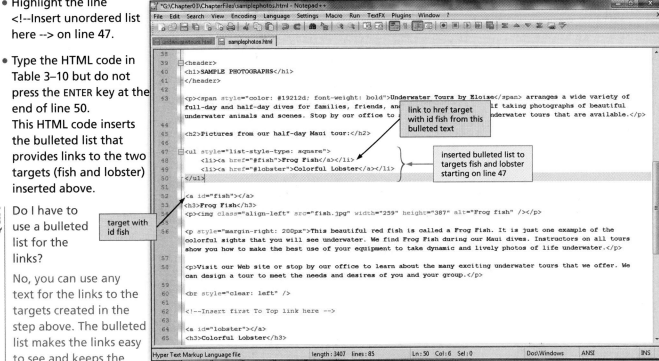

Figure 3–43

To Add Links to a Target at the Top of the Page

In this step, you add two To top links to provide a quick way to move back to the top of the Web page. To make these links, you first set the target at the top of the page, and then create the links to that target. You will also use an inline style to make the link text smaller than the regular font-size. The following steps illustrate how to add links to a target at the top of the page.

1

- Highlight the line <!--Insert Top target here --> on line 35.

- Type <a id= "top"></a> as the tag that will create a target at the top of the Web page named top (Figure 3–44).

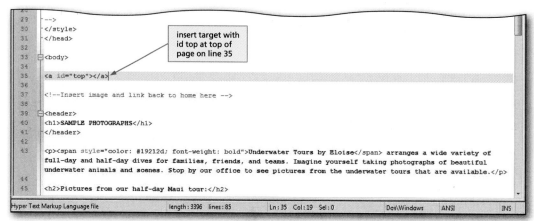

Figure 3–44

2

- Highlight the line <!--Insert first To Top link here --> on line 62.

- Type <p><a href= "#top"><span style="font- size: small">To top</span></a> </p> as the tag (Figure 3–45).

Q&A Why do you use a small size font for this link?

The link back to the top of the page should be subtle yet distinguishable from the other text on the page. Notice that the text link at the very bottom of the Web page to return to the home page is the same small size.

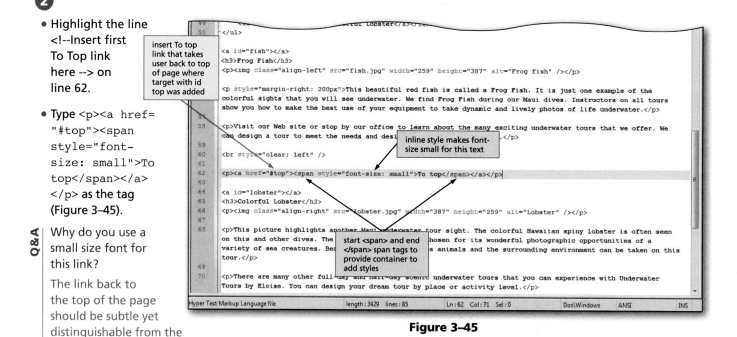

Figure 3–45

To Copy and Paste HTML Code

The copy and paste feature can be very useful for entering the same code in different places. The following step shows how to copy and paste the link code to another line in the HTML code.

1

- Highlight the HTML code <p><a href= "#top"><span style="font-size: small">To top</span></a> </p> on line 62.

- Click Edit on the menu bar and then click Copy.

- Highlight the line <!--Insert second To top link here --> on line 74 to position the pointer.

- Click Edit on the menu bar and then click Paste to paste the HTML code that you copied into line 74 (Figure 3–46).

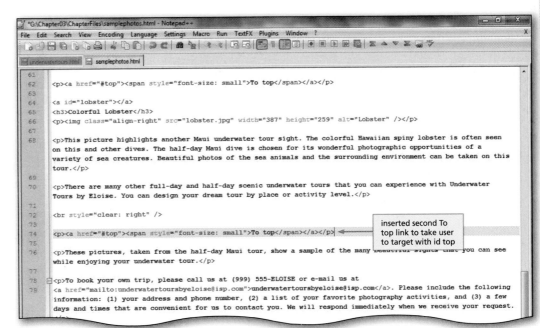

Figure 3–46

To Add an Image Link to a Web Page

The last step is to add an image link from the Sample Photographs Web page back to the Underwater Tours by Eloise home page. The style for links that you set with an embedded style sheet earlier set the link background color to dark blue and the text to light blue. For an image link, however, this would not be appropriate. To override the embedded style sheet for just this one instance, you will use an inline style to set a background-color that is transparent with text-decoration of none (no underline). Remember that according to the style precedence rules, an inline style takes precedence over an embedded style sheet. These two styles in the <a> tag (background-color: transparent; text-decoration: none) together with the border-color: transparent style in the <img> tag ensure that no border appears around the image and there is no line under the link image. Remember that the <div> </div> tags create a container that defines logical divisions in your Web page. The <div> tag is similar to a paragraph tag, but it allows you to divide the page into larger sections and to define the style of whole sections within your Web page. You could define a section of your page and give that section a different style from the surrounding text. When you use the <div> </div> tags, you are able to design a layout that uses CSS properties. You use the <div> </div> tags in this case to insert the image that will be used as a link on the Web page. Table 3–11 shows the code used to insert the image link.

Table 3–11 HTML Code to Insert Image Link to Home	
Line	**HTML Tag and Text**
37	`<div>`
38	`<a href="underwatertours.html" style="background-color: transparent; text-decoration: none">`
39	`<img style="border-color: transparent" src="underwaterlogosm.jpg" width="158" height="49" alt="Back to home page" /></a>`
40	`</div>`

The following step shows how to create an image link at the top of the Sample Photographs Web page.

- Highlight the line <!--Insert image and link back to home here --> on line 37.

- Type the HTML code in Table 3–11 but do not press the ENTER key at the end of line 40. This HTML code inserts a link back to home from the image underwaterlogosm. jpg. This image is a smaller version of the underwaterlogo .jpg image that you used on the home page (Figure 3–47).

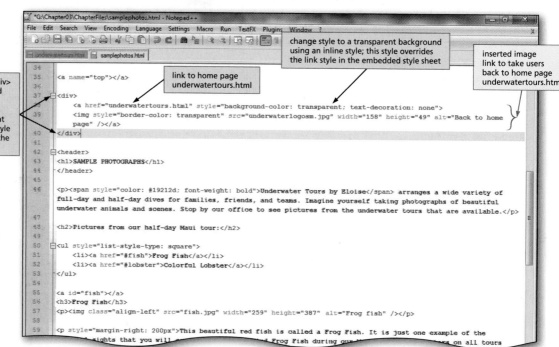

Figure 3–47

To Save, Validate, and Print the HTML File

With the HTML code for the Sample Photographs Web page complete, the HTML file should be saved, the Web page should be validated at w3.org, and a copy of the file should be printed as a reference.

1 Click File on the menu bar, and then click Save to save the HTML file as samplephotos. html.

2 Open a new browser window and go to validator.w3.org.

3 Click the Validate by File Upload tab, browse to the samplephotos.html Web page, and then click Open.

4 Click the Check button to determine if the Web page is valid. If the file is not valid, make corrections, re-save, and revalidate.

5 Click the Notepad++ button on the taskbar to display the samplephotos.html code. Click File on the menu bar, click Print, and then click the Print button in the Print dialog box to print the HTML code.

To View and Test a Web Page

With the HTML code validated and saved, you should view the Web page and test the links.

1 Click the Internet Explorer button on the taskbar to view the samplephotos.html page in your browser.

2 Click the Refresh button in the Address bar to display the changes made to the Web page, which should now look like Figure 3–1b on page HTML 89.

3 Verify that all internal links work correctly. Click the two links in the bulleted list at the top of the Web page. Then scroll down and click each To top link to check its function. Finally, verify that the image link to the home page works.

Q&A How can I tell if internal links are working when the link and target are displayed in the same browser window?

To see movement to a target within a page, you might need to restore down and resize the browser window so that the target is not visible, then click the link.

To Print a Web Page

1 Click the Print button on the Command bar to print the Web page (Figure 3–48).

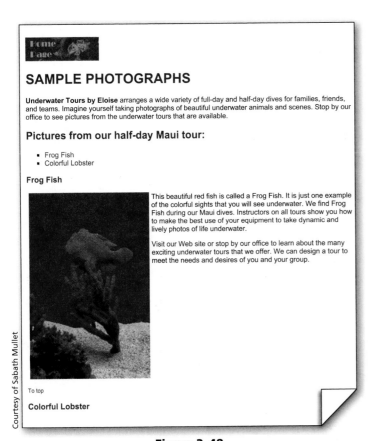

Courtesy of Sabath Mullet

Figure 3–48

BTW

Quick Reference
For a list of HTML tags and their associated attributes, see the HTML Quick Reference (Appendix A) at the back of this book, or visit the HTML Quick Reference on the Book Companion Site Web page for this book at cengagebrain.com. For a list of CSS properties and values, see Appendix D.

To Quit Notepad++ and a Browser

1 In Notepad++, click the File menu, then Close All.

2 Click the Close button on the Notepad++ title bar.

3 Click the Close button on all open browser windows.

Chapter Summary

In this chapter, you have learned how to develop a two-page Web site with links, images, and formatted text. You learned how to use inline and embedded style sheets and style classes to format elements in each Web page. The items listed below include all the new HTML and CSS skills you have learned in this chapter.

1. Add a Banner Image (HTML 102)
2. Add a Text Link to Another Web Page Within the Same Web Site (HTML 106)
3. Add an E-mail Link (HTML 107)
4. Add a Text Link to a Web Page in Another Web Site (HTML 109)
5. Add Embedded Style Sheet Statements (HTML 117)
6. Add an Inline Style for Color (HTML 119)
7. Test Links on a Web Page (HTML 123)
8. Wrap Text Around Images Using CSS Classes (HTML 134)
9. Clear Text Wrapping (HTML 136)
10. Set Link Targets (HTML 138)
11. Add Links to Link Targets Within a Web Page (HTML 139)
12. Add Links to a Target at the Top of the Page (HTML 140)
13. Copy and Paste HTML Code (HTML 140)
14. Add an Image Link to a Web Page (HTML 141)

Learn It Online

Test your knowledge of chapter content and key terms.

Instructions: To complete the following exercises, please visit www.cengagebrain.com. At the CengageBrain.com home page, search for *HTML5 and CSS 7th Edition* using the search box at the top of the page. This will take you to the product page for this book. On the product page, click the Access Now button below the Study Tools heading. On the Book Companion Site Web page, select Chapter 3, and then click the link for the desired exercise.

Chapter Reinforcement TF, MC, and SA
A series of true/false, multiple choice, and short answer questions that test your knowledge of the chapter content.

Flash Cards
An interactive learning environment where you identify chapter key terms associated with displayed definitions.

Practice Test
A series of multiple choice questions that test your knowledge of chapter content and key terms.

Who Wants To Be a Computer Genius?
An interactive game that challenges your knowledge of chapter content in the style of a television quiz show.

Wheel of Terms
An interactive game that challenges your knowledge of chapter key terms in the style of the television show, *Wheel of Fortune.*

Crossword Puzzle Challenge
A crossword puzzle that challenges your knowledge of key terms presented in the chapter.

Apply Your Knowledge

Reinforce the skills and apply the concepts you learned in this chapter.

Adding Text Formatting to a Web Page Using Inline Styles

Instructions: Start Notepad++. Open the file apply3-1.html from the Chapter03\Apply folder of the Data Files for Students. See the inside back cover of this book for instructions on downloading the Data Files for Students, or contact your instructor for information about accessing the required files. The apply3-1.html file is a partially completed HTML file that you will use for this exercise. Figure 3–49 shows the Apply Your Knowledge Web page as it should be displayed in a browser after the additional HTML tags and attributes are added.

Perform the following tasks:

1. Enter G:\Chapter03\Apply\apply3-1.html as the URL to view the Web page in your browser.

2. Examine the HTML file in Notepad++ and its appearance in the browser.

3. In Notepad++, change the HTML code to make the Web page look similar to the one shown in Figure 3–49.

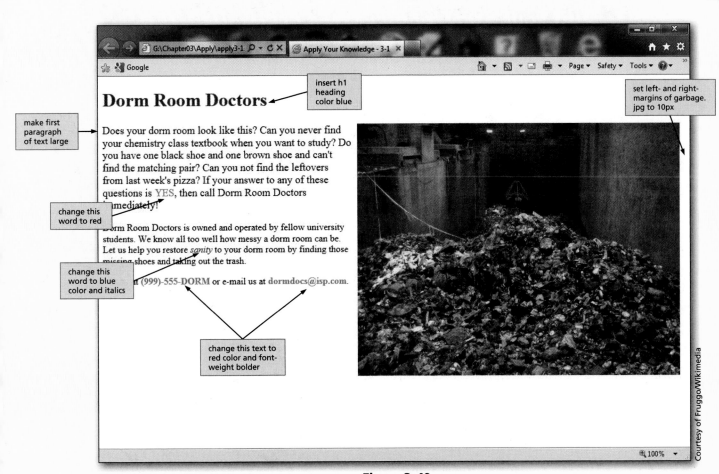

Figure 3–49

Courtesy of Fruggo/Wikimedia

Continued >

Apply Your Knowledge *continued*

4. Use an inline style to create the h1 heading, Dorm Room Doctors, and make it blue.

5. Using the <div></div> container, right-align the image garbage.jpg (width=560, height=420). Give the image right- and left-margins of 10 pixels. (*Hint:* Make sure to use the alt attribute.)

6. Make the first paragraph a large font. Color the word YES red in that paragraph. (*Hint:* Use the <span> tag.)

7. The second paragraph should be normal font, but make the word sanity blue and italic.

8. In the third paragraph, make the phone number and e-mail address red and in a bolder font-weight.

9. Save the revised HTML file in the Chapter03\Apply folder using the file name apply3-1solution.html.

10. Validate your code.

11. Print the revised HTML file.

12. Enter G:\Chapter03\Apply\apply3-1solution.html as the URL to view the revised Web page in your browser.

13. Print the Web page.

14. Submit the revised HTML file and Web page in the format specified by your instructor.

Extend Your Knowledge

Extend the skills you learned in this chapter and experiment with new skills.

Creating Targets and Links

Instructions: Start Notepad++. Open the file extend3-1.html from the Chapter03\Extend folder of the Data Files for Students. See the inside back cover of this book for instructions on downloading the Data Files for Students, or contact your instructor for information about accessing the required files. This sample HTML file contains all of the text for the Web page shown in Figure 3–50. You will add the necessary tags to make this Web page appear with left- and right-aligned images, text formatting, and links, as shown in Figure 3–50.

Perform the following tasks:

1. Insert the following embedded styles:

    body   {font-family: Garamond, Arial, Verdana;

                    font-size: 12pt;}

    h1, h2   {color: red;

                    font-variant: small-caps;}

    .align-right   {float: right;

                    margin-left: 15px;

                    margin-right: 15px;}

    .align-left   {float: left;

                    margin-left: 15px;

                    margin-right: 15px;}

    a   {text-decoration: underline;

                    color: red;}

    a:hover   {background: red;

                    color: white;}

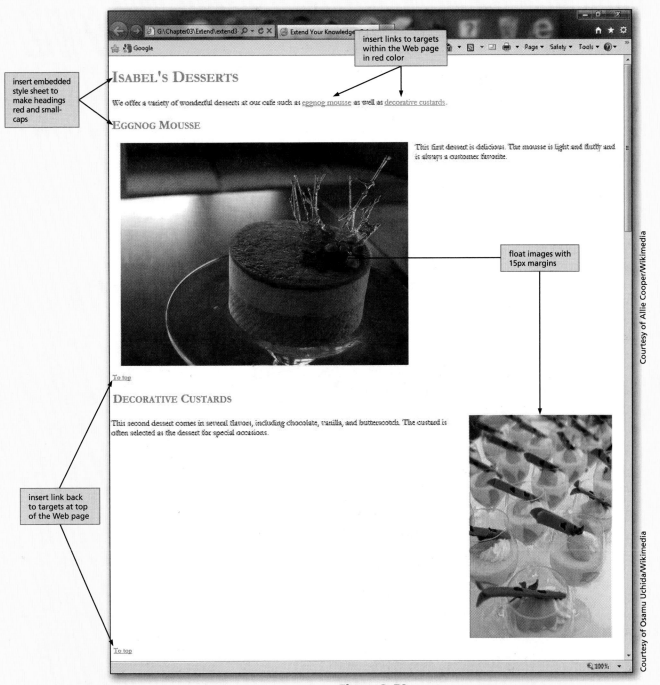

insert embedded style sheet to make headings red and small-caps

insert links to targets within the Web page in red color

float images with 15px margins

insert link back to targets at top of the Web page

Courtesy of Allie Cooper/Wikimedia

Courtesy of Osamu Uchida/Wikimedia

Figure 3–50

2. Make sure to use inline styles for all other styles. Add code to align the first picture on the left and the second picture on the right, with margins of 15px. (*Hint:* Remember to clear alignment for both images.)

3. Add the HTML code to create three targets (one at the top of the Web page, one near the first h2 heading, and the last near the second h2 heading). Create links from the first paragraph to the heading for each dessert. Also create two link(s) back to the top with font-size small, as shown in Figure 3–50.

4. Validate your HTML code and test all links.

5. Save the revised document as extend3-1solution.html and submit it in the format specified by your instructor.

Make It Right

Analyze a document; correct all errors and improve the design.

Correcting the Egypt Vacation Web Page

Instructions: Start Notepad++. Open the file makeitright3-1.html from the Chapter03\MakeItRight folder of the Data Files for Students. See the inside back cover of this book for instructions on downloading the Data Files for Students, or contact your instructor for information about accessing the required files. The Web page is a modified version of what you see in Figure 3–51 on the next page. Make the necessary corrections to the Web page to make it look like the figure. The background color is #e5aa64, and the h1 color is #4a7493 for this Web page. Use an inline style to float the images and provide margins of 15 pixels on both right and left sides. The Web page uses the images egypt1.jpg and egypt2.jpg, which both have widths and heights of 512 and 384.

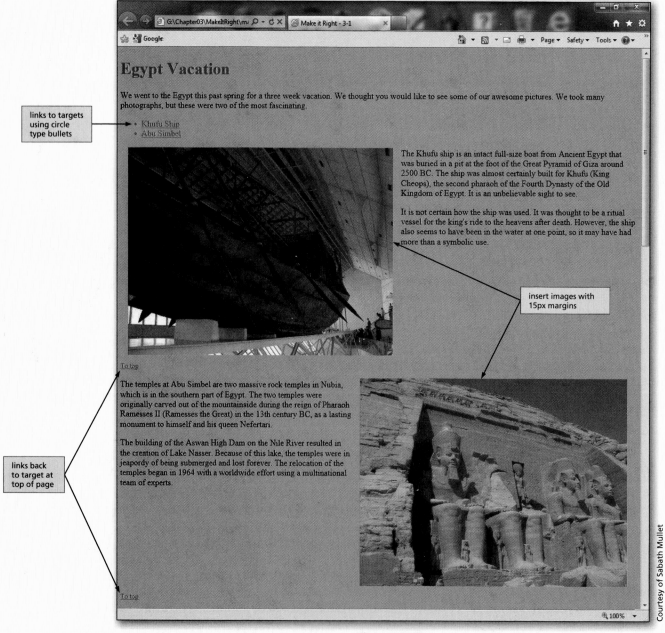

Figure 3–51

In the Lab

Lab 1: Creating a Web Page with Links

Problem: Your instructor wants you to create a Web page demonstrating your knowledge of link targets. You have been asked to create a Web page to demonstrate this technique, similar to the one shown in Figure 3–52. Use inline styles for all styles in the Web page.

Instructions: Perform the following steps:

1. Start Notepad++ and create a new HTML file with the title, Lab 3-1, in the head section.

2. Begin the body section by adding the image recycle.png and aligning it to the left. Use the margin-left and -right with values of 10 pixels.

3. Add the heading Help the Earth - Recycle. Format the heading to use the Heading 1 style, left-aligned, italic, with the font color black.

4. Add an unordered list with the three list items, as shown in Figure 3–52. These three items will be used to link to the three sections of text below them.

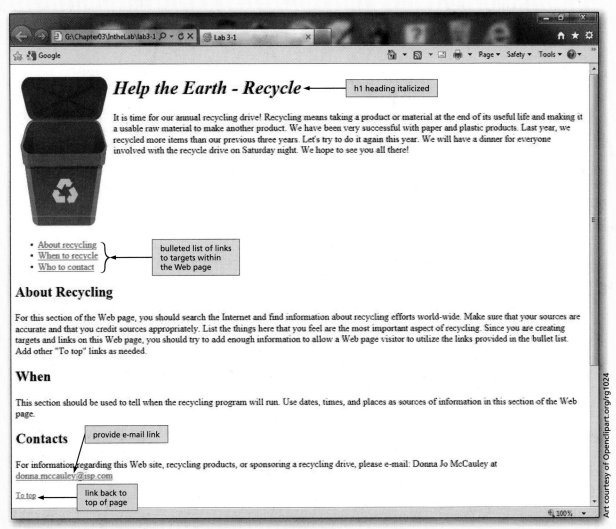

Art courtesy of Openclipart.org/rg1024

Figure 3–52

Continued >

In the Lab *continued*

5. Add a Heading 2 style heading, About Recycling, and set a link target named about. Type a paragraph of text based on your research of the topic, as shown in Figure 3–52.

6. Add a Heading 2 style heading, When, and set a link target named when. Type a paragraph based on your research of the topic, as shown in Figure 3–52.

7. Add a Heading 2 style heading, Contacts, and set a link target named contact. Type the paragraph, as shown in Figure 3–52.

8. Create a link target at the top of the page named top.

9. Create a To top link at the bottom of the page, as shown in Figure 3–52. Set the link to direct to the top target at the top of the page.

10. Create links from the bulleted list to the three targets.

11. Create an e-mail link, as shown in Figure 3–52.

12. Save the HTML file in the Chapter03\IntheLab folder using the file name lab3-1solution.html.

13. Validate the lab-3-1solution.html file.

14. Print the lab3-1solution.html file.

15. Enter the URL G:\Chapter03\IntheLab\lab3-1solution.html to view the Web page in your browser.

16. Print the Web page.

17. Submit the HTML file and Web page in the format specified by your instructor.

In the Lab

Lab 2: Creating a Web Page with Links

Problem: Your instructor wants you to create a Web page demonstrating your knowledge of link targets. You have been asked to create a Web page to demonstrate this technique, similar to the one shown in Figure 3–53.

Instructions: Perform the following steps:

1. Start Notepad++ and create a new HTML file with the title, Lab 3-2, in the head section.

2. Begin the body section by adding an h1 heading that is left-aligned.

3. Add the following code into an embedded style. Notice that all text links have the same background color as the h1 heading at the top of the Web page. This is because of the code that you put in the embedded style, as follows:

```
body            {font-family: Arial, Verdana, Garamond;
                font-size: 11pt;}
h1, h2, h3      {color: #19212d;}
a               {color: black;}
a:hover         {background: #19212d;
                color: white;}
img.align-right {float: right;
                margin-left: 5px;
                margin-right: 5px;}
img.align-left  {float: left;
                margin-left: 5px;
                margin-right: 5px;}
```

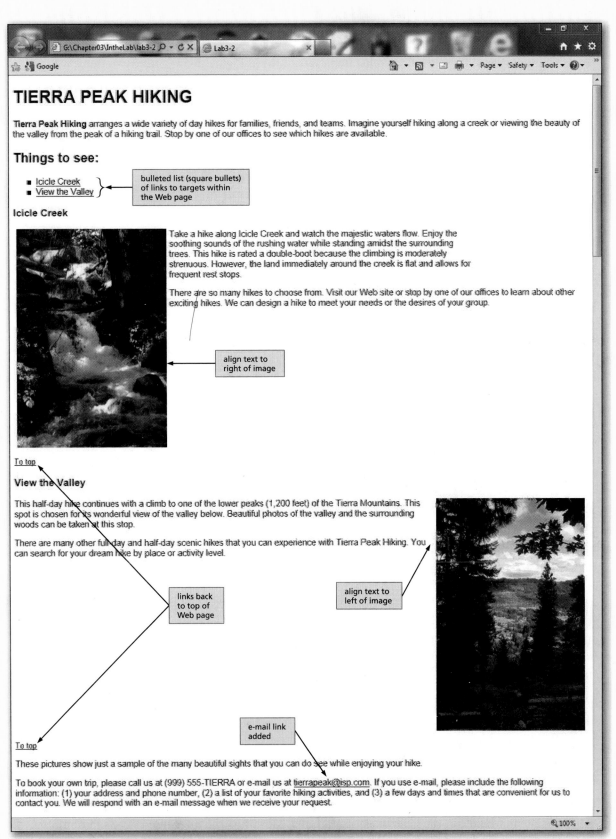

Figure 3–53

Continued >

In the Lab continued

4. Add an unordered list with the two list items, as shown in Figure 3–53. These two items will be used to link to the two sections of text below them. (*Hint:* Note that the bullets are square.)

5. Add one h1 heading, one h2 heading, and two h3 headings.

6. Add an inline style sheet changing the first three words of the first paragraph to be color #19212d and font-weight of bold. (*Hint:* Use the <span></span> container.)

7. Add the two images provided (creek.jpg and valley.jpg).

8. Create a link target at the top of the page named top.

9. Add two To top links, one after each section, as shown in Figure 3–53. Set the link to direct to the top target at the top of the page.

10. Create links from the bulleted list to the two targets. (*Hint:* Remember to insert a unique id for both targets.)

11. Create an e-mail link, as shown in Figure 3–53.

12. Save the HTML file in the Chapter03\IntheLab folder using the file name lab3-2solution.html.

13. Validate the lab3-2solution.html file.

14. Print the lab3-2solution.html file.

15. View the Web page in your browser.

16. Print the Web page.

17. Submit the HTML file and Web page in the format specified by your instructor.

In the Lab

Lab 3: Creating Two Linked Web Pages

Problem: Your Communications instructor has asked each student in the class to create a two-page Web site to help students in the class get to know more about the subject area in which you are majoring in school. She suggested using the basic template shown in Figures 3–54a and 3–54b as a starting point. The first Web page (Figure 3–54a) is a home page that includes basic information about your major. Really try to answer the questions listed (for example, why you chose this major), as shown on the Web page. If you can, add an image related to your chosen field somewhere on the Web page. Add a link to the second Web page. The second Web page (Figure 3–54b) includes a paragraph of text and numbered lists with links.

Instructions: Perform the following steps:

1. Start Notepad++ and create a new HTML file with the title Lab 3-3 in the head section.

2. In the first Web page, include a Heading style 1 heading, similar to the one shown in Figure 3–54a, and a short paragraph of text. Experiment and use any color for the heading (navy is shown). (*Hint:* Review the text-align: center property and value in Appendix D and online.)

3. Create a text link to the second Web page, lab3-3specifics.html.

4. Save the HTML file in the Chapter03\IntheLab folder using the file name lab3-3solution.html. Validate the lab3-3solution.html file. Print the lab3-3solution.html file.

5. Start a new HTML file with the title Lab 3-3 Specifics in the head section.

(a) First Web page.

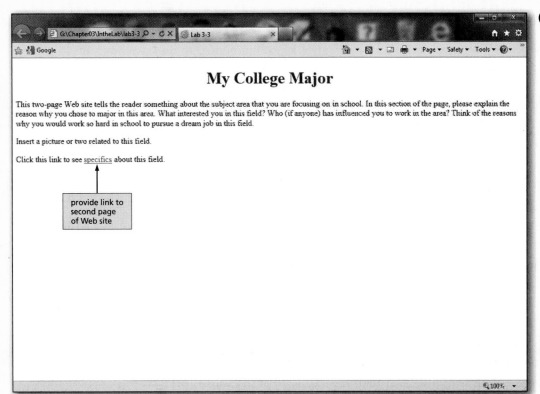

(b) Second Web page.

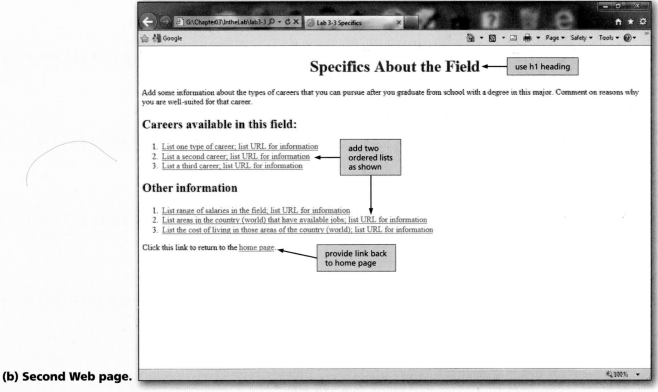

Figure 3–54

Continued >

In the Lab *continued*

6. In the second Web page, include a Heading style 1 heading, similar to the one shown in Figure 3–54b on the previous page, a short paragraph of text, and two Heading style 2 headings. From the standpoint of consistency, you may want to make those h2 headings all the same color. (*Hint:* Use an inline style sheet sheet for this.)

7. Create two ordered (numbered) lists with at least two items each that serve as links to Web pages on another (external) Web site. Add a link back to the first Web page, as shown in Figure 3–54b.

8. Save the HTML file in the Chapter03\IntheLab folder using the file name lab3-3specifics.html. Validate the lab3-3specifics.html file. Print the lab3-3specifics.html file.

9. View the home page in your browser. Click the text link to the second Web page. Click the links in the lists to test them.

10. Print the Web pages.

11. Submit the HTML files and Web pages in the format specified by your instructor.

Cases and Places

Apply your creative thinking and problem-solving skills to design and implement a solution.

1: Create a Web Page with Text Formatting

Academic

You recently got a work-study position developing Web pages for your academic department at school. Your professor has asked you to update the home page for the department's Web site to make it more visually appealing. As a first step, you plan to create a Web page with sample text formats, such as the ones shown in Figure 3–19 on page HTML 111, to share with your professor and get her input on which types of formatting she prefers. Include text formatted as bold, italic, underlined, superscript, and subscript on the Web page, using different colors and sizes for each type of text. Use CSS styles for most of your styles, but also use some of the text formatting tags shown in the chapter. Determine why you would choose to use one over the other (i.e., styles versus formatting tags). Be sure to include one sample using the font-weight bold style and one using bolder to see how they compare when displayed together. Compare those to using <bold> or <strong> as formatting tags. Be creative and make sure that the Web page looks good but that the new styles do not distract from the content. Utilize a sampling of different font-families on the Web page to show contrast. Be prepared to explain why some font-families (e.g., a curvy script style) might not be appropriate.

2: Create a Web Page with Text Links and Define Link Colors

Personal

You are starting a small business to provide you with some income while in school. You have asked a friend to design your logo, and you would like the link colors on your Web page to match the colors you chose. Create a Web page similar to Figure 3–3 on page HTML 92, with three text links to a Web page in an external Web site. Add the appropriate link styles to define the link colors to match your logo. Also, explain why you might not want to change the colors of the links from the standard blue and violet but show ways that you can accommodate different colors and not confuse users.

3: Create a Prototype Web Site with Five Pages

Professional

Your manager at Uptown Enterprises has asked you to create a simple five-page prototype of the Web pages in the new Entertainment section for the online magazine CityStuff. The home page should include headings and brief paragraphs of text for Arts, Music, Movies, and Dining. Within each paragraph of text is a link to one of the four detailed Web pages for each section (for example, the Arts link should connect to the Arts Web page). The home page also includes an e-mail link at the bottom of the page. Add a To top link that connects to a target at the top of the page. The four detailed Web pages should include links to external Web sites of interest and a link back to the home page. If possible, also find appropriate images to use as a background or in the Web page, and set text to wrap around the images. Remember to use CSS. Determine during the design phase whether it would be better to use inline or embedded style sheets or both for this Web site.

4 Creating Tables in a Web Site Using an External Style Sheet

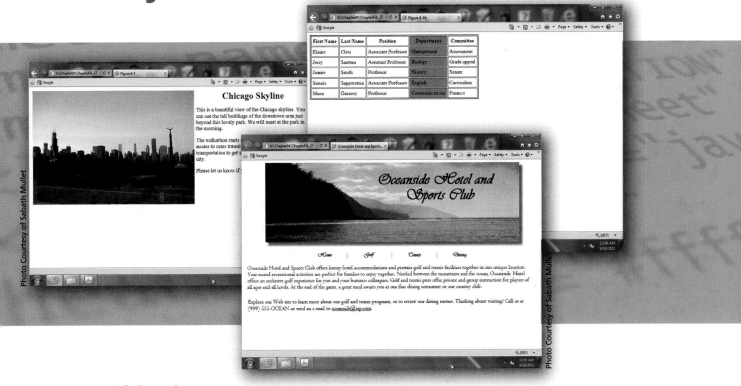

Objectives

You will have mastered the material in this chapter when you can:

- Define table elements

- Describe the steps used to plan, design, and code a table

- Create a borderless table for a horizontal navigation bar with text links

- Create an external style sheet to define styles across a Web site

- Utilize classes to give you more control over styles

- Link an external style sheet to Web pages where you want its styles applied

- Create a table with borders and insert text

- Use the box-shadow property to alter the appearance of an image

- Alter the spacing between and within cells using the border spacing and padding properties

- Utilize inline styles to alter the style of individual elements on a Web page

- Add background color to rows and cells

- Insert a caption below a table

- Create headings that span rows using the rowspan attribute

4 Creating Tables in a Web Site Using an External Style Sheet

Introduction

So far, you have learned how to make a basic Web page and how to link one Web page to another, both within the same Web site and external to the Web site. You also learned how to create inline styles and embedded (internal) style sheets to alter the appearance of Web page elements. In this chapter's project, you will create an external (linked) style sheet to set the style for elements across multiple Web pages. The project adds to your HTML knowledge by teaching you how to organize and present information on a Web page using tables with rows and columns. In this chapter, you will learn about the elements used in a table and how to plan, design, and code a table. You will learn how to use a table to create a horizontal navigation bar with image links, and to create tables to organize text and images. You will enhance the Web site by manipulating the properties and attributes of tables and paragraphs, altering borders, colors, and spacing, and adding a table caption. You will use the new CSS3 box-shadow property to give a unique look to the banner image.

Project — Oceanside Hotel and Sports Club Web Site

Having a reliable Web site makes it easier for a company's customers to find the establishment, provides a way to communicate the company's brand, and allows the company to provide additional services. As advertising director for Oceanside Hotel and Sports Club, you want to enhance Oceanside's Web site to increase the hotel's exposure to current and new customers and to incorporate ideas gathered from customer feedback surveys. The new site will allow customers to browse through tables of information that outline the golf, tennis, and dining options offered by the hotel and sports club.

As shown in Figure 4–1a, the Oceanside Hotel and Sports Club home page includes a company logo banner and a borderless table that contains a navigation bar under the logo. The borderless table gives users easy access to all pages in the Web site. This table is available on every Web page in the Web site. The Golf, Tennis, and Dining Web pages (Figures 4–1b, 4–1c, and 4–1d) each include the company logo banner and the same borderless table at the top, as well as one table with borders that displays the contents of that particular Web page. In this project, you will create the oceanside.html and golf.html Web pages. You will edit the tennis.html Web page (Figure 4–1c) to add border spacing and padding properties, thereby adjusting the spacing between cells. The dining.html Web page file (Figure 4–1d) is also edited to add a caption with information about the table and to use the rowspan attribute to create headings that span several rows.

As you read through this chapter and work on the project, you will learn how to plan, design, and code tables to create a user-friendly Web site. You also will learn to format tables and to combine table features to make the pages more readable. In addition, you will learn to create a navigation bar with image links.

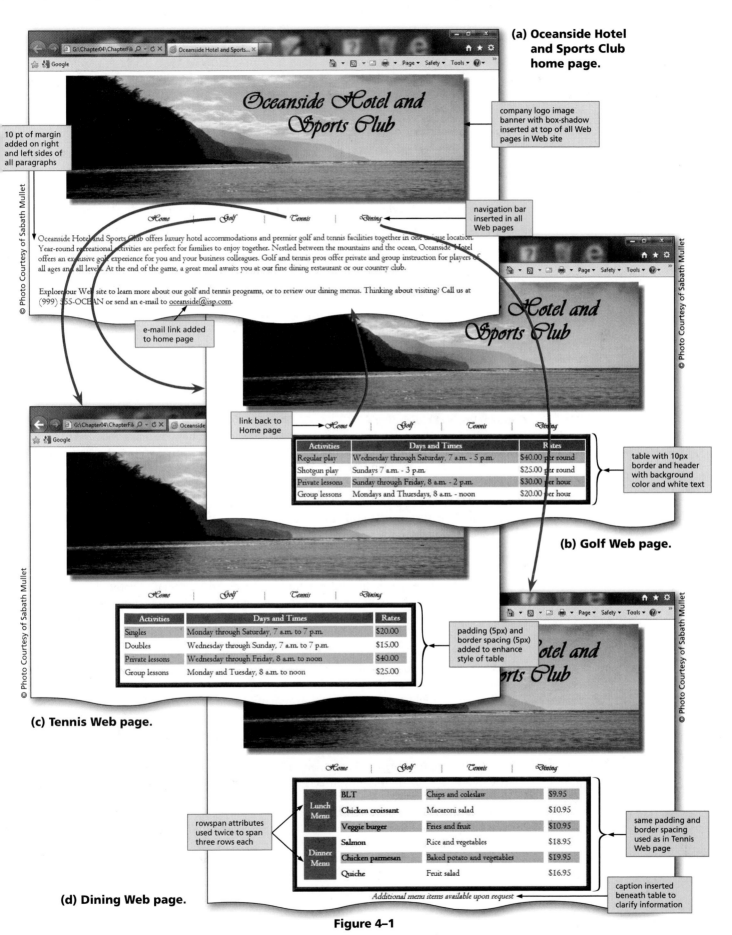

(a) Oceanside Hotel and Sports Club home page.

company logo image banner with box-shadow inserted at top of all Web pages in Web site

10 pt of margin added on right and left sides of all paragraphs

navigation bar inserted in all Web pages

e-mail link added to home page

link back to Home page

table with 10px border and header with background color and white text

(b) Golf Web page.

padding (5px) and border spacing (5px) added to enhance style of table

(c) Tennis Web page.

rowspan attributes used twice to span three rows each

same padding and border spacing used as in Tennis Web page

caption inserted beneath table to clarify information

(d) Dining Web page.

Figure 4–1

Overview

As you read this chapter, you will learn how to create the Web pages shown in Figures 4–1a through 4–1d on the previous page by performing these general tasks:

- Enter HTML code into the Notepad++ window.
- Save the file as an HTML file.
- Enter basic HTML tags and add text to the file.
- Add a horizontal navigation bar with image links.
- Create a table with borders to display information in an organized manner.
- Create an external style sheet to set the style for all Web pages in the Web site.
- Use classes to give more control over the styles used.
- Link an external style sheet to Web pages.
- Utilize inline styles to alter the style of individual elements on the Web page.
- Add HTML tags that enhance a table with padding and border spacing.
- Enhance a Web table with rowspanning.
- Add a caption to a table.
- Print the HTML code and Web pages

Plan Ahead

General Project Guidelines

When creating a Web page, the actions you perform and decisions you make will affect the appearance and characteristics (the styles) of the finished page. As you create Web pages, such as those shown in Figures 4–1a through 4–1d, you should follow these general guidelines:

1. **Complete Web page planning.** Before developing a Web page, you must know the purpose of the Web site, identify the users of the site and their computing environments, and decide who owns the information on the Web page.

2. **Analyze the content and organization of the Web page.** In the analysis phase of the Web development life cycle, you should analyze what content to include on the Web page and how to organize that information. In this phase, you need to determine what information you want to convey so that you can highlight that information on the Web page using different techniques. Refer to Table 1–4 on page HTML 15 for information on the phases of the Web development life cycle.

3. **Choose the content and organization for the Web page.** Once you have completed the analysis, you need to determine specifically what content to include on the Web page. With tables, you are able to display the Web page content in a very organized manner. Tables can be used to display text only, as well as graphical images or combinations of text and images. Some text is better highlighted by using different colors for column or row headings. Other information is displayed more effectively with row- and column-spanning techniques. This should all be determined before coding the Web pages.

4. **Identify how to format various elements of the Web page.** The overall appearance or style of a Web page significantly affects its ability to communicate clearly. Additionally, you want to provide easy navigation for your Web site visitors. Adding images and color helps to communicate your message and adding a navigation bar with links to the other Web pages within the Web site makes it easy to navigate the Web site. Determine what style sheets to use for the overall appearance or style, including external, embedded, and inline style sheets. Also determine which formatting tag attributes need to be implemented.

Plan
Ahead

(continued)

5. **Determine where to save the Web page.** You can store a Web page permanently, or save it on a variety of storage media, including a hard disk, USB flash drive, CD, or DVD. You can also indicate a specific location on the storage media for saving the Web page. Recognize the appropriate absolute and relative addressing that you will need as determined by your analysis.

6. **Create the Web page and links.** After analyzing and designing the Web site, you need to develop the individual Web pages. It is important to maintain a consistent look throughout the Web site. Use graphics and links consistently so that your Web site visitor does not become confused.

7. **Test all Web pages within the Web site.** An important part of Web development is testing to assure that you are following XHTML standards. This book uses the World Wide Web Consortium (W3C) validator that allows you to test your Web page and clearly explains any errors you have. Additionally, you should check all content for accuracy and test all links.

When necessary, more specific details concerning the above guidelines are presented at appropriate points in the chapter. The chapter will also identify the actions performed and decisions made regarding these guidelines during the creation of the Web pages shown in Figures 4–1a through 4–1d on page HTML 155.

Planning and Designing a Multipage Web Site

The Web site that you create in this chapter consists of four Web pages: oceanside.html, golf.html, tennis.html, and dining.html. With a multipage Web site, you need to design the overall look of the Web site itself, as well as the individual Web pages. You will use both formatting tag attributes and style sheets to create the overall appearance (or style) of the Web site. An **external style sheet** is used to define styles for multiple pages in a Web site. With external (linked) style sheets, you create the style sheet first in a separate file saved with a .css extension. You then link this style sheet into any Web page in which you want to use it.

In Chapters 2 and 3, you learned how to insert inline and embedded (internal) style sheets into your Web pages. Recall that inline style sheets are used to change the style of an individual HTML tag. An embedded style sheet is inserted between the <head> and </head> tags of a single Web page within the style container (<style> and </style>). Embedded (or internal) style sheets are used to change the style for elements on an entire Web page. For the project in this chapter, where you have a multipage Web site, you will learn how to create an external, or linked, style sheet.

Creating Web Pages with Tables

Tables allow you to organize information on a Web page using HTML tags. Tables are useful when you want to arrange text and images into rows and columns in order to make the information straightforward and clear to the Web page visitor. You can use tables to create Web pages with newspaper-type columns of text or structured lists of information. Tables can be complex, with text or images spanning rows and columns, background colors in cells, and borders (Figure 4–2a on the next page). Tables can also be simple, with a basic grid format and no color (Figure 4–2b). The purpose of the table helps to define what formatting is appropriate.

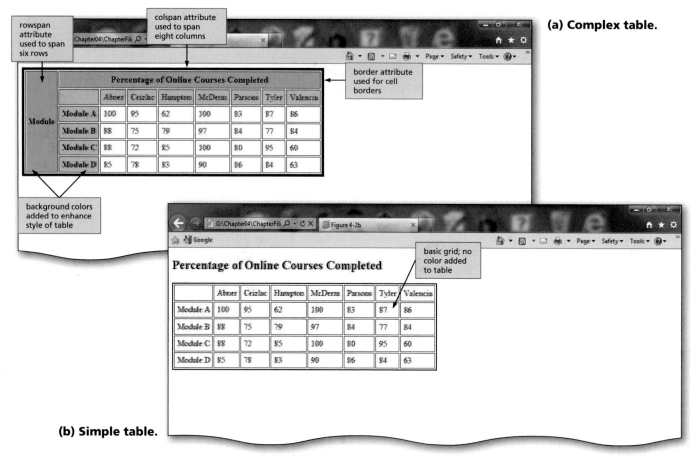

(a) Complex table.

(b) Simple table.

Figure 4–2

In Chapter 3, you learned how to wrap text around an image. You can also use tables to position text and images, such as the one shown in Figure 4–3; this is a borderless table used to position text to the right of the image. One advantage of using a table to position text and images instead of just wrapping the text around the image is that you have greater control over the placement of the text and image. However, CSS is the preferred method for structuring Web sites; tables are often found in legacy (i.e., older) Web sites.

Figure 4–3   Image and text positioned in table.

Table Elements

Tables consist of rows, columns, and cells, much like spreadsheets. A **row** is a horizontal line of information. A **column** is a vertical line of information. A **cell** is the intersection of a row and a column. Figure 4–4 shows examples of these three elements. In Figure 4–4a, the fifth row in the table has a green background. In Figure 4–4b, the fourth column has a blue background. In Figure 4–4c, the cell at the intersection of column 2 and row 6 has an orange background.

As shown in Figure 4–4c, a cell can be one of two types: a heading cell or a data cell. A **heading cell** displays text as bold and center-aligned. A **data cell** displays normal text that is left-aligned.

Understanding the row, column, and cell elements is important as you create a table using HTML. Properties and attributes are set relative to these table elements. For example, you can set attributes for an entire row of information, for a single cell, or for one or more cells within a row. Appendix A lists all attributes not supported by HTML5, indicated by a double asterisk (**). Review that appendix for more information.

BTW

Tables
Tables are useful for a variety of purposes. They can store information in tabular form or create a layout on a Web page.

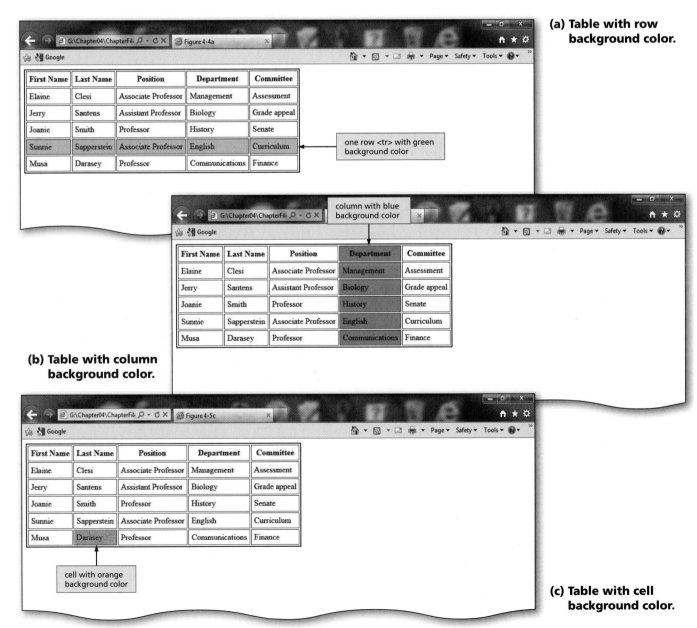

(a) Table with row background color.

(b) Table with column background color.

(c) Table with cell background color.

Figure 4–4

Adding Style to Table Elements

As discussed earlier, there are many ways to set the style (or appearance) of a Web page element. You can use formatting tag attributes (e.g., setting the border in the <table> tag or setting colspan in the <td> or <th> tag) to set the appearance or style. You can also use inline, embedded, or external (linked) style sheets to set the style. During the design phase of the Web development life cycle, you will determine how to set the styles for the elements on your Web pages.

HTML5 established a major change in how tables are formatted. All <table> tag attributes (as indicated in Appendix A) have been eliminated in HTML5 except for the border attribute. In this book, you will utilize the new tags and properties available in HTML5 when formatting tables. For instance, instead of using the cellspacing attribute, which is not supported in HTML5, to increase the space between cells, you will use the border-spacing property in an inline style. If you used the cellspacing attribute in your HTML code and tried to validate the file using an HTML5 DOCTYPE, you would get an error that said, "The cellspacing attribute on the table element is obsolete. Use CSS instead." In this book we do not use any attributes that are unsupported in HTML5.

In addition, you will use a new CSS3 property to add a style to the banner image used in this chapter project. The box-shadow property is a very exciting new addition with CSS3 and can be used in a variety of ways. For this Web site, it gives the banner image a very unique look as shown in Figure 4–1a on page HTML 155.

Figure 4–5a shows an example of a table of information in which no border has been added. In Figure 4–5b, you see a table in which the border has been set to 1 pixel. As you can see, just adding that one style has changed the table dramatically. Figure 4–5c shows a table in which many styles were set to enhance the look of the table. By using a combination of inline styles and an external style sheet, the table looks much more appealing and professional. In this chapter, you will use an external (linked) style sheet to set styles for the tables across the entire Web site.

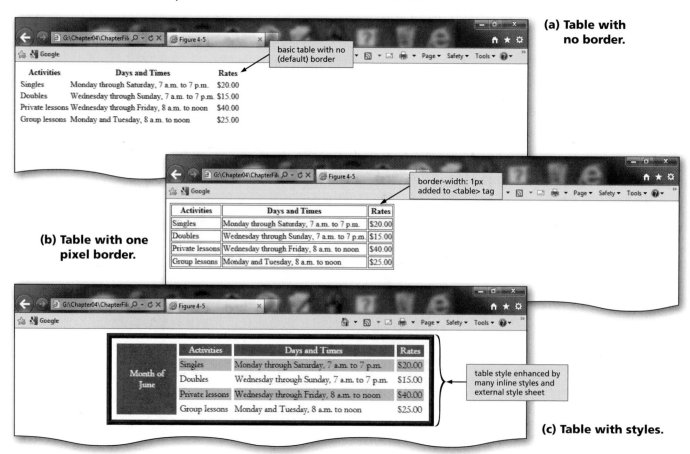

(a) Table with no border.

(b) Table with one pixel border.

(c) Table with styles.

Figure 4–5

Table Borders, Headers, Captions, and Rules

Tables not only contain columns and rows, but they also include features such as table borders, table headers, and table captions (Figure 4–6). A **table border** is the line that encloses the perimeter of the table. A **table header** is the same as a heading cell — it is any cell with bold, centered text that indicates the purpose of the row or column. A header row is used to identify the meaning of the numbers in each column, and headings that span columns and rows are used to provide additional information. Headers also are used by nonvisual browsers to identify table content. See the guidelines in Appendix C for specific information about making your Web pages accessible to those with disabilities. A **table caption** is descriptive text located above or below the table that further describes the purpose of the table.

Tables can use these features individually or in combination. The purpose for the table dictates which of these features are used. For example, the table shown in Figure 4–6 lists columns of numbers. A header row is used to identify the meaning of the numbers in each column, and headings that span columns and rows are used to provide additional information. Finally, the table caption explains that each number is based on thousands (that is, the 10 listed in the table represents 10,000).

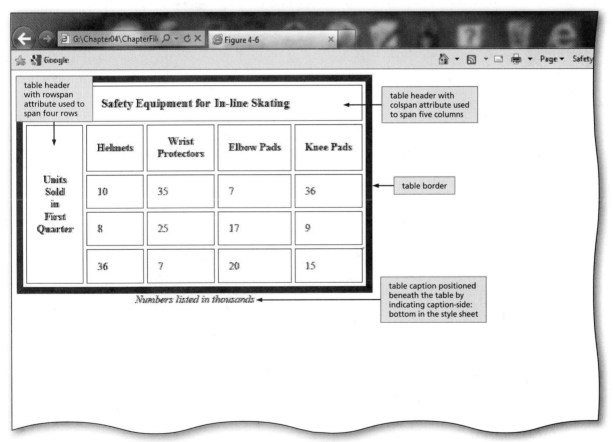

Figure 4–6 Table headers, border, and caption.

Determining the Need for, Planning, and Coding a Table

Creating tables for a Web page is a three-step process: (1) determining if a table is needed, (2) planning the table, and (3) coding the table. Each of these steps is discussed in detail in the following sections.

Determining if a Table Is Needed

First, you must determine whether a table is necessary. Not all Web pages require the use of tables. A general rule is that a table should be used when it will help organize information or Web page elements in such a way that it is easier for the Web page visitor to read. Tables generally are useful on a Web page if the Web page needs to display a structured, organized list of information or includes text and images that must be positioned in a very specific manner. Figures 4–7a and 4–7b show examples of information displayed as text in both a table and a bulleted list. To present this information, a table (Figure 4–7a) would be the better choice. The bulleted list (Figure 4–7b) might give the Web page an acceptable look, but the table presents the information more clearly.

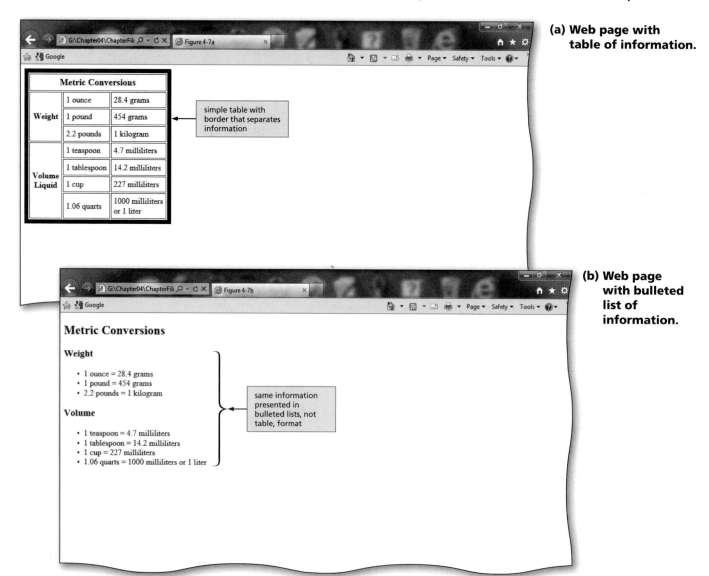

(a) Web page with table of information.

(b) Web page with bulleted list of information.

Figure 4–7

Planning the Table

To create effective tables, you must plan how the information will appear in the table and then create a good design. Before writing any HTML code, sketch the table on paper. After the table is sketched on paper, it is easier to see how many rows and columns to create, if the table will include headings, and if any of the headings span rows or columns. Conceptualizing the table on paper first saves time when you try to determine which HTML table tags to use to create the table.

For example, to create a simple table that lists the times run by various cross-country team members, you might sketch the table shown in Figure 4–8a. If runners participate in two different race lengths, such as 5K and 10K, that information can be included in a table designed as shown in Figure 4–8b. If the table needs to include different race dates for each race length, that information can be included in a table such as the one shown in Figure 4–8c. Finally, to make the table easier for the Web page visitor to understand, the table should include headings that span rows and columns. For instance, in Figure 4–8b, the headings 5K and 10K each span two columns of data. Because column spanning is used, you can easily see which runners ran in the 5K or 10K races. In Figure 4–8c, because of row spanning, you can easily tell what date each race was run. Design issues such as these should be considered in the planning stage before any HTML code is entered. Figure 4–9, on the next page, shows how the table might look after it is coded. You will use a variety of style sheets together with formatting tag attributes to create the tables for the project in this chapter.

NAME1	NAME2	NAME3	NAME4
TIME	TIME	TIME	TIME

(a) Simple table.

5K		10K	
NAME1	NAME2	NAME3	NAME4
TIME	TIME	TIME	TIME

(b) Column spanning added.

		5K		10K	
		NAME1	NAME2	NAME3	NAME4
Meet Dates	MAY 5	TIME	TIME	TIME	TIME
	MAY 12	TIME	TIME	TIME	TIME
	MAY 19	TIME	TIME	TIME	TIME
	MAY 26	TIME	TIME	TIME	TIME

(c) Row spanning added.

Figure 4–8

BTW

Table Tutorial
Table tutorials are available through online sources. Tutorials take you step-by-step through the table creation process. Search the Web for the phrase HTML Table Tutorial to find excellent sources of information.

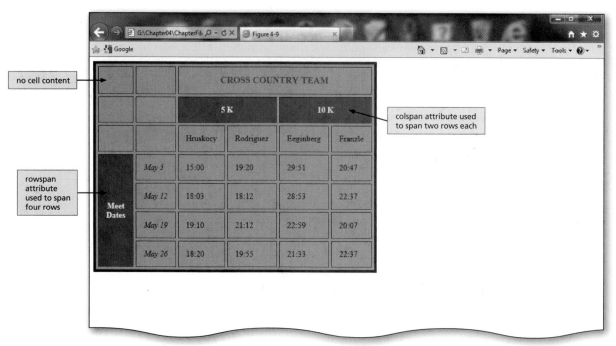

Figure 4–9 Table with row and column spanning.

Coding the Table

After you have completed the table design, you can begin coding the table using HTML tags. Table 4–1 shows the four main HTML tags used to create a table. Some of the tags have attributes, which are discussed later in this chapter.

Table 4–1 HTML Table Tags	
Tag	**Function**
<table> </table>	• Indicates the start and end of a table • All other table tags are inserted within these tags
<tr> </tr>	• Indicates the start and end of a table row • Rows consist of heading or data cells
<th> </th>	• Indicates the start and end of a table heading (also called a heading cell) • Table headings default to bold text and center-alignment
<td> </td>	• Indicates the start and end of a data cell in a table • Data cells default to normal text and left-alignment

Figure 4–10a shows an example of these tags used in an HTML file, and Figure 4–10b shows the resulting Web page. As shown in Figure 4–10b, the table has four rows (a table header and three rows of data cells) and two columns. The rows are indicated in the HTML file in Figure 4–10a by the start **<tr>** tags and the end **</tr>** tags. For this simple table, the number of columns in the table is determined based on the number of cells within each row. As shown in Figure 4–10b, each row has two cells, which results in a table with two columns. (Later in this chapter, you will learn how to indicate the number of columns within the <table> tag.)

As shown in the HTML in Figure 4–10a, the first row includes table heading cells, as indicated by the start **<th>** tag and end **</th>** tag. In the second, third, and fourth rows, the cells contain data, indicated by the start **<td>** tag and end **</td>** tag. In the resulting table, as shown in Figure 4–10b, the table header in row 1 appears as bold and centered text. The text in the data cells in rows 2 through 4 is left-aligned and normal text. The

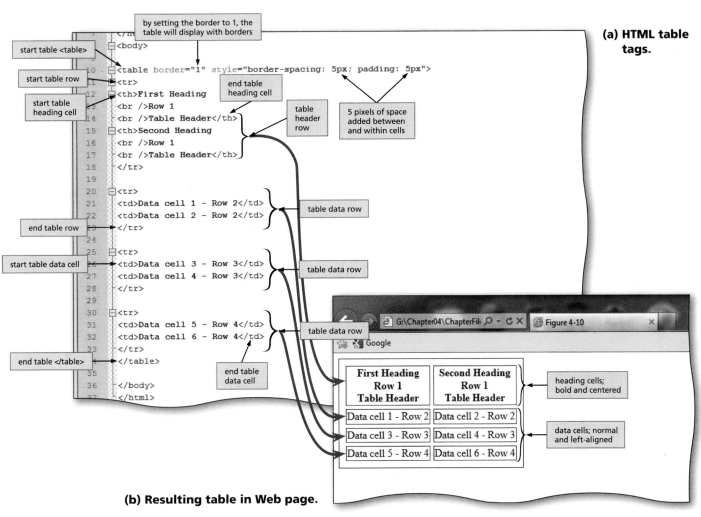

(a) HTML table tags.

by setting the border to 1, the table will display with borders

start table <table>

start table row

start table heading cell

end table heading cell

table header row

5 pixels of space added between and within cells

table data row

end table row

start table data cell

table data row

table data row

end table </table>

end table data cell

(b) Resulting table in Web page.

heading cells; bold and centered

data cells; normal and left-aligned

Figure 4–10

table in Figure 4–10b has a border, and using inline styles, the border-spacing and padding was set to 5 pixels each to highlight further differences between the cells. You will learn about border-spacing and padding styles later in the chapter.

Table Tag Attributes

Prior to HTML5, the four table tags had many attributes that could be used to format tables. These attributes are all shown in Appendix A. However, HTML5 does not support most of those attributes, and it is recommended that you use Cascading Style Sheets to style tables in a Web page. With HTML5:

- the <table> tag only allows the use of the border attribute
- the <tr> tag has no attributes still in use
- the <th> and <td> tags still allow use of the rowspan, colspan, and headers attributes

Table 4–2 lists the CSS properties and values that can be used to style tables. You use the border-spacing property in this chapter project to create more space between borders in the table. Many other styles are added to style the tables in the Web site in this chapter by using a combination of HTML5 supported attributes along with inline styles and an external style sheet.

Table 4–2 Table Properties and Values		
Property	**Description**	**Values**
border-collapse	Specifies whether or not table borders should be collapsed, i.e., if table cells should have their own border, or share a common border	**separate** collapse inherit
border-spacing	Specifies the distance between the borders of adjacent cells	**not specified** length inherit
caption-side	Specifies the placement of a table caption	**top** bottom inherit
empty-cells	Specifies whether or not to display borders and background on empty cells in a table	**show** hide inherit
table-layout	Sets the layout algorithm to be used for a table	**auto** fixed inherit

Plan Ahead

Identify the purpose of various Web page elements.

Before inserting tables or graphical elements in a Web page, you should plan how you want to use them to present the content of the page. By effectively utilizing tables and graphics, you can better organize the most important topics on the Web page. Consider the following formatting suggestions:

- **Effectively utilize graphics.** An important part of Web development is the use of graphics to call attention to a Web page. Generally, companies utilize the same logo on their Web site as they use on print material associated with the company, such as business cards and letterheads. Using the same graphical image on all marketing materials, including the Web site, is a good way to provide a consistent visual image and brand message to customers. Colorful company logos can also add an attention-grabbing element to a Web page.

- **Format tables to present Web page content.** Sometimes it is better to have no border around the table, while other times borders enhance the look of the table, depending on the content and purpose of the table. For example, when creating a table containing image links, you may not want a border to break up the images. In other cases, you may want only separators (e.g., pipe symbols) between the links to visually organize them for the viewer. In this chapter, you will use both bordered and borderless tables. Another consideration is where to place the table (left-, right-, or center-aligned).

- **Identify what links are needed.** Each Web page in a multipage Web site should have a link back to the home page of the Web site. Web developers often use the company logo to link back to the home page. In this project, the logo is also the central image of the Web pages. Because of that, a better option might be to provide a link called Home that visitors can use to return to the home page. Each Web page should include links to the other pages on the Web site. Putting these links in a table at the top of each Web page helps visitors navigate easily, and providing the navigation bar across all Web pages in the Web site is also important for consistency. Again, the purpose of providing links is to make it easy to navigate the Web site.

Creating a Home Page with Banner Logo and Borderless Navigation Table

The first Web page developed in this chapter's project is the home page of the Oceanside Hotel and Sports Club Web site. As you have learned, the home page is the main page of a Web site and is what Web site visitors generally view first. Visitors then click links to move from the home page to the other Web pages in the site. The Oceanside Hotel and Sports Club home page includes the company logo as a banner image and a borderless table that contains a navigation bar with four image links. Three of the links allow the user to navigate to other pages: the Golf Web page, the Tennis Web page, and the Dining Web page. The navigation bar also includes a link to return to the Home page. In addition to these links, the home page also provides an e-mail link, so visitors can contact Oceanside Hotel and Sports Club easily.

To Start Notepad++

The first step in creating the Oceanside Hotel and Sports Club Web site is to start Notepad++ and ensure that word wrap is enabled. The following steps, which assume Windows 7 is running, start Notepad++ based on a typical installation. You may need to ask your instructor how to start Notepad++ for your computer.

1 Click the Start button on the Windows taskbar to display the Start menu.

2 Click All Programs at the bottom of the left pane on the Start menu to display the All Programs list.

3 Click Notepad++ in the All Programs list to expand the folder.

4 Click Notepad++ in the expanded list to start the Notepad++ program.

5 If the Notepad++ window is not maximized, click the Maximize button on the Notepad++ title bar to maximize it.

6 Click View on the menu bar and verify that the Word wrap command has a check mark next to it. If it does not, click Word wrap.

To Enter Initial HTML Tags to Define the Web Page Structure

Just as you did in Chapters 2 and 3, you start your file with the initial HTML tags that define the structure of the Web page. Table 4–3 contains the tags and text for this task.

Line	HTML Tag and Text
Table 4–3 Initial HTML Tags	
1	`<!DOCTYPE HTML>`
2	
3	`<html>`
4	`<head>`
5	`<meta charset="utf-8" />`
6	`<title>Oceanside Hotel and Sports Club</title>`
7	`</head>`
8	

Table 4–3 Initial HTML Tags (continued)	
Line	**HTML Tag and Text**
9	`<body>`
10	
11	`</body>`
12	`</html>`

The following steps illustrate how to enter the initial tags that define the structure of the Web page.

① Enter the HTML code shown in Table 4–3. Press ENTER at the end of each line.

② Position the insertion point on the blank line between the <body> and </body> tags (line 10) and press the ENTER key to position the insertion point on line 11 (Figure 4–11).

③ Compare your screen with Figure 4–11 and correct any errors.

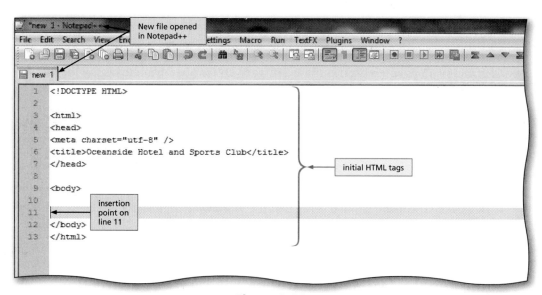

Figure 4–11

To Save an HTML File

With the initial HTML code for the Oceanside Hotel and Sports Club home page entered, you should save the file. Saving the file frequently ensures you won't lose your work. Saving a file in Notepad++ also adds color to code that can help you identify different elements more easily. The following steps save an HTML file in Notepad++.

① Click File on the menu bar, click Save, and then type `oceanside.html` in the File name text box (do not press ENTER).

② Navigate to storage device and folder (Chapter04\ChapterFiles) where you save your Data Files and then click the Save button in the Save As dialog box to save the file.

Using the Box-Shadow Property

A new property with CSS3 is the box-shadow (see Border Properties in Appendix D). The box-shadow property allows designers to easily implement multiple drop shadows (outer or inner) on box elements, specifying values for color, size, blur, and offset to a <div> element. Table 4–4 lists the values that can be used with the box-shadow property.

Table 4–4 Box-Shadow Property	
Value	**Description**
h-shadow	Required. The position of the horizontal shadow. Negative values are allowed. If positive, shadow will be on the right of the box; if negative, shadow is on the left of the box.
v-shadow	Required. The position of the vertical shadow. Negative values are allowed. If negative, shadow will be above the box; if positive, shadow is below the box.
blur	Optional. The blur distance. If set to 0 (zero), shadow will be sharp; the higher the number, the more blurred it will be.
spread	Optional. The size of shadow.
color	Optional. The color of the shadow.
insert	Optional. Changes the shadow from an outer shadow (outset) to an inner shadow.

You can use the box-shadow property to give an image a shadow. You can use an inline style within the <img> tag to set a box-shadow around the oceanside.jpg banner image as shown in Figure 4-12a on the next page. The following inline style is added to the <img> tag:

```
<img src="oceansidelogo.jpg" style="box-shadow: 10px 10px 12px
#888888" />
```

(Note: All of the <img> tags shown in this section would also include the height, width, and alt attributes for the image as per good coding standards. They are not shown here for clarity.) In the box-shadow property, the horizontal and vertical shadows are both set to 10 pixels as shown in Figure 4–12a. The blur value is set to 12 pixels, and the shadow color is set to gray (#888888). Figure 4–12b shows an example of the same code except that the horizontal and vertical shadows are set to –10 pixels each as shown below.

```
<img src="oceansidelogo.jpg" style="box-shadow: -10px -10px
12px #888888" />
```

Finally, you can also layer shadows by using multiple box-shadow values separated by a comma. When more than one shadow is specified, the shadows are layered front to back. The following code offers an example of how the box-shadow property can be customized for a unique effect as shown in Figure 4–12c.

```
<img src="oceansidelogo.jpg" style="box-shadow: 20px 20px 12px
darkgreen, -20px -20px 12px darkblue" />
```

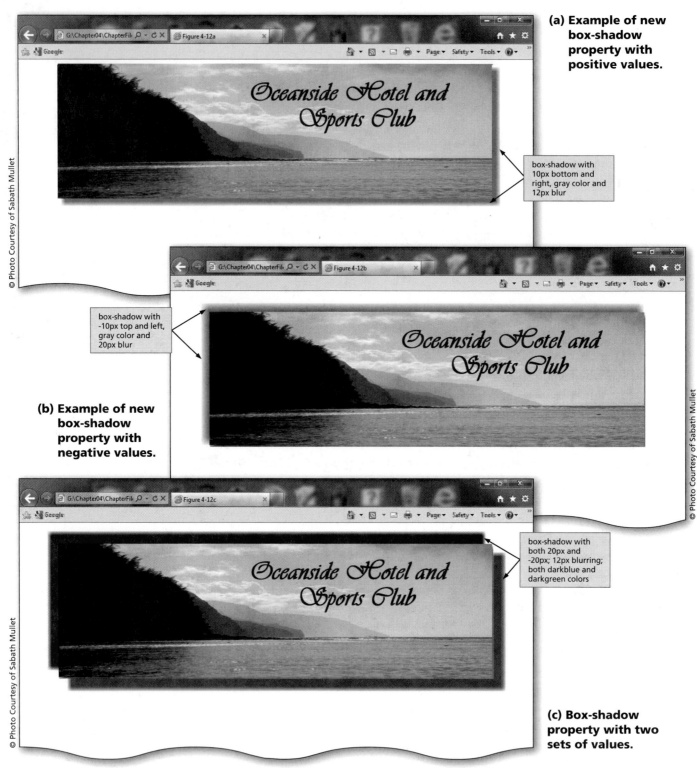

(a) Example of new box-shadow property with positive values.

box-shadow with 10px bottom and right, gray color and 12px blur

box-shadow with -10px top and left, gray color and 20px blur

(b) Example of new box-shadow property with negative values.

box-shadow with both 20px and -20px; 12px blurring; both darkblue and darkgreen colors

(c) Box-shadow property with two sets of values.

© Photo Courtesy of Sabath Mullet

© Photo Courtesy of Sabath Mullet

© Photo Courtesy of Sabath Mullet

Figure 4–12

To Insert, Center, and Style an Image with a Box-Shadow

The first task for the Oceanside Hotel and Sports Club home page is to insert the company logo banner, oceansidelogo.jpg. As stated earlier in the book, the company logo is generally used in all communication that represents the company, including on the Web site, on business cards, and on company letterheads. Table 4–5 contains the HTML code to add the centered logo banner image.

Table 4–5 HTML Code for Adding and Centering an Image

Line	HTML Tag and Text
11	`<div style="text-align: center">`
12	`<img src="oceansidelogo.jpg" width="866" height="259" alt="Oceanside logo" style="box-shadow: 10px 10px 12px #888888" />`
13	`</div>`

The following step shows how to add a centered banner image.

1

- With the insertion point on line 11, enter the HTML code shown in Table 4–5, pressing ENTER at the end of each line. Make sure to indent the second line of code by using the TAB key. This separates the start and end <div> tag from the <img> tag, highlighting the image insertion. Press the ENTER key twice at the end of line 13 to position the insertion point on line 15 (Figure 4–13).

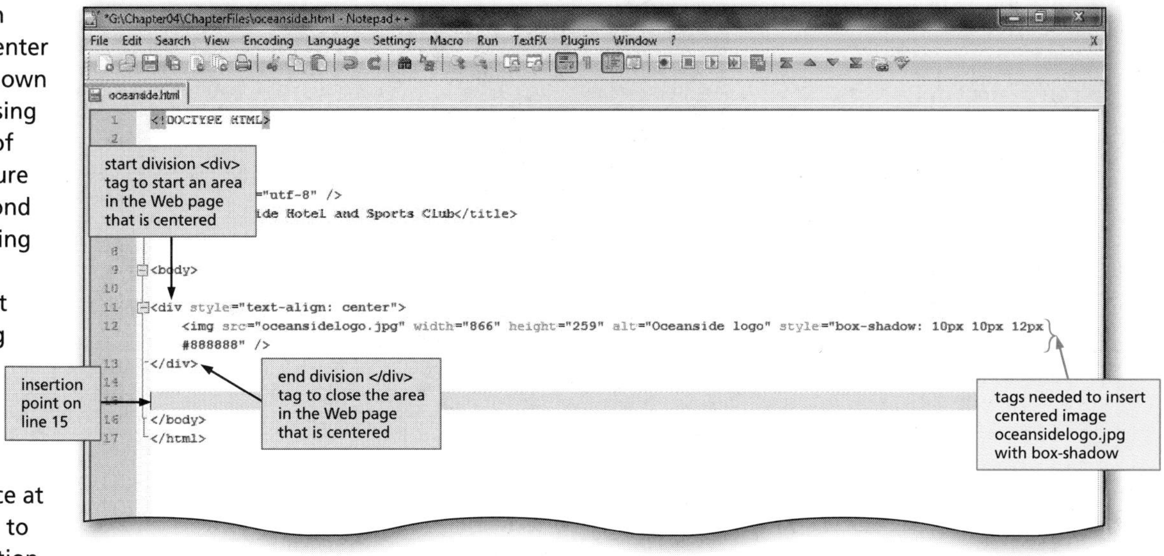

start division <div> tag to start an area in the Web page that is centered

insertion point on line 15

end division </div> tag to close the area in the Web page that is centered

tags needed to insert centered image oceansidelogo.jpg with box-shadow

Figure 4–13

Q&A When I pressed ENTER at the end of line 12, Notepad++ indented line 13 also. How do I remove the indent?

You have to press the left arrow key or Backspace to get back to the left margin before you insert the </div> tag.

Q&A How can I determine the height and width of an image?

There are several ways to determine the height and width of an image. The first way is to click on the image in Windows Explorer; the height and width display in the status bar. Another way is to right-click the image in Windows Explorer, select Properties, and display the Details tab. A third way is to open the image in a paint or image-editing program and view the dimensions in the status bar or via a command in the program. Although you can adjust the width and height by using the width and height attributes in the <img> tag, doing so might cause the image to look distorted on the Web page.

Using a Table to Create a Horizontal Navigation Bar

The Web site created in this project consists of four Web pages. Visitors should be able to move easily from one Web page to any of the other three Web pages. Providing a navigation bar prominently across the top of the Web page (Figure 4–14) gives the visitor ready access to navigation links. You will create a table to hold the navigation bar links.

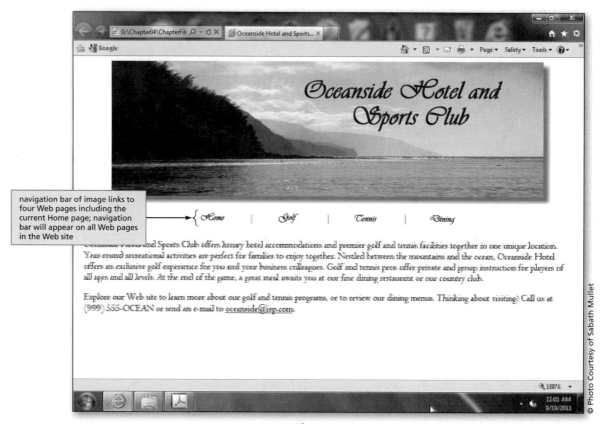

navigation bar of image links to four Web pages including the current Home page; navigation bar will appear on all Web pages in the Web site

Figure 4–14

BTW

Navigation
Studies have been conducted to assess the best location on a Web page to place navigation bars and lists. The research results are varied, with indications that navigation options on the top, side, and bottom of a Web page show slight differences in visitor usability. The most important aspect of Web page navigation is to make the options easy enough to locate so visitors do not have to search for them.

All of the styles for this and other tables are set in the external style sheet that you will create in the next section of this chapter. The horizontal navigation bar table is borderless (the border-style is set to "none"), and has one row and seven columns (each of the four link options is in a column, as is each of the three dividers). To better align the navigation bar with the Oceanside Hotel and Sports Club logo, the table is set to 60% of the window's width, so that it is not as wide as the logo. The navigation bar has four links — Home, Golf, Tennis, and Dining — that link to the Web pages oceanside.html, golf.html, tennis.html, and dining.html, respectively. Each link has its own image file, including home.gif, golf.gif, tennis.gif, and dining.gif. Each link image is inserted in a single column (cell). The | (pipe) symbol is included in a column between each of the four links to separate them visually. Although you could have used plain text for these links, using images allows you to create a consistent visitor experience across all browsers, regardless of whether a visitor has the Vivaldi font installed. The link images were created using a simple paint program. All four images are equal in size and utilize the same font family (Vivaldi) as shown in the logo.

The width of each column (cell) in the table is specified as a class in the external style sheet, which will be linked to the home page and all other Web pages in this Web site later in the chapter. (If you do not define the width for these cells, the width defaults to the size of the word, image, or symbol in the cell.) The menuicon and menupipe classes need to be inserted in the navigation bar in order to adopt the styles as defined in the external style sheet. The class menuicon will be used to set each of the cells in which there are images to 23% of the width of the table. The menupipe class will be used to set each of the cells in which there are pipe symbols to 1% of the size of the table. When you specify sizes in percentages, it is generally best not to set the width to 100% as it will fill the entire width of the browser window.

Just as you did in Chapter 3, you will add the class names to your Web pages before you create the classes, in this case, in the external style sheet. All navigation bar styles are controlled with the external style sheet. If you didn't use an external style sheet, you would have to type each style into each navigation bar on each Web page in the Web site. The advantage of using an external (linked) style sheet is that if you need to make a change across the entire Web site, you make that change only once — in the external style sheet. The change then takes effect in every Web page into which the external (linked) style sheet has been linked. Using an external style sheet, you will create the .css file once and link it with one line of code into each Web page.

To Create a Horizontal Menu Bar with Image Links

Table 4–6 shows the HTML code for the horizontal navigation bar table.

Table 4–6 HTML Code to Insert a Menu Bar

Line	HTML Tag and Text
15	` <table class="menu" style="border-style: none">`
16	`<tr>`
17	`<td class="menuicon"><a href="oceanside.html"><img src="home.gif" width="50" height="21" alt="Home" /></a></td>`
18	`<td class="menupipe">|</td>`
19	`<td class="menuicon"><a href="golf.html"><img src="golf.gif" width="50" height="21" alt="Golf" /></a></td>`
20	`<td class="menupipe">|</td>`
21	`<td class="menuicon"><a href="tennis.html"><img src="tennis.gif" width="50" height="21" alt="Tennis" /></a></td>`
22	`<td class="menupipe">|</td>`
23	`<td class="menuicon"><a href="dining.html"><img src="dining.gif" width="50" height="21" alt="Dining" /></a></td>`
24	`</tr>`
25	`</table>`

The following step shows how to create a table that contains image links to four pages on the Web site, separated by pipe symbols. The pipe symbol is usually found above the ENTER key; it is inserted when you press Shift and the \ (backslash) key.

1

- With the insertion point on line 15, enter the HTML code, as shown in Table 4–6, pressing ENTER after each line. Use the TAB key to indent the code, as shown in the table. Press the ENTER key once more after line 26 (Figure 4–15) to position the insertion point on line 27.

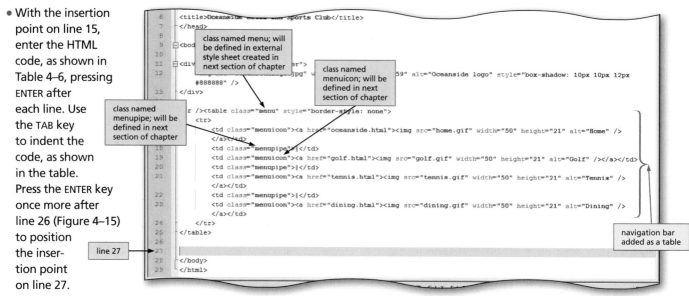

Figure 4–15

Q&A Why indent my code with the TAB key?

Indenting is a good way to organize your code so sections are recognizable. You can immediately see what lines of code are related to a single row in the table, as contained within the indented <tr> </tr> tags. This is helpful when you have many rows in the table, as in the dining.html file, which you will encounter later in the chapter.

To Add Paragraphs of Text

Next, two paragraphs of text must be added to the Web page. The text is displayed beneath the navigation bar of links that you just inserted. You will use a paragraph <p> tag to insert a blank line between the navigation bar and the text. Table 4–7 contains the code to add the paragraphs of text. In line 29, you will enter an inline style in the <span> tag to set the link text-decoration to underline. Although links appear as underlined text by default, you will set text-decoration to none for all links when you create the external style sheet in the next section. The inline style inserted on line 29 overrides that external style sheet link style and sets just this e-mail link to be underlined.

Table 4–7 HTML Code to Add Paragraphs of Text

Line	HTML Tag and Text
27	`<p>Oceanside Hotel and Sports Club offers luxury hotel accommodations and premiere golf and tennis facilities together in one unique location. Year-round recreational activities are perfect for families to enjoy together. Nestled between the mountains and the ocean, Oceanside Hotel offers an exclusive golf experience for you and your business colleagues. Golf and tennis pros offer private and group instruction for players of all ages and all levels. At the end of the game, a great meal awaits you at our fine dining restaurant or our country club.</p>`
28	
29	`<p>Explore our Web site to learn more about our golf and tennis programs, or to review our dining menus. Thinking about visiting? Call us at (999) 555-OCEAN or send an e-mail to <a href="mailto:oceanside@isp.com"><span style="text-decoration: underline">oceanside@isp.com</span></a>.</p>`

The following step illustrates how to add paragraphs of text.

1 With the insertion point on line 27, enter the HTML code, as shown in Table 4–7, to insert the paragraphs of text, pressing the ENTER key after each line, including line 29 (Figure 4–16).

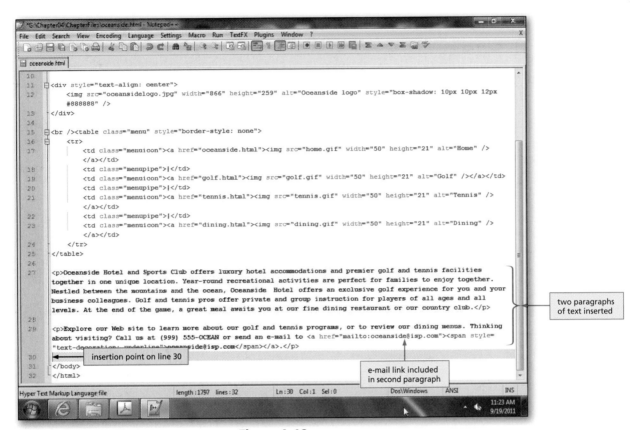

Figure 4–16

To Save the HTML File

With the HTML code for the Oceanside Hotel and Sports Club home page complete, you should resave the file. The following step shows how to save an HTML file that has been previously saved.

1 Click the Save icon on the Notepad++ toolbar to save the most recent version of oceanside.html on the same storage device and in the same folder as the last time you saved it (Figure 4–17).

Save icon

G:\Chapter04\ChapterFiles\oceanside.html - Notepad++

File Edit Search View Encoding Language Settings Macro Run TextFX Plugins Window ?

oceanside.html
filename inserted

oceanside.html

```
10
11      <div style="text-align: center">
12          <img src="oceansidelogo.jpg" width="866" height="259" alt="Oceanside logo" style="box-shadow: 10px 10px 12px
            #888888" />
13      </div>
14
15  <br /><table class="menu" style="border-style: none">
16          <tr>
17              <td class="menuicon"><a href="oceanside.html"><img src="home.gif" width="50" height="21" alt="Home" />
                </a></td>
18              <td class="menupipe">|</td>
19              <td class="menuicon"><a href="golf.html"><img src="golf.gif" width="50" height="21" alt="Golf" /></a></td>
20              <td class="menupipe">|</td>
21              <td class="menuicon"><a href="tennis.html"><img src="tennis.gif" width="50" height="21" alt="Tennis" />
                </a></td>
22              <td class="menupipe">|</td>
23              <td class="menuicon"><a href="dining.html"><img src="dining.gif" width="50" height="21" alt="Dining" />
                </a></td>
24          </tr>
```

Figure 4–17

Viewing the Web Page and Testing Links

After you save the HTML file for the Oceanside Hotel and Sports Club home page, it should be viewed in a browser to confirm the Web page appears as desired. You do not validate or print the Web page yet because you still have one statement (the link to the external style sheet) to add to the file. It is also important to test the four links on the Oceanside Hotel and Sports Club home page to verify they function as expected.

To View a Web Page

The following steps illustrate how to view the HTML file in a browser.

1 In Internet Explorer, click the Address bar to select the URL on the Address bar.

2 Type G:\Chapter04\ChapterFiles\oceanside.html or the location of your file on the Address bar of your browser and press ENTER to display the Web page (Figure 4–18).

Web page as completed thus far without any styles added

inserted company logo image with box-shadow

Oceanside Hotel and Sports Club

navigation bar left-aligned with text decoration (bordered image links)

Home | Golf | Tennis | Dining

two paragraphs of text in normal font displayed in 100% (default) of window

Oceanside Hotel and Sports Club offers luxury hotel accommodations and premier golf and tennis facilities together in one unique location. Year-round recreational activities are perfect for families to enjoy together. Nestled between the mountains and the ocean, Oceanside Hotel offers an exclusive golf experience for you and your business colleagues. Golf and tennis pros offer private and group instruction for players of all ages and all levels. At the end of the game, a great meal awaits you at our fine dining restaurant or our country club.

Explore our Web site to learn more about our golf and tennis programs, or to review our dining menus. Thinking about visiting? Call us at (999) 555-
mail to oceanside@isp.com

© Photo Courtesy of Sabath Mullet

Figure 4–18

To Test Links on a Web Page

The following steps show how to test the links on the Oceanside Hotel and Sports Club home page to verify that they work correctly.

1 With the Oceanside Hotel and Sports Club's home page displayed in the browser, point to the e-mail link, oceanside@isp.com and click the link to open the default e-mail program with the address oceanside@isp.com in the To: text box.

2 Click the Close button in the new message window. If a dialog box asks if you want to save changes, click No.

3 With the USB flash drive in drive G, click the Tennis link from the home page just created. Click Home to return to the home page from the Tennis page. Next, click the Dining link from the Home page. Click Home to return to the home page from the Dining page. The link for the Golf page will not work because that Web page is not yet created; you will create it later in this chapter. The links work on the Tennis and Dining Web pages as those pages were supplied in the Data Files with the navigation already coded.

External Style Sheets

External style sheets are the most comprehensive type of style sheet and can be used to control the consistency and look of many Web pages within a Web site. Adding an external style sheet to a Web page involves a two-step process of creating an external style sheet and then linking this style sheet to the desired Web pages. The most beneficial feature of the external style sheet is that you can easily change the style (appearance) of all Web pages into which the style sheet is linked just by changing the external style sheet. For instance, the font-family and font-size for all four Web pages in this chapter's project are set in the external style sheet. If the owners of the Web site decide that they do not like the look (or style) of that font-family or font-size, you only have to make the change in one file — the external style sheet. Compare that process to having the font-family and font-size inserted into every single Web page in a Web site either with embedded style sheets or (worst case) inline styles. To make a change to all font-family and font-size styles, you would have to change those in every single place that the styles reside. External (linked) style sheets are the most efficient and powerful way to change styles for an entire Web site.

An external style sheet is a text file that contains the selectors and declarations for the styles you want to apply across the Web site. The sample code that follows shows an example of an external style sheet used to set table, paragraph, image, and link formatting. Note the use of classes (e.g., menu, menuicon, menupipe) in this external style sheet that provides a finer level of control within a table used for navigation.

```
body        {font-family: Centaur, "Century Gothic", Arial;
             font-size: 14pt;}
p           {margin-left: 10pt;
             margin-right: 10pt;}
a           {text-decoration: none;
             color: black;}
img         {border-color: transparent;}
```

BTW

Classes
Note that the classes are named with a period (.) after the element is defined. Thus, the table .menu statement identifies a class named menu that will be used with the table elements.

```
table        {width: 65%;

             margin-left:auto;

             margin-right:auto;

             border-color: #545859;

             border-style: ridge;

             border-width: 10px;}

             .menu    {text-align: center;

                      width: 60%;}

             .menuicon  {width: 23%;}

             .menupipe  {width: 1%;}

th           {color: white;

             background-color: #757775;}

tr.stripe    {background-color: #d8d8ce;}

td.bolder    {font-weight: bold;}

caption      {caption-side: bottom;

             font-style: italic;}
```

The format of the external style sheet is very similar to the format of an embedded style sheet. An external style sheet, however, does not need <style> </style> tags to start and end the style sheet; it only needs the style statements.

To create an external style sheet, enter all of the style statements in a text file using Notepad++ or another text editor, and then save the text file with a .css (for Cascading Style Sheets) extension. The code shown above, for example, can be saved with the file-name stylesch4.css and then linked onto multiple Web pages.

Remember that the <head> tag is used for a variety of purposes. The information contained within the <head> </head> container of your HTML document provides information to browsers and search engines but is not displayed on the Web page itself. The following tags can be used within the <head> </head> container: <base>, <link>, <meta>, <script>, <style>, and <title>. For each Web page to which you want to apply the styles in an external style sheet, a <link /> tag similar to the sample code below must be inserted within the <head> </head> tags of the Web page:

```
<link rel="stylesheet" type="text/css" href="stylesch4.css" />
```

The <link /> tag indicates that the style sheet stylesch4.css should be applied to this Web page. The property-value statement rel="stylesheet" defines the relationship of the linked document (that is, it defines it as a style sheet). The property-value statement type="text/css" indicates the content and language used in the linked document. The property-value statement href="stylesch4.css" indicates the name and location of the linked style sheet, stylesch4.css. To apply this style sheet to other pages in the Web site, you would insert the same <link /> tag between the <head> </head> tags of each Web page.

**Plan
Ahead**

Determine what type of style sheets or other formatting to use in your Web pages.

- **Determine which styles will be common across the Web pages in the Web site.** Web sites should strive for a consistent experience across all pages. For instance, if tables are used, the style of the tables should be common or consistent throughout the Web site. A font-family style is also something that is generally common across all Web pages in a Web site. Consider using external (or linked) style sheets for styles that will encompass all Web pages in a multipage Web site. Because it is a four-page Web site, the project in this chapter is a perfect application for external (or linked) style sheets. You will use an external style sheet in this project to set styles for the body, paragraphs, links, images, and tables. *(Note: Although it is important to maintain consistency across a Web site, the three tables created in the Web pages in this project will all be different, so that you will learn different table techniques.)*

- **Identify elements that need to differ from the style used across the Web site.**

  - Consider using embedded style sheets for Web pages in which the styles apply only to one particular Web page. You can use embedded style sheets when you want elements within one Web page to look similar to one another. In the projects in this chapter, however, you do not use embedded style sheets.

  - Consider using inline styles for any style that is unique for a single element, such as when you want one word or paragraph on one Web page to look different than all others. In this project, you will use inline styles to align images and vary some text.

Adding an External Style Sheet

The next step is to create an external style sheet (.css file) and link it to the Web pages where it will be used. The external (linked) style sheet will set the style for body text, paragraphs, links, images, and table format.

Because the font-family and font-size style is used for all text on all Web pages, you can put that style in the body element, identified on the external style sheet as body. All links (identified using the a tag in the external style sheet) will be black through all states (normal, visited, and active) and use no text decoration (i.e., the text links will not be underlined). Note that you overrode this style on the home page by adding an inline style to the e-mail address link. Your inline style adds underlining to the e-mail link. Most of the tables will have a 65% width relative to the window. The exception is the navigation bar table that you created earlier, which will be slightly smaller (60% width). Finally, you will use classes, as discussed in Chapter 3, to have more control over particular elements of the tables in the Web site. You will use a class named menu for the navigation bar links. You also want to separate the navigation bar table cells with pipe symbols. To do that, you will use classes named menuicon and menupipe to specify the width of each of those cells. Note that the classes are named with a period (.) after the element is defined. Thus, the table.menu statement identifies a class named menu that will be used with the table elements.

BTW

Adding Comments
If your instructor wants you to add your name to the CSS code file, you can do that by adding your name within a comment line. Use /* and */ to surround the added information (e.g., your name), marking it as a comment.

**Plan
Ahead**

Create and link an external style sheet.
The external style sheet is the most powerful style sheet and has the lowest precedence. You can easily create a common look across a Web site by creating an external (.css) style sheet and linking it to all Web pages.

- **Create the .css file.** The first step is to create the external style sheet itself. This file, which contains all of the style statements that you want, has to be saved with a filename extension of .css. Make sure to store this file in the same folder as the other Web pages.

- **Link the external style sheet onto the Web pages.** The second step is to link the external style sheet (.css file) onto the Web pages where you want the styles to be applied. The link statement is placed between the <head> and </head> tags.

To Create an External Style Sheet

Table 4–8 shows the style statements for an external style sheet for the Oceanside Hotel and Sports Club Web site. To create an external style sheet, you will open a new text file and enter the CSS code for the style statements that define the Web page style. After coding the style statements, you will save the file with the file extension .css to identify it as a CSS file.

Table 4–8 Code for an External Style Sheet	
Line	**CSS Properties and Values**
1	body {font-family: Centaur, "Century Gothic", Arial;
2	font-size: 14 pt;}
3	
4	p {margin-left: 10pt;
5	margin-right: 10pt;}
6	
7	a {text-decoration: none;
8	color: black;}
9	
10	img {border-color: transparent;}
11	
12	table {width: 65%;
13	margin-left: auto;
14	margin-right: auto;
15	border-color: #545859;
16	border-style: ridge;
17	border-width: 10px;}
18	
19	.menu {text-align: center;
20	width: 60%;}
21	
22	.menuicon {width: 23%;}
23	
24	.menupipe {width: 1%;}
25	
26	th {color: white;
27	background-color: #757775;}
28	
29	tr.stripe {background-color: #d8d8ce;}
30	
31	td.bolder {font-weight: bold;}
32	
33	caption {caption-side: bottom;
34	font-style: italic;}

The following steps illustrate how to create, save, and validate an external style sheet. You must use a different w3.org validation service to validate a .css file. You will use jigsaw.w3.org/css-validator/#validate_by_upload for the .css file type. The validation result page looks very similar to the ones you saw in the HTML validation process.

1

- If necessary, click the Notepad++ button on the taskbar to display oceanside.html. Click File on the navigation bar and then click New.

- Enter the CSS code, as shown in Table 4–8, using the TAB key to align text, as shown (Figure 4–19).

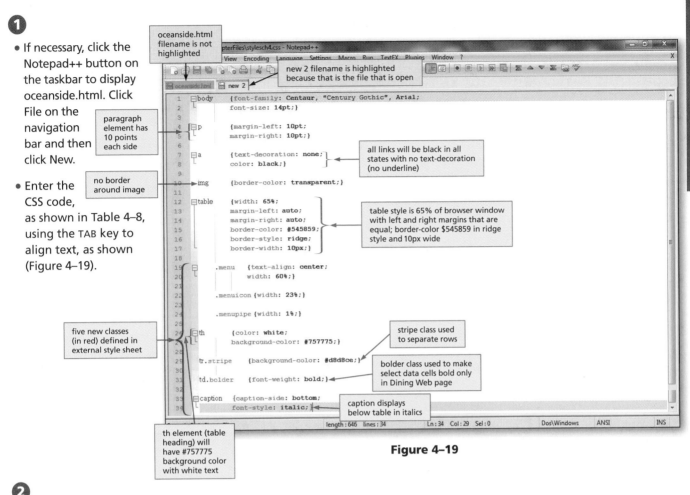

Figure 4–19

2

- With the USB drive plugged into your computer, click File on the menu bar and then click Save As. Type `stylesch4.css` in the File name text box. If necessary, navigate to the G:\Chapter04\ChapterFiles folder. Click the Save button in the Save As dialog box to save the file as stylesch4.css.

- Open Internet Explorer and navigate to jigsaw.w3.org/css-validator/#validate_by_upload.

- Validate the stylesch4.css file.

- Return to the stylesch4.css Notepad++ file and print a hard copy of the style sheet (Figure 4–20).

```
body{font-family: Centaur, "Century Gothic", Arial;
        font-size: 14pt;}

p       {margin-left: 10pt;
        margin-right: 10pt;}

a       {text-decoration: none;
        color: black;}

img     {border-color: transparent;}

table{width: 65%;
        margin-left: auto;
        margin-right: auto;
        border-color: #545859;
        border-style: ridge;
        border-width: 10px;}

    .menu   {text-align: center;
            width: 60%;}

    .menuicon {width: 23%;}

    .menupipe {width: 1%;}

    th      {color: white;
            background-color: #757775;}
```

Figure 4–20

Examining the External Style Sheet

Because the CSS code for the external style sheet is complex, a review is necessary to learn what it does. The CSS code that you entered, which is shown in Table 4-8 on page HTML 180 defines a new style for five main elements on a Web page: body, paragraphs, links, images, and tables. It is a good idea (but not a requirement) to insert your styles in order in the external style sheet.

The first style statement on lines 1 and 2 is entered as:

```
body    {font-family: Centaur, "Century Gothic", Arial;
        font-size: 14pt;}
```

to change the font-family and font-size for the text throughout the Web site. You use the body element because you want these styles to apply to text across the Web site (Figure 4-19). If you wanted to apply one font-family or font-size to paragraphs of text and another font-family and font-size to the text in links, you would use the paragraph (p) and link (a) elements rather than body to create those styles. This project uses three different font-family styles (Centaur, Century Gothic, and Arial) just in case the computer on which the Web page is viewed does not have the first (Centaur) or second (Century Gothic) font-family. If the computer does not have any of the three font-families, then the normal (default browser) font-family is used.

The next styles are applied to the paragraph (p) element on lines 4 and 5:

```
p       {margin-left: 10pt;
        margin-right: 10pt;}
```

With this style, you are adding right and left margins that are 10 points wide. This pulls the paragraph text in 10 points both from the left and right. To see what that style statement does to the look of the home page for this Web site, look at Figure 4–18 on page HTML 176 compared to Figure 4–1a on page HTML 155.

Lines 7 and 8 define the styles for all links by using the link (a) element:

```
a       {text-decoration: none;
        color: black;}
```

Colors
To find the exact color, you can open the logo in a graphic image editing program and use one of the tools (such as the eye dropper tool) to click on the logo itself. If you then look at the color box, you should see the six-digit hexadecimal code for that color.

This statement sets links to have no text-decoration (no underlines) and makes all link states (normal, visited, and active) black in color. With a text-decoration setting of none, the browser will not display lines under any links. Setting the link color to black throughout eliminates the blue and purple (normal and visited) link colors that you would normally have. The next statement, on line 10 in the external style sheet, sets the border color of the image tag to transparent. With that setting, no border will display around any images.

```
img     {border-color: transparent;}
```

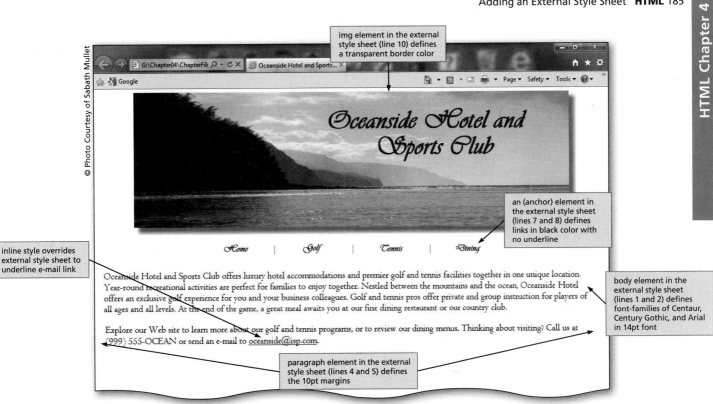

Figure 4–21

In this external style sheet, all table-related styles are inserted together from lines 12 through 34:

table	{width: 65%;
	margin-left: auto;
	margin-right: auto;
	border-color: #545859;
	border-style: ridge;
	border-width: 10px;}
.menu	{text-align: center; width: 60%;}
.menuicon	{width: 23%;}
.menupipe	{width: 1%;}
th	{color: white;
	background-color: #757775;}
tr.stripe	{background-color: #d8d8ce;}
td.bolder	{font-weight: bold;}
caption	{caption-side: bottom;
	font-style: italic;}

Lines 12 through 17 identify the general style for all tables on the Web pages. The width of all tables (with the exception of the navigation bar) will be 65% of the browser window. You control the width of the navigation bar table separately by naming a class called menu (remember this can be any arbitrary name). The margin: auto statements horizontally center the element table with respect to the edges of the window. The values used for each side are equal because of the auto designator. You also set the table border color to #545859, with a ridge style and a width of 10 pixels.

On lines 19 through 24, beneath the table element, are three named classes: menu, menuicon, and menupipe. Those lines are indented so that you can easily see that these classes are related to the table element. On line 20, the width of the menu class is designated to be 60% of the browser window, instead of the 65% width of all the other tables. Line 19 tells the browser to center the navigation image links (Home, Golf, Tennis, and Dining) within the cells of the table instead of the default setting of left-alignment. See the differences created by these styles in Figure 4–22.

The menuicon class sets the width of that column to 23%. The menupipe class sets the column containing the pipe symbol to 1%. You can utilize these classes (menu, menuicon, and menupipe) with the HTML code that you just typed in the oceanside.html file.

In lines 26 and 27, you identify styles for all table headers (<th>) and rows (<tr>). You designate a background color of #757775 (which is a dark gray) with text color that is white. Line 29 creates a table row class named stripe. That will be used to set every other row to a light gray color to distinguish them from the rows that are default white in color (Figure 4–22). Line 31 creates a table data cell named bolder that is used in the Dining Web page as shown in Figure 4-1d on page HTML 155.

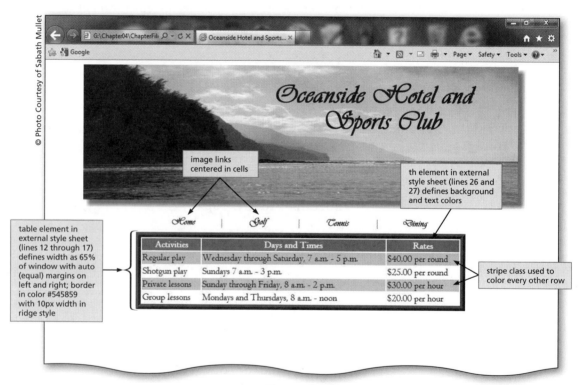

Figure 4–22

The final section of CSS code, lines 33 and 34, defines the styles to be applied to table captions. You want all captions to be aligned beneath the table and italicized.

Linking to the External Style Sheet

Four Web pages in the Oceanside Hotel and Sports Club Web site require the same style: oceanside.html, golf.html, tennis.html, and dining.html. Linking the external style sheet to each of these Web pages gives them the same styles for margins, paragraph text, links, images, and tables.

To link to the external style sheet, a <link /> tag must be inserted onto each of these four Web pages. The <link /> tag used to link an external style sheet is added within the <head> </head> tags of the Web page HTML code. The general format of the <link /> tag is:

```
<link rel="stylesheet" type="text/css" href="stylesch4.css" />
```

where rel="stylesheet" establishes that the linked document is a style sheet, type="text/css" indicates that the CSS language is used in the text file containing the style sheet, and href="stylesch4.css" provides the name and location (URL) of the linked style sheet. To link a style sheet to a Web page, the <link /> tag must use "stylesheet" as the value for the rel property and text/css as the value for the type property. The URL used as the value for the href property varies, based on the name and location of the file used as the external style sheet. The URL used here indicates that the external style sheet, stylesch4.css, is located in the main or root directory of the Web site.

To Link to an External Style Sheet

After creating and saving the external style sheet, .css file, you use a <link /> tag to link the external style sheet to any Web pages to which you want to apply the style. Notice that the link tag is one of those (like the <img /> tag) that does not have a separate end tag (e.g., <body> and </body>). You therefore should use the / after a space and before the > in the tag to indicate the end of the tag.

The following step illustrates how to add a link to an external style sheet using a <link /> tag:

1

- Click the oceanside .html tab in Notepad++ to make it the active window.

- With the oceanside .html file open, click the end of line 6 after the > and press the ENTER key twice. Your insertion point should be positioned on line 8.

- Type <link rel="stylesheet" type="text/css" href="stylesch4 .css" /> as the HTML code and then press the ENTER key, as shown in Figure 4–23.

- Click the Save button on the Notepad++ toolbar.

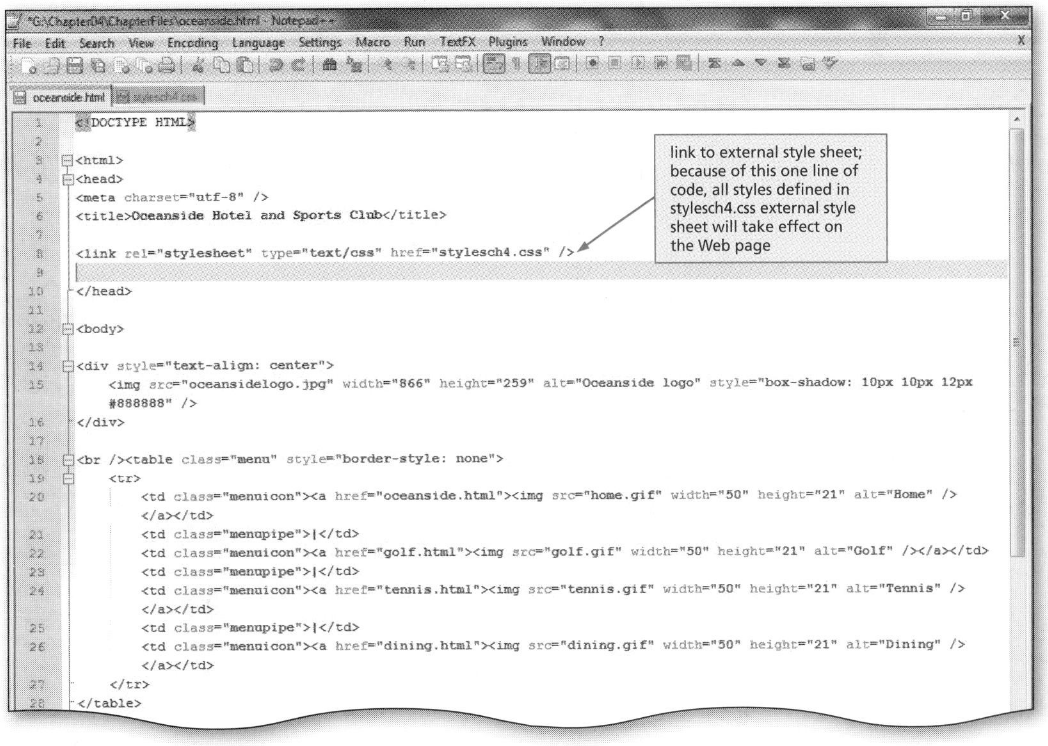

Figure 4–23

Is that all it takes to use an external style sheet — to insert that link statement?

Yes, that is all you need to do to use the styles identified in the external style sheet. The styles specified in the external style sheet will apply to that page, unless an embedded or inline style sheet takes precedence. Also remember that if you want to change a style, you just change it in the external (linked) style sheet itself. It automatically takes effect in any Web page that is linked to the external style sheet. (Remember to click the Refresh button if that Web page is already open in the browser.)

Will the table styles from the stylesch4.css file take effect for all tables within the Web site?

As long as you insert the style sheet link statement onto the Web page, then the table styles will take effect. Remember that you can override those styles with either an embedded or an inline style sheet. You would do this if there is a table that you want to vary from all other tables in the Web site.

Why is an external style sheet sometimes called a linked style sheet?

The style sheet that you created above is external to (as opposed to inline or embedded in) the Web page in which it is used. That's why it is called an external style sheet. The external style sheet is used by linking it into a Web page. It is called linked because you use a <link /> tag to insert it.

Validating and Printing the HTML, Viewing the Web Page, and Testing Links

After you save the HTML file for the Oceanside Hotel and Sports Club home page, it should be validated to ensure that it meets the current standards applied throughout this text and viewed in a browser to confirm the Web page displays as desired. It is also important to test the links in the Oceanside Hotel and Sports Club home page to verify that they function as expected.

To Validate a Web Page

The following steps illustrate how to validate an HTML file:

1 Open Internet Explorer and navigate to the Web site validator.w3.org.

2 Click the Validate by File Upload tab.

3 Click the Browse button.

4 Locate the oceanside.html file on your storage device, click the filename, and then click the Open button in the Choose File to Upload dialog box and the filename will be inserted into the File box.

5 Click the Check button.

What if my HTML code does not pass the validation process?

If your file does not pass validation, make changes to the file to correct your errors. You should then revalidate the file.

To Print an HTML File

After your HTML code has passed validation, it is a good idea to make a hard copy printout of it.

1 Click the Notepad++ button on the taskbar to activate the Notepad++ window.

2 Click File on the menu bar, click the Print command, and then click the Print button to print a hard copy of the HTML code (Figure 4–24).

```html
<!DOCTYPE HTML>

<html>
<head>
<meta charset="utf-8" />
<title>Oceanside Hotel and Sports Club</title>

<link rel="stylesheet" type="text/css" href="stylesch4.css" />

</head>

<body>

<div style="text-align: center">
    <img src="oceansidelogo.jpg" width="866" height="259" alt="Oceanside logo" style=
    "box-shadow: 10px 10px 12px #888888" />
</div>

<br /><table class="menu" style="border-style: none">
    <tr>
        <td class="menuicon"><a href="oceanside.html"><img src="home.gif" width="50"
        height="21" alt="Home" /></a></td>
        <td class="menupipe">|</td>
        <td class="menuicon"><a href="golf.html"><img src="golf.gif" width="50" height=
        "21" alt="Golf" /></a></td>
        <td class="menupipe">|</td>
        <td class="menuicon"><a href="tennis.html"><img src="tennis.gif" width="50"
        height="21" alt="Tennis" /></a></td>
        <td class="menupipe">|</td>
        <td class="menuicon"><a href="dining.html"><img src="dining.gif" width="50"
        height="21" alt="Dining" /></a></td>
    </tr>
</table>

<p>Oceanside Hotel and Sports Club offers luxury hotel accommodations and premier golf
and tennis facilities together in one unique location. Year-round recreational
activities are perfect for families to enjoy together. Nestled between the mountains
and the ocean, Oceanside Hotel offers an exclusive golf experience for you and your
business colleagues. Golf and tennis pros offer private and group instruction for
players of all ages and all levels. At the end of the game, a great meal awaits you at
our fine dining restaurant or our country club.</p>

<p>Explore our Web site to learn more about our golf and tennis programs, or to review
our dining menus. Thinking about visiting? Call us at (999) 555-OCEAN or send an e-mail
to <a href="mailto:oceanside@isp.com"><span style="text-decoration: underline">
oceanside@isp.com</span></a>.</p>

</body>
</html>
```

Figure 4–24

To View, Test, and Print a Web Page

① Click the Internet Explorer button on the Windows taskbar to activate Internet Explorer.

② In Internet Explorer, click the Address bar to select the URL in the Address bar.

③ Type G:\Chapter04\ChapterFiles\oceanside.html (or the specific path to your file) to display the new URL in the Address bar and then press the ENTER key.

④ Click the Tennis link and then click the Back button. Click the Dining link and then click the Back button.

Q&A Why isn't the Tennis Web page formatted with the styles in the external style sheet?
In order for the external style sheet to take effect, you have to insert the <link> statement into the HTML code in the Tennis file.

⑤ Click the Print button on the Internet Explorer Command bar to print the Web page (Figure 4–25).

Figure 4–25

© Photo Courtesy of Sabath Mullet

Creating a Second Web Page

You have created the Oceanside Hotel and Sports Club home page with a horizontal navigation bar of image links for easy navigation to other pages in the site and an external style sheet. Now it is time to create one of those linked pages — the Golf page (Figure 4–26 on the next page). Like the home page, the Golf page includes the logo image and a horizontal navigation bar of text links. Having the Oceanside Hotel and Sports Club logo and the horizontal navigation bar at the top of each page provides consistency throughout the Web site. The navigation bar lists the four Web pages — Home, Golf, Tennis, and Dining — with a | (pipe) symbol between links. Beneath the navigation bar is a table listing the golf options that are available at Oceanside Hotel and Sports Club.

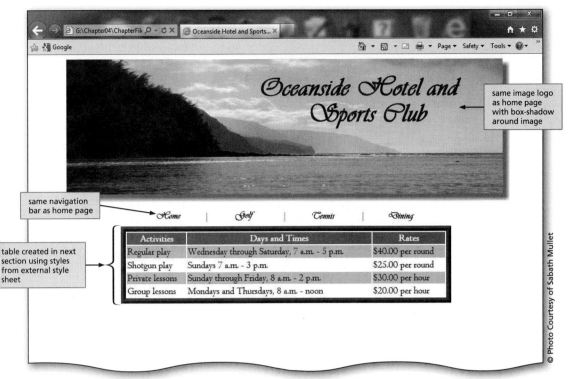

same image logo as home page with box-shadow around image

same navigation bar as home page

table created in next section using styles from external style sheet

© Photo Courtesy of Sabath Mullet

Figure 4–26

The first step in creating the Golf Web page is to add the HTML tags to define the Web page structure, the Oceanside Hotel and Sports Club logo banner image, and the horizontal navigation bar. Because the logo banner image and navigation bar are the same as on the home page, you can copy and paste HTML code from the Home page and then edit it for the Golf page. You would copy/paste this code because you have already tested it by opening the oceanside.html file in the browser, and you know the code works. Rather than retyping the code, and possibly getting errors, a copy/paste will assure that it is correct.

To Copy and Paste HTML Code to a New File

The following steps show how to copy the HTML tags to define the Web page structure and the horizontal menu table from the HTML file, oceanside.html, to a new HTML file.

1 If necessary, click the Notepad++ button on the taskbar and click the oceanside.html tab to make it the active window.

2 Click immediately to the left of the < in the <!DOCTYPE> html tag on line 1.

3 Drag through the </table> tag on line 28 to highlight lines 1 through 28.

4 Press CTRL+C to copy the selected lines to the Clipboard.

5 Click File on the Notepad++ menu bar and then click New.

6 Press CTRL+V to paste the contents from the Clipboard into a new file. Press the ENTER key twice to position the insertion point on line 30.

7 After the words Oceanside Hotel and Sports Club in the <title> on line 6, add ~ Golf (using the tilde ~ character).

To Save an HTML File

With the HTML code for the structure code and menu table added, the golf.html file should be saved. For this Web page, the end body </body> and end HTML </html> tags will be added later.

1 With a USB drive plugged into the computer, click File on the menu bar and then click Save As. Type `golf.html` in the File name text box.

2 If necessary, click USB (G:) (or the drive where you store your data files) in the Save in list. Double-click the Chapter04 folder and then double-click the ChapterFiles folder in the list of available folders. Click the Save button in the Save As dialog box (Figure 4–27).

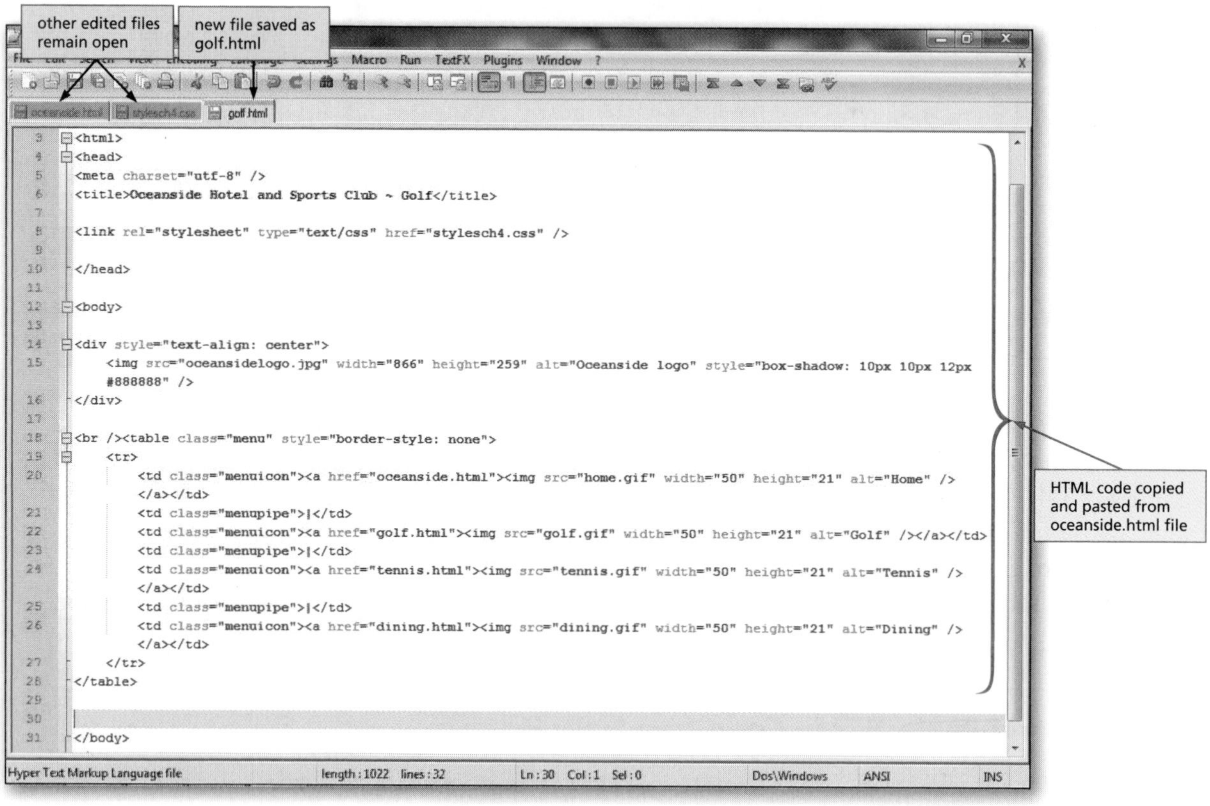

Figure 4–27

Plan Ahead

Determine what styles are needed for the second Web page.
Prior to adding more code to the Golf Web page, think through what styles you have defined and determine if there is anything in this Web page that needs to differ from the external style sheet. Any differences can be inserted as a formatting attribute, an inline style, or as an embedded style sheet that will override the styles defined in the external style sheet.

• **Review the table formatting in the external style sheet to see if it is appropriate for this page.** Borderless tables are often appropriate when the tables are used to position text and image elements. In other instances, such as when a table is used to structure columns and rows of information, borders are appropriate.

• **Identify any other styles that may need to be applied to tables on this page.** It is important to make your tables clear enough that users can easily identify the information that they need. You may want to start with the basic table format and add options as necessary.

Adding a Table with Borders

The borderless table style defined in the stylesch4.css external style sheet works well for the horizontal navigation bar that appears on every page. However, the borderless format would be less effective in presenting the three columns and five rows of information about available golf options at Oceanside Hotel and Sports Club. Figure 4–28a shows this information in a table with borders. Figure 4–28b shows the same information in a table without borders and with a distinct background color in every other row. As shown in this figure, using a table with borders makes the information on the Golf Web page easier to read and provides a frame that gives the table a three-dimensional appearance.

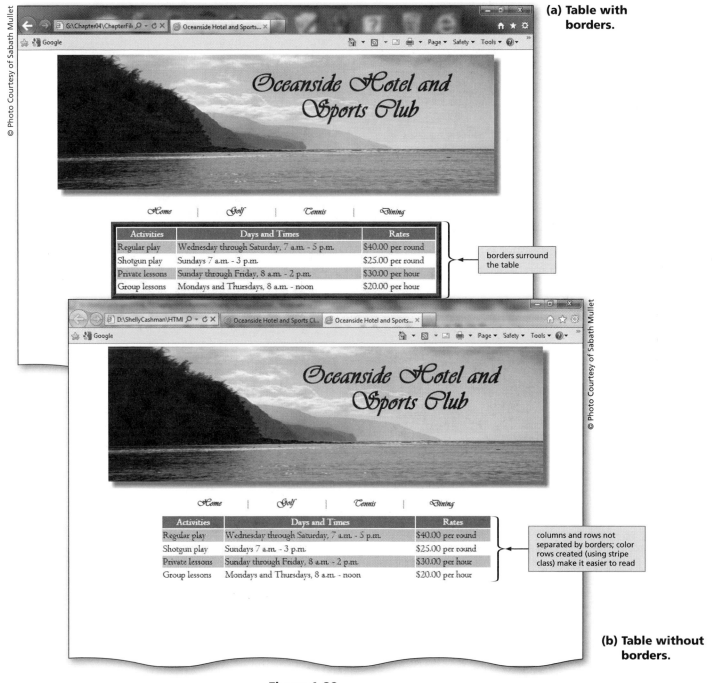

(a) Table with borders.

borders surround the table

columns and rows not separated by borders; color rows created (using stripe class) make it easier to read

(b) Table without borders.

Figure 4–28

To Create a Table with Borders and Insert Text

Creating the table shown in Figure 4–28a involves first creating a table with three columns and five rows. The first row of the table is for column headings; the other rows are for data. As you have learned, table heading cells <th> differ from data cells <td> in their appearance. Text in a heading cell appears as bold and centered, while text in a data cell appears as normal and left-aligned. In the external style sheet stylesch4.css that you created in an earlier section of the project, you gave table header cells a background color of #757775 and white text. Table 4–9 contains the HTML tags and text used to create the table of golf options on the Golf Web page.

Line	HTML Tag and Text
Table 4–9 HTML Code to Create a Table	
30	`<table>`
31	`<tr>`
32	`<th>Activities</th>`
33	`<th>Days and Times</th>`
34	`<th>Rates</th>`
35	`</tr>`
36	
37	`<tr class="stripe">`
38	`<td>Regular play</td>`
39	`<td>Wednesday through Saturday, 7 a.m. - 5 p.m.</td>`
40	`<td>$40.00 per round</td>`
41	`</tr>`
42	
43	`<tr>`
44	`<td>Shotgun play</td>`
45	`<td>Sundays 7 a.m. - 3 p.m.</td>`
46	`<td>$25.00 per round</td>`
47	`</tr>`
48	
49	`<tr class="stripe">`
50	`<td>Private lessons</td>`
51	`<td>Sunday through Friday, 8 a.m. - 2 p.m.</td>`
52	`<td>$30.00 per hour</td>`
53	`</tr>`
54	
55	`<tr>`
56	`<td>Group lessons</td>`
57	`<td>Mondays and Thursdays, 8 a.m. - noon</td>`
58	`<td>$20.00 per hour</td>`
59	`</tr>`
60	`</table>`
61	
62	`</body>`
63	`</html>`

The following step illustrates how to create a table with borders and insert text into heading and data cells.

1

- With the insertion point on line 30, enter the HTML code for the Golf table, as shown in Table 4–9, using TAB to create indents, and pressing ENTER after each line except the last line (line 63) (Figure 4–29).

Are there other attributes that can be used in the <table>, <tr>, <th>, and <td> tags?

Most table attributes are no longer supported by HTML5. You can still change the style of tables by using Cascading Style Sheets as is done in this chapter project.

Why are we using a white font color for the headings?

Because the background color is so dark (#757775), you could not easily read the heading if it was the default color of black. Changing the font color to white on a dark background color makes it easier to read.

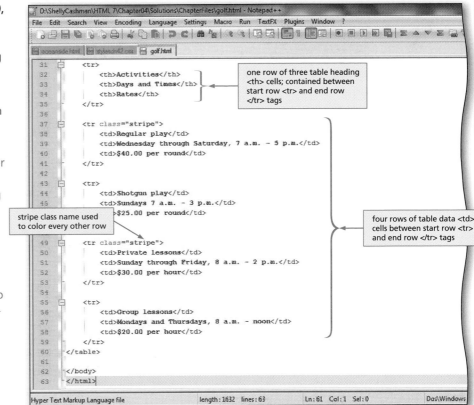

Figure 4–29

To Save, Validate, View, and Print the Web Page

After adding the remaining HTML code, perform the following steps to save, validate, view, and print the Golf Web page.

1 In Notepad++, save the golf.html file.

2 Click the Internet Explorer button on the taskbar.

3 Use the W3C validator service to validate the golf.html Web page.

4 Return to Notepad++ and print the golf.html Notepad++ file (Figure 4–30).

5 Return to the Oceanside's home page, click the Golf link to show the most recent file, and then print the Web page, as shown in Figure 4–31 on the next page.

```
<!DOCTYPE HTML>

<html>
<head>
<meta charset="utf-8" />
<title>Oceanside Hotel and Sports Club ~ Golf</title>

<link rel="stylesheet" type="text/css" href="stylesch4.css" />

</head>

<body>

<div style="text-align: center">
    <img src="oceansidelogo.jpg" width="866" height="259" alt="Oceanside logo" style=
    "box-shadow: 10px 10px 12px #888888" />
</div>

<br /><table class="menu" style="border-style: none">
    <tr>
        <td class="menuicon"><a href="oceanside.html"><img src="home.gif" width="50"
        height="21" alt="Home" /></a></td>
        <td class="menupipe">|</td>
        <td class="menuicon"><a href="golf.html"><img src="golf.gif" width="50" height=
        "21" alt="Golf" /></a></td>
        <td class="menupipe">|</td>
        <td class="menuicon"><a href="tennis.html"><img src="tennis.gif" width="50"
        height="21" alt="Tennis" /></a></td>
        <td class="menupipe">|</td>
        <td class="menuicon"><a href="dining.html"><img src="dining.gif" width="50"
        height="21" alt="Dining" /></a></td>
    </tr>
</table>

<table>
    <tr>
        <th>Activities</th>
        <th>Days and Times</th>
        <th>Rates</th>
    </tr>

    <tr class="stripe">
        <td>Regular play</td>
        <td>Wednesday through Saturday, 7 a.m. - 5 p.m.</td>
        <td>$40.00 per round</td>
    </tr>

    <tr>
        <td>Shotgun play
        <td>Sundays 7 a.m
        <td>$25.00 per ro
    </tr>
```

Figure 4–30

Oceanside Hotel and Sports Club ~ Golf

Page 1 of 1

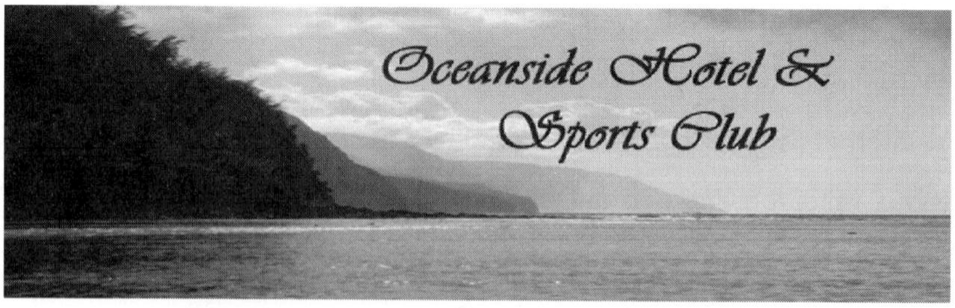

Home | Golf | Tennis | Dining

Activities	Days and Times	Rates
Regular play	Wednesday through Saturday, 7 a.m. - 5 p.m.	$40.00 per round
Shotgun play	Sundays 7 a.m. - 3 p.m.	$25.00 per round
Private lessons	Sunday through Friday, 8 a.m. - 2 p.m.	$30.00 per hour
Group lessons	Mondays and Thursdays, 8 a.m. - noon	$20.00 per hour

Figure 4–31

To Test Links on a Web Page

After confirming that the Web page appears as desired, the four links on the horizontal navigation bar should be tested to verify that they function as expected. The following steps show how to test the links on the golf.html Web page. Compare Figure 4–32a (the starting Web page) to Figure 4–32b (the ending Web page after the HTML code is entered in the next section).

1 Click the Home link to change to the Oceanside Hotel and Sports Club home page.

2 Click the Golf link to return to the golf.html Web page.

3 Click the Dining link.

4 Click the Tennis link (Figure 4–32a).

Q&A Why aren't the Dining and Tennis Web pages formatted with the styles in the external style sheet?

In order for the external style sheet to take effect, you have to insert the <link> statement into the HTML code in the Dining and Tennis files.

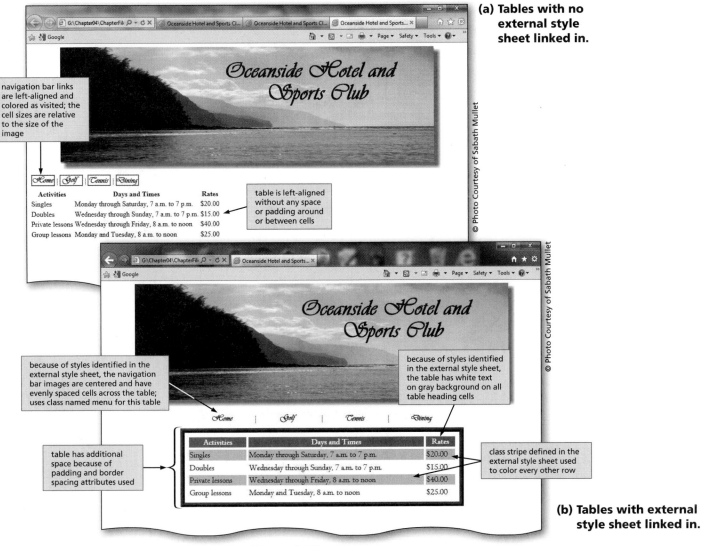

(a) Tables with no external style sheet linked in.

navigation bar links are left-aligned and colored as visited; the cell sizes are relative to the size of the image

table is left-aligned without any space or padding around or between cells

© Photo Courtesy of Sabath Mullet

because of styles identified in the external style sheet, the navigation bar images are centered and have evenly spaced cells across the table; uses class named menu for this table

because of styles identified in the external style sheet, the table has white text on gray background on all table heading cells

table has additional space because of padding and border spacing attributes used

class stripe defined in the external style sheet used to color every other row

(b) Tables with external style sheet linked in.

Figure 4–32

Adding a Link, Border Spacing, Padding, and Row Color

The table of information on the Golf Web page did not use any additional spacing or padding styles. The size of each data cell, therefore, automatically was set to the minimum size needed for the text inserted in the data cell. The tennis.html Web page, however, should be modified to use border spacing and padding by adding an inline style to the <table> tag. **Border spacing** specifies the distance between the borders of adjacent cells in a table. (See Table Properties in Appendix D for more information about border spacing.) Additional spacing makes the borders around each cell look thicker (see the thickness of the borders in Figure 4–33b versus Figure 4–33a). **Padding** is shorthand to set the top, right, bottom, and left padding around an element (see Margin and Padding Properties in Appendix D for more information). In other words, if you add padding, you give more space around the content within that cell. Figures 4–33a and 4–33b illustrate how adding an inline style with border spacing and padding in the <table> tag can affect a table's appearance. Adding the class, stripe, to certain rows also helps to differentiate one row from another using color and gives the table a unique style.

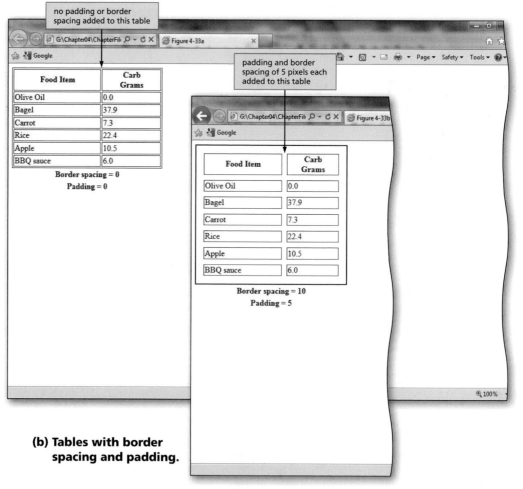

(a) Tables without border spacing and padding.

(b) Tables with border spacing and padding.

Figure 4–33

- **Determine if you need to use padding, border spacing, or both.** The first thing you should consider is if you need these spacing properties at all. If your content is getting across to the users without any modification to the spacing, then maybe you do not need to do this. Look again at the golf.html Web page. The information there is completely readable, and there is no padding or border spacing.

- **Determine what type of spacing to use.** If you decide that you do need to insert space within or around the cells of data, then you should next consider how much space to provide within the table. Border spacing is the distance between the borders of adjacent cells. Padding sets the top, right, bottom, and left padding around an element. Both properties serve the purpose of making the table of information easier to read. No rule of thumb says how much padding or border spacing should be used. Try various values to see the effect on the table.

- **Determine whether to use color in the table.** Color can be used to separate or highlight information in a table. The row colors used in this Web page help viewers differentiate rows from one another.

To Open an HTML File

In the following step, you will activate Notepad++ and open the tennis.html Web page file.

1 Switch to Notepad++ and open tennis.html, located in the Chapter04\ChapterFiles folder (Figure 4–34).

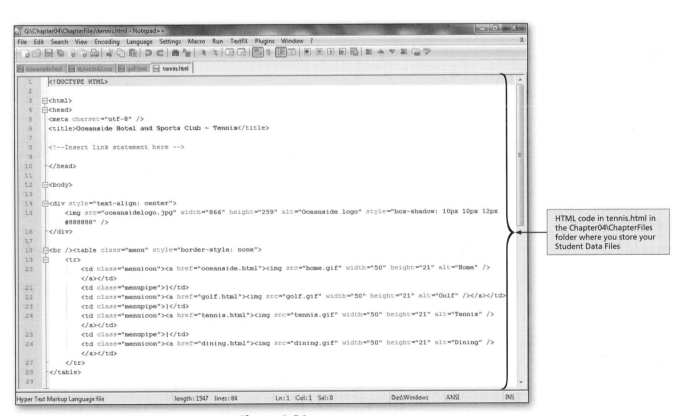

HTML code in tennis.html in the Chapter04\ChapterFiles folder where you store your Student Data Files

Figure 4–34

To Link to an External Style Sheet

The first thing you need to do in this Web page is link to the external style sheet that contains the overall styles you want this Web page to have.

1 Highlight the phrase `<!--Insert link statement here -->` on line 8.

2 Type `<link rel="stylesheet" type="text/css" href="stylesch4.css" />` to enter the link to the external style sheet. Do not press the ENTER key.

Q&A Remind me, what does this link statement do?

This statement links this Web page to the external style sheet that you created earlier. You need this link to the external (or linked) style sheet in order to apply those styles to the Web page.

To Add Border Spacing, Padding, and Row Color to a Table

With the tennis.html file open, the HTML code to add border spacing, padding, and row color can be added. The following step shows how to add border spacing, padding, and decorative color stripes to a table.

- Click immediately to the right of the e in the `<table>` tag on line 30 and then press the SPACEBAR.

- Type `style="border-spacing: 5px; padding: 5px"` as the properties and values but do not press the ENTER key (Figure 4–35).

- Click immediately to the right of the r in `<tr>` on line 37 and press the spacebar.

- Type `class="stripe"` and do not press the ENTER key.

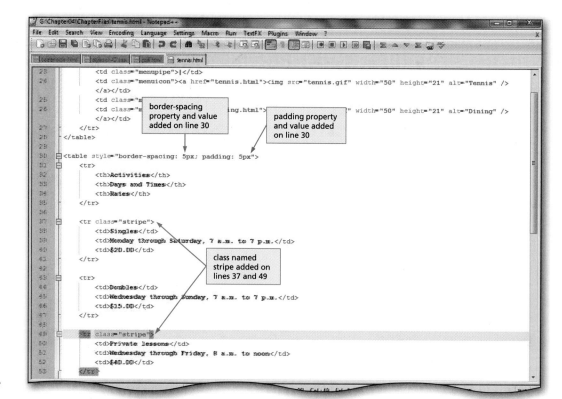

Figure 4–35

- Click immediately to the right of the r in `<tr>` on line 49 and press the spacebar.

- Type `class="stripe"` and do not press the ENTER key.

Q&A Can I set the padding and border spacing differently for different cells?

With the flexibility of inline styles, you can adjust the border spacing and padding at the table header or table data cell level.

To Save, Validate, Print, and View the HTML File and Print the Web Page

1 With the USB drive plugged into your computer, click File on the menu bar and then click Save to save the tennis.html file.

2 Display the Oceanside Hotel and Sports Club's ~ Tennis page in Internet Explorer.

3 Validate the Web page using the W3C validator service.

4 Return to the Oceanside Hotel and Sports Club's ~ Tennis page, refresh the Web page, and then print it.

5 Return to Notepad++ and print the file.

Adding a Caption and Spanning Rows

If you need to add information to a table that does not fit into the table data cells, a caption can be a good option. For example, look at the dining.html Web page in Figure 4–1d on page HTML 155. The caption indicates that additional menu items are available upon request. That "additional menu items" information does not fit into either the heading or data cells for the table. It is also not appropriate to have that information as an h1 or h2 heading. Putting that information in a caption is a perfect solution. The <caption> tag defines a table caption. The <caption> tag must be inserted immediately after the <table> tag and only one caption may be specified per table. By default, the caption will be centered above the table. In this project, you previously inserted the caption-side property in the external style sheet to align the caption at the bottom of (beneath) the table.

When you want to merge several cells into one, you can use row or column spanning. You can span rows or columns anywhere in a table. Generally, row and column spanning is used to create headings in tables. The **rowspan attribute** of the <th> or <td> tag sets a number of rows spanned by a cell. Although the chapter project uses only row spanning, you can also span columns. The **colspan attribute** of the <th> or <td> tag sets a number of columns spanned by a cell. Figure 4–9 on page HTML 164 shows examples of both column and row spanning. Notice that both the 5K and 10K headings span (or go across) two columns each. The heading Meet Dates spans (or goes across) four rows of information.

Figure 4–36, on the next page, shows what the dining.html Web page looks like at the start of the process. All of the table content is present, but there is no row or column spanning. You decide during the design phase that this table would benefit from row spanning, but that column spanning is unnecessary. You will enter the HTML code to complete the row spanning. In Figure 4–37, on the next page, the heading Lunch Menu is an example of row spanning. In this case, this heading spans three rows. In the same figure, the words Dinner Menu also span three rows of information.

The "stripe" class is already added to every other row to give the table a unique style. In addition, in this section of the project, you will insert the <td> class "bolder" (line 31 in the stylech4.css file) to make the text in certain cells bolder than the surrounding text. This helps to highlight the name of the main dish in every row, as shown in Figure 4-37. You could have added individual inline styles specifying the bold font weight to each data cell that you wanted to make bolder, but using a class in the external style sheet allows you to apply that same font weight in other tables, if it is appropriate.

BTW

Row and Column Spanning
Creating headings that span rows and columns defines tables more clearly. Many Web sites contain information about row and column spanning. For more information about row and column spanning, search the Web.

no styles from stylesch4.css external style sheet inserted until link statement is added

no rowspanning heading cells inserted

© Photo Courtesy of Sabath Mullet

Figure 4–36   Dining Web page before enhancements.

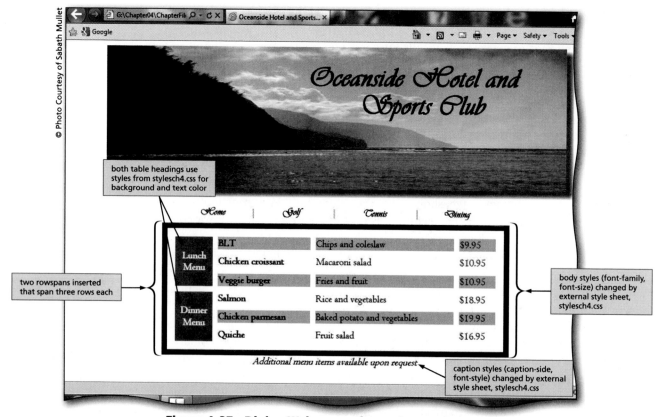

© Photo Courtesy of Sabath Mullet

both table headings use styles from stylesch4.css for background and text color

two rowspans inserted that span three rows each

body styles (font-family, font-size) changed by external style sheet, stylesch4.css

caption styles (caption-side, font-style) changed by external style sheet, stylesch4.css

Figure 4–37   Dining Web page after enhancements.

The first step when deciding to span rows or columns is to sketch the table design on a piece of paper, as shown in Figure 4–38. Again, for this Web page, it was determined that column spanning was unnecessary. The table organizes menu items by lunch and dinner and thus should have rowspanning for those two row headings.

	BLT	Chips and coleslaw	$9.95
Lunch Menu	Chicken croissant	Macaroni salad	$10.95
	Veggie burger	Fries and fruit	$10.95
	Salmon	Rice and vegetables	$18.95
Dinner Menu	Chicken parmesan	Baked potatoes and vegetables	$19.95
	Quiche	Fruit salad	$16.95

Figure 4–38

After defining the main sections of the table, you must determine how many rows each heading should span. In this project, the headings, Lunch Menu and Dinner Menu, should span three rows. In the following steps, you will open the file dining.html, link the external style sheet stylesch4.css, and add rowspan attributes to create table headings that span rows.

Plan Ahead

- **Determine if a caption is needed.** A caption can help clarify the table's purpose. For some tables, such as the table used to position images and the tables used to create navigation bars, captions are not appropriate. Tables used to structure columns and rows of information, such as the dining table, can benefit from having a caption to clarify or add information about the contents of the table. The caption tag must be inserted directly after the <table> tag.

- **Determine whether to use row and column spanning.** The purpose of the table determines whether you need to add row or column spanning. If the content is broken into logical segments of information, you may also need to include row or column spanning in order to make the content clear. If you decide to add row or column spanning, it is best to sketch your ideas on paper first. This could help you understand more clearly what tags you need to use where.

- **Determine if different colors are needed for backgrounds.** You can help visitors more easily read a table full of information by varying the background colors effectively. If you use the same color background for the same level (or type) of information, it can help visually organize the information. Again, you may have to use a light font color if the background color is very dark.

To Open an HTML File

1 Switch to Notepad++ and open dining.html, located in the Chapter04\ChapterFiles folder.

To Link the External Style Sheet

The first thing you need to do in this Web page is link to the external style sheet that contains the styles that you want for this Web page.

1 Highlight the text <!--Insert link statement here --> on line 8.

2 Type `<link rel="stylesheet" type="text/css" href="stylesch4.css" />` to enter the link to the external style sheet. Do not press the ENTER key.

To Add a Table Caption

Captions are added to tables using the <caption> </caption> tags to enclose the caption text. The formatting to make the caption italic and align it at the bottom of the table is included in the external style sheet (stylesch4.css) that is now linked to this page. The following step shows how to add a caption below the menu table.

- Highlight the text <!--Insert caption statement here --> on line 32.

- Type `<caption> Additional menu items available upon request </caption>` as the tag to add the italic caption below the table (Figure 4–39).

Experiment

- By default, captions are aligned at the top (above) a table. You changed the style of the caption in the external style sheet to align the caption on the bottom. To see what the caption would look like at the top of the table, insert an inline style sheet in the <caption> tag and use the caption-side property to align the caption at the top. (Hint: You could also remove lines 33 and 34 in the stylesch4.css file.)

```
8    <link rel="stylesheet" type="text/css" href="stylesch4.css" />
9
10   </head>
11
12   <body>
13
14   <div style="text-align: center">
15       <img src="oceansidelogo.jpg" width="866" height="259" alt="Oceanside logo" style="box-shadow: 10px 10px 12px
         #888888" />
16   </div>
17
18   <br /><table class="menu" style="border-style: none">
19       <tr>
20           <td class="menuicon"><a href="oceanside.html"><img src="home.gif" width="50" height="21" alt="Home" />
             </a></td>
21           <td class="menupipe">|</td>
22           <td class="menuicon"><a href="golf.html"><img src="golf.gif" width="50" height="21" alt="Golf" /></a></td>
23           <td class="menupipe">|</td>
24           <td class="menuicon"><a href="tennis.html"><img src="tennis.gif" width="50" height="21" alt="Tennis" />
             </a></td>
25           <td class="menupipe">|</td>
26           <td class="menuicon"><a href="dining.h        "50" height="21" alt="Dining" />
             </a></td>
27       </tr>
28   </table>
29
30   <table style="border-spacing: 10px; padding: 5px">
31
32   <caption>Additional menu items available upon request</caption>
33
34       <tr class="stripe">
35   <!--Insert first rowspan heading here -->
36           <td>BLT</td>
```

inserted link statement to stylesch4.css, the external style sheet with all styles defined

caption element inserted into Web page; styles for caption will be taken from the stylesch4.css, the external style sheet

next step to insert HTML code here on line 35

Figure 4–39

To Create the Headings That Span Rows

The following steps illustrate how to enter HTML code to create two headings that each span three rows:

1

- Highlight <!--Insert first rowspan heading here --> on line 35.

- Press the TAB key twice and then type <th rowspan="3">Lunch and then press the ENTER key; the next line is automatically indented to the same level.

- Type
Menu and then press the ENTER key.

- Type </th> as the HTML code but do not press the ENTER key (Figure 4–40).

Q&A

What is the purpose of the <br /> tag in the steps above?

The <br /> tag moves the word Menu to a second line so that the first column is not too much wider than the other columns in the table.

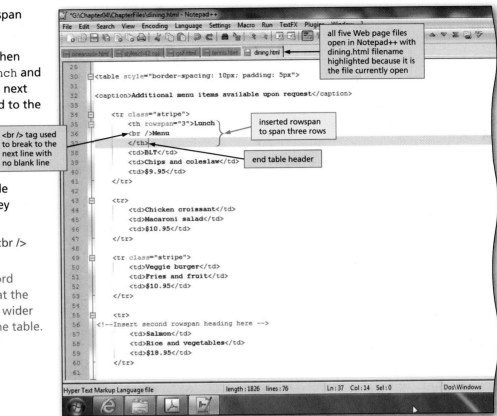

Figure 4–40

2

- Highlight <!--Insert second rowspan heading here --> on line 56.

- Press the TAB key twice and then type <th rowspan="3">Dinner and then press the ENTER key.

- Type
Menu and then press the ENTER key.

- Type </th> as the HTML code but do not press the ENTER key (Figure 4–41).

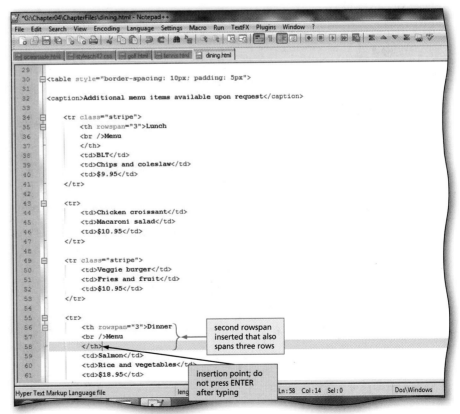

Figure 4–41

Q&A Why isn't there an extra pair of <tr> </tr> tags between the rowspan title (Lunch Menu) and the line of HTML code for data (BLT)?

The words Lunch Menu and BLT are on the same row (row 1) that is being spanned. Row 2 contains the line with Chicken croissant; row 3 is the line with Veggie burger. Therefore, the rowspan value is set to 3. The text that spans the rows (Lunch Menu and Dinner Menu) is always aligned with the first row of text.

 Experiment

- Remove the <br /> tag from the HTML code that you entered on lines 36 and 57. See how this changes the look of the table.

- Change the <br /> tag on lines 36 and 57 to a <p> tag (don't forget the </p>). See what that does to the look of the table.

To Add the Bolder Class to Data Cells

The class bolder was defined in the external style sheet, stylesch4.css. Although we want the text in the data cells to be left-justified (the default option of the <td> tag), we also want to highlight that text by making it more bold than the other text in the table data cells. The following step illustrates how to enter HTML code to insert the class bolder to six data cells.

1

- Click just after the d in <td> on line 38.

- Type class="bolder" and do not press the ENTER key.

- Repeat these steps for lines 44, 50, 59, 65, and 71 as shown in Figure 4–42.

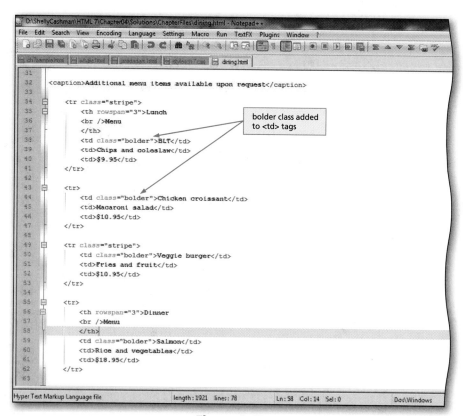

Figure 4–42

To Save, Validate, and Print the HTML File

1 With the USB drive plugged into your computer, click the Save icon on the Notepad++ toolbar to save the dining.html file.

2 Validate the HTML file using the validator.w3.org Web page.

3 Print the Notepad++ file.

To View and Print the Web Page

1 Click the Internet Explorer button on the taskbar.

2 Click the Dining link on the navigation bar to display the Dining Web page.

3 Print the Web page with rowspan attributes entered (Figure 4–43).

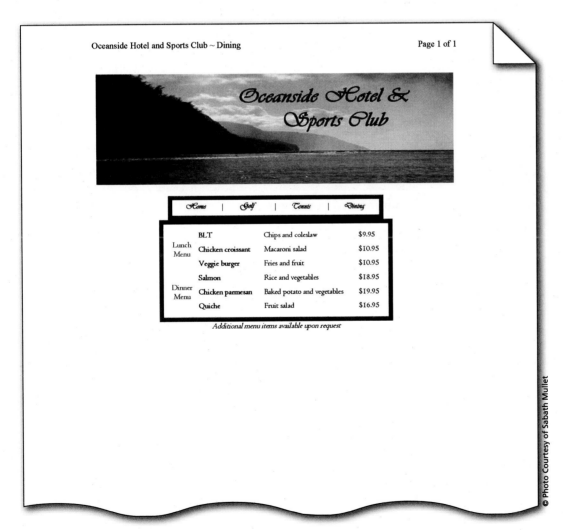

Figure 4–43

To Quit Notepad++ and a Browser

1 In Notepad++, click the File menu, then Close All.

2 Click the Close button on the Notepad++ title bar.

3 Click the Close button on the browser title bar. If necessary, click the Close all tabs button.

Chapter Summary

In this chapter, you learned how to create and link an external style sheet. You learned about about table elements, and the necessary steps to plan, design, and code a table in HTML. You also learned to enhance a table with background color, border spacing, padding, a caption, classes, and headers that span rows. The items listed below include all the new HTML skills you learned in this chapter.

1. Insert, Center, and Style an Image with a Box-Shadow (HTML 170)
2. Create a Horizontal Menu Bar with Image Links (HTML 173)
3. Create an External Style Sheet (HTML 180)
4. Link to an External Style Sheet (HTML 185)
5. Copy and Paste HTML Code to a New File (HTML 189)
6. Create a Table with Borders and Insert Text (HTML 192)
7. Add Border Spacing, Padding, and Row Color to a Table (HTML 198)
8. Add a Table Caption (HTML 202)
9. Create Headings That Span Rows (HTML 202)
10. Add the Bolder Class to Data Cells (HTML 204)

Learn It Online

Test your knowledge of chapter content and key terms.

Instructions: To complete the following exercises, please visit www.cengagebrain.com. At the CengageBrain.com home page, search for *HTML5 and CSS 7th Edition* using the search box at the top of the page. This will take you to the product page for this book. On the product page, click the Access Now button below the Study Tools heading. On the Book Companion Site Web page, select Chapter 4, and then click the link for the desired exercise.

Chapter Reinforcement TF, MC, and SA
A series of true/false, multiple choice, and short answer questions that test your knowledge of the chapter content.

Flash Cards
An interactive learning environment where you identify chapter key terms associated with displayed definitions.

Practice Test
A series of multiple choice questions that test your knowledge of chapter content and key terms.

Who Wants To Be a Computer Genius?
An interactive game that challenges your knowledge of chapter content in the style of a television quiz show.

Wheel of Terms
An interactive game that challenges your knowledge of chapter key terms in the style of the television show, *Wheel of Fortune*.

Crossword Puzzle Challenge
A crossword puzzle that challenges your knowledge of key terms presented in the chapter.

Apply Your Knowledge

Reinforce the skills and apply the concepts you learned in this chapter.

Editing a Table on a Web Page

Instructions: Start Notepad++. Open the file apply4-1.html from the Chapter04\Apply folder of the Data Files for Students. See the inside back cover of this book for instructions on downloading the Data Files for Students, or contact your instructor for information about accessing the required files.

The apply4-1.html file is a partially completed HTML file that you will use for this exercise. Figure 4–44 shows the Apply Your Knowledge Web page as it should display in a browser after the additional HTML tags, attributes, and styles are added.

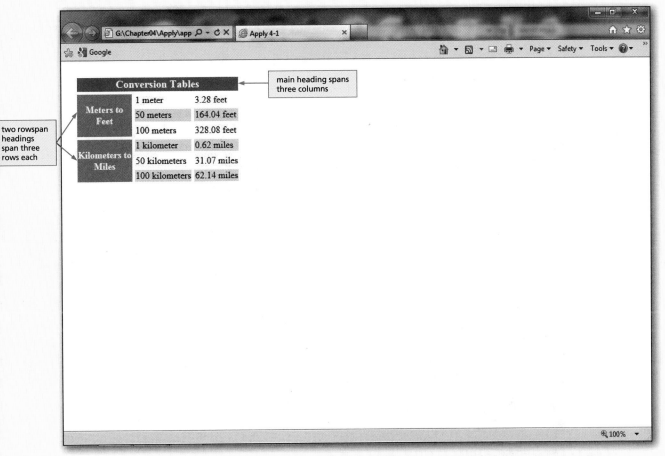

Figure 4–44

Perform the following tasks:

1. Enter the URL G:\Chapter04\Apply\apply4-1.html to view the Web page in your browser.

2. Examine the HTML file and its appearance as a Web page in the browser.

3. Add a border width of 10, border spacing of 5, and padding of 15 in an inline style to the table.

4. Add any HTML code necessary for additional features shown on the Web page in Figure 4–44. Your changes should include a colspan heading that spans three columns of information and two rowspan headings that span three rows each. The main heading is font-size large.

Continued >

Apply Your Knowledge *continued*

5. Colors used for the headings are colspan - #bc4676; first and second rowspan - #87aaae (experiment with the colors if you wish). The background color of the striped rows is #ddecef. All text in those colored cells is white.

6. Save the revised file in the Chapter04\Apply folder using the filename apply4-1solution.html.

7. Validate the code using the W3C validator service.

8. Print the revised HTML file.

9. Enter the URL G:\Chapter04\Apply\apply4-1solution.html to view the Web page in your browser.

10. Print the Web page.

11. Submit the revised HTML file and Web page in the format specified by your instructor.

Extend Your Knowledge

Extend the skills you learned in this chapter and experiment with new skills.

Creating a Table with Rules

Instructions: Start Notepad++. Open the file extend4-1.html from the Chapter04\Extend folder of the Data Files for Students. See the inside back cover of this book for instructions on downloading the Data Files for Students, or contact your instructor for information about accessing the required files. This sample HTML file contains all of the text for the Web page shown in Figure 4–45. You will add the necessary tags to make this Web page display the table, as shown in Figure 4–45.

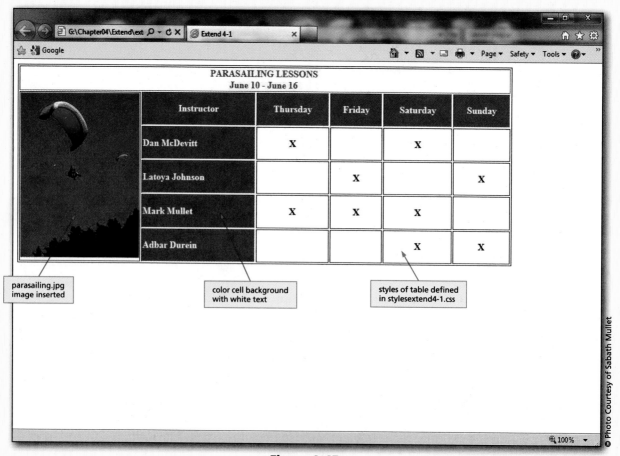

parasailing.jpg image inserted

color cell background with white text

styles of table defined in stylesextend4-1.css

Figure 4–45

Perform the following tasks:

1. Add HTML code to align the table on the left of the Web page. Give the table a border of 1 with padding of 15 pixels. Add a heading spanning six columns in color #4174ab.

2. Insert the image parasailing.jpg in to a new table header cell that spans five rows. Determine the width and height of the image using methods discussed in the chapter.

3. Create an external style sheet that contains the following styles and save it as stylesextend4-1.css. Validate the CSS code.

4. Link stylesextend4-1.css into the Web page extend4-1solution.html.

```
table              {text-align: center;}
.twentyfive        {width: 25%;}
.twelve            {width: 12%;}
th.blue            {background-color: #4174ab;
                    color: white;}
td.instructors     {font-weight: bold;
                    text-align: left;
                    color: white;
                    background-color: #4174ab;}
```

5. Add the class, twentyfive, to the first two columns (image and instructors). Add the classes, twelve and blue, in the next four columns (days of week). (Hint: Separate multiple class names with a comma.)

6. Add the class, instructors, to the table cells that contain the instructor names.

7. Save the revised document as extend4-1solution.html and validate the code using the W3C validator service.

8. Resave extend4-1solution.html. Print the revised HTML file and Web page and submit them in the format specified by your instructor.

Make It Right

Analyze a document and correct all errors and/or improve the design.

Correcting the Golf Course Tournament Schedule

Instructions: Start your browser. Open the file makeitright4-1.html from the Chapter04\MakeItRight folder of the Data Files for Students. See the inside back cover of this book for instructions on downloading the Data Files for Students, or contact your instructor for information about accessing the required files. The Web page is a modified version of what you see in Figure 4–46 on the next page. Make the necessary corrections to the Web page to make it look like Figure 4–46, using inline styles for all styles. The Web page should include the six columns of information with a main heading that spans all six columns. The second row contains the image golfcourse.png in the first cell. The second row also has a line break between the person's first and last name. (*Hint:* Use the <br /> tag.) Move the caption to the bottom in italics. Make every other row of the table color #9ecc39. Save the file as makeitright4-1solution.html and validate the code. Submit the files in the format requested by your instructor.

Continued >

Make It Right *continued*

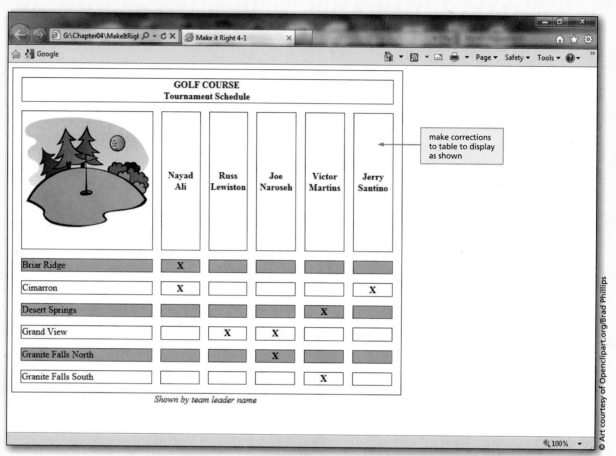

Figure 4–46

In the Lab

Lab 1: Creating a Table with Multiple Images

Problem: The owners of Beautiful Backyards want to review the potential for the use of tables on their company home page. You have been asked to create a Web page that shows the two images and how tables can be used to display them and the associated text, as shown in Figure 4–47.

Instructions: Perform the following steps:

1. Start a new HTML file with the title Lab 4-1 in the main heading section.

2. The heading <h1> should be color #00934a.

3. Insert the text shown in the top lines of the Web page using a font size of large.

4. Add a centered borderless table with two columns and two rows and padding of 15.

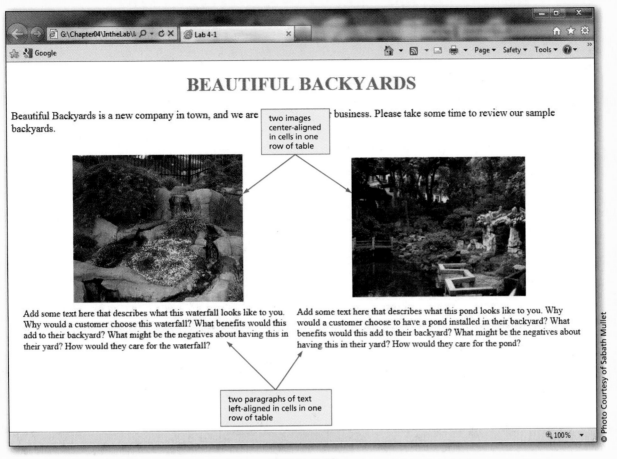

© Photo Courtesy of Sabath Mullet

Figure 4–47

5. Insert the image largewaterfall.jpg in the first column of the first row. (*Hint:* You can use the techniques discussed in this chapter to determine the width and height of each image.)

6. Add the second image pond.jpg to that same row in a second column.

7. Start a new row and add a paragraph of text for each of the images.

8. Save the HTML file in the Chapter04\IntheLab folder using the filename lab4-1solution.html.

9. Validate the Web page using the W3C validator service.

10. Print the lab4-1solution.html file.

11. Open the lab4-1solution.html file in your browser to view it as a Web page.

12. Print the Web page.

13. Submit the revised HTML file and Web page in the format specified by your instructor.

In the Lab

Lab 2: Creating Two Linked Pages

Problem: Your manager at Clocks Beyond has asked you to create two Web pages, similar to the ones shown in Figures 4–48a and 4–48b. The first Web page is a home page that presents information about Clocks Beyond, together with two links. The Prices link on the first page will be linked to a price list of items found at the clock store. The second link, called Links, should direct the Web page visitor to another Web page of your choosing that has to do with clocks. You may select a museum or another similar site of your choosing. For this project, use a combination of inline style sheets and external (linked) style sheets in order to accomplish the tasks.

Instructions: Perform the following steps:

1. Start a new HTML file with the title Lab 4-2a in the main heading section.

2. Create a one-row, two-column borderless table with the image clock.jpg in the left-hand data cell. Use the box-shadow property to create the two-tone shadow around the top and bottom of the image. The values are: -20px -20px 15px #122973 and 20px 20px 15px #9a9391. (*Hint:* Make sure to separate the two value strings with a comma.) Insert the words Clocks Beyond using text color #122973 and font size xx-large in the right-hand data cell.

3. Create a second one-row, two-column borderless table with border-spacing of 10 pixels. In the first column, use the background color #eddaa7 and include two text links: Prices (which links to lab4-2bsolution.html) and Links (which links to a clock-related Web site of your choosing). In the second column, add the text and an e-mail link, as shown in Figure 4–48a.

4. Create an external style sheet with the following styles. Save it as lab4-2styles.css. Link this external style sheet into the Web page.

body	{font-family: Arial, Verdana, Garamond;
	font-size: 11pt;}
a	{text-decoration: none;
	color: #122973;}
table	{width: 65%;
	margin-left: auto;
	margin-right: auto;}
.menu	{text-align: left;
	width: 20%;}
.content	{width: 80%;}

5. Save the HTML file using the filename lab4-2asolution.html in the Chapter04\IntheLab folder. Validate the file using the W3C validator service. Print the HTML file.

6. Start a new HTML file with the title Lab 4-2b in the main heading section. Link the external style sheet lab4-2styles.css into the file.

7. Create a five-row, two-column table with a border of 1, padding of 15 pixels, and border-spacing of 5 pixels.

8. Span the first heading across both columns, as shown in Figure 4–48b, using a text color of #122973, a background color of #eddaa7, and font size large.

9. Enter the headings, Item and Price, along with the additional information, in the appropriate table cells, as shown in Figure 4–48b. Make sure to include a link (font size small and center-aligned) back to the home page.

10. Save the HTML file in the Chapter04\IntheLab folder using the filename lab4-2bsolution.html. Validate the HTML and CSS files using the W3C validator services. Print the HTML file.

11. Open the file lab4-2asolution.html in your browser and test that Prices links to the lab4-2bsolution.html Web page and that the link, Back to home, links to lab2-4asolution.html.

12. Print both Web pages.

13. Submit the HTML files, .css file, and Web pages in the format specified by your instructor.

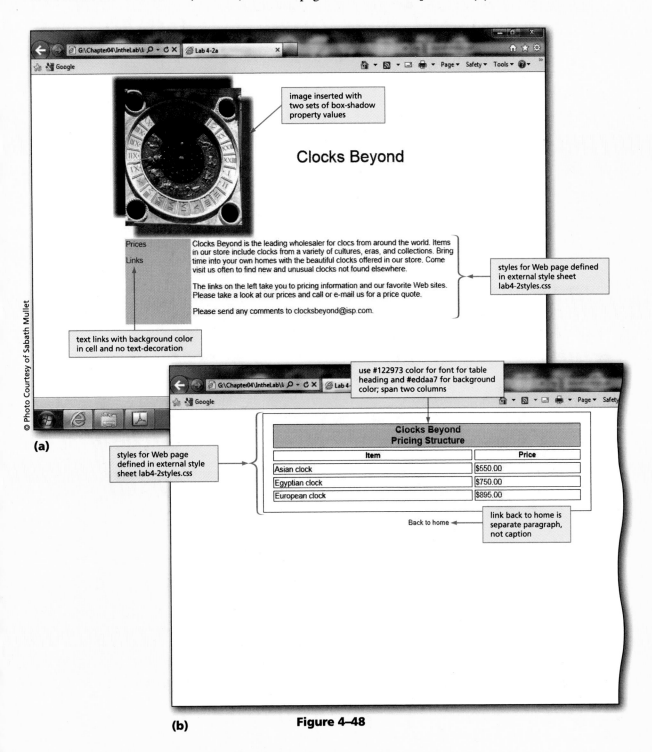

© Photo Courtesy of Sabath Mullet

Figure 4–48

In the Lab

Lab 3: Creating Schedules

Problem: You want to create a Web page and an external style sheet that lists your piano practice and volunteer schedule, similar to the one shown in Figure 4–49. The Web page will use a table with images that span several rows and columns to organize the information.

Instructions: Perform the following steps:

1. Start a new HTML file with the title Lab 4-3 in the main heading section.

2. In the Web page, create a bordered table that displays in 90% of the browser, as shown in Figure 4–49.

3. Insert an inline style into the <table> tag that assigns the border a color of #194a70, a border width of 20 pixels, and a border style of groove. Give the table a rounded-edge look by using the border-radius property (see Appendix D). The radius should be 25 pixels.

4. Include the headings and data cells as shown, with valid information (i.e., real days and times as per a normal schedule of activities) in the data cells. The main headings (Piano Practice Schedule and Kid Camp Schedule) should be center-aligned across three columns and have a line height of 30 pixels. The data, other than the main headings, will have an indent of 10 pixels when the style sheet is coded and attached.

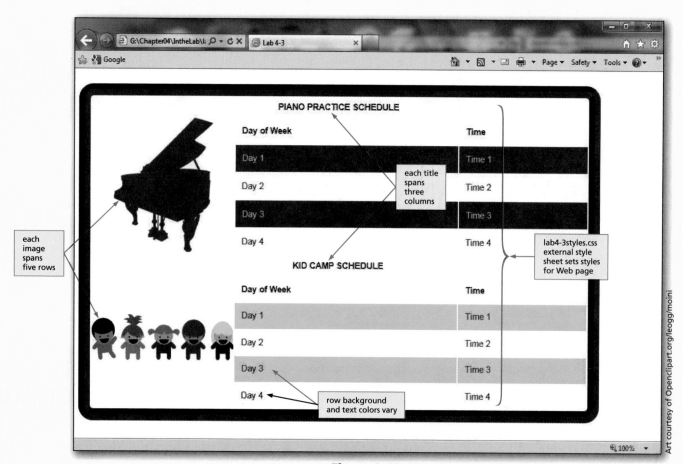

Figure 4–49

5. Add two images, piano.png and kids.png, with all appropriate image attributes, each spanning five rows.

6. The external style sheet should contain the following styles and be saved as lab4-3styles.css:

body	{font-family: Arial, Verdana, Garamond;
	font-size: 11 pt;}
th.subtitle	{text-align: left; text-indent: 10px;}
td	{text-indent: 10px;}

(*Hint:* The <th> element aligns text left. Where would you use that class named subtitle?)

7. Link lab4-3styles.css to the HTML file, and save the HTML file as lab4-3solution.html.

8. Validate the HTML and CSS files using the W3C validator services.

9. Print the HTML and CSS files.

10. Print the Web page from your browser.

11. Submit the HTML file, .css file, and Web page in the format specified by your instructor.

Cases and Places

Apply your creative thinking and problem-solving skills to design and implement a solution.

1: Finding Tables on the Web

Academic

The Dean of your school wants to update the Web pages for the school's Web site. She has asked your help in doing this and wants to see a proposal. You think that tables would provide the perfect format for displaying the various academic programs available in your school, potential class schedules, and a calendar of events. Browse the Web to find examples of tables used for information such as what is needed on your school's Web site. Print those pages so that you have concrete examples to show the Dean. Prepare a document that explains to the Dean how you would use such tables for your school's particular needs. Try using a storyboard (a series of illustrations or images, displayed in sequence, that visually depicts your ideas). Sketch a Web page design (see Figure 4–8 on page HTML 163 and Figure 4–38 on page HTML 201) that incorporates tables for your purpose.

2: Creating a Time Schedule

Personal

Your computer club wants you to create a table that lists meeting, open lab, and lab class times for the computer labs. Sketch a basic table format to use for this purpose and ask a few friends (or classmates) what they think. Once you have determined a good design for the Web page, begin to code the table needed. As you begin to build the Web page, you should start thinking about other table properties that could make the Web pages look even better. Create a Web page with a basic five-row, two-column table with a border. Review additional properties listed in Appendix D that can be used with tables. Find information on those properties on other Web sites, including the W3C Web site (w3.org). Modify the basic table on your Web page to incorporate at least four of these properties.

Continued >

Cases and Places *continued*

3: Creating a Gift Shop Web Site

Professional

Your design team at Webber Design has been asked to create a proposal that explains the value of using Cascading Style Sheets to an existing customer. Select a Web site with which you are familiar. Verify which of the three types of style sheets the Web site uses. Develop a graphic of the Web site hierarchy. Determine how the three types of style sheets could possibly be used differently in this Web site and develop an outline explaining how they could enhance pages or sections of the site, add style consistency, or make the site easier to maintain. Write a proposal to the owners of the Web site that describes the features you could add with style sheets and the benefits of doing so, relative to the formatting techniques currently used in the Web site. Use ideas as discussed in the chapter to emphasize the other benefits of style sheets. Write the proposal in the form of a bid, giving time estimates and costs associated with the development effort. Include your hierarchy chart and style sheet outline as appendices to the proposal.

Special Feature 1

Attracting Visitors to Your Web Site

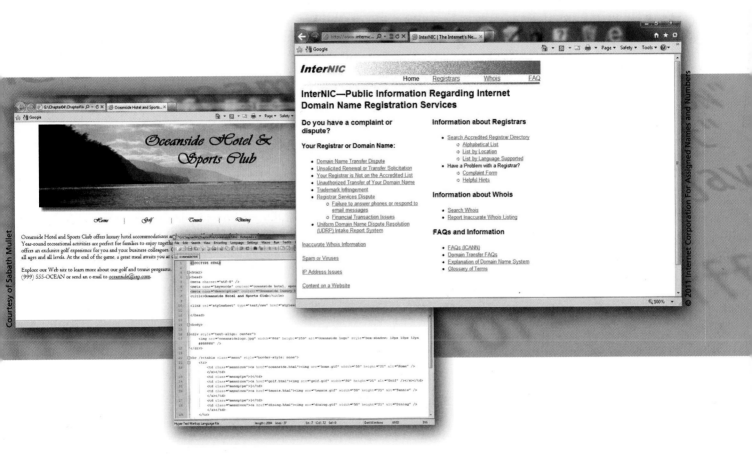

Objectives

You will have mastered the material in this special feature when you can:

- Add keywords and descriptions to your Web pages
- Find appropriate Web site servers
- Determine the availability of a domain name
- Discuss Web page publishing options
- Develop a marketing plan to get the word out about your Web site

Introduction

In Chapter 4, you developed the Oceanside Hotel and Sports Club Web site, which consisted of four Web pages. In this special feature, you will learn how to fine-tune that Web site to make sure that it will attract visitors. A Web site is a passive marketing tool; it serves no purpose if no one knows that it is there. It is not enough to just develop a Web site. You also have to make modifications to the Web pages to ensure that they will attract visitors.

Project — Attracting Visitors

Web sites have become an important means of worldwide communication. Businesses utilize Web sites to communicate with their customers and vendors. Teachers create Web sites to communicate with other teachers and their students, and private users create Web sites to share aspects of their personal life with family, friends, and others.

In Chapter 4, you created the Oceanside Hotel and Sports Club home page, oceanside.html, as shown in Figure 1. The project in this feature shows you how to utilize <meta /> tags to add keywords and descriptions to this page to help Web site visitors who are looking for such topics to find your Web page.

Overview

As you read through this feature, you will learn how to add two new meta tags that will include keywords and descriptions to attract visitors to the Oceanside Web site. The new meta tags are added after the meta tag that you previously added (Figure 1a) to the Web page. You will also learn how to find a hosting site, determine a domain name, publish the Web pages, and determine a marketing plan by performing these general tasks:

- Decide what meta names (keywords and descriptions) you should use.
- Insert the keywords and descriptions into the meta tags.
- Identify available domain names.
- Determine an appropriate hosting situation for your Web site.
- Establish a marketing plan.

Special Feature 1

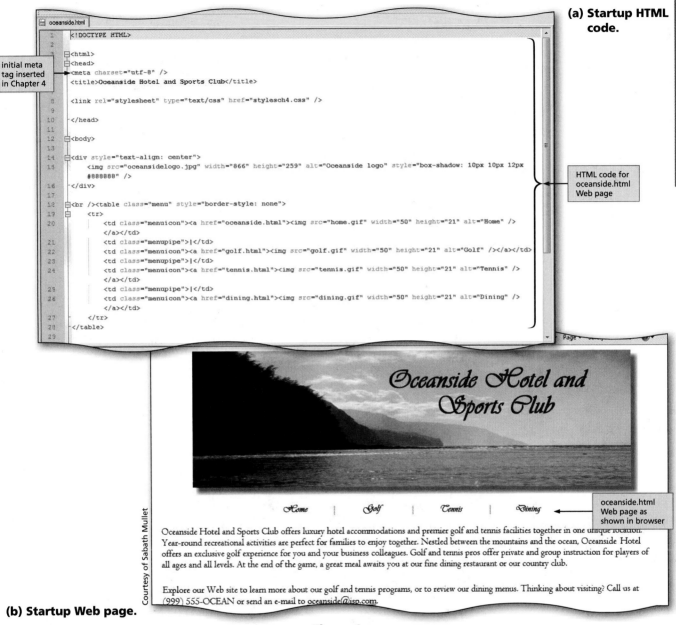

(a) Startup HTML code.

initial meta tag inserted in Chapter 4

HTML code for oceanside.html Web page

Courtesy of Sabath Mullet

oceanside.html Web page as shown in browser

(b) Startup Web page.

Figure 1

Plan Ahead

General Project Guidelines

In the Oceanside Hotel and Sports Club home page in Chapter 4, you added a title, Oceanside Hotel and Sports Club that included the keywords "hotel" and "sports club" in it. The words "hotel" and "sports club" identify the main subject matter for the Web site, but while your topic is clear, more must be done to your Web site. Once your Web page is complete, you need to publish it and attract visitors. There are several ways to attract visitors, which you will accomplish in the following project. In preparation for this project, you should follow these general guidelines:

1. **Identify the meta names you should use.** There are different meta names that you can use within the <meta /> tag, including keywords and description. In this step, you will determine whether to use keywords or description or to use both keywords and description in different meta tags.

(continued)

(continued)

2. **Determine the keywords and descriptions that reflect the purpose of the Web site.** Review your Web site and determine the keywords and the description that best apply to the Web site. Consider what Web users will type into search engines when searching for Web sites like yours and use those words/phrases as your keywords and description. The keywords and description are included in addition to the relevant phrases already in the Web page title or body content.

3. **Decide the available domain names.** A Web page address or URL is an important part of marketing your Web page. You can register your domain name, which will make it easier for Web users to find your site. You need to decide on a few possibilities and then determine if those domain names are already registered. If the name you choose is not registered, you can purchase and register it.

4. **Assess your Web hosting alternatives.** Many Web developers have access to their own Web servers. If you do, then you do not have to consider other Web hosting options. If this is not an option, then you need to find a Web server on which to host your Web pages.

5. **Establish a marketing plan.** You have many choices for publicizing your Web pages. Most companies include their URL in all corporate correspondence, including letterheads, advertisements, and products. Sharing links with a related Web site also helps get visitors. You need to determine a plan that will incorporate the best techniques to effectively publicize your Web pages. Keep in mind that a Web site is just one component of a corporate marketing plan. The plan that you establish here should flow into the larger marketing plan.

Adding Keywords

You have already created the HTML file that is used in this special feature. You will use the file oceanside.html that you created in Chapter 4. The page includes a number of keywords: you added the words "hotel" and "sports club" to the title on the Web page; you also used the words and phrases "oceanside hotel," "sports club," "golf," and "tennis" in the Web page content. Any of these words or phrases might be used by visitors searching for hotels that have golf and tennis facilities. You can explicitly identify the keywords that you want the search engine to find by adding additional keywords and phrases to your <meta /> tag.

As with other projects, you use Notepad++ to enhance this file by adding keywords and descriptions. To include additional information in your Web page, you will follow these general steps:

1. Open the oceanside.html file in Notepad++.
2. Add the keywords and description to new <meta /> tags.
3. Save and validate the file.

To Open the File

For this project, you will add keywords and a description to the oceanside.html Web page already created. The following steps show you how to add keywords.

1 Start Notepad++.

2 Open the oceanside.html file in the Chapter04\ChapterFiles folder that you stored on the G:\ drive (Figure 2). If necessary, enable Word wrap in Notepad++.

Q&A What if I did not create the oceanside.html file from Chapter 4?
Your instructor should have a copy of the oceanside.html file.

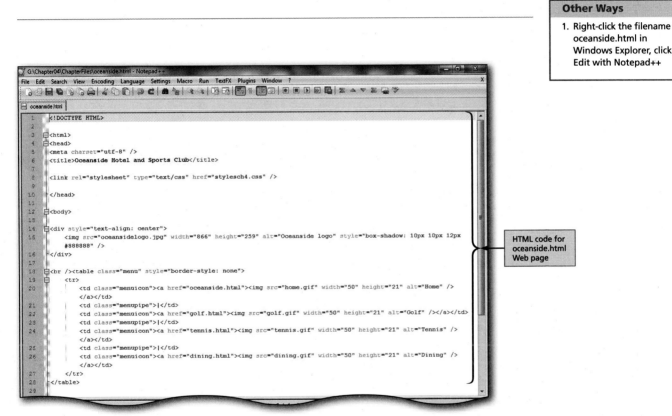

Other Ways

1. Right-click the filename oceanside.html in Windows Explorer, click Edit with Notepad++

Figure 2

Meta Names

The meta tag derives from the word, metadata, which is data (or information) about data. You already included one meta tag in the initial HTML code that you inserted into every Web page created thus far. The

```
<meta charset="utf-8" />
```

line has been included in all Web pages throughout the book. As mentioned earlier, this statement declares the character-encoding as UTF-8. The Unicode Transformation Format (UTF) is a compressed format that allows computers to display and manipulate text. When the browser encounters this meta tag, it will display the Web page properly, based on the particular UTF-8 encoding embedded in the tag. UTF-8 is the preferred encoding standard for Web pages, e-mail, and other applications.

The meta tag also allows you to specify the keywords, description, and author for the Web page through the use of the name and content attributes. Some of the more frequently

SEO

SEO is an acronym for search engine optimization. SEO is the process of improving the amount of traffic that you get on your Web site by improving the ranking of your site in search engine results. Optimizing a Web site involves editing the content and HTML in the Web page to increase its relevance to specific keywords and to remove barriers to the page indexing functions of search engines. To find more information, search for SEO on the Internet.

used meta name values are listed in Table 1. In this project, you will use two of those meta name values: description and keywords. The keywords are used by some search engines to find your Web pages. Other search engines use the keywords included in the content of your Web pages. The best plan includes putting keywords in both places. The description, on the other hand, is what some search engines add next to your Web page URL to describe the content of the Web page. Visitors often look at that description to determine whether they want to click that particular link (or URL) from the list of URLs in the search engine results. The format that is used for each name and content attribute pair is:

```
<meta name="keywords" content="oceanside hotel, sports club,
golf, tennis" />
<meta name="description" content="Oceanside luxury hotel, golf,
tennis for family."
```

where name identifies the type of information in the content attribute, and content identifies the specific phrases or words that you want to appear as metadata. It is important to note that these two attributes must be used in conjunction with one another—the content attribute cannot be defined if the name attribute is not.

Table 1 Meta Names and Their Functions	
Meta Name	**Function**
author	Supplies the name of the document author
description	Provides a description of the document
keywords	Provides a list of keywords that a user might type in a search engine to search for the document

To Add Keywords

The following step illustrates how to add keywords to the oceanside.html Web page:

- Click after the > at the end of line 5 and press the ENTER key to position the insertion point on line 6.

- Type `<meta name="keywords" content="oceanside hotel, sports club, golf, tennis"/>` and then press the ENTER key (Figure 3).

Figure 3

To Add a Description

The following step illustrates how to add a meta tag description to your Web page.

- If necessary, position the insertion point on line 7.

- Type <meta name="description" content="Oceanside luxury hotel, golf, tennis for family."/> but do not press the ENTER key (Figure 4).

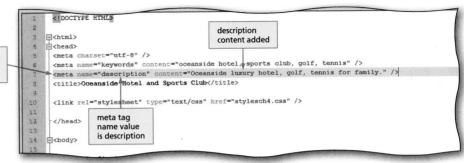

Figure 4

Q&A Is there a difference between keywords and description?

Yes. Search engines use keywords to find your Web pages, while descriptions are displayed next to their respective Web page URLs in a search results list.

Q&A If I have relevant keywords in the content of my Web page, why should I add other words to the <meta /> tags?

It always helps to have keywords identified in both places for those search engines that rely on the meta tag for keywords versus those that rank results by analyzing the page content.

To Save, Validate, and Print a Document

You are finished entering the meta tags. As with all Web development projects, you now need to save, validate, and print the file.

1 In Notepad++, click the Save icon on the toolbar to save the file with the new meta tags.

2 Validate the file using the w3.org validation service.

3 Once the file is successfully validated, print the file (Figure 5).

4 Close Notepad++.

```
<!DOCTYPE HTML>

<html>
<head>
<meta charset="utf-8" />
<meta name="keywords" content="oceanside hotel, sports club" />
<meta name="description" content="Oceanside luxury hotel, golf, tennis for family."  />
<title>Oceanside Hotel and Sports Club</title>

<link rel="stylesheet" type="text/css" href="stylesch4.css" />

</head>

<body>

<div style="text-align: center">
    <img src="oceansidelogo.jpg" width="866" height="259" alt="Oceanside logo" style=
    "box-shadow: 10px 10px 12px #888888" />
</div>

<br /><table class="menu" style="border-style: none">
    <tr>
        <td class="menuicon"><a href="oceanside.html"><img src="home.gif" width="50"
        height="21" alt="Home" /></a></td>
        <td class="menupipe">|</td>
        <td class="menuicon"><a href="golf.html"><img src="golf.gif" width="50" height=
        "21" alt="Golf" /></a></td>
        <td class="menupipe">|</td>
        <td class="menuicon"><a href="tennis.html"><img src="tennis.gif" width="50"
        height="21" alt="Tennis" /></a></td>
        <td class="menupipe">|</td>
        <td class="menuicon"><a href="dining.html"><img src="dining.gif" width="50"
        height="21" alt="Dining" /></a></td>
    </tr>
</table>
```

Figure 5

Determining a Domain Name

A **domain name** is the server name portion of a URL. You can use the domain name of the server on which you publish your Web pages together with a path to your specific pages for your Web page address. However, this Web page address option can result in a URL that is long, hard to remember, and not representative of your Web site or business. You can register your own domain name on the Internet for minimal cost per year. A unique domain name can make it easier for visitors to find your Web pages. In the case of the oceanside.html file, you could register a unique domain name for your Oceanside Hotel and Sports Club Web site, if you can find a name that is both suitable and available.

To determine if the domain name you are considering is available, you can start your search at InterNIC. InterNIC is a registered service mark of the U.S. Department of Commerce. The InterNIC Web site (www.internic.net) is operated by the Internet Corporation for Assigned Names and Numbers (ICANN) to provide information to the public regarding Internet domain name registration services. ICANN is responsible for managing and coordinating the Domain Name System (DNS) to ensure that every Internet address is unique, and that all users of the Internet can find all valid addresses.

BTW

InterNIC
InterNIC contains trusted public information regarding Internet domain name registration services. The InterNIC Web site has a FAQ section, information about domain name registrars, as well as links for domain name disputes.

Check Domain Name Availability

In order to check to see if a domain name is available, complete the following steps:

1

- Type `http://www.internic.net` into the address bar of the browser and press ENTER, as shown in Figure 6.

- Review the FAQ section of the Web site to better understand the domain naming process.

- Click the Whois link to see what domain names have previously been registered for oceansidehotel. Type `oceansidehotel.com` into the text box provided on the Whois Web page and click the Submit button to see if the domain name has been registered. Next, type `oceanside-hotel.net` into the text box and view that result. Finally, try oceansidehotel.org and view the results.

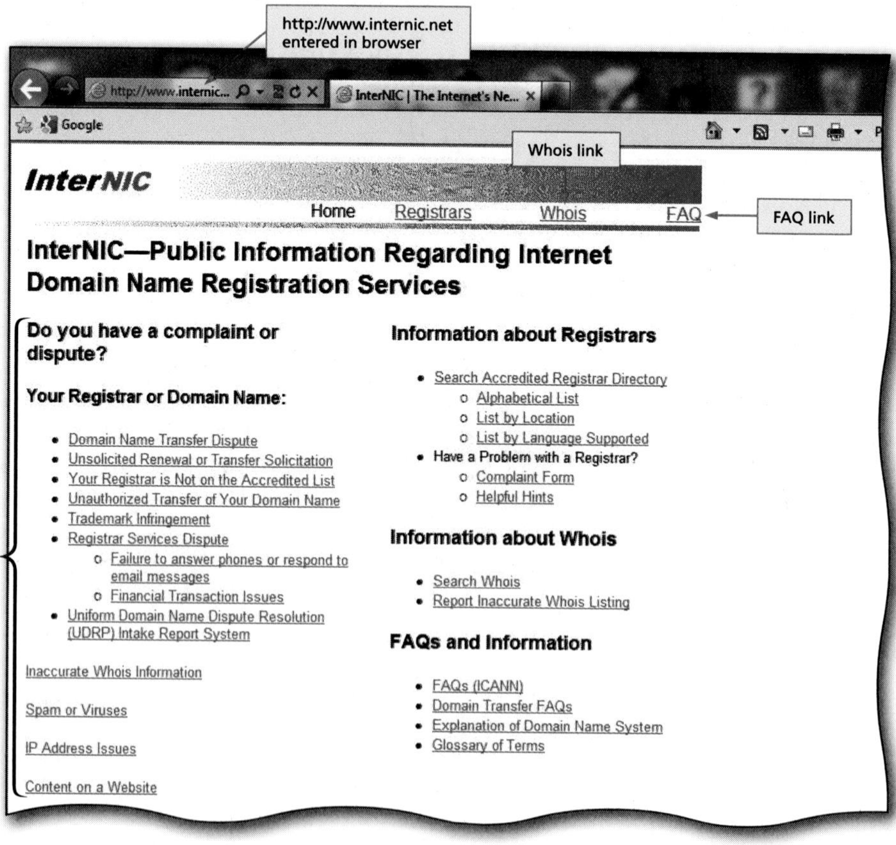

Figure 6

Finding a Web Hosting Site

The next step in the Web development process is to publish your Web pages so that visitors can see them. In order to publish your Web site, you need hosting services. There are many options available for Web hosting. You will need access to a Web server onto which you can upload all of the Web pages in your Web site.

One option is to use the ISP that you use to connect to the Internet. ISPs sometimes provide space for their clients to host a Web site. If you registered your own domain name, you can have your ISP set up a virtual domain, or shared Web hosting, on their server with your new domain name. Your ISP's server may be set up to allocate hosting services and bandwidth to more than one Web site by using a virtual domain. In other words, although you register the domain name oceansidehotel.com, your ISP would host it on its own Web server. Virtual Web hosting is a less expensive option because you do not have to pay for a dedicated server to host just your Web site. You can check with your ISP for details. A second option is to use a company that charges for Web site hosting. There are thousands of companies that provide Web hosting services. Most charge a monthly fee, but some offer free Web hosting in exchange for advertising on your Web site. A final option is for you to set up your own Web server. You would have to know enough about the technology to set it up and keep it running.

Whether you choose to utilize your ISP to host your Web site, to use a Web hosting service, or to set up your own Web server, you need to consider the following:

- What is the total cost? Compare monthly or annual costs; the highest cost may not always provide the best service.
- How much space is available to you? You need to assess your current needs (i.e., file sizes, sizes of graphics) and also your future needs (i.e., how much more information you will create).
- How fast is the connection speed? The speed of the connection to the Internet is important to efficiently serve your visitors.
- How much total bandwidth transfer is available? The number and size of Web pages in your Web site together with the number and size of graphical images is important to consider.
- Is technical support provided? You may occasionally need help, especially in the beginning.
- Are tracking services provided? Many hosting companies allow you to see how visitors utilize your Web site by viewing a tracking log.

After you have selected a Web hosting service, you need to transfer your files to that server.

BTW

Web Site Hosting
There are a variety of Web site hosting options available today. To search for Web hosting services, use different search engines to find different alternatives. Make sure to use the checklist shown on this page to assess the hosting services and fees.

Publishing Your Web Site

Once you have determined a Web hosting strategy, the next step is to publish your Web pages so that visitors can see them. **Publishing** your Web site means transferring your files to the Web server. There are many options available for file transfers. You could use a File Transfer Protocol (FTP) program such as WS_FTP for Windows (Figure 7 on the next page) or Fetch for Mac (for more information about FTP programs, see Appendix E). In addition, many Web page editors also provide publishing functionality. Once your Web pages are published, the last step is to market their location to attract visitors.

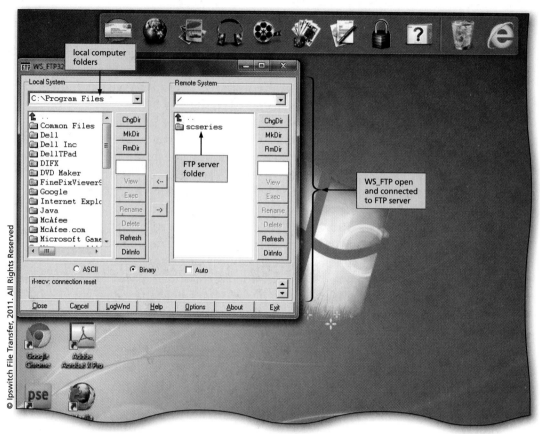

Figure 7

Marketing Your Web Site

Now that your Web pages are published, you need to get the word out to potential Web site visitors. You need to determine a comprehensive marketing plan. It serves no purpose for you to publish a Web site if no one visits it. There are several ways to start a marketing campaign:

- Put your URL on your business cards, company brochures, stationery, and e-mail signature.
- Advertise your URL in newsletters and print articles.
- Tell people verbally about your Web site.
- Find and get listed on targeted directories and search engines specific to your industry.
- Buy banner ads.
- Negotiate reciprocal links in which you agree to link to a Web site if they agree to link to your Web site.
- Utilize newsgroups specific to your industry.

BTW

Search Engines
Both Google and Yahoo! contain information about optimizing your Web sites. Review their Webmaster guidelines and resources for great ideas on registering with their search engines.

Registering with Search Engines

You are finished entering the meta tags, publishing, and marketing your Web site. The next step is to register your Web site with the two most popular search engines, Google and Yahoo! It is also a good idea to register your site with search engines that specialize in subject matter related to your Web site.

To Register Your Web Site with Search Engines

The next steps show you how to register your Web pages with the Google and Yahoo! search engines. Note that both Google and Yahoo! search engines require or recommend that you register with their site before you can submit a Web site to the search engine.

- In Internet Explorer, type http://www.google.com/addurl.html in the address bar and press the ENTER key (Figure 8).

- Click the Learn more link. Some of the worthwhile links on that page are: Google Basics and Webmaster FAQ. These links provide excellent starting points. This page also contains articles and links to other valuable resources, including tools and contacts for Webmasters.

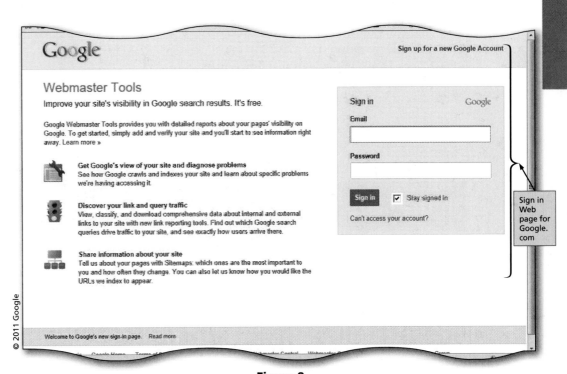

Figure 8

- For the Yahoo! registration, type http://search.yahoo.com/info/submit.html in the address bar and press the ENTER key (Figure 9).

- Follow the directions to add your URL.

- Close the browser.

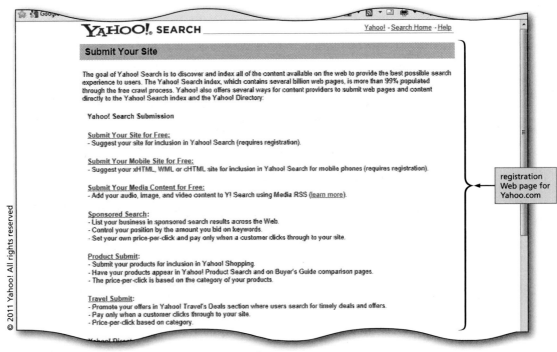

Figure 9

Feature Summary

In this feature, you have learned how to insert keywords and description meta tags into your Web page. You also learned about domain names, what questions to ask of a potential a Web host, how to publish your Web page, ways to market your Web site, and how to register your site with search engines. The items listed below include all the new skills you have learned in this feature.

1. Add Keywords (HTML 226)
2. Add a Description (HTML 226)
3. Check Domain Name Availability (HTML 228)
4. Register Your Web Site with Search Engines (HTML 230)

In the Lab

Design and/or create a document using the guidelines, concepts, and skills presented in this chapter. Labs are listed in order of increasing difficulty.

Lab 1: Creating a Publishing and Marketing Plan

Problem: Your assignment is to apply the ideas and suggestions listed in this special feature to write a comprehensive publishing and marketing plan. This plan should be presented in a Word file that can be submitted to your instructor.

Instructions:

1. Determine a domain name that is available to use for your Oceanside Hotel and Sports Club Web site.

2. Research and identify several possible Web hosting options. Answer all six questions covered in this special feature section for each of your hosting options.

3. Research and identify the specifics about registering your Web site with both Google and Yahoo!.

4. Write a marketing plan that addresses specific ways that you can get the word out about your Web site. Specific plans should include:

   a. Locating targeted directories and search engines specific to the industry reflected in the Web site

   b. Investigating the pros and cons of buying banner ads

   c. Determining Web sites to which you could have possible reciprocal links

   d. Finding newsgroups specific to the industry reflected in the Web site

5. Save the file with the name Lab SF1-1 Marketing.docx. Submit the file in the format specified by your instructor.

In the Lab

Lab 2: Attracting Visitors to Another Web Site

Problem: In this assignment, you will assess another Web site to complete the same basic steps as taken in this feature to improve the site's visibility on the Internet.

Instructions:

1. Select a Web site that is of interest to you and open the site's home page.

2. Review the meta tags (if any) that are used on the home page. (*Hint:* View the page source to review those tags.) Determine how you can utilize additional meta tags for this Web page. What keywords and descriptions would be good to use? What keywords and descriptions do other related Web sites use?

3. Write a marketing plan that addresses specific ways that you can get the word out about this Web site. Specific plans should include:

   a. Locating targeted directories and search engines specific to the industry reflected in the Web site

   b. Determining Web sites to which you could have possible reciprocal links

   c. Finding newsgroups specific to the industry reflected in the Web site

4. Save the file with the name Lab SF1-2 Marketing.docx. Submit the file in the format specified by your instructor.

Appendix A
HTML Quick Reference

HTML Coding Standards

HTML is the original language used for publishing hypertext on the World Wide Web. It is a nonproprietary format based on Standard Generalized Markup Language (SGML). HTML documents can be created with a wide variety of tools, from simple text editors such as Notepad and Notepad++, to sophisticated WYSIWYG authoring tools such as Adobe Dreamweaver. Extensible Markup Language (XML) is a markup language that uses tags to describe the structure and content of a document, not just the format.

Extensible Hypertext Markup Language (XHTML) is a reformulation of HTML so it conforms to XML structure and content rules. By combining HTML and XML, XHTML provides the display features of HTML and the stricter coding standards required by XML.

HTML5 is the newest version of HTML. HTML5 is a very flexible language that does not have coding standards like the XHTML standards defined by the World Wide Web Consortium (W3C). For instance, with HTML5, you can combine lowercase, uppercase, or mixed-case lettering in your tags and attributes. Despite the HTML5 flexibility, this book adheres to good coding practices (other than the XHTML <!DOCTYPE> tag) that would make it easy to convert to XHTML standards if they should one day override HTML5. The coding practices to which the book adheres are shown in Table A–1. The projects in this book use the HTML5 <!DOCTYPE> tag and follow the standards outlined in Table A–1. This information is also shown in Table 1–3 in Chapter 1.

Table A–1 Coding Practices

Practice	Invalid Example	Valid Example
All tags and attributes must be written in lowercase	\<IMG HEIGHT="346" />	\<img height="346" />
All attribute values must be enclosed by single or double quotation marks	\<img height=346 />	\<img height="346" />
All tags must be closed, including tags such as img, hr, and br, which do not have end tags, but which must be closed as a matter of practice	\ \<hr> \<p>This is another paragraph	\ \<hr /> \<p>This is another paragraph\</p>
All elements must be nested properly	\<p>\This is a bold paragraph\</p>\	\<p>\This is a bold paragraph\\</p>

HTML Tags and Attributes

HTML uses tags such as <h1> and <p> to structure text into headings, paragraphs, lists, hypertext links, and so on. Many HTML tags have attributes that can be defined in different ways to further structure the content of the Web page. Attributes are the parts of HTML elements that define them. Attributes provide additional information that a browser can use to determine things like how to display an element. As an example, the height and width attributes in the <img> tag describe the size of the image. **Global attributes** are those that can be used with most (there are exceptions) HTML tags. HTML4 had a number of global attributes, and HTML5 has added some new ones (as indicated below). Table A–2 lists the HTML5 global attributes. This is a comprehensive list of attributes that are common to all HTML5 elements (with some exceptions).

Table A–2 HTML5 Global Attributes		
Attribute	**Value**	**Description**
accesskey	character	Specifies a shortcut key to access an element
class	classname	Refers to a class specified in a style sheet
[NEW] contenteditable	true false inherit	Specifies whether a user can edit the content of an element or not
[NEW] contextmenu	menu_id	Specifies a context menu for an element; the value must be the id of a <menu> element
dir	ltr rtl auto	Specifies the text direction for the content in an element
[NEW] draggable	true false auto	Specifies whether a user is allowed to drag an element or not
[NEW] dropzone	copy move link	Specifies what happens when dragged items/data are dropped in the element
[NEW] hidden	hidden	Specifies that an element should be hidden
id	id	Specifies a unique id for an element
lang	language_code	Specifies the language of the element's content
[NEW] spellcheck	true false	Specifies if the element must have its spelling and grammar checked
style	style_definitions	Specifies an inline style for an element
tabindex	number	Specifies the tab order of an element
title	text	Specifies extra information about an element

As the W3C continually updates the HTML specifications, HTML tags are added to, deleted, and replaced by newer tags. Table A–3 lists HTML tags and their associated attributes. The list provides a brief description of each tag and its values. The default value for each attribute is indicated by bold text in the Description column. Certain tags and elements listed in Table A–3 are highlighted as follows:

| NEW | The NEW icon indicates tags or attributes that are new with HTML5 and validate successfully with the HTML5 DOCTYPE. Note that these tags may not work with all browsers. |

* Deprecated tags are indicated by an asterisk. Those are tags that have been replaced by newer elements and validate successfully with the Transitional DOCTYPE.

** Two asterisks indicate tags and attributes not supported (or absent) in HTML5. Using these tags with an HTML5 DOCTYPE will result in validation errors. However, these tags will validate with the Transitional DOCTYPE. They remain in Table A–3 because you will encounter them in Web pages that you maintain.

Deprecated elements are still available for use, and most browsers still support them. Browsers will probably continue to support deprecated tags and attributes in the near future, but eventually these tags may become obsolete, so future support cannot be guaranteed. It is therefore best not to use deprecated tags.

For a comprehensive list of HTML tags and attributes, more thorough descriptions, examples of HTML tags, and XHTML coding standards, visit the W3C Web site at w3.org.

Table A–3 HTML Tags and Attributes

HTML Tag and Attributes	Description	
<!DOCTYPE>	Indicates the version of HTML used	
<!--Text here-->	Inserts comments that are ignored by browsers	
<a>....</a>	Anchor; creates a hyperlink or fragment identifier	
charset=*character set* **	Specifies the character encoding of the linked resource	
href=*URL*	Hyperlink reference that specifies the target URL	
media=*media_query*	Specifies what media/device the target URL is optimized for	NEW
id=*text*	Specifies an id for enclosed text, allowing it to be the target of a hyperlink	
rel=*relationship*	Indicates the relationship going from the current page to the target	
rev=*relationship* **	Indicates the relationship going from the target to the current page	
target=_blank, _self, _parent, _top, *framename*	Defines the name of the window or frame in which the linked resource will appear	
type=*MIME_type*	Specifies the MIME type of the target URL	NEW
<address>....</address>	Used for information such as authorship, e-mail addresses, or addresses; enclosed text appears italicized and indented in some browsers	
<area>....</area>	Creates a clickable area, or hotspot, on a client-side image map	
alt=*text*	Specifies an alternate text for the area	NEW
coords=*value1, value2*	Specifies the coordinates that define the edges of the hotspot; a comma-delimited list of values	
href=*URL*	Hyperlink reference that specifies the target URL	
hreflang=*language_code*	Specifies the language of the target URL	NEW
media=*media query*	Specifies what media/device the target URL is optimized for	NEW
nohref**	Indicates that no link is associated with the area	
shape=*circle, poly, rect*	Identifies the shape of the area	
target=_blank, _self, _parent, _top, *framename*	Defines the name of the window or frame in which the linked resource will appear	
type=*MIME_type*	Specifies the MIME type of the target URL	NEW
<article>...</article>	Defines an article	

NEW   New with HTML5   * Deprecated tags   ** Not supported in HTML5

Table A–3 HTML Tags and Attributes (continued)

HTML Tag and Attributes	Description
NEW **<aside>...</aside>**	Defines content aside from the main page content
NEW **<audio>...</audio>**	Defines sound content
autoplay=autoplay	Specifies that the audio should start playing as soon as it is ready
controls=controls	Specifies that playback controls should be displayed
loop=loop	Specifies that the audio should start over again, when it is finished
preload=auto, metadata, none	Specifies whether or not the audio should be loaded when the page loads
src=URL	Specifies the URL of the audio to play
<b>....</b>	Specifies text to appear in bold
<base />	Identifies the base in all relative URLs in the document
href=URL	Specifies the absolute URL used to resolve all relative URLs in the document
target=_blank, _self, _parent, _top, framename	Defines the name for the default window (or frame*) in which the hyperlinked pages are displayed
<big>....</big> **	Increases the size of the enclosed text to a type size bigger than the surrounding text; exact display size depends on the browser and default font
<blockquote>....</blockquote>	Sets enclosed text to appear as a quotation, indented on the right and left
cite=URL	Specifies the source of the quotation
<body>....</body>	Defines the start and end of a Web page's content
alink=color **	Defines the color of an active link
background=URL **	Identifies the image to be used as a background
bgcolor=color **	Sets the document's background color
link=color **	Defines the color of links not yet visited
vlink=color **	Defines the color of visited links
**
**	Inserts a line break
NEW **<canvas>...</canvas>**	Defines graphics
height=pixels	Specifies the height of the canvas
width=pixels	Specifies the width of the canvas
<caption>....</caption>	Creates a caption for a table
align=position **	Sets caption position
<center>....</center> **	Centers the enclosed text horizontally on the page
<cite>....</cite>	Indicates that the enclosed text is a citation; text is usually displayed in italics
<code>....</code>	Indicates that the enclosed text is a code sample from a program; text is usually displayed in fixed width font such as Courier
<col>....</col>	Organizes columns in a table into column groups to share attribute values
align=position **	Sets horizontal alignment of text within the column
span=number	Sets the number of columns that span the <col> element
valign=position **	Specifies vertical alignment of text within the column
width=pixels **	Sets the width of each column in the column group
<colgroup>....</colgroup>	Encloses a group of <col> tags and groups the columns to set properties
align=position **	Specifies horizontal alignment of text within the column
char=character **	Specifies a character on which to align column values (for example, a period is used to align monetary values)

NEW   New with HTML5   * Deprecated tags   ** Not supported in HTML5

Table A–3 HTML Tags and Attributes *(continued)*

HTML Tag and Attributes	Description	
<colgroup>....</colgroup> *(continued)*		
charoff=*value* **	Specifies a number of characters to offset data aligned with the character specified in the char property	
span=*number*	Sets the number of columns the <col> element spans	
valign=*position* **	Specifies vertical alignment of text within the column	
width=*pixels* **	Sets the width of each column spanned by the colgroup statement	
<command>...</command>	Defines a command button	NEW
checked=checked	Defines if the command is checked or not; use only if type is radio or checkbox	
disabled=disabled	Defines if the command is available or not	
icon=*URL*	Defines the URL of an image to display as the command	
label=*name*	Defines a name for the command; the label is visible	
radiogroup=*groupname*	Defines the name of the radiogroup this command belongs to; use only if type is radio	
type=checkbox, command, radio	Defines the type of command; default value is command	
<datalist>...</datalist>	Defines a dropdown list	NEW
<dd>....</dd>	Indicates that the enclosed text is a definition in the definition list	
<details>...</details>	Defines details of an element	NEW
<div>....</div>	Defines block-level structure or division in the HTML document	
align=*position* **	Specifies alignment of the content block	
<dl>....</dl>	Creates a definition list	
<dt>....</dt>	Indicates that the enclosed text is a term in the definition list	
....	Indicates that the enclosed text should be emphasized; usually appears in italics	
<embed>...</embed>	Defines external interactive content or plugin	NEW
height=*pixels*	Specifies the height of the embedded content	
src=*URL*	Specifies the URL of the embedded content	
type=*MIME_type*	Specifies the MIME type of the embedded content	
width=*pixels*	Specifies the width of the embedded content	
<fieldset>....</fieldset>	Groups related form controls and labels	
disabled=disabled	Specifies that a fieldset should be disabled	
form=*form_id*	Specifies one or more forms that a fieldset belongs to	
name=*text*	Specifies the name of the fieldset	
<figcaption>...</figcaption>	Defines the caption of a figure element	NEW
<figure>...</figure>	Defines a group of media content, and their captions	NEW
<font>....</font> **	Defines the appearance of enclosed text	
color=*color* **	Sets the font color; can be a hexadecimal value (#rrggbb) or a word for a predefined color value	
face=*list* **	Identifies the font face; multiple entries should be separated by commas	
point-size=*value* **	Sets the point size of text for downloaded fonts	
size=*value* **	Sets the font size in absolute terms (1 through 7) or as a relative value	
weight=*value* **	Sets the weight of the font, ranging from 100 (lightest) to 900 (heaviest)	
<footer>...</footer>	Defines a footer for a section or page	NEW

NEW New with HTML5   * Deprecated tags   ** Not supported in HTML5

Table A–3 HTML Tags and Attributes *(continued)*

HTML Tag and Attributes	Description
\<form\>....\</form\>	Marks the start and end of a Web page form
action=*URL*	Specifies the URL of the application that will process the form; required attribute
[NEW] autocomplete=on, off	Specifies whether or not the form should have autocomplete enabled
enctype=*encoding*	Specifies how the form element values will be encoded
method=get, post	Specifies the method used to pass form parameters (data) to the server
name=*form_name*	Specifies the name for a form
[NEW] novalidate=novalidate	If present the form should not be validated when submitted
target=_blank, _self, _parent, _top, *framename*	Specifies the frame or window that displays the form's results
\<frame\>....\</frame\> **	Delimits a frame within a frameset
frameborder=*option* **	Specifies whether the frame border is displayed
marginheight=*value* **	Adds *n* pixels of space above and below the frame contents
marginwidth=*value* **	Adds *n* pixels of space to the left and the right of the frame contents
name=*text* **	Specifies the name of the frame
noresize **	Prevents the user from resizing the frame
scrolling=*option* **	Adds scroll bars or not—always, never, or add when needed
src=*URL* **	Defines the URL of the source document that is displayed in the frame
\<frameset\>....\</frameset\> **	Defines a collection of frames in a frameset
cols=*value1, value2,...* **	Defines the number and width of frames within a frameset
frameborder=*option* **	Specifies whether the frame border is displayed
rows= *value1, value2,...* **	Defines the number and height of frames within a frameset
\<head\>....\</head\>	Delimits the start and end of the HTML document's head
[NEW] **\<header\>...\</header\>**	Defines a header for a section or page
[NEW] **\<hgroup\>...\<hgroup\>**	Defines information about a section in a document
\<h*n*\>....\</h*n*\>	Defines a header level *n*, ranging from the largest (h1) to the smallest (h6)
align=left, center, right **	Specifies the header alignment
\<hr /\>	Inserts a horizontal rule
align=left, center, right **	Specifies the alignment of the horizontal rule
noshade=noshade **	Specifies to not use 3D shading and to round the ends of the rule
size=*value* **	Sets the thickness of the rule to a value in pixels
width=*pixels, %* **	Sets the width of the rule to a value in pixels or a percentage of the page width; percentage is preferred
\<html\>....\</html\>	Indicates the start and the end of the HTML document
[NEW] manifest=*URL*	Specifies the URL of the document's cache manifest
version=*data* **	Indicates the HTML version used; not usually used
\<i\>....\</i\>	Sets enclosed text to appear in italics
\<iframe\>....\</iframe\> *	Creates an inline frame, also called a floating frame or subwindow, within an HTML document
height=*pixels*	Sets the frame height to a value in pixels
marginheight=*value* **	Sets the margin between the contents of the frame and its top and bottom borders to a value in pixels
marginwidth=*value* **	Sets the margin between the contents of the frame and its left and right borders to a value in pixels

[NEW] New with HTML5   * Deprecated tags   ** Not supported in HTML5

Table A–3 HTML Tags and Attributes *(continued)*

HTML Tag and Attributes	Description	
<iframe>....</iframe> * *(continued)*		
name=*text* *	Assigns a name to the current frame	
noresize *	Prevents the user from resizing the frame	
sandbox=*allow-option*	Specifies restrictions to the frame content	NEW
scrolling=*option* **	Adds scroll bars or not—always, never, or add when needed	
seamless=seamless	Specifies that the iframe should be seamlessly integrated	NEW
src=*URL* *	Defines the URL of the source document that is displayed in the frame	
srcdoc=*HTML_code*	Specifies the HTML of the document showing in the iframe	NEW
width=*pixels* *	Sets the frame width to a value in pixels	
<img>....</img>	Inserts an image into the current Web page	
align=*type* **	Defines image alignment in relation to the text or the page margin	
alt=*text*	Provides a text description of an image if the browser cannot display the image; should always be used	
border=*value* **	Sets the thickness of the border around the image to a value in pixels; value is 0 or 1; developers discouraged from using this	
height=*pixels*	Sets the height of the image to a value in pixels (not percentages); should always be used	
src=*URL*	Specifies the URL of the image to be displayed; required	
usemap=#*mapname*	Specifies the map of coordinates and links that defines the href within this image	
width=*pixels*	Sets the width of the image to a value in pixels (not percentages); should always be used	
<input>....</input>	Defines controls used in forms	
alt=*text*	Provides a short description of the control or image button; for browsers that do not support inline images	
autocomplete=on, off	Specifies whether or not the input field should have focus on page load	NEW
autofocus=autofocus	Specifies that the input field should have focus on page load	NEW
checked=checked	Sets radio buttons and check boxes to the checked state	
disabled=disabled	Disables the control	
form=*form_id*	Specifies one or more forms the input element belongs to	NEW
formaction=*URL*	Overrides the form's action attribute. Defines where to send the data when the form is submitted (for type="submit" and type="image")	NEW
formenctype=*encoding*	Overrides the form's enctype attribute. Defines how form data should be encoded before sending it to the server (for type="submit" and type="image")	NEW
formmethod=get, post	Overrides the form's method attribute. Defines the HTTP method for sending data to the action URL (for type="submit" and type="image")	NEW
formnovalidate= formnovalidate	Overrides the form's novalidate attribute. Defines that the input element should not be validated when submitted	NEW
formtarget=_blank, _self, _parent, _top, *framename*	Overrides the form's target attribute. Defines the target window to use when the form is submitted (for type="submit" and type="image")	NEW
height=*pixels*, %	The height of an input element (for type="image")	NEW
list=*datalist_id*	Refers to a datalist that contains predefined options for the input element	NEW
max=*number, date*	Specifies a maximum value for an input field	NEW
maxlength=*number*	Sets a value for the maximum number of characters allowed as input for a text or password control	

NEW New with HTML5   * Deprecated tags   ** Not supported in HTML5

Table A–3 HTML Tags and Attributes *(continued)*

HTML Tag and Attributes	Description
<input>....</input> *(continued)*	
multiple=*multiple*	If present, the user is allowed more than one value
name=*text*	Assigns a name to the control
NEW pattern=*regexp_pattern*	Specifies a pattern or format for the input field's value
NEW placeholder=*text*	Specifies a hint to help users fill out the input field
readonly=*readonly*	Prevents changes to the control
NEW required=*required*	Indicates that the input field's value is required in order to submit the form
size=*number*	Sets the initial size of the control to a value in characters
NEW step=*number*	Specifies the legal number intervals for the input field
src=*URL*	Identifies the location of the image if the control is set to an image
type=*type*	Defines the type of control
value=*value*	Sets the initial value of the control
<ins>....</ins>	Identifies and displays text as having been inserted in the document in relation to a previous version
cite=*URL*	Specifies the URL of a document that has more information on the inserted text
datetime=*datetime*	Date and time of a change
<kbd>....</kbd>	Sets enclosed text to display as keyboard-like input
NEW **<keygen>...</keygen>**	Defines a generated key in a form
autofocus=*autofocus*	Makes the input field focused on page load
challenge=*challenge*	Specifies that the value of the keygen is set to be challenged when submitted
disabled=*disabled*	Disables the keytag field
form=*form_id*	Defines one or more forms the input field belongs to
keytype=*rsa, dsa, ec*	Specifies the security algorithm of the key (for example, rsa generates an RSA key)
name=*text*	Defines a unique name for the input element; the name attribute is used to collect the field's value when submitted
<label>....</label>	Creates a label for a form control
for=*element_id*	Indicates the name or ID of the element to which the label is applied
form=*form_id*	Specifies one or more forms the label field belongs to
<legend>....</legend>	Assigns a caption to a fieldset element, as defined by the <fieldset> tags
<li>....</li>	Defines the enclosed text as a list item in a list
value=*value*	Inserts or restarts counting with value
<link />	Establishes a link between the HTML document and another document, such as an external style sheet
charset=*character set* **	Specifies the character encoding of the linked resource
href=*URL*	Defines the URL of the linked document
name=*text*	Names the current anchor so that it can be the destination for other links
rel=*relationship*	Indicates the relationship going from the current page to the target
rev=*relationship* **	Indicates the relationship going from the target to the current page
NEW sizes=*heightxwidth, any*	Specifies sizes (height and width) of the linked resource
target=*name* **	Defines the name of the frame into which the linked resource will appear
type=*MIME_type*	Indicates the data or media type of the linked document (for example, text/css for linked style sheets)

NEW New with HTML5   * Deprecated tags   ** Not supported in HTML5

Table A–3 HTML Tags and Attributes *(continued)*

HTML Tag and Attributes	Description	
<map>....</map>	Specifies a client-side image map; must enclose <area> tags	
name=*text*	Assigns a name to the image map	
<mark>...</mark>	Defines marked text	NEW
<menu>...</menu>	Defines a list/menu of commands	
label=*menulabel*	Specifies a visible label for the menu	NEW
type=context, toolbar, list	Specifies which type of menu to display	NEW
<meta />	Provides additional data (metadata) about an HTML document	
charset=*character_set*	Specifies the character encoding for the HTML document	NEW
content=*text*	Specifies the value for the <meta> information; required	
http-equiv=content-type, default-style, refresh	Specifies the HTTP-equivalent name for metadata; tells the server to include that name and content in the HTTP header when the HTML document is sent to the client	
name=*text*	Assigns a name to metadata	
scheme=*text* **	Provides additional context for interpreting the information in the content attribute	
<meter>...</meter>	Defines measurement within a predefined range	NEW
form=*form_id*	Specifies which form this meter belongs to	
high=*number*	Specifies at which point the measurement's value is considered a high value	
low=*number*	Specifies at which point the measurement's value is considered a low value	
max=*number*	Specifies the maximum value; default value is 1.0	
min=*number*	Specifies the minimum value; default value is 0	
optimum=*number*	Specifies which measurement's value is the best value	
value=*number*	Required. Specifies the measurement's current or "measured" value	
<nav>...</nav>	Defines navigation links	NEW
<noframes>....</noframes> **	Defines content to be displayed in browsers that do not support frames	
<object>....</object>	Includes an external object in the HTML document such as an image, a Java applet, or other external object	
data=*URL*	Identifies the location of the object's data	
form=*form_id*	Specifies one or more forms the object belongs to	NEW
height=*pixels*	Sets the height of the object to a value in pixels	
name=*text*	Assigns a control name to the object for use in forms	
type=*MIME_type*	Specifies the content or media type of the object	
usemap=*#mapname*	Associates an image map as defined by the <map> element	
width=*pixels*	Sets the width of the object to a value in pixels	
<ol>....</ol>	Defines an ordered list that contains numbered list item elements (<li>)	
reversed=reversed	Specifies that the list order should be descending	NEW
start=*start*	Specifies the start value of an ordered list	
type=*option* **	Sets or resets the numbering format for the list	
<optgroup>...</optgroup>	Defines an option group	NEW
disabled=disabled	Specifies that an option group should be disabled	NEW
label=*text*	Specifies a label for the option group	NEW

NEW New with HTML5   * Deprecated tags   ** Not supported in HTML5

Table A–3 HTML Tags and Attributes *(continued)*

HTML Tag and Attributes	Description
<option>....</option>	Defines individual options in a selection list, as defined by the <select> element
disabled=disabled	Disables the option items
label=*text*	Provides a shorter label for the option than that specified in its content
selected=selected	Sets the option to be the default or the selected option in a list
value=*text*	Sets a value returned to the server when the user selects the option
NEW **<output>...</output>**	Defines some types of output
for=*element_id*	Specifies one or more elements the output field relates to
form=*form_id*	Specifies one or more forms the output field belongs to
name=*text*	Specifies a name for the object (to use when a form is submitted)
<p>....</p>	Delimits a paragraph; automatically inserts a blank line between text
align=*position* ★★	Aligns text within the paragraph
<param>....</param>	Passes a parameter to an object or applet, as defined by the <object>
name=*text*	Defines the name of the parameter required by an object
type=*MIME_type* ★★	Specifies the content or media type of the object
value=*data*	Sets the value of the parameter
valuetype=data, ref, object ★★	Identifies the type of parameter used in the value attribute
<pre>....</pre>	Preserves the original format of the enclosed text; keeps line breaks and spacing the same as the original
NEW **<progress>...</progress>**	Defines progress of a task of any kind
max=*number*	Defines the value of completion
value=*number*	Defines the current value of the progress
<q>....</q>	Sets enclosed text as a short quotation
cite=*URL*	Specifies the source URL of the quote
NEW **<rp>...</rp>**	Used in ruby annotations to define what to show if a browser does not support the ruby element
NEW **<rt>...</rt>**	Defines explanation to ruby annotations
NEW **<ruby>...</ruby>**	Defines ruby annotations, which are used for East Asian typography
<s>...</s>	Defines text that is no longer correct, accurate, or relevant
<samp>....</samp>	Sets enclosed text to appear as sample output from a computer program or script; usually appears in a monospace font
<script>....</script>	Inserts a client-side script into an HTML document
NEW async=async	Defines if the script should be executed asynchronously or not
defer=defer	Indicates that the browser should defer executing the script
src=*URL*	Identifies the location of an external script
type=*MIME_type*	Specifies the MIME type of the script
NEW **<section>...</section>**	Defines a section
<select>....</select>	Defines a form control to create a multiple-choice menu or scrolling list; encloses a set of <option> tags to define one or more options
NEW autofocus=autofocus	Makes the select field focused on page load
disabled=disabled	Disables the selection list
form=*form_id*	Defines one or more forms the select field belongs to
multiple=multiple	Sets the list to allow multiple selections

NEW New with HTML5   ★ Deprecated tags   ★★ Not supported in HTML5

Table A–3 HTML Tags and Attributes *(continued)*

HTML Tag and Attributes	Description	
\<select\>....\</select\> *(continued)*		
name=*text*	Assigns a name to the selection list	
size=*value*	Sets the number of visible options in the list	
\<small\>....\</small\>	Sets enclosed text to appear in a smaller typeface	
\<source\>...\</source\>	Defines media resources	NEW
media=*media_query*	Specifies what media/device the media resource is optimized for; default value: all	
src=*URL*	The URL of the media	
type=*MIME_type*	Specifies the MIME type of the media resource	
\<span\>....\</span\>	Creates a user-defined container to add inline structure to the HTML document	
\<strike\>....\</strike\> **	Sets enclosed text to appear with strong emphasis; usually displayed as bold text	
\<strong\>....\</strong\>	Sets enclosed text to appear with strong emphasis; usually displayed as bold text	
\<style\>....\</style\>	Encloses embedded style sheet rules for use in the HTML document	
media=*media_query*	Identifies the intended medium of the style	
scoped=*scoped*	If present, the styles should only apply to this element's parent element and its child elements	NEW
type=text/css	Specifies the MIME type of the style sheet	
\<sub\>....\</sub\>	Sets enclosed text to appear in subscript	
\<summary\>...\</summary\>	Defines the header of a "detail" element	NEW
\<sup\>....\</sup\>	Sets enclosed text to appear in superscript	
\<table\>....\</table\>	Marks the start and end of a table	
align=*position* **	Aligns the table text	
border=*value*	Specifies if the table cells have borders or not; the only values are " " and 1	
cellpadding=*pixels* **	Sets padding around each cell's contents to a value in pixels	
cellspacing=*pixels* **	Sets spacing between cells to a value in pixels	
frame=*option* **	Defines which parts of the outer border (frame) to display	
rules=*option* **	Specifies which inner borders are to appear between the table cells	
summary=*text* **	Provides a summary of the table's purpose and structure	
width=*pixels, %* **	Sets table width in pixels or a percentage of the window	
\<tbody\>....\</tbody\>	Defines a groups of rows in a table body	
align=*option* **	Aligns text	
char=*character* **	Specifies a character on which to align column values (for example, a period is used to align monetary values)	
charoff=*value* **	Specifies a number of characters to offset data aligned with the character specified in the char property	
valign=*position* **	Sets vertical alignment of cells in a group	
\<td\>....\</td\>	Defines a data cell in a table; contents are left-aligned and normal text by default	
abbr=*text* **	Provides an abbreviated version of the cell's contents that browsers can use if space is limited	
align=*position* **	Specifies horizontal alignment	

NEW New with HTML5   * Deprecated tags   ** Not supported in HTML5

Table A–3 HTML Tags and Attributes (continued)

HTML Tag and Attributes	Description
<td>....</td> (continued)	
bgcolor=color **	Defines the background color for the cell
char=character **	Specifies a character on which to align column values (for example, a period is used to align monetary values)
charoff=value **	Specifies a number of characters to offset data aligned with the character specified in the char property
colspan=value	Defines the number of adjacent columns spanned by the cell
headers=header_id	Defines the list of header cells for the current cell
rowspan=value	Defines the number of adjacent rows spanned by the cell
scope=option **	Specifies cells for which the element defines header cells
valign=position **	Sets vertical alignment of cells in the group
width=pixels, % **	Sets the width of the table in either pixels or a percentage of the whole table width
<textarea>....</textarea>	Creates a multiline text input area within a form
NEW autofocus=autofocus	Specifies that the text area field should have focus on page load
cols=value	Defines the number of columns in the text input area
disabled=disabled	Disables the element
NEW form=form_id	Specifies one or more forms the text area belongs to
NEW maxlength=number	Specifies the maximum number of characters allowed in the text area
name=text	Assigns a name to the text area
NEW placeholder=text	Specifies a hint to help users fill out the input field
readonly=readonly	Prevents the user from editing content in the text area
NEW required=required	Indicates that the input field's value is required in order to submit the form
rows=value	Defines the number of rows in the text input area
NEW wrap=hard, soft	Specifies how the text in the text area is wrapped, and if it should be wrapped when submitted in a form
<tfoot>....</tfoot>	Identifies and groups rows into a table footer
align=position **	Specifies horizontal alignment
char=character **	Specifies a character on which to align column values (for example, a period is used to align monetary values)
charoff=value **	Specifies a number of characters to offset data aligned with the character specified in the char property
valign=position **	Sets vertical alignment of cells in a group
<th>....</th>	Defines a table header cell; contents are bold and center-aligned by default
colspan=value	Defines the number of adjacent columns spanned by the cell
NEW headers=header_id	Specifies one or more header cells a cell is related to
rowspan=value	Defines the number of adjacent rows spanned by the cell
NEW scope=col, colgroup, row, rowgroup	Specifies whther a header cell is a header for a column, row, or group of columns or rows
width=pixels, % **	Sets the width of the table in either pixels or a percentage of the whole table width

NEW   New with HTML5   * Deprecated tags   ** Not supported in HTML5

Table A–3 HTML Tags and Attributes *(continued)*

HTML Tag and Attributes	Description
<thead>....</thead>	Identifies and groups rows into a table header
align=*position* **	Specifies horizontal alignment
char=*character* **	Specifies a character on which to align column values (for example, a period is used to align monetary values)
charoff=*value* **	Specifies a number of characters to offset data aligned with the character specified in the char property
valign=*position* **	Sets vertical alignment of cells in a group
<time>...</time> `NEW`	Defines a date/time
datetime=*datetime*	Specifies the date or time for the time element; this attribute is used if no date or time is specified in the element's content
pubdate=pubdate	Specifies that the date and time in the <time> element is the publication date and time of the document (or the nearest ancestor article element)
<title>....</title>	Defines the title for the HTML document; should always be used
<tr>....</tr>	Defines a row of cells within a table
align=*position* **	Specifies horizontal alignment
bgcolor=*color* **	Defines the background color for the cell
char=*character* **	Specifies a character on which to align column values (for example, a period is used to align monetary values)
charoff=*value* **	Specifies a number of characters to offset data aligned with the character specified in the char property
valign=*position* **	Sets vertical alignment of cells in a group
<tt>....</tt> **	Formats the enclosed text in teletype- or computer-style monospace font
<u>....</u> **	Sets enclosed text to appear with an underline
<ul>....</ul>	Defines an unordered list that contains bulleted list item elements (<li>)
type=circle, disc, square **	Sets or resets the bullet format for the list
<var>....</var>	Indicates the enclosed text is a variable's name; used to mark up variables or program arguments
<video>...</video> `NEW`	Defines a video
autoplay=autoplay	If present, then the video will start playing as soon as it is ready
controls=controls	If present, controls will be displayed, such as a play button
height=*pixels*	Sets the height of the video player
loop=loop	If present, the video will start over again, every time it is finished
muted=muted	Specifies the default state of the the audio. Currently, only "muted" is allowed
poster=*URL*	Specifies the URL of an image representing the video
preload=auto, metadata, none	Specifies whether or not the video should be loaded when the page loads
src=*URL*	The URL of the video to play
width=*pixels*	Sets the width of the video player
<wbr>...</wbr> `NEW`	Defines a possible line break

`NEW` New with HTML5   * Deprecated tags   ** Not supported in HTML5

Appendix B
Browser-Safe Color Palette

Browser-Safe Colors

Three hardware components help deliver color to a computer user: the processor, the video card, and the monitor. Because of the wide variety of components that exist, the color quality that users see varies greatly. The software on a user's computer, specifically the Web browser, also affects the way that color is displayed on a monitor. It is very difficult, if not impossible, to plan for all possible color variations created by a Web browser. In the past, Web developers had to make sure that they used browser-safe colors. These browser-safe colors restricted the number of colors used on a Web page and minimized the impact of color variations. The trend for monitors today is to display "true color," which means that any of 16 million colors can be displayed on the monitor. Few people use 8-bit monitors anymore, so you generally do not have to limit yourself to browser-safe colors.

A total of 216 browser-safe colors appear the same on different monitors, operating systems, and browsers—including both Windows and Macintosh operating systems and Internet Explorer, Apple Safari, Google Chrome, and Mozilla Firefox browsers. When using color on your Web site, keep in mind that using only the 216 browser-safe colors can be very restrictive. On those 8-bit monitors, only the browser-safe colors will be displayed. If you decide to use a non-browser-safe color, the browser will try to create the color by combining (a process called dithering) any number of the 216 acceptable colors. The resulting color could be slightly different from the color you had intended.

For a complete list of the 216 browser-safe colors, see Table B–1 on the next page or visit the Book Companion Site Web page for this book at www.cengagebrain.com.

Note that you can use either the color name or the color number when identifying a particular color to use. For instance, you can use the number #000099 (see color sample on the following page) or the word "navy" to specify the same color. Also note that to comply with XHTML standards, color names such as "navy" or "silver" must be all lowercase letters and all colors, whether identified by name or number, should be enclosed within quotation marks. Although the book teaches HTML5, for which the XHTML standards do not apply, we still stress using lowercase letters and quotation marks.

Table B–1 Browser-Safe Colors

#ffffff	#ffffcc	#ffff99	#ffff66	#ffff33	#ffff00
#ffccff	#ffcccc	#ffcc99	#ffcc66	#ffcc33	#ffcc00
#ff99ff	#ff99cc	#ff9999	#ff9966	#ff9933	#ff9900
#ff66ff	#ff66cc	#ff6699	#ff6666	#ff6633	#ff6600
#ff33ff	#ff33cc	#ff3399	#ff3366	#ff3333	#ff3300
#ff00ff	#ff00cc	#ff0099	#ff0066	#ff0033	#ff0000
#ccffff	#ccffcc	#ccff99	#ccff66	#ccff33	#ccff00
#ccccff	#cccccc	#cccc99	#cccc66	#cccc33	#cccc00
#cc99ff	#cc99cc	#cc9999	#cc9966	#cc9933	#cc9900
#cc66ff	#cc66cc	#cc6699	#cc6666	#cc6633	#cc6600
#cc33ff	#cc33cc	#cc3399	#cc3366	#cc3333	#cc3300
#cc00ff	#cc00cc	#cc0099	#cc0066	#cc0033	#cc0000
#99ffff	#99ffcc	#99ff99	#99ff66	#99ff33	#99ff00
#99ccff	#99cccc	#99cc99	#99cc66	#99cc33	#99cc00
#9999ff	#9999cc	#999999	#999966	#999933	#999900
#9966ff	#9966cc	#996699	#996666	#996633	#996600
#9933ff	#9933cc	#993399	#993366	#993333	#993300
#9900ff	#9900cc	#990099	#990066	#990033	#990000
#66ffff	#66ffcc	#66ff99	#66ff66	#66ff33	#66ff00
#66ccff	#66cccc	#66cc99	#66cc66	#66cc33	#66cc00
#6699ff	#6699cc	#669999	#669966	#669933	#669900
#6666ff	#6666cc	#666699	#666666	#666633	#666600
#6633ff	#6633cc	#663399	#663366	#663333	#663300
#6600ff	#6600cc	#660099	#660066	#660033	#660000
#33ffff	#33ffcc	#33ff99	#33ff66	#33ff33	#33ff00
#33ccff	#33cccc	#33cc99	#33cc66	#33cc33	#33cc00
#3399ff	#3399cc	#339999	#339966	#339933	#339900
#3366ff	#3366cc	#336699	#336666	#336633	#336600
#3333ff	#3333cc	#333399	#333366	#333333	#333300
#3300ff	#3300cc	#330099	#330066	#330033	#330000
#00ffff	#00ffcc	#00ff99	#00ff66	#00ff33	#00ff00
#00ccff	#00cccc	#00cc99	#00cc66	#00cc33	#00cc00
#0099ff	#0099cc	#009999	#009966	#009933	#009900
#0066ff	#0066cc	#006699	#006666	#006633	#006600
#0033ff	#0033cc	#003399	#003366	#003333	#003300
#0000ff	#0000cc	#000099	#000066	#000033	#000000

Appendix C
Accessibility Standards and the Web

Making the Web Accessible

Nearly 15% of the world population has some sort of disability, a physical condition that limits the individual's ability to perform certain tasks. The U.S. Congress passed the Rehabilitation Act in 1973, which prohibits discrimination for those with disabilities. In 1998, Congress amended this act to reflect the latest changes in information technology. Section 508 requires that any electronic information developed, procured, maintained, or used by the federal government be accessible to people with disabilities. Disabilities that inhibit a person's ability to use the Web fall into four main categories: visual, hearing, motor, and cognitive. This amendment has had a profound effect on how Web pages are designed and developed.

Although Section 508 is specific to Web sites created and maintained by the federal government, all competent Web developers adhere to the Section 508 guidelines. It is important to include everyone as a potential user of your Web site, including those with disabilities. To ignore the needs of nearly 15% of our population is just poor practice. However, some portions of Section 508 are not supported by HTML5. For example, longdesc (§ 1194.22a) and frames (§ 1194.22i) are no longer supported by HTML5. A Web developer would not use those elements, which renders those Section 508 requirements null.

The World Wide Web Consortium (W3C) sponsors its own initiative, called the Web Accessibility Initiative (WAI), that develops guidelines and support materials for accessibility standards. These guidelines, known as the Web Content Accessibility Guidelines (WCAG), cover many of the same issues defined in the Section 508 rules and expand on them relative to superior Web site design.

Section 508 Guidelines Examples

The 13 parts of the Section 508 guidelines are as follows:

- Subpart A—General
  - 1194.1 Purpose.
  - 1194.2 Application.
  - 1194.3 General exceptions.
  - 1194.4 Definitions.
  - 1194.5 Equivalent facilitation.

● Subpart B—Technical Standards

- 1194.21 Software applications and operating systems.
- 1194.22 Web-based intranet and Internet information and applications. 16 rules.
- 1194.23 Telecommunications products.
- 1194.24 Video and multimedia products.
- 1194.25 Self contained, closed products.
- 1194.26 Desktop and portable computers.

● Subpart C—Functional Performance Criteria

- 1194.31 Functional performance criteria.

● Subpart D—Information, Documentation, and Support

- 1194.41 Information, documentation, and support.

Web developers should review these guidelines thoroughly. We focus on the specific guidelines for intranet and Internet development in the following sections.

Subsection **§ 1194.22** of Section 508, **Web-based intranet and Internet information and applications**, is the segment of the amendment that impacts Web design. There are 16 paragraphs within § 1194.22, which are lettered (a) through (p). These 16 paragraphs describe how each component of a Web site should be designed to ensure accessibility. The following is a list of the 16 paragraphs:

§ 1194.22 (a) A text equivalent for every non-text element shall be provided (e.g., via "alt", "longdesc", or in element content).

Graphical images that contain Web page content should include a text alternative. For good Web development practice, all images should include the alt attribute to describe that image, as shown in Chapter 2. As mentioned earlier, longdesc is not supported by HTML5.

§ 1194.22 (b) Equivalent alternatives for any multimedia presentation shall be synchronized with the presentation.

Audio clips should contain a transcript of the content; video clips need closed captioning.

§ 1194.22 (c) Web pages shall be designed so that all information conveyed with color is also available without color, for example from context or markup.

Although color is an important component of most Web pages, you need to consider those site visitors with forms of color blindness if the color contributes significantly to the Web site content.

§ 1194.22 (d) Documents shall be organized so they are readable without requiring an associated style sheet.

Style sheets have an important role in Web development. Some browsers, however, allow users to create their own customized style sheets, which could alter the style sheets that you have designated. When developing a Web site using style sheets, ensure that the site maintains its functionality, even if your specified style sheets have been turned off.

§ 1194.22 (e) Redundant text links shall be provided for each active region of a server-side image map.
and

§ 1194.22 (f) Client-side image maps shall be provided instead of server-side image maps except where the regions cannot be defined with an available geometric shape.

This means that it is preferable for the Web developer to use client-side image maps unless the map uses a shape that the client-side will not allow. If the Web developer chooses to use server-side image maps, the developer should provide text alternatives for each link on the image map.

§ 1194.22 (g) Row and column headers shall be identified for data tables.
and

§ 1194.22 (h) Markup shall be used to associate data cells and header cells for data tables that have two or more logical levels of row or column headers.

You should structure your tables so that they appear in a linear fashion. In other words, the table content should be displayed one cell at a time, working from left to right across each row before moving to the next row.

§ 1194.22 (i) Frames shall be titled with text that facilitates frame identification and navigation.

Although frames are not supported by HTML5, it is important to understand what the law requires. Nonvisual browsers open frame sites one frame at a time. It is therefore important that the Web developer gives a name to each frame, and that the name reflects the contents of that frame. You can use either the title or the id, but because nonvisual browsers differ in which attribute they use, the Web developer should use both attributes.

§ 1194.22 (j) Pages shall be designed to avoid causing the screen to flicker with a frequency greater than 2 Hz and lower than 55 Hz.

Animations on a Web page can be irritating to many people. However, they can also be quite harmful to people who have certain cognitive or visual disabilities or seizure disorders. You should therefore ensure that animations fall within the ranges stated, and you should limit the use of animations when possible. You also should make certain that necessary page content is available without the animations.

§ 1194.22 (k) A text-only page, with equivalent information or functionality, shall be provided to make a Web site comply with the provisions of this part, when compliance cannot be accomplished in any other way. The content of the text-only pages shall be updated whenever the primary page changes.

If you cannot comply with the other 15 guidelines, you should provide a text-only page to display the content of the page. You should also provide an easily accessible link to that text-only Web page.

§ 1194.22 (l) When pages utilize scripting languages to display content, or to create interface elements, the information provided by the script shall be identified with functional text that can be read by assistive technology.

Scripts are often used to create a more interesting and dynamic Web page. You should ensure that the functionality of the script is still available for any person using nonvisual browsers.

§ 1194.22 (m) When a Web page requires that an applet, plug-in, or other application be present on the client system to interpret page content, the page must provide a link to a plug-in or applet that complies with 1194.21 (a) through (l).

Any applet or plug-in that is used on your Web pages should also comply with Section 508. The Web developer should provide a link to the applet or plug-in that is compliant with Section 508.

§ 1194.22 (n) When electronic forms are designed to be completed on-line, the form shall allow people using assistive technology to access the information, field elements, and functionality required for completion and submission of the form, including all directions and cues.

Forms need to be accessible to anyone, including those using nonvisual browsers. You should therefore include value attributes or alternative text for buttons, input boxes, and text area boxes on any form included on your Web page.

§ 1194.22 (o) A method shall be provided that permits users to skip repetitive navigation links.

It can be helpful to provide text links at the very top of a Web page so that users of nonvisual browsers can quickly link to the content of the Web site. Some Web developers use a link that allows users to skip to the main content of the Web page immediately by using a transparent image.

§ 1194.22 (p) When a timed response is required, the user shall be alerted and given sufficient time to indicate that more time is required.

Users need to be given sufficient time to react to a time-out from inactivity by notifying users that the process will soon time out. The user should then be given a way to easily request additional time.

WAI Guidelines

The WAI identifies 12 guidelines for Web developers, known as Web Content Accessibility Guidelines (WCAG) 2.0. The Web Content Accessibility Guidelines (WCAG) documents explain how to make Web content more accessible to people with disabilities. Web **content** generally refers to the information in a Web page or Web application, including text, images, forms, sounds, and such. All Web developers should review the information at the official Web site at w3.org/WAI/intro/wcag.php for complete information on these guidelines, and should apply the guidelines to their Web page development.

The 12 WCAG 2.0 guidelines are organized under four principles: perceivable, operable, understandable, and robust. Anyone who wants to use the Web must have content that is:

Perceivable: Information and user interface components must be presentable to users in ways they can perceive. Users must be able to perceive the information being presented (it can't be invisible to all of their senses).

Operable: User interface components and navigation must be operable. Users must be able to operate the interface (the interface cannot require interaction that a user cannot perform).

Understandable: Information and the operation of the user interface must be understandable. Users must be able to understand the information as well as the operation of the user interface (the content or operation cannot be beyond their understanding).

Robust: Content must be robust enough that it can be interpreted reliably by a wide variety of user agents, including assistive technologies. Users must be able to access the content as technologies advance (as technologies and user agents evolve, the content should remain accessible).

If any of these are not true, users with disabilities will not be able to use the Web.

For each guideline, there are testable success criteria, which are at three levels: A, AA, and AAA. In order for a Web page to conform to WCAG 2.0, all of the following conformance requirements must be satisfied:

- **Level A:** For Level A conformance (the minimum level of conformance), the Web page satisfies all the Level A Success Criteria, or a conforming alternate version is provided.

- **Level AA:** For Level AA conformance, the Web page satisfies all the Level A and Level AA Success Criteria, or a Level AA conforming alternate version is provided.

- **Level AAA:** For Level AAA conformance, the Web page satisfies all the Level A, Level AA, and Level AAA Success Criteria, or a Level AAA conforming alternate version is provided.

Table C–1 contains a summary of the WCAG 2.0 guidelines and the corresponding level of conformance.

Table C–1

WCAG 2.0 Guidelines	Level
Principle 1: Perceivable—Information and user interface components must be presentable to users in ways they can perceive.	
Guideline 1.1 Text Alternatives: Provide text alternatives for any non-text content so that it can be changed into other forms people need, such as large print, braille, speech, symbols or simpler language.	
1.1.1 Nontext Content: All nontext content that is presented to the user has a text alternative that serves the equivalent purpose.	A
Guideline 1.2 Time Based Media: Provide alternatives for time-based media.	
1.2.1 Audio-only and Video-only (Prerecorded): An alternative for time-based media is provided that presents equivalent information for prerecorded audio-only or video-only content.	A
1.2.2 Captions (Prerecorded): Captions are provided for all prerecorded audio content in synchronized media, except when the media is a media alternative for text and is clearly labeled as such.	A
1.2.3 Audio Description or Media Alternative (Prerecorded): An alternative for time-based media or audio description of the prerecorded video content is provided for synchronized media, except when the media is a media alternative for text and is clearly labeled as such.	A
1.2.4 Captions (Live): Captions are provided for all live audio content in synchronized media.	AA
1.2.5 Audio Description (Prerecorded): Audio description is provided for all prerecorded video content in synchronized media.	AA
1.2.6 Sign Language (Prerecorded): Sign language interpretation is provided for all prerecorded audio content in synchronized media.	AAA
1.2.7 Extended Audio Description (Prerecorded): Where pauses in foreground audio are insufficient to allow audio descriptions to convey the sense of the video, extended audio description is provided for all prerecorded video content in synchronized media.	AAA

Table C–1 *(continued)*

WCAG 2.0 Guidelines	Level
1.2.8 Media Alternative (Prerecorded): An alternative for time-based media is provided for all prerecorded synchronized media and for all prerecorded video-only media.	AAA
1.2.9 Audio-only (Live): An alternative for time-based media that presents equivalent information for live audio-only content is provided.	AAA
Guideline 1.3 Adaptable: Create content that can be presented in different ways (for example simpler layout) without losing information or structure.	
1.3.1 Info and Relationships: Information, structure, and relationships conveyed through presentation can be programmatically determined or are available in text.	A
1.3.2 Meaningful Sequence: When the sequence in which content is presented affects its meaning, a correct reading sequence can be programmatically determined.	A
1.3.3 Sensory Characteristics: Instructions provided for understanding and operating content do not rely solely on sensory characteristics of components such as shape, size, visual location, orientation, or sound.	A
Guideline 1.4 Distinguishable: Make it easier for users to see and hear content including separating foreground from background.	
1.4.1 Use of Color: Color is not used as the only visual means of conveying information, indicating an action, prompting a response, or distinguishing a visual element.	A
1.4.2 Audio Control: If any audio on a Web page plays automatically for more than 3 seconds, either a mechanism is available to pause or stop the audio, or a mechanism is available to control the audio volume independently from the overall system volume level.	A
1.4.3 Contrast (Minimum): The visual presentation of text and images of text has a contrast ratio of at least 4.5:1 (for specific exceptions, refer to w3.org/TR/WCAG).	AA
1.4.4 Resize text: Except for captions and images of text, text can be resized without assistive technology up to 200 percent without loss of content or functionality.	AA
1.4.5 Images of Text: If the technologies being used can achieve the visual presentation, text is used to convey information rather than images of (for specific exceptions, refer to w3.org/TR/WCAG).	AA
1.4.6 Contrast (Enhanced): The visual presentation of text and images of text has a contrast ratio of at least 7:1 (for specific exceptions, refer to w3.org/TR/WCAG).	AAA
1.4.7 Low or No Background Audio: For prerecorded audio-only content in which 1) the audio does not contain background sounds, 2) the background sounds can be turned off, or 3) the background sounds are at least 20 decibels lower than the foreground speech content.	AAA
1.4.8 Visual Presentation: For the visual presentation of blocks of text, a mechanism is available to manipulate the look of the page (e.g., background colors, text size) easily.	AAA
1.4.9 Images of Text (No Exception): Images of text are only used for pure decoration or where a particular presentation of text is essential to the information being conveyed.	AAA
Principle 2: Operable—User interface components and navigation must be operable.	
Guideline 2.1 Keyboard Accessible: Make all functionality available from the keyboard.	
2.1.1 Keyboard: All functionality of the content is operable through a keyboard interface without requiring specific timings for individual keystrokes, except where the underlying function requires input that depends on the path of the user's movement and not just the endpoints.	A
2.1.2 No Keyboard Trap: If keyboard focus can be moved to a component of the page using a keyboard interface, then focus can be moved away from that component using only a keyboard interface, and, if it requires more than unmodified arrow or tab keys or other standard exit methods, the user is advised of the method for moving focus away.	A
2.1.3 Keyboard (No Exception): All functionality of the content is operable through a keyboard interface without requiring specific timings for individual keystrokes.	AAA

Table C–1 *(continued)*	
WCAG 2.0 Guidelines	**Level**
Guideline 2.2 Enough Time: Provide users enough time to read and use content.	
2.2.1 Timing Adjustable: The user should be able to easily change each time limit that is set by the content.	A
2.2.2 Pause, Stop, Hide: The user should be able to pause, stop, or hide moving, blinking, scrolling, or auto-updating information.	A
2.2.3 No Timing: Timing is not an essential part of the event or activity presented by the content, except for noninteractive synchronized media and real-time events.	AAA
2.2.4 Interruptions: Interruptions can be postponed or suppressed by the user, except interruptions involving an emergency.	AAA
2.2.5 Re-authenticating: When an authenticated session expires, the user can continue the activity without loss of data after re-authenticating.	AAA
Guideline 2.3 Seizures: Do not design content in a way that is known to cause seizures.	
2.3.1 Three Flashes or Below Threshold: Web pages do not contain anything that flashes more than three times in any one second period, or the flash is below the general flash and red flash thresholds.	A
2.3.2 Three Flashes: Web pages do not contain anything that flashes more than three times in any one second period.	AAA
Guideline 2.4 Navigable: Provide ways to help users navigate, find content, and determine where they are.	
2.4.1 Bypass Blocks: A mechanism is available to bypass blocks of content that are repeated on multiple Web pages.	A
2.4.2 Page Titled: Web pages have titles that describe topic or purpose.	A
2.4.3 Focus Order: If a Web page can be navigated sequentially and the navigation sequences affect meaning or operation, focusable components receive focus in an order that preserves meaning and operability.	A
2.4.4 Link Purpose (In Context): The purpose of each link can be determined from the link text alone or from the link text together with its programmatically determined link context, except where the purpose of the link would be ambiguous to users in general.	A
2.4.5 Multiple Ways: More than one way is available to locate a Web page within a set of Web pages except where the Web Page is the result of, or a step in, a process.	AA
2.4.6 Headings and Labels: Headings and labels describe topic or purpose.	AA
2.4.7 Focus Visible: Any keyboard operable user interface has a mode of operation where the keyboard focus indicator is visible.	AA
2.4.8 Location: Information about the user's location within a set of Web pages is available.	AAA
2.4.9 Link Purpose (Link Only): A mechanism is available to allow the purpose of each link to be identified from link text alone, except where the purpose of the link would be ambiguous to users in general.	AAA
2.4.10 Section Headings: Section headings are used to organize the content.	AAA
Principle 3: Understandable—Information and the operation of user interface must be understandable.	
Guideline 3.1 Readable: Make text content readable and understandable.	
3.1.1 Language of Page: The default human language of each Web page can be programmatically determined.	A
3.1.2 Language of Parts: The human language of each passage or phrase in the content can be programmatically determined except for proper names, technical terms, words of indeterminate language, and words or phrases that have become part of the vernacular of the immediately surrounding text.	AA

Table C–1 *(continued)*

WCAG 2.0 Guidelines	Level
3.1.3 Unusual Words: A mechanism is available for identifying specific definitions of words or phrases used in an unusual or restricted way, including idioms and jargon.	AAA
3.1.4 Abbreviations: A mechanism for identifying the expanded form or meaning of abbreviations is available.	AAA
3.1.5 Reading Level: When text requires reading ability more advanced than the lower secondary education level after removal of proper names and titles, supplemental content, or a version that does not require reading ability more advanced than the lower secondary education level, is available.	AAA
3.1.6 Pronunciation: A mechanism is available for identifying specific pronunciation of words where the meaning of the words, in context, is ambiguous without knowing the pronunciation.	AAA
Guideline 3.2 Predictable: Make Web pages appear and operate in predictable ways.	
3.2.1 On Focus: When any component receives focus, it does not initiate a change of context.	A
3.2.2 On Input: Changing the setting of any user interface component does not automatically cause a change of context unless the user has been advised of the behavior before using the component.	A
3.2.3 Consistent Navigation: Navigational mechanisms that are repeated on multiple Web pages within a set of Web pages occur in the same relative order each time they are repeated, unless a change is initiated by the user.	AA
3.2.4 Consistent Identification: Components that have the same functionality within a set of Web pages are identified consistently.	AA
3.2.5 Change on Request: Changes of context are initiated only by user request or a mechanism is available to turn off such changes.	AAA
Guideline 3.3 Input Assistance: Help users avoid and correct mistakes.	
3.3.1 Error Identification: If an input error is automatically detected, the item that is in error is identified and the error is described to the user in text.	A
3.3.2 Labels or Instructions: Labels or instructions are provided when content requires user input.	A
3.3.3 Error Suggestion: If an input error is automatically detected and suggestions for its correction are known, then the suggestions are provided to the user, unless it would jeopardize the security or purpose of the content.	AA
3.3.4 Error Prevention (Legal, Financial, Data): For Web pages that cause legal commitments or financial transactions for the user to occur, that modify or delete user-controllable data in data storage systems, or that submit user test responses, a mechanism is available for reviewing, confirming, and correcting information before finalizing the submission.	AA
3.3.5 Help: Context-sensitive help is available.	AAA
3.3.6 Error Prevention (All): For Web pages that require the user to submit information, a mechanism is available for reviewing, confirming, and correcting information before finalizing the submission.	AAA
Principle 4: Robust—Content must be robust enough that it can be interpreted reliably by a wide variety of user agents, including assistive technologies.	
Guideline 4.1 Compatible: Maximize compatibility with current and future user agents, including assistive technologies.	
4.1.1 Parsing: In content implemented using markup languages, elements have complete start and end tags, elements are nested according to their specifications, elements do not contain duplicate attributes, and any IDs are unique, except where the specifications allow these features.	A
4.1.2 Name, Role, Value: For all user interface components (including but not limited to: form elements, links, and components generated by scripts), the name and role can be programmatically determined; states, properties, and values that can be set by the user can be programmatically set; and notification of changes to these items is available to user agents, including assistive technologies.	A

Appendix D
CSS Properties and Values

This appendix provides a brief review of Cascading Style Sheets (CSS) concepts and terminology, and lists CSS level 1, 2, and 3 properties and values. The CSS3 properties and values are indicated with a NEW icon. CSS3 utilizes a modularized approach to style sheets, which allows CSS to be updated in a more timely and flexible manner. Many of the new properties are not supported by all browsers as of yet. As stated previously, CSS3, like HTML5, is a moving target. Browsers adapt new properties on an ongoing basis and will continue to do so.

CSS Concepts and Terminology

CSS supports three types of style sheets: inline, embedded (or internal), and external (or linked). A **style** is a rule that defines the appearance of an element on a Web page. Inline styles are used to change the appearance (or style) for individual elements, such as a heading or a paragraph. A **style sheet** is a series of rules that defines the style for a Web page or an entire Web site. The **style statement** changes that specific element, but does not affect other elements in the document. With an embedded style sheet, you add the style sheet within the <style></style> container between the <head></head> tags of the HTML document. An embedded, or internal, style sheet allows you to define the style for an entire Web page. With a linked, or external, style sheet, you create a text file that contains all of the styles that you want to apply, and save the text file with the file extension .css. You then add a link to this external style sheet on any Web page in the Web site in which you want to use those styles. External style sheets give you the most flexibility and are ideal to apply the same formats to all of the Web pages in a Web site. External style sheets also make it easy to change formats quickly across Web pages.

The part of the style statement that identifies the page element that you want to change is called the selector. In the example below, the selector is the h1 (heading size 1) element. The part of the style statement that identifies how the element(s) should appear is called the declaration. In this example, the declaration is everything between the curly brackets {color: red}. This includes the property named color and the value named red.

```
h1    {color: red;}
```

You could use the statement above in both an embedded and an external style sheet. With an external (linked) style sheet, you save the file with the selectors and declarations as a .css file. You then link that file into any Web page into which you want those styles to apply. To add the same style statement into an embedded style sheet, you have to put the selector and declaration within the <style></style> container as shown below. This code would be inserted within the <head></head> container.

```
<style type="text/css">
  h1   {color: red;}
</style>
```

These two style sheets (embedded and external) give you the most flexibility. For instance, if you want all h1 and h2 headings to be the color red, you would simply add the code below:

```
h1, h2      {color: red;}
```

You could also make the style change to the h1 heading as an inline style. You insert that code within the body of the Web page in the following format:

```
<h1 style="color: red">
```

Although inline styles can be very useful, understand that you would have to insert the same declaration for every h1 (or h2 or h3) heading within the Web page. That makes the inline style less flexible than the other style sheets.

As shown in Table D–1, the three style sheets supported by CSS control the appearance of a Web page at different levels. Each style sheet type also has a different level of precedence or priority in relationship to the others. An external style sheet, for example, is used to define styles for multiple pages in a Web site. An embedded style sheet is used to change the style of one Web page, but overrides or takes precedence over any styles defined in an external style sheet. An inline style sheet is used to control the style within an individual HTML tag and takes precedence over the styles defined in both embedded and external style sheets.

Table D–1 CSS Precedence

Type	Level and Precedence
Inline	• Changes the style within an individual HTML tag • Overrides embedded and external style sheets
Embedded	• Changes the style of one Web page • Overrides external style sheets
External	• Changes the style of multiple pages in a Web site

Because style sheets have different levels of precedence, all three types of style sheets can be used on a single Web page. For example, you may want some elements of a Web page to match the other Web pages in the Web site, but you also may want to vary the look of certain sections of that Web page. You can do this by using the three types of style sheets.

For a more comprehensive list of CSS properties and values, see the Web site of the World Wide Web Consortium (w3.org). In addition to an abundance of information about CSS levels 1 and 2, the W3C site also has extensive information about CSS3, from its history to its use with browsers today. The Web site also includes many online tutorials for learning CSS levels 1 and 2 as well as CSS3.

CSS Properties

Tables D–2 through D–30 show the property names, descriptions, and valid values for various categories of CSS properties. Properties shown with the NEW icon are new to CSS3. The NEW icon next to a table name indicates that all properties in the table are new with CSS3. Values listed in bold are the default.

Acceptable Units of Measure

Table D–2 Units of Measure

Property Name	Description	Values
color	A color is either a keyword or a numerical hexidecimal, RGB, RGBA, HSL, or HSLA color specification	[keyword] [#rrggbb]
length	Indicates both relative (em, ex, px) and absolute (in, cm, mm, pt, pc) lengths	em – relative to size of capital M of browser default font ex – relative to small x of browser default font px – represents one pixel, smallest unit of measure in – one inch cm – one centimeter mm – one millimeter pt – 1/72 of an inch pc – 1/12 of an inch
percentage	Values are always relative to another value	percentage of width or height of parent element; if only one value is given, the second is set to "auto"

Animation Properties

NEW | Table D–3 Animation Properties

Property Name	Description	Values
@keyframes	Specifies the animation	[animationname] [keyframes-selector] [css-styles]
animation	A shorthand property for all the animation properties below, except the animation-play-state property	
animation-delay	Specifies when the animation will start	[time]
animation-direction	Specifies whether or not the animation should play in reverse on alternate cycles	**normal** alternate
animation-duration	Specifies how many seconds or milliseconds an animation takes to complete one cycle	[time]
animation-iteration-count	Specifies the number of times an animation should be played	[n] infinite
animation-name	Specifies a name for the @keyframes animation	[keyframename] **none**
animation-play-state	Specifies whether the animation is running or paused	paused **running**
animation-timing-function	Specifies the speed curve of the animation	linear **ease** ease-in ease-out ease-in-out cubic-bezier

Background and Color Properties

Table D–4 Background and Color Properties

Property Name	Description	Values
background	The background property is a shorthand property for setting the individual background properties	
background-attachment	Sets the background image to fixed or scrolls with the page	**scroll** fixed inherit
NEW background-clip	Specifies the painting area of the background	
background-color	Sets the background color of an element	**transparent** [color]
background-image	Sets an image as the background	**none** [URL]
NEW background-origin	Specifies the positioning area of the background images	
background-position	Sets the starting position of a background image	[length] [percentage] bottom center left right top

Table D–4 Background and Color Properties *(Continued)*

Property Name	Description	Values	
background-repeat	Sets if/how a background image will be repeated	**repeat** repeat-x repeat-y no-repeat inherit	
background-size	Specifies the size of the background images		NEW

Border Properties

Table D–5 Border Properties

Property Name	Description	Values	
border	Set all the border properties in one declaration		
border-color	Shorthand property for setting the color of the four borders in one declaration; can have from one to four colors	[color] transparent	
border-bottom-color border-left-color border-right-color border-top-color	Sets the respective color of the top, right, bottom, and left borders individually	[color]	
border-image	A shorthand property for setting all the border-image-*n* properties		NEW
border-image-outset	Specifies the amount by which the border image area extends beyond the border box	[length] [number]	NEW
border-image-repeat	Specifies whether the image-border should be repeated, rounded, or stretched	**stretch** repeat round	NEW
border-image-slice	Specifies the inward offsets of the image-border	[number] [percentage] fill	NEW
border-image-source	Specifies an image to be used as a border	**none** [image]	NEW
border-image-width	Specifies the widths of the image-border	[number] [percentage] auto	NEW
border-radius	A shorthand property for setting all the four border-*n*-radius properties		NEW
border-bottom-left-radius border-bottom-right-radius border-top-left-radius border-top-right-radius	Sets the shape of the border of the bottom-left, bottom-right, top-left, and top-right corners individually	[percentage] [length]	NEW NEW NEW NEW
border-style	Shorthand property for setting the style of the four borders in one declaration; can have from one to four styles	**none** dashed dotted double groove inset outset ridge solid	

Table D–5 Border Properties *(Continued)*

Property Name	Description	Values
border-bottom-style border-left-style border-right-style border-top-style	Sets the respective style of the top, right, bottom, and left borders individually	**none** dashed dotted double groove inset outset ridge solid
border-width	Shorthand property for setting the width of the four borders in one declaration; can have from one to four values	**medium** [length] thick thin
border-bottom-width border-left-width border-right-width border-top-width	Sets the respective width of the top, right, bottom, and left borders individually	**medium** [length] thick thin
NEW box-decoration-break		
NEW box-shadow	Attaches one or more drop-shadows to the box	[h-shadow] [v-shadow] [blur] [spread] [color] inset

Box Properties

NEW   **Table D-6 Box Properties**

Property Name	Description	Values
overflow-style	Specifies the preferred scrolling method for elements that overflow	**auto** scrollbar panner move marquee
overflow-x	Specifies whether or not to clip the left/right edges of the content, if it overflows the element's content area	**visible** hidden scroll auto no-display no-content
overflow-y	Specifies whether or not to clip the top/bottom edges of the content, if it overflows the element's content area	**visible** hidden scroll auto no-display no-content

Table D-6 Box Properties (Continued)

Property Name	Description	Values
rotation	Rotates an element around a given point defined by the rotation-point property	[angle]
rotation-point	Defines a point as an offset from the top-left border edge	left top left center left bottom right top right center right bottom center top center center center bottom

Classification Properties

Table D–7 Classification Properties

Property Name	Description	Values
display	Describes how/if an element is displayed on the canvas, which may be on a printed page, a computer monitor, etc.	**block** inline list-item none
white-space	Declares how white-space inside the element is handled: the 'normal' way (where white-space is collapsed), as *pre* (which behaves like the <pre> element in HTML) or as *nowrap* (where wrapping is done only through elements)	**normal** pre nowrap

Color Properties

Table D-8 Color Properties

NEW

Property Name	Description	Values
color-profile	Permits the specification of a source color profile other than the default	
opacity	Sets the opacity level for an element	[value] inherit
rendering-intent	Permits the specification of a color profile rendering intent other than the default	

Content for Paged Media Properties

NEW   **Table D-9 Paged Media Properties**

Property Name	Description	Values
bookmark-label	Specifies the label of the bookmark	
bookmark-level	Specifies the level of the bookmark	
bookmark-target	Specifies the target of the bookmark link	
float-offset	Pushes floated elements in the opposite direction of the where they have been floated with float	
hyphenate-after	Specifies the minimum number of characters in a hyphenated word after the hyphenation character	
hyphenate-before	Specifies the minimum number of characters in a hyphenated word before the hyphenation character	
hyphenate-character	Specifies a string that is shown when a hyphenate-break occurs	
hyphenate-lines	Indicates the maximum number of successive hyphenated lines in an element	
hyphenate-resource	Specifies a comma-separated list of external resources that can help the browser determine hyphenation points	
hyphens	Sets how to split words to improve the layout of paragraphs	
image-resolution	Specifies the correct resolution of images	
marks	Adds crop and/or cross marks to the document	

Dimension Properties

NEW   **Table D-10 Dimension Properties**

Property Name	Description	Values
height	Sets the height of an element	**auto** [length] [percentage] inherit
max-height	Sets the maximum height of an element	**none** [length] [percentage] inherit
max-width	Sets the maximum width of an element	**none** [length] [percentage] inherit
min-height	Sets the minimum height of an element	[length] [percentage] inherit
min-width	Sets the minimum width of an element	[length] [percentage] inherit
width	Sets the width of an element	**auto** [length] [percentage] inherit

Flexible Box Properties

Table D-11 Flexible Box Properties			NEW
Property Name	**Description**	**Values**	
box-align	Specifies how to align the child elements of a box	start end center baseline **stretch**	
box-direction	Specifies in which direction the children of a box are displayed	**normal** reverse inherit	
box-flex	Specifies whether the children of a box is flexible or inflexible in size	[value]	
box-flex-group	Assigns flexible elements to flex groups	[integer]	
box-lines	Specifies whether columns will go onto a new line whenever it runs out of space in the parent box	**single** multiple	
box-ordinal-group	Specifies the display order of the child elements of a box	[integer]	
box-orient	Specifies whether the children of a box should be laid out horizontally or vertically	horizontal vertical **inline-axis** block-axis inherit	
box-pack	Specifies the horizontal position in horizontal boxes and the vertical position in vertical boxes	**start** end center justify	

Font Properties

Table D–12 Font Properties			
Property Name	**Description**	**Values**	
font	Shorthand property for setting font properties		
@font-face	A rule that allows Web sites to download and use fonts other than the "Web-safe" fonts		NEW
font-family	A prioritized list of font-family names and/or generic family names for an element	[family-name] cursive fantasy monospace sans-serif serif	
font-size	Sets the size of a font	[length] [percentage] large larger **medium** small smaller x-large x-small xx-large xx-small inherit	

Table D–12 Font Properties *(Continued)*

	Property Name	Description	Values
NEW	font-size-adjust	Preserves the readability of text when font fallback occurs	[number] **none** inherit
NEW	font-stretch	Selects a normal, condensed, or expanded face from a font family	
	font-style	Sets the style of a font	**normal** italic oblique
	font-variant	Displays text in a small-caps font or a normal font	**normal** small-caps
	font-weight	Sets the weight of a font	**normal** bold bolder lighter

Generated Content Properties

Table D-13 Generated Content Properties

	Property Name	Description	Values
	content	Used with the :before and :after pseudo-elements, to insert generated content	none normal counter attr [string] open-quote close-quote no-open-quote [URL] inherit
	counter-increment	Increments one or more counters	**none** [id number] inherit
	counter-reset	Creates or resets one or more counters	**none** [id number] inherit
NEW	crop	Allows a replaced element to be just a rectangular area of an object, instead of the whole object	
NEW	move-to	Causes an element to be removed from the flow and reinserted at a later point in the document	
NEW	page-policy	Determines which page-based occurrence of a given element is applied to a counter or string value	
	quotes	Sets the type of quotation marks for embedded quotations	none [string] inherit

Grid Properties

Table D-14 Grid Properties   NEW

Property Name	Description	Values
grid-columns	Specifies the width of each column in a grid	[length] [percentage] **none** inherit
grid-rows	Specifies the height of each column in a grid	[length] [percentage] **none** inherit

Hyperlink Properties

Table D-15 Hyperlink Properties   NEW

Property Name	Description	Values
target	A shorthand property for setting the target-name, target-new, and target-position properties	
target-name	Specifies where to open links (target destination)	**current** root parent new modal [name]
target-new	Specifies whether new destination links should open in a new window or in a new tab of an existing window	**window** tab none
target-position	Specifies where new destination links should be placed	**above** behind front back

Linebox Properties

Table D-16 Linebox Properties   NEW

Property Name	Description	Values
alignment-adjust	Allows more precise alignment of elements	
alignment-baseline	Specifies how an inline-level element is aligned with respect to its parent	
baseline-shift	Allows repositioning of the dominant-baseline relative to the dominant-baseline	
dominant-baseline	Specifies a scaled-baseline-table	
drop-initial-after-adjust	Sets the alignment point of the drop initial for the primary connection point	
drop-initial-after-align	Sets which alignment line within the initial line box is used at the primary connection point with the initial letter box	

Table D-16 Linebox Properties *(Continued)*

Property Name	Description	Values
drop-initial-before-adjust	Sets the alignment point of the drop initial for the secondary connection point	
drop-initial-before-align	Sets which alignment line within the initial line box is used at the secondary connection point with the initial letter box	
drop-initial-size	Controls the partial sinking of the initial letter	
drop-initial-value	Activates a drop-initial effect	
inline-box-align	Sets which line of a multiline inline block align with the previous and next inline elements within a line	
line-stacking	A shorthand property for setting the line-stacking-strategy, line-stacking-ruby, and line-stacking-shift properties	
line-stacking-ruby	Sets the line-stacking method for block elements containing ruby annotation elements	
line-stacking-shift	Sets the line-stacking method for block elements containing elements with base-shift	
line-stacking-strategy	Sets the line-stacking strategy for stacked line boxes within a containing block element	
text-height	Sets the block-progression dimension of the text content area of an inline box	

List Properties

Table D–17 List Properties

Property Name	Description	Values
list-style	A shorthand property for setting list-style-image, list-style-position, and list-style-type in one declaration	
list-style-image	Sets an image as the list-item marker	**none** [URL]
list-style-position	Indents or extends a list-item marker with respect to the item's content	**outside** inside
list-style-type	Sets the type of list-item marker	**disc** circle square decimal lower-alpha lower-roman upper-alpha upper-roman

Margin and Padding Properties

Table D–18 Margin and Padding Properties

Property Name	Description	Values
margin	Shorthand property for setting margin properties	
margin-bottom margin-left margin-right margin-top	Sets the top, right, bottom, and left margin of an element individually	[length] [percentage] auto inherit
padding	Shorthand property for setting padding properties in one declaration	
padding-bottom padding-left padding-right padding-top	Sets the top, right, bottom, and left padding of an element individually	[length] [percentage] inherit

Marquee Properties

Table D-19 Marquee Properties   `NEW`

Property Name	Description	Values
marquee-direction	Sets the direction of the moving content	
marquee-play-count	Sets how many times the content moves	
marquee-speed	Sets how fast the content scrolls	
marquee-style	Sets the style of the moving content	

Multicolumn Properties

Table D-20 Multicolumn Properties   `NEW`

Property Name	Description	Values
column-count	Specifies the number of columns an element should be divided into	[number] **auto**
column-fill	Specifies how to fill columns	**balance** auto
column-gap	Specifies the gap between the columns	[length] **normal**
column-rule	A shorthand property for setting all the column-rule-*n* properties	
column-rule-color	Specifies the color of the rule between columns	[color]
column-rule-style	Specifies the style of the rule between columns	**none** hidden dotted dashed solid double groove ridge inset outset

Table D-20 Multicolumn Properties *(Continued)*

Property Name	Description	Values
column-rule-width	Specifies the width of the rule between columns	thin **medium** thick [length]
column-span	Specifies how many columns an element should span across	**1** all
column-width	Specifies the width of the columns	**auto** [length]
columns	A shorthand property for setting column-width and column-count	

Paged Media Properties

NEW   **Table D-21 Paged Media Properties**

Property Name	Description	Values
fit	Gives a hint for how to scale a replaced element if neither its width nor its height property is auto	
fit-position	Determines the alignment of the object inside the box	
image-orientation	Specifies a rotation in the right or clockwise direction that a user agent applies to an image	
page	Specifies a particular type of page where an element should be displayed	
size	Specifies the size and orientation of the containing box for page content	

Positioning Properties

Table D-22 Positioning Properties

Property Name	Description	Values
bottom	Specifies the bottom position of a positioned element	**auto** [length] [percentage] inherit
clear	Specifies the sides of an element where other floating elements are not allowed	left right both **none** inherit
clip	Clips an absolutely positioned element	[shape] **auto** inherit

Table D-16 D-22 Positioning Properties *(Continued)*

Property Name	Description	Values
cursor	Specifies the type of cursor to be displayed	[URL] **auto** crosshair default e-resize help move n-resize ne-resize nw-resize pointer progress s-resize se-resize sw-resize text w-resize wait inherit
display	Specifies the type of box an element should generate	none block **inline** inline-block inline-table list-item run-in table table-caption table-cell table-column table-column-group table-footer-group table-header-group table-row table-row-group inherit
float	Specifies whether or not a box should float	left right **none** inherit
left	Specifies the left position of a positioned element	**auto** [length] [percentage] inherit
overflow	Specifies what happens if content overflows an element's box	**visible** hidden scroll auto inherit
position	Specifies the type of positioning method used for an element (static, relative, absolute, or fixed)	**static** absolute fixed relative inherit

Table D-22 Positioning Properties *(Continued)*

Property Name	Description	Values
right	Specifies the right position of a positioned element	**auto** [length] [percentage] inherit
top	Specifies the top position of a positioned element	**auto** [length] [percentage] inherit
visibility	Specifies whether or not an element is visible	**visible** hidden collapse inherit
z-index	Sets the stack order of a positioned element	**auto** [number] inherit

Print Properties

Table D-23 Print Properties

Property Name	Description	Values
orphans	Sets the minimum number of lines that must be left at the bottom of a page when a page break occurs inside an element	
page-break-after	Sets the page-breaking behavior after an element	**auto** always avoid left right inherit
page-break-before	Sets the page-breaking behavior before an element	**auto** always avoid left right inherit
page-break-inside	Sets the page-breaking behavior inside an element	**auto** avoid inherit
widows	Sets the minimum number of lines that must be left at the top of a page when a page break occurs inside an element	

Ruby Properties

Table D-24 Ruby Properties   NEW

Property Name	Description	Values
ruby-align	Controls the text alignment of the ruby text and ruby base contents relative to each other	
ruby-overhang	Determines whether, and on which side, ruby text is allowed to partially overhang any adjacent text in addition to its own base, when the ruby text is wider than the ruby base	
ruby-position	Controls the position of the ruby text with respect to its base	
ruby-span	Controls the spanning behavior of annotation elements	

Speech Properties

Table D-25 Speech Properties   NEW

Property Name	Description	Values
mark	A shorthand property for setting the mark-before and mark-after properties	
mark-after	Allows named markers to be attached to the audio stream	
mark-before	Allows named markers to be attached to the audio stream	
phonemes	Specifies a phonetic pronunciation for the text contained by the corresponding element	
rest	A shorthand property for setting the rest-before and rest-after properties	
rest-after	Specifies a rest or prosodic boundary to be observed after speaking an element's content	
rest-before	Specifies a rest or prosodic boundary to be observed before speaking an element's content	
voice-balance	Specifies the balance between left and right channels	
voice-duration	Specifies how long it should take to render the selected element's content	
voice-pitch	Specifies the average pitch (a frequency) of the speaking voice	
voice-pitch-range	Specifies variation in average pitch	
voice-rate	Controls the speaking rate	
voice-stress	Indicates the strength of emphasis to be applied	
voice-volume	Refers to the amplitude of the waveform output by the speech syntheses	

Table Properties

Table D-26 Table Properties

Property Name	Description	Values
border-collapse	Specifies whether or not table borders should be collapsed	collapse **separate** inherit
border-spacing	Specifies the distance between the borders of adjacent cells	[length] inherit
caption-side	Specifies the placement of a table caption	**top** bottom inherit
empty-cells	Specifies whether or not to display borders and background on empty cells in a table	hide **show** inherit
table-layout	Sets the layout algorithm to be used for a table	**auto** fixed inherit

Text Properties

Table D–27 Text Properties

	Property Name	Description	Values
	color	Sets the color of text	[color] inherit
	direction	Specifies the text direction/writing direction	**ltr** rtl inherit
NEW	hanging-punctuation	Specifies whether a punctuation character may be placed outside the line box	none first last allow-end force-end
	letter-spacing	Increases or decreases the space between characters	**normal** [length] inherit
	line-height	Sets the line height	**normal** [length] [number] [percentage] inherit
NEW	punctuation-trim	Specifies whether a punctuation character should be trimmed	none start end allow-end adjacent
	text-align	Specifies the horizontal alignment of text	left right center justify inherit

Table D–27 Text Properties (*Continued*)

Property Name	Description	Values	
text-align-last	Describes how the last line of a block or a line right before a forced line break is aligned when text-align is "justify"		NEW
text-decoration	Adds decoration to text	**none** blink line-through overline underline inherit	
text-indent	Indents the first line of text in an element	[length] [percentage] inherit	
text-justify	Specifies the justification method used when text-align is "justify"	**auto** interword interideograph intercluster distribute kashida none	
text-outline	Specifies a text outline	**none** [thickness] [blur] [color]	
text-overflow	Specifies what should happen when text overflows the containing element	**clip** ellipsis [string]	
text-shadow	Adds shadow to text	[h-shadow] [v-shadow] [blur] [color]	NEW
text-transform	Controls text capitalization	**none** capitalize lowercase uppercase inherit	
text-wrap	Specifies line breaking rules for text	**normal** none unrestricted suppress	NEW
vertical-align	Sets the vertical positioning of text	**baseline** [length] [percentage] bottom middle sub super text-bottom text-top top inherit	
white-space	Specifies how white-space inside an element is handled	**normal** nowrap pre preline prewrap inherit	

Table D–27 Text Properties (*Continued*)		
Property Name	**Description**	**Values**
NEW word-break	Specifies the line breaking rules for non-CJK scripts	**normal** break-all hyphenate
word-spacing	Increases or decreases the space between words	**normal** [length] inherit
NEW word-wrap	Allows long, unbreakable words to be broken and wrap to the next line	**normal** break-word

2D/3D Transform Properties

NEW Table D-28 2D/3D Transform Properties		
Property Name	**Description**	**Values**
backface-visibility	Defines whether or not an element should be visible when not facing the screen	**visible** hidden
perspective	Specifies the perspective on how 3D elements are viewed	
perspective-origin	Specifies the bottom position of 3D elements	[x-axis] [y-axis]
transform	Applies a 2D or 3D transformation to an element	
transform-origin	Allows you to change the position on transformed elements	[x-axis] [y-axis] [z-axis]
transform-style	Specifies how nested elements are rendered in 3D space	**flat** preserve-3d

Transition Properties

NEW Table D-29 Transition Properties		
Property Name	**Description**	**Values**
transition	A shorthand property for setting the four transition properties	
transition-delay	Specifies when the transition effect will start	[time]
transition-duration	Specifies how many seconds or milliseconds a transition effect takes to complete	[time]
transition-property	Specifies the name of the CSS property the transition effect is for	none **all** property
transition-timing-function	Specifies the speed curve of the transition effect	linear **ease** ease-in ease-in-out ease-out cubic-bezier

User-Interface Properties

Table D-30 User-Interface Properties NEW

Property Name	Description	Values
appearance	Allows you to make an element look like a standard user interface element	**normal** icon window button menu field
box-sizing	Allows you to define certain elements to fit an area in a certain way	**content-box** border-box inherit
icon	Provides the author with the ability to style an element with an iconic equivalent	**auto** [URL] Inherit
nav-down	Specifies where to navigate when using the arrow-down navigation key	**auto** [id] [target-name] inherit
nav-index	Specifies the tabbing order for an element	**auto** [number] inherit
nav-left	Specifies where to navigate when using the arrow-left navigation key	**auto** [id] [target-name] inherit
nav-right	Specifies where to navigate when using the arrow-right navigation key	**auto** [id] [target-name] inherit
nav-up	Specifies where to navigate when using the arrow-up navigation key	**auto** [id] [target-name] inherit
outline-offset	Offsets an outline, and draws it beyond the border edge	[length] inherit
resize	Specifies whether or not an element is resizable by the user	**none** both horizontal vertical

Appendix E
Publishing Web Pages to a Web Server

Publishing your Web site means transferring your files to a Web server (Web host) that will make your pages available 24/7 on the Web. Publishing involves two basic steps: choosing a Web host and uploading your Web site files (usually via FTP) to that host.

Choosing a Web Host

There are many options available for Web hosting, as detailed in the "Finding a Web Hosting Site" section of the Special Feature on "Attracting Visitors to Your Web Site." Common options are to use the ISP that you use to connect to the Internet or to use a Web hosting service.

Your Internet service provider (ISP) may provide space for its clients to host a Web site. If it does, you should contact the network system administrator or technical support staff at your ISP to determine if their Web server supports FTP, and to obtain necessary permissions to access the Web server. There are other options for hosting Web sites as well. You can search for free Web hosts using any browser and search engine. Whatever Web host you choose, you must secure a username and password in order to gain access to the host.

Uploading Files to the Host

Once you have chosen a Web host, you'll need a program to transfer your files to the Web server. The most common file transfer program is called FTP. **File Transfer Protocol (FTP)** is an Internet standard that allows computers to exchange files with other computers on the Internet. FTP was developed to promote file sharing across a variety of computers reliably and efficiently. FTP programs that run on personal computers are sometimes called FTP clients.

There are many FTP programs available for free on the Internet. Search for FTP using any search engine, and you will find a variety of programs. Read the documentation to ensure that the program works with your computer and operating system. Then download and install the FTP program of your choice.

Now you can use your FTP program to upload your Web pages to the server. Be sure to include all HTML files, CSS files, and any graphic files that make up your Web site. Table E–1 shows the steps to use FTP to upload your files. All of the necessary information (e.g., username) should be provided to you by the network administrator for the Web host. Specific keystrokes or mouse clicks to accomplish each step may vary among FTP clients.

Table E–1 Using FTP to Upload Your Web Files

1. Start your FTP program.

2. Type in the host name/address as provided by the network administrator.

3. Select the host type.

4. Enter your FTP user ID and password as provided by the network administrator.

5. You should see both a local system (your computer) as well as the remote system (the Web host) in the FTP dialog box.

6. Navigate your local drive to find the folders in which you stored your files; then locate the folders on the remote system.

7. Highlight the files that you want to upload and copy the files to the remote system.

Index

Note
- Page numbers in bold type indicate definitions.
- Page numbers followed by "t" indicate tables.
- Page numbers followed by "BTW" indicate margin notes.
- Page numbers followed by "+t" or "+BTW" indicate discussions plus tables or margin notes.

Symbols